Lionheart

The Diaries of Richard I

Edited by Chris Manson

First published in 2014 by Habton Publishing

A CIP catalogue record for this title is available from the British Library.

ISBN 978-1-910256-56-5

Editor's note

The original manuscripts are in Latin.

Richard the Lionheart dictated these diaries to his scribe, Armande. It is likely that he dictated in the language he used in everyday life, Norman French.

However, quills and ink in this period were difficult to use and therefore transcribing the diaries would have taken considerable time. From what we know of Richard, it seems unlikely that he would have been sufficiently patient to wait for Armande to catch up. Instead, it appears that Armande made notes from Richard's dictation and then translated these notes into Latin, the universal language of the written word in the Middle Ages.

The Latin that Armande and Richard use is typical of the late twelfth century. In translating it, I have attempted to provide a modern English version that is faithful to the original in that it sounds as if it is someone speaking aloud, but alone and in confidence, to a trusted retainer.

Under the terms of the agreement under which I purchased the original Latin manuscripts, they will be given as a bequest to the British Museum in 2050. Until then, to protect the identity of the previous German owners of the manuscripts, they will remain in the care of a Swiss bank.

There were twenty-seven bound volumes of Latin manuscripts buried with Berengaria. Unfortunately, damp and mildew over the course of the past seven centuries so damaged twenty-one of the volumes that they are illegible. Six volumes remain in a good state of repair and it is these that are published here, together with Richard's last letter to Berengaria, which was folded inside the last volume.

Contents

The diaries open in the eighteenth year of the reign of Henry II.

Henry, the father of Richard, was the pre-eminent ruler in Western Europe. As King of England, Duke of Normandy, Count of Anjou, Count of Maine, Lord of Ireland and Duke of Aquitaine his writ ran from Hadrian's Wall to the Pyrenees.

Early in his reign he had married Eleanor of Aquitaine, only eight weeks after her marriage to Louis VII of France had been annulled. Their relationship was widely known to have been tempestuous, but they had five sons and three daughters.

The eldest son, William, died at the age of two. Henry, known at this time as Henry the Young King, was seen as heir apparent. Richard was born on 8 September 1157 in Oxford. He appears to have spent his formative years either at the palace of Woodstock or in Aquitaine under the care of his mother. Geoffrey was born one year after Richard, and John, later King John, some nine years later. Henry II's three daughters were born between Geoffrey and John.

The early part of Henry's reign had been hugely successful as he expanded his territories and brought to bear a much more efficient royal administration.

But the murder of his former close adviser, Thomas Becket, increasing tension over the succession after he named his second son Henry as the Young King, and regular discord with his wife were to make the second half of his reign much more difficult.

1 June 1172

Limoges

I stand here in the flickering candlelight, not quite sure how to begin. At a desk in the corner sits Armande, who has this very instant started to write down everything I say. He is new to me, this Armande. I found him hovering uncertainly outside my rooms as I staggered up the spiral stairs from the banquet below.

He stammered as he first spoke, telling me that he is the scribe who my father, King Henry, promised to send me to assist me in keeping a record of my actions. My father had written to me saying that he thinks it appropriate to try to counter some of the more malicious and salacious stories coming from the French court of King Louis VII, and that the best way to do this is to keep an accurate record oneself. He has been in the habit of keeping such a journal since his fifteenth birthday. Now that I am approaching fifteen, I too am to keep such a record.

Armande has told me he is a monk, and has been for thirteen years, since he was twelve years old. He is small, and thin, in sharp contrast to most of his brother monks, who have grown fat on the work of others. His countenance is rather doleful, the result, I suspect, of soft brown eyes and a gentle, perhaps shy, demeanour.

How ironic that my father should send me a monk to record my every action. He has always taken pleasure in embarrassing the Church, but equally he has always known how to use its creatures.

This is indeed an auspicious day on which to begin my journal for today I have been confirmed as Duke of Aquitaine and Count of Poitou in the most glorious of ceremonials in the cathedral of Limoges. Glorious in part for the pageantry and theatricality of the occasion, but mainly because the mutinous barons had no choice but to come and kneel at my feet and swear their undying devotion to me, the second surviving son, to whom they had, until recently, paid scant attention.

How delicious as Count Raymond V of Toulouse knelt at my feet and uttered the words: 'I pledge to you, My Lord...' It must have galled him to the core to have to kneel before me, when I must seem to him just a naïve youth.

A sudden thought occurs as the wine begins to clear slightly from my head. Perhaps Armande is here to report on me to my father?

He has glanced up at me. Perhaps he is terrified to be called a spy by a rebellious boy wanting to defy his all-powerful father? His discomfort is almost as delicious to me as that of old Raymond of Toulouse kneeling at my feet earlier today.

2 June 1172

Limoges

I woke this morning a couple of hours after dawn to find Armande still in my room. He was standing at the window and had pulled the heavy drapes back in order to peer out. The daylight is what had woken me. This annoyance, and the after-effects of last night, did not put me in a good frame of mind.

As I remembered that Armande had been sent by my father, I rose from my bed furious, flung the contents of my chamber pot in his direction and hurled insults after him as he scuttled through the door and down the stairs. Not for the first time, I was too quick to anger, as I realised almost immediately.

Once I had breakfasted, I began to see more clearly that I would have to play the situation a little more cleverly.

I sought out Armande later in the day. I had half expected him to be lurking in the kitchens, begging scraps from some pretty serving girl. However, to his credit, I found him in the cathedral. Maybe he knew that I would be coming for him, and that the cathedral would be a good place to be found. Or maybe he is genuinely pious.

I went up behind him and touched him on the shoulder as he was praying. He started slightly, which makes me believe that his prayers were at least part genuine. I raised my shoulders in a sort of half shrug, which is about as close as an Angevin can get to an apology. He looked scared, which made me feel guilty. I looked down and saw that some of the contents of my chamber pot had soiled the bottom of his monk's habit. My guilt deepened.

I muttered something about perhaps starting again and took his nervous nod to be a form of relieved assent.

My father must be nervous of what my mother Eleanor is doing here in Aquitaine. They have not seen each other since the autumn of 1170, some twenty-one months ago. I was present when the rift between them became permanent, although my father does not know to this day that I was there.

Two years ago, when I was a lusty thirteen-year-old, I was hiding in my mother's apartment after she had come in unexpectedly, almost catching me with her young mistress of the bedchamber, Lysette. I had to dive under the bed as Lysette hurriedly rearranged the bedclothes and moved into the washroom, just as the main door to the apartment opened, and my mother entered in her customary imperious fashion.

She moved about her apartment issuing instructions for what seemed like an eternity. In reality it was probably about ten minutes. She sounded as if she were skittishly excited about something. It suggested to me that something had come of one of her various intrigues.

Then she took a sharp intake of breath as she heard the thundering footsteps of what could only have been my father approaching, together with his raised voice shouting: 'What have you been doing to Rosamunde?'

My mother, as part of the chicanery surrounding her Courts of Love, had decided to try to persuade one of her finest knights to approach and seduce Rosamunde Clifford, my father's long-term mistress.

Unfortunately, the knight whom she had selected was so devoted to my mother, and the mythology that surrounds her, that he took this task to be a kind of quest.

Doubly unfortunately, he had proved to be remarkably adept at his task.

Not only did he manage to seduce Rosamunde, but he captured her heart to such an extent that even my father, normally so inattentive to the feelings of others, noticed the change in Rosamunde.

Evidently, Rosamunde had confessed to my father. He was now in a fury of which I, and I suspect, my mother, had never seen the like before. He raged around the room, turning over the furniture, ripping the drapes from their hangings, tearing at the bed sheets with his sword. He swiped at my mother with the back of his hand, but caught her only a glancing blow.

I have to admit that my reaction was not particularly worthy, for I cowered ever lower beneath the bed, catching the occasional glimpse of what was happening in the mirror positioned against the inside wall.

Unfortunately, just as my father's rage was beginning to abate, Lysette made a noise in the washroom. My father roared into the washroom, grabbed Lysette by the hair, and tugged her screaming into the bedroom. He commanded my mother to sit on the bed. She hesitated, and he bellowed at the top of his voice for her to sit.

He took a dagger from his belt, put it to Lysette's throat, and with his other hand, ripped her skirts from her waist. He drew a little blood with the point of the dagger on her throat, then threw the dagger on the bed, pushed her roughly down next to it, and began to unbuckle himself.

At this point, I closed my eyes, and could only listen to the sound of my father, the most powerful man in the world, raping a girl with whom I had recently been intimate, while my mother looked on and I hid under the bed.

Although part of me felt that I should leap out to halt this dreadful scene, another part of me recognised that what I was witnessing was my father as an elemental force, and that I was simply not ready to challenge such a force.

He had forged a great empire through his energy, endeavour, brutality and cunning. I have spent much of the last two years wondering whether I will grow into such an elemental force, and if so, whether I will be able to control the dark side of that force better than my father did on this occasion.

When my father had finished, he leaned over and, slowly and deliberately, untied the silk scarf that was wound around my mother's neck, put it to his groin and wiped himself, before throwing the scarf back at her.

There was silence for a few moments after he had left, broken only by the muffled sobs of poor Lysette. Eventually, I saw my mother's feet come off the bed and on to the floor. She escorted Lysette, firmly, it must be said, from the room. Then she went into the bathroom, and I could hear the sound of retching into a bucket. Even my mother, with her legendary sangfroid, had been distressed by the scene.

I slid out from under the bed, and was creeping to the door when my mother called out. I hesitated before turning back to face her as she stood in the door to the washroom. Her jaw was set, and her eyes were icily blue. She nodded at me once, then turned away.

Almost two years later I can still feel the strength of that look.

23 June 1172

Poitou

My father is in England currently, but even so the nature and extent of his cruelty become more apparent with every passing day. The events of today illustrate his genius for malign scheming.

A party of six travellers arrived late last night, after I had retired. I heard them clattering in the courtyard and muffled snatches of conversation drifted up towards me. However, I was not aware of any visitors expected, and, slightly soporific from the evening's wine, I drifted off.

As I woke this morning I could not quite believe my eyes.

Undoubtedly, the events following my fumblings with Lysette had made me rather cautious about repeating the experience. In fact, I had intended for Lysette to be my first conquest, but we never got that far. As a consequence, nearly two years later, I remained, almost fifteen, a virgin. Much to the amusement of my fellow knights.

However, this morning was something different. I pulled the blanket down from over my head to find a naked woman standing next to the bed. She had full breasts with extremely large nipples, which she was teasing with her fingers.

She had absolutely no pubic hair, and I watched fascinated as she drew one of her hands from her breast to her mouth, wet her forefinger and then ran that down to the area where the hair should have been. I was transfixed as she began to play with herself, to arch her back, to moan slightly.

It was only now, as she arched back into the brighter light, that I saw that she was wearing a scarf over her head, so that I could not see her face. I could see impressions of her nose and mouth, but nothing more.

She moved on to my bed, crouching above me on her knees with her hand now working more quickly at her crotch about three or four inches from my face. She took her hand away and positioned herself over my face and I began tentatively to lick at her. She seemed to like this, pulling at my hair and grinding herself gently on me.

Then, suddenly, she heaved herself up, turned herself round so that she was facing down my body and threw back the blankets.

She took my penis in her right hand and leaned down to it. I could feel her alternately licking and blowing her way down the shaft, and then giving the same treatment to my balls.

She came back up the shaft, took a firm grip with her left hand and drew it deep into her mouth. By this stage I was clawing at the mattress with my hands in an effort to keep myself in. However, as she drew back to take a breath, I exploded and it must have hit her full in the face.

I lay panting with her slumped on the mattress. We must have lain there for a few minutes.

Then the door opened, and my mother bustled in talking loudly about I know not what. As she caught sight of the tableau before her, she came to a sudden halt.

There was a moment or two when nobody moved. Then in a slightly shrill voice, my mother said: 'I see that you are wearing one of my scarves. Kindly return it to me at once.'

My companion raised up her torso and lifted one leg over me, managing to retain some dignity as she slowly unwound the scarf from her head.

As she came to what would clearly be the last unwinding before the scarf fell free, the faces of my mother and I must have been a picture of anticipation.

There was an audible gasp from my mother, and a kind of stifled groan from me, as the scarf fell away to reveal Rosamunde Clifford, my father's mistress.

She wiped her face free of my smears using the scarf, and then proffered it to my mother, saying: 'This was my Lord Henry's wish.'

24 June 1172
Poitou

Rosamunde left this morning. I know that my mother was tempted to have her badly harmed, but in the end she confined herself to making Rosamunde dress in the old hair shirt that my father used to say that he wore during Lent. She was also forced to travel on a ploughman's cart, with an escort of only four lightly armed squires.

My mother has long cavilled at Rosamunde's taste for expensive dresses and large retinues of knights, so she must have taken some small pleasure out of inflicting these slights. However, I suspect that Rosamunde considered them low punishment compared to what my father had made her do to me.

The rape of Lysette and now the degrading of Rosamunde have made clear to me the extent of the hatred between my mother and father.

I know that my father thinks of me as my mother's creature. It is not altogether surprising, given that I have spent most of my life at her court rather than with him. However, I now understand that my mother is beginning to wonder whether I will remain on her side. First, she finds me with a girl in her bedchamber, and then she finds me with her husband's mistress. She may feel that I am slipping from her. I suspect she calculates that by saying nothing to me of either incident, she is less likely to push me away.

10 July 1172

Poitou

For almost a week now, we have had two brothers staying with us, Hubert and Theobald Walter. Hubert is the same age as me. Theobald is younger, and appears to be somewhat in his brother's shadow.

Hubert and I have spent a reasonable amount of time together. He lives with his uncle, Ranulf de Glanville, who is close to my father. Hubert does not appear to have had much formal schooling. Indeed, he seems to be rather embarrassed by it, but he strikes me as a person of rare intelligence and perception. Or at least he laughs at my jokes, which in my view comes to much the same thing.

He is not much to look at: shorter than me, with Celtic fair skin, but of the type that burnishes readily in summer, and a shock of dark wiry hair. I suspect he will run to fat in later life – he certainly has a large appetite.

We have developed a kind of unspoken pact. I teach him the rudiments of swordsmanship and coach him while riding. Indeed, I have even passed him some of my armour since my new pieces from London arrived. In return, he fills me in on the view from England and the goings-on at my father's court.

Of my father's lands, England is both the richest and the easiest to govern. It will be interesting to see to whom it falls when my father dies. Currently, my oldest brother, Henry the Young King, has not been granted any land by my father, although he has been crowned in England in a mock coronation, set up by my father as part of his campaign against Becket in exile. My brother has long seen his lack of land as a real insult to his position, particularly now that he is married and maintains his own court. I know that he was spitting mad at my confirmation as Duke of Aquitaine and Count of Poitou.

Geoffrey, the brother between John, the youngest, and me, has Brittany and seems content with it, for now.

The assumption is that England will go to Henry, but my father will not pass it to him yet, mostly because he needs the money that flows from it, but partly also because he feels the need to consolidate his position following the Becket incident. Almost everybody can see that this is a sensible standpoint. Unfortunately, the one person who cannot see it is Henry himself.

Hubert Walter is interesting on this point. He seems to think that a conflict between Henry and my father is inevitable. He also mentioned to me a couple of times that I need to think about my position in the event of such a conflict. I have to confess that the thought had not even occurred to me. I will try over the coming days to get some advice from Hubert on this. Obliquely, of course. A prince cannot ask directly for advice.

15 July 1172

Poitou

Today was a significant day. Hubert Walter and I went out on our own on a long day's hunting. We set out early, about an hour before dawn. The morning went well, but it was hot, and we found a shaded spot to eat and rest.

After eating, we lay on the grass. Spontaneously, I decided to tell Hubert the real story behind the Becket saga. I have never spoken to anyone before of my involvement in it. It was in some ways a release to talk of it openly.

It is worth retelling the story of Becket to place the facts on record, and also to help myself make sense of it. Although my father is a man of swift temper capable of calculated cruelty, the Becket incident has given him a darker reputation than the real story justifies.

From about five years before my birth, Thomas Becket had been close to my father. They had met during the negotiations through which my father became king. Becket, at that time, was in the household of Theobald, Archbishop of Canterbury, and my father appointed him as chancellor on his coronation in December 1154.

They had grown close through a shared love of hunting and hawking, and Becket was his constant companion through the early years of my childhood. Becket was also a notorious drinker and womaniser. My mother described him once as appealing to my father's darker nature. He certainly shared my father's obsessive streak. For example, Becket was famously attached to his hawk, and there is a story of his hawk falling in its cage into a river when the cart it was in toppled from a bridge. Becket dived in after it despite not being able to swim. He nearly died, but he rescued the bird. The two men driving the cart were left to drown.

For three or four years after my father's coronation, he and Becket were virtually inseparable, and my father granted him a succession of titles and land. Becket was extraordinary in the role of chancellor. His aptitude for the work, combined with the increasing wealth of the country, brought in record revenues. All the while, he continued to hunt, stage the occasional tournament and plough his way through the various women at court.

Becket was fierce in asserting my father's rights over the rights of the Church, and as a consequence riled many churchmen who had formerly aided his progress. This would leave him short of friends when his relationship with my father began to deteriorate.

During these years, everything went well from my father's point of view, up until Becket's visit to the court of the King Louis in Paris, where he was received like a king. This infuriated my father, and he became increasingly disenchanted with Becket's grand ambitions. It may well be that Louis had played on my father's sensitivities by staging such a lavish entrance to Paris, knowing that it would put pressure on the relationship between king and chancellor. If it was a deliberate strategy, it worked to the extent that my father and Becket spent less and less time together.

Some three years later, when Theobald, Archbishop of Canterbury died, my father was torn between appointing Becket or Gilbert Foliot. Becket was seen at this time as clearly unsuited to the post, given his personal behaviour and his greedy financial attacks on the Church. Furthermore, he was not even a priest, whereas Foliot was a well-known monk and pious theologian, and, more importantly, was widely respected in the Church.

My father dithered for a year, but eventually plumped for Becket, largely, I believe, because he saw it as an opportunity to bring Becket back into the fold. In the event, however, even the archbishopric was not enough to satisfy Becket's ambition.

I remember meeting Becket a few times, and although I was young, he made a definite impression on me. His physical appearance was ordinary, but he had the capacity to bend people to his will simply through the sheer force of his personality. But he seemed unable to admit any error whatsoever, or even to be able to gloss over things that had not gone his way, and to move on. As a consequence, although my father had extended the olive branch by making him Archbishop of Canterbury, he did the exact opposite of what everyone, including my father, had expected, and became a fierce protector of the Church's so-called rights.

In my view, and that of my mother, he felt he had been baulked by my father in his rise up the secular ladder. He had reached the top of the ladder and found my father there, determined to keep him in his place. By switching sides to the Church, he felt he had an opportunity to be treated as an equal. Of course, my father had not seen this when offering him the archbishopric. My father was merely indulging his oldest friend in the hope of winning him back.

Things came to a head fairly quickly, at a meeting in the palace at Woodstock in July 1163, thirteen months after Becket's accession. The battleground issue turned out to be the Church's protection of churchmen who had committed crimes.

In itself, it was not that important an issue to my father. The real argument was between two old friends. I suspect that Becket had rewritten history in his own mind to the extent that he felt that he had helped to make my father king during the negotiations before his accession. Equally, my father had begun, after nine years of kingship, to feel more comfortable in the role and to feel able to do without Becket, who could not accept that his progress had been slowed.

I will not detail here all the claims and counterclaims that followed Woodstock. Suffice it to say that Becket escaped one night across the Channel and sought the protection of King Louis. There he remained, in inglorious exile, until two years ago.

During his exile, Becket was little more than a minor irritant to my father. But I do know that he was sad at the fracture of the relationship, because he mentioned it to me a few times on our occasional hunting or hawking trips together.

The pressure for a resolution of the problem came because both King Louis and my father wanted to establish a permanent peace, so that they could go on Crusade together. Becket obstinately disrupted progress towards a solution several times. Eventually, in December 1170, Becket was free to return to Canterbury under the terms of the peace established with my father. Almost immediately, however, Becket set about reasserting his rights. I was with my father at his Christmas court near Bayeux and news trickled in slowly from England.

Firstly, Becket had tried to visit the Christmas court of my brother Henry at Winchester, with the intention of staying for the festive period. Henry had been perfectly happy to receive him, but his advisers didn't think it wise to host Becket while he was still complaining about the way Henry had been crowned as the Young King during his exile.

Then the news arrived that Becket had excommunicated all of the bishops who had continued in their positions during his exile. In fact, we discovered later that he had suspended them rather than excommunicated them, and that some bishops had not been included on the list at all. Nevertheless, the impact on my father at the time was significant.

We had just dined on Christmas Day, and it had been a particularly good feast, when the messenger from England was brought before us. The atmosphere had been one of celebration, but now my father exploded at the news of the excommunications. He was drinking at the time and I remember he spat out his wine in his indignation. The entire hall fell silent as he ranted for five full minutes about the betrayal of trust, of friendship, of shared times and of his generosity in settling with Becket at all.

This last complaint didn't ring true to my ears, as I knew that my father had had to settle in order to achieve his ends, but I kept quiet.

Towards the end of his diatribe he began to turn his anger on those in the hall: 'What miserable drones and traitors have I nurtured and promoted in my household who let their lord be treated with such shameful contempt by a low-born clerk?'

With that he stormed from the hall, and we heard the shouts of his attendants as he summoned his horse. The court remained in cowering silence. I managed to stop myself from making some facetious quip. Two examples of restraint in one day; I was pleased with myself.

Later that evening, a party was due to set out for England to confront Becket with a list of complaints and to arrest him if he did not comply. The party, which included William de Tracy, Reginald FitzUrse and Hugh de Morville, was to be led by William de Mandeville, the Earl of Essex, and Richard de Humet, the Constable of Normandy.

De Tracy came to me that evening as we milled around the fire in the Great Hall and asked if I wanted to go with them. I had recently spent many hours practising swordsmanship with de Tracy. He was some ten years older than me and I rather looked up to him and admired his gallantry.

Looking back, he was mad to invite me. He must have done it as a spontaneous gesture of goodwill. For me such an opportunity was not only a chance of adventure but also a chance to impress my father. I think William must have been so naïve that he thought that my father would be pleased when he found out. I knew different, of course, but I was not about to let de Tracy know of the recklessness of his invitation. As things turned out, I rather wish I had.

De Tracy's idea was to tell the rest of the party that I was his young cousin, whom he was charged with returning to England. We figured that if I stayed in the shadows (we left two hours before midnight) and wore a hooded cloak we could maintain the subterfuge for long enough that we would be too far gone for the party to turn back when they found out the truth.

His plan worked better than we had expected. By dawn, I still remained undiscovered. As we approached the coast, I thought about revealing myself to William de Mandeville. But, partly because of my nervous excitement at the escapade, and partly because I so wanted to be part of a successful expedition to arrest my father's greatest irritant, I decided to curb my tongue a while longer.

The weather that night was calm and the voyage across to Kent was uneventful, but as I was coming down the gangway to disembark, a sudden gust of wind blew back my hood. Just at that moment, William de Mandeville, at the vanguard of our group, turned and saw me. He did a double take as if unable to believe his eyes and then came marching back up the gangway, barging the other members of the party out of the way. It was too late to hide under my hood again, and he came right up to me, placing both hands on my shoulders. His eyes burned into me. De Mandeville is a tall man and, although I was only thirteen years old, I was already unusually tall myself, but he towered over me. I felt a wave of guilt wash over me, as I stared challengingly back at him. He was one of my father's most trusted nobles; he was, with William the Marshal, the most respected soldier in our dominions. Yet now, he could be undone by the foolish prank of a boy prince and his older and dashing but imprudent friend.

He held me by the shoulders for five or ten seconds, while he assessed the situation.

I dared to speak first: 'It was all my idea; please don't blame de Tracy.'

I believe that the sound of my words startled him back into action. He turned away, indicating with his arm that I should follow on with the others.

He marched back down the gangway and leapt on to the quayside, where de Tracy awaited him nervously. De

Mandeville headed straight for de Tracy and seized him by the hair with both hands. He looked wildly around him until he lit upon an upturned oak stump into which was set an axe for chopping logs for the brazier around which the quayside workers were gathered.

De Mandeville dragged de Tracy to the tree stump and smashed his head three times into it. I thought at first that he intended to behead de Tracy there and then. But with de Tracy now unconscious, de Mandeville took de Tracy's right hand and laid it out on the stump, spreading the fingers as he did so.

He summoned me: 'My Lord Prince Richard.'

I stepped gingerly forward. He nodded at the axe. I thought he meant that I was to use it, but he then asked me to pass him the axe. Almost relieved that I was not to be the one, I passed it to him and closed my eyes as he hauled it two-handed above his head and with a guttural roar brought it crashing down.

Something flew past me and hit Reginald FitzUrse in the face. I realised a second later, as I looked at de Tracy, that it must have been one of the four fingers of his hand. All were now gone. Only the thumb and a bloody stump remained.

De Mandeville turned towards me, stared me full in the face, dropped the axe, which clattered loudly on the quay, and walked away.

Later that afternoon, he summoned me to his tent and told me of his plans. I was to ride with him to Winchester where he would deposit me with Henry, before hastening on to meet the others at Saltwood Castle near Canterbury. He was going to send a message back to my father telling him of what had happened and what his plans were.

He was still extraordinarily angry; it was clearly only my rank that prevented him from meting out a similar punishment to de Tracy's.

I nodded my assent, and silently turned and walked out. The adventure was over. I would get none of the credit for arresting Becket, and no doubt my father would be angry about my departure. But his anger would blow over. Soon the episode would be forgotten, I thought.

I went to see de Tracy next. He was conscious now, and his hand had been bound up, but he was still in great pain. He had drunk a lot of brandy, and it looked as if he had been crying. He had instantly understood upon coming round that his life as a knight was over. No knight could fight with a sword or hold a lance or pluck a crossbow with no fingers on his right hand. De Tracy's kind-hearted folly had led to the shattering of his dreams. Indeed, he looked like a shattered man already. That night I was overcome with remorse; my casual acceptance of his foolish plan had had dire consequences for him.

In the morning we travelled to Winchester, arriving late at night. My brother Henry was surprised to see me and took some pleasure in my discomfort at the situation. He can never quite forget the fact that Aquitaine and Poitou will be mine, albeit with him as my overlord.

De Mandeville left early the following morning for the two-day trip to Canterbury, and I settled gently into my brother's regime of mannered courtliness.

It was four days later that we heard the news from Canterbury. The four knights had overnighted at Saltwood Castle, but instead of remaining there, they had almost immediately moved on to Canterbury. Presumably, they thought that they could impress de Mandeville if they had already arrested Becket by the time de Mandeville had made it across country. Or perhaps they were worried that Becket would receive word of their arrival and would disappear as he had done once before.

They arrived in Canterbury, with the garrison knights and troops from Saltwood, on the afternoon of the 28th of December. Ranulf de Broc, who owned Saltwood, took the gatehouse and the others hurried into the cathedral complex. They found that Becket had just finished his midday meal and had retired to his chambers with some of his advisers. They were ushered into his presence, but Becket ostentatiously ignored them. They were understandably incensed by his snubbing of them, the King's messengers, and the insults began to fly.

Becket, apparently, began by referring to the knights as clerks here to do their lord's business, implying that he did not recognise the same lord and was somehow above them. But this they could have endured, had they not known that Becket himself was low-born, and had just reaffirmed his recognition of my father's position as part of the terms that saw him return from exile.

The argument escalated until Becket and Reginald FitzUrse stood toe to toe screaming into each other's faces. Becket's household staff and the other knights eventually dragged them apart, and the knights hurried FitzUrse from the room to seek reinforcements from the troops at the gatehouse. Becket's advisers realised that an arrest was imminent, and sought to get him into the cathedral, so that he would be safe. The knights in turn realised that Becket and his group were seeking sanctuary in the cathedral, and that they needed to stop him.

They were too late. They drew up outside the entrance from the south cloister as the last of Becket's group went into the cathedral and closed the heavy oak doors on them. They shuffled about outside, unsure of what to do next.

There the matter might have rested. But then they heard Becket's voice from inside the cathedral, commanding his men to open the doors.

Shortly afterwards the doors opened, and there stood Becket, his arms outstretched, in the position of the Cross, his figure illuminated from behind by the weak midwinter sun filtering through the windows. The knights were momentarily stilled by this powerful image, as it played on their mortal fear of crossing the threshold of a church when armed.

However, then Becket began to laugh; a staged, mocking laugh. At this, some of his household slipped away, most notably John of Salisbury, who had always been a reluctant supporter.

His laughter intensified when FitzUrse shouted the King's demand that the excommunicated bishops be reinstated.

Finally, de Tracy could bear it no longer. He broke from the group of knights, drawing his sword with difficulty as he crossed the threshold.

Becket's mocking laugh grew louder as he observed de Tracy fumbling for his sword with his bloody bandaged hand. The mockery must have driven de Tracy on. He finally got a good grip on his sword, raised it above his head, paused for a second, and then brought it crashing down on to Becket's head. The blow took a large slice of Becket's head clean off. One of his men, Edward Grim, stepped forward to try to stop de Tracy's second blow and he lost part of his arm, as the sword carved down again into Becket's skull.

The other knights were stunned by de Tracy's action. They had not calculated that his disgrace had signalled the end of his chivalrous dreams, and that he was, as a consequence, a dangerous man. Half crazed with pain, and half drunk with brandy to blot out the pain, he had forced himself to go along with the knights in the hope of redeeming himself in the eyes of my father. Once there, the goading of the insufferable Becket had caused him to lose control.

With the benefit of hindsight, it is strange to think that the despair of one man could have had such a profound political effect. Without de Tracy's actions, the encounter with Becket would have been just one more frustrating stand-off.

Now, however, the knights were quick to recognise that there was no going back. They swiftly withdrew to Saltwood Castle, where they arrived at exactly the same time as William de Mandeville, who gathered the knights together and swore them to a solemn oath. In order to protect me and the King, the knights would have to lie about the circumstances of Becket's death. They were to say that all of them had simultaneously attacked Becket, thus protecting de Tracy and keeping secret my involvement.

De Mandeville also ordered an officer of the household to return to Canterbury immediately to ensure that the body was buried quickly. He was concerned not only that the body would be examined and that the new story would be challenged, but also that parts of the body would be taken and hoarded for later sale in the event of Becket becoming a martyr.

He ordered the knights to make their way to Knaresborough in Yorkshire, the seat of Hugh de Morville, whilst he returned to Winchester to collect me.

The first I knew of Becket's death was from de Mandeville himself. Immediately upon his return he requested an audience with Henry the Young King and myself, and relayed the story. Henry immediately saw a chance to damage me, by saying that he was not sure that de Mandeville's story to protect me was a good idea, and that he felt that his conscience would lead him to disclose the truth. Pompous ass. He is as irreligious as my father, but, also like my father, he is happy to invoke God's name when it suits him.

Credit is due to de Mandeville, however. He stood up to my brother's blustering and boldly asserted that he was sure that his plan would meet with the approval of my father, and that only my father could countermand the plan. Henry eventually acquiesced, albeit sulkily. When it comes to it, he does not have the spine for confrontation, despite his formidable parentage and his ambition.

De Mandeville and I left the following morning and returned to Bayeux. Our journey took three days, and de Mandeville was polite but cold to begin with, but he began to thaw as the journey progressed. He talked of his having had to take firm action against de Tracy in order to maintain his authority, but he did not feel that he could determine the punishment for the other knights. Since their disobedience had led to such a dangerous situation, only the King could deal with them. He added: 'And as for yourself, sire, only your father can deal with you.'

I told him a little of the remorse that I felt because de Tracy had suffered because I had agreed to his idea. He let me brood on it for a while and then said: 'You could have said no, sire, but there are not many young men your age who would turn down an adventure. The fact is, de Tracy was and is a liability. He is like an excitable dog, bouncing up, sticking his head in your crotch. Someone was going to slap him down hard someday. It just happened to be me. And it is my fault that I did not realise that it would send him over the edge. The other knights should also have seen it and stopped him. But what is done is done.'

Despite his kind words, I still dreaded my father's reaction.

When we arrived in Bayeux, my father was out hunting. On his return from the hunt, de Mandeville went to see him and explained the story to him. De Mandeville had displayed no sign of it, but I now realise that he must have feared my father's reaction as much, if not more, than me.

They were closeted together for the whole evening, and eventually I took myself off to bed, although I hardly slept. In the morning, again there was no word from my father. It was not until noon that I was called before him. As I entered the room, I saw that my father was seated in his favourite wooden, high-backed chair, positioned near the window, with its back to the door. He called me to the chair. When I was about ten feet away, he commanded me to stop. I did. I waited. And waited.

I prayed that I would not let my bladder go. There I was, supposedly a great Prince of Christendom in the making, brought before his all-powerful father to answer for his part in the greatest scandal the country had known, and all I could concentrate on was not wetting myself. My father knew the impact his silence would have, and he enjoyed the power of it.

Eventually, he spoke.

'I am disappointed that you chose to disobey me. De Mandeville tells me that your motives were good, but that you lacked judgement.'

With that, he rose from his chair and turned to face me.

'Knightly virtue and adventure make for a great story

to entertain the ladies at court. But never forget that judgement and discipline are what make a king great.'

He considered me for a moment.

'You are to go to your mother at once. I want you to exercise judgement and discipline at her court. If you can do it there, with all its fripperies, you will be able to do it anywhere.'

With that, he dismissed me.

He knew, of course, that the greatest punishment that a father can lay on a son is his disappointment, and he did not stint on this occasion.

The others were not so lucky. The exception was William de Mandeville who continues to prosper to this day. When he is not at my father's side at court, he is on an embassy for him, a sign of the trust he holds.

As Becket's legend has grown over the past two and a half years, so too has the story of the curse on the four knights present at his murder. The story goes that Becket cursed them with his dying breath, and they could only lift the curse by seeking expiation at the Church of the Holy Sepulchre in Jerusalem.

At first the knights prevaricated, but as the pressure on them grew, they decided one by one to embark on the pilgrimage, but they all died en route. Reginald FitzUrse was set upon in Italy and died of stab wounds. Hugh de Morville supposedly died after eating a surfeit of bad oysters. Richard de Brito drowned whilst bathing, but the most horrible death was reserved for de Tracy. His naked body was found staked out in the middle of a cornfield in Normandy, partly devoured by a pack of hunting dogs. No one dared to bury him.

Something my father said recently hinted that one of his men had been responsible for their deaths. I am inclined to believe this, as it would have ensured that the curse was fulfilled, thus satisfying a public bloodlust and eliminating the knights before the story could grow any larger to include my father himself, or me.

As for Becket's reputation, this venal, scheming hypocrite looks set to become a saint. Almost immediately, stories began circulating that Becket's blood had miraculous curative powers. The monks of Canterbury were selling vials of his 'blood' to the ever-increasing throngs to the shrine that they had rapidly established. My father and I joked the last time I saw him that Becket's blood had been spattered liberally over the four knights, but its curative power did not seem to have done much for their health.

But we have to be careful not to be seen to stand in the way of his myth, however repugnant it is that someone so undeserving should be so revered. My father recently, when in his cups, made so bold as to ask Gilbert Foliot, whom he knew had disapproved of Becket, an interesting question:

'How is it that Becket, who, as chancellor, had been the most severe of them all against the Church, now surpasses all other saints in the number and magnitude of his miracles?'

Foliot replied: 'The Archbishop suffered many injuries culminating in his cruel death. If St Peter and the thief on the Cross could obtain God's pardon for their sins, surely Becket has atoned for his much less serious transgressions?'

My father grunted unhappily, cast a look at me, and kept his counsel.

Later, Foliot caught my arm in the corridor and expanded on the theme, saying: 'The tyrant dies and his rule is over; the martyr dies and his rule begins.'

Perhaps Becket had recognised this, and saw his chance to finally beat my father. Perhaps that explains why he seemed so intent on provoking the knights by opening the doors of the cathedral and mocking them.

This, then, is the full story, that I told to Hubert Walter this afternoon. He was clearly by turns fascinated and appalled. He also quickly realised that possession of this knowledge has admitted him to an exclusive circle. He took it as a compliment and an indication of my regard for him that I have chosen to tell him.

He also recognised, I think, that he is now bound to me by this knowledge.

Armande too must realise he has a choice. Silence and my trust. Or death.

30 July 1172

Limoges

Hubert Walter left today to return to Ranulf de Glanville in England. I shall miss him.

He is different from the knights whom my mother attracts to her court. They tend to be of the flighty, superficial type, so unlike herself, with her purpose and resolve. Maybe opposites attract. Or maybe, it is the only type of knight that my mother can attract, being a woman. The more ambitious knight will head to where the real power is, at my father's court. After the split between my mother and father of two years ago, they see the power as naturally sitting with my father. This riles my mother and she is increasingly beginning to encourage my brothers and me to assert ourselves.

We shall have to wait for a suitable opportunity, however, and Hubert counselled caution on this. He sees Henry as impetuous and therefore likely to make mistakes, whereas Geoffrey, the next oldest to me, is, of less concern. He is happy with what he has. John the youngest will get the scraps.

I must bide my time and pick my moment.

8 September 1172

Limoges

Today is my fifteenth birthday. My mother has arranged a feast. Some three hundred will be attending in the Great Hall, and she has sent out carts bearing wine to ten local villages.

My father has sent me the traditional gift of a horse for reaching man's estate: a beautiful white charger from the Camargue. I took him out this morning: his power and speed were immediately obvious. I named him Arthur, which pleased my mother, who is fond of Arthurian legend.

My father also sent a message. My mother and I are to attend his Christmas court, at Chinon. It will be the first time my mother has seen my father since the Lysette incident just over two years ago, and it will also be the first time I have seen him since our rather uncomfortable interview after Becket's death, almost two years ago.

Is my father trying to bring my mother back into the fold, as he did unsuccessfully with Becket? Or is he trying to keep her close, so that he knows what she is up to?

Whatever his motives, my mother seems determined to resist any change to the current hostile atmosphere. She is capable of providing astonishing support to those on her side, but once crossed, she remains steadfast in her hatred.

I would have thought my father would have known this. After all, he has seen it all before. When my mother was married to the French King Louis as a young woman, so determined was she to support her husband that she even took the extraordinary step of accompanying him on the Second Crusade. She was also largely responsible for raising the funds that took the vast army overland to Constantinople.

However, when King Louis crossed her by refusing to commit troops to the defence of Antioch, ruled by her uncle Raymond, she was livid. Particularly since Louis's motivation after his huge defeat in Anatolia appeared to have been simply to get to Jerusalem to discharge his pilgrim's vows, rather than to achieve anything more constructive.

A grudge held by my mother is a serious matter. So serious that it fractured their marriage and the two were divorced in 1152 on the specious grounds that they were too closely related. The reality was that they could stand each other no longer.

Ever since, King Louis and his chroniclers have been claiming that my mother was having an affair with her uncle Raymond and that it was this great scandal that undermined the whole Crusade. It is more likely that Louis's inability to father a son lay at the root of the problem. Louis, of course, looked slightly foolish when, shortly after the divorce, my mother married my father and bore him five sons in swift succession.

So my mother is not a woman to cross lightly. Maybe my father is seeking to avoid crossing her further with his invitation. Or maybe he thinks he is so far above it all now that he has not heeded this lesson from the past. Either way, it will be an interesting Christmas.

Two more presents. One from my mother: a magnificent sword. Allegedly it is the original Excalibur used by King Arthur. Everyone is suspicious of its real provenance, but my mother wants to believe it once belonged to King Arthur. Regardless of its true origin, it is a beautiful and mighty weapon in its own right.

The second was from Hodierna, who wet-nursed me from birth with her son Alexander Neckam. It was Alexander himself who brought it, a manuscript of Boethius's *Consolations of Philosophy*, which we had studied together at St Alban's for a year, when we were eleven. It was a kind and thoughtful gift. He is going on to Paris shortly to study there.

Alexander and I were born on the same day and were nursed for two years by the same woman. Yet we have nothing else in common. He is quiet and bookish and deeply God-fearing. I am not any of these, and he is none of the things I am. Nevertheless, we have this unspoken bond. I shall miss him.

27 November 1172
Limoges

News arrived today for my mother by messenger from King Louis. They seem to be more warmly inclined towards each other than has been the case for a long time. Messages have been going backwards and forwards since the summer, but until now my mother has not allowed me to be privy to their contents. Clearly she now thinks the time is right to include me.

The news itself is sensational. Henry, the Young King has met with King Louis, who has been encouraging him to rebel against our father. Apparently they met on the Norman/French border some ten days ago. Henry has not yet decided what to do, but Louis has given him assurances that he will lend him the support 'when the time comes'.

Henry has been in a fury ever since our father granted three castles that were nominally in Henry's control to my younger brother John, who is only five years old. My father's defence is that he needs the castles to provide for John and his fiancée, the daughter of Count Humbert of Maurienne.

However, it is a thin argument that a five-year-old already needs three castles. Henry quite rightly believes it is a ruse for my father to keep the castles himself. He sees our father, who is still under forty years old, forever keeping him short of what he thinks is his entitlement. It is astonishing to me that he cannot show more patience. But then I am only the second son. And second sons have to learn patience.

By encouraging Henry to rebel, I have nothing to lose. If he is successful I will have been his supporter. If not, then I have only Aquitaine and Poitou, and they are held more from my mother than from my father.

Hubert Walter was right. Decision time is approaching.

10 December 1172

Limoges

Messengers arrived today from Henry the Young King. Although he is capable of being a monstrous fool, I have to say that currently he is showing signs of building a credible alliance against my father. He has already secured the support of King Louis. Admittedly not a difficult task, but still no mean feat for Henry. I believe that he has the support of Geoffrey, as well as myself. If he can get my mother's support, then he may have sufficient strength to force some concessions out of my father. However, Henry will almost certainly squander any advantages he currently has. He always wastes opportunities.

It is a curious thing, how different we four brothers are. Physically we are much the same, much taller than average and of the same heavy build as our father. In terms of character, however, we are very different. Henry is the one with all of the advantages. He is the firstborn son, or at least the oldest one to survive, as William died at two and a half. Perhaps as a consequence of William's early death, Henry became very much the apple of my father's eye and travelled constantly with him.

I have always spent more time with my mother, and so have not been much in Henry's company. However, the time we have spent together has always been coloured by his insistence on pressing the fact that he is the eldest son. Even in childhood games he would make a point of how he had to go first as he was the oldest, or how he had to have the last piece of cake as he was the oldest, or that he should use a steel sword to our wooden swords as he was the oldest.

From childhood through adolescence, he maintained this extraordinary ability to rile everyone by saying the wrong thing at the wrong time, or by giving out the wrong signals. It is as if he has no sensitivity to how others react to him. This was even the case with my father, who found him increasingly difficult to be with. As Henry realised this, he became shriller in his demands, such that he is now setting himself up for a struggle with my father. I am sure that both of them would rather be close, but neither of them can quite allow it.

15 December 1172
Limoges

We set off for Chinon today. I shall enjoy seeing what happens when my parents meet again after so long.

It will also be interesting to see if my mother dares to support Henry in his coming struggle against my father. I talked to Hubert Walter about it. He tells me that it would be impossible for no queen has ever gone against her husband. True enough. But there has never been a queen quite like my mother.

20 December 1172
Chinon

We arrived at Chinon to find my father out hunting. He did not return at nightfall, which greatly annoyed my mother. She is excellent at masking her emotions before the court, but I know every little sign now. The constant twitching of her rings on the way here betrayed her edginess. The sharp rebukes for her servants while they settled her into her quarters betrayed her frustration at finding my father had snubbed her again by being absent when she arrived.

Late in the evening, a messenger came with an order to join my father tomorrow in hunting from a lodge some ten miles away. I will set off at dawn, taking Arthur and a hunting horse with me.

21 December 1172
Ten miles from Chinon

A bitterly cold day. An hour or more in the saddle to meet my father, then a change of horse and off hunting with barely a grunt of acknowledgement from him.

It was only at lunch that he deigned to talk to me, and then only perfunctorily. I had comported myself well in the morning, but I knew that my father wanted to see how I would keep up with him through to the end of the day. Maybe it is to test me. Or maybe, now that he is nearly forty, it is to test himself.

In fact, we had an exhilarating afternoon, running down and spearing a large male wild boar that had given us two hours of hard pursuit. I think it was the happiest I have seen my father, patently tired, but fit and lean and flushed by his success.

In the evening, in the rather cramped hunting lodge, he quizzed me, politely but firmly, about the state of affairs in Aquitaine. I could see he was leading towards questions about my mother, but I managed to remain non-committal about her intentions. Mostly because I do not actually know what her intentions are.

However, he is definitely as anxious about seeing her, as she is about seeing him. I hope that the mutual anxiety does not spark an almighty conflagration. Or maybe I should hope for that.

Interestingly, he did not once mention Henry the Young King. Maybe as a test of my filial loyalty, my father was waiting for me to mention him. If it was a test, I failed.

Tomorrow we head back to Chinon.

22 December 1172

Chinon

My father and I arrived back mid-morning. There was no great fanfare, we just drifted back in. There is to be a great feast tomorrow, at which my mother and father will finally meet. She has been grilling me this afternoon for information from my day with him yesterday. She seemed disappointed that I had not learnt more and slightly suspicious that I was holding something back. But she probably knows as well as I do that my father plays his cards close to his chest.

Henry the Young King arrived this afternoon with an enormous entourage. He insisted, apparently, that the trumpeters should sound him into the town. My father pointedly did not appear to greet him, but my mother did go down and make a great fuss of him. I decided to take the middle course, so I did not go down while he was in the main square, but I did go to his quarters soon afterwards.

He was barely civil, asking me only if Geoffrey and John were here. His exact words were: 'Are the other children with you?'

Indeed, he does not help himself to win friends.

23 December 1172

Chinon

11 am

Today dawned bright and cold, perfect conditions for the feast, which will overflow from the Great Hall into two large covered areas set up in the main courtyard. Our family, together with the most senior noblemen, will of course be within the Great Hall. Nevertheless it was satisfying for my father, and indeed all of us, to see that the greatest Christmas court for years would be blessed by good weather. The peasants who will gather outside to watch proceedings will doubtless see it as a sign of God's favour on our family. They have an interest in the feast going well too, as they will receive the leftovers.

One innovation this year is my father's decision to employ four peasants to taste all of his food for him. When I told my mother this on my return yesterday, she commented wryly: 'He really does not trust us, does he?'

9 pm

What a day! As an example to the rest of the world of the dignity and power of our family, the feast was a triumph. The French court could never have managed such a spectacle, and my father cleverly invited the Count of Flanders, who is King Louis's most senior courtier, so that he could report back to King Louis. Perhaps only the Holy Roman Emperor, Frederick Barbarossa himself, could have managed such a display. And maybe not even he.

It began about a mile outside the town. The road was lined with tens of thousands of ordinary folk, all dressed in their finest clothes. The procession was led by the Bishop of London, Gilbert Foliot, together with about forty other bishops and senior clerics.

'Not a thin one amongst them,' my father grunted at me as we waited our turn to set off. He sees the corpulence of many churchmen as a physical sign of their corruption.

The bishops were followed by a choir of boys chanting psalms. Again my father grunted: 'It is lucky they put the bishops ahead of the boys. How the crowds would have laughed to see the bishops chasing the young boys up the road.'

Then came the lower squires and knights, in their finery, followed by the more senior nobility.

Finally it was our turn.

Firstly young John, riding a pony. Then Geoffrey, on a horse. Then myself, on Arthur. I had not paid much attention to the preparations for this procession, which was my mistake. Fortunately my mother had given instructions for my armour to be buffed and for me to have a new cloak. Carrying Excalibur unsheathed I looked and felt the part of a prince for perhaps the first time. I could certainly feel the attention of the crowd on me. And I enjoyed it.

My mother had rebuked me this morning: 'You and I know that this procession and the dressing up are just for show. But don't forget how important the show is. It demonstrates to the peasants, the merchants, to the nobles where the real power lies. Don't ever underestimate the power of a display.'

She is right. If I have never seen the like of this before, when I live with it every day, then I can imagine how the lower orders must be amazed by it.

After me came Henry. There had been a fracas as he belatedly insisted on processing at the same time as my father. My father gave him short shrift and sent him ahead, so Henry no doubt now harbours a further grudge.

And finally came my father in white ermine, and, at the last minute, my mother appeared at his side dressed in black on a white horse. They both wore crowns. They processed into town with my father rather gallantly holding my mother's hand up at shoulder level so that everyone could see they were united. The crowds were in ecstatic awe.

Then inside to the feast. For some reason, there was a delay with the food, which made my father increasingly irritable. He is irascible at the best of times, but catch him when he is hungry and the results can be explosive.

The delay meant that the wine and beer began to have an effect more quickly than usual. Even the ladies seemed to be caught up with the success of the procession and were sipping at the wine, which I suspect was stronger than usual too. Within half an hour the atmosphere was quite lively.

Even my father relaxed. After an hour or so, I saw him chatting animatedly, almost flirtatiously, with my mother. Who would have thought that possible?

I had the misfortune of sitting with Henry's wife, Margaret, the daughter of King Louis. She really is no great beauty. She has virtually no breasts, a long angular nose, and breath that makes one take a step back if one has not been forewarned. Henry got the raw end of that deal, to be sure.

I was civil to her, of course, but no more. Geoffrey, my younger brother, was on the other side of her. He is quite the most handsome of us all and has an easy charm with the ladies that escapes me even though I am a full year older. A mischievous streak runs through him too. He spent the whole of dinner trying to flirt with Margaret, in order to provoke Henry. However, Margaret is such a dry old stick that she did not react at all.

On my other side was the voluptuous Sarah, wife of the Count of Flanders. She is an exciting creature, with long blonde hair, an ample bosom and a coquettish smile. The drawback is her teeth, which are awful: yellow, with two gold replacement teeth right at the front. She obviously knows it, though, for she is adept at keeping her teeth hidden. It is only when she laughs that one really gets the full effect. I spent the whole meal trying to be charming, feigning interest in her two children. I think I made something of an impression.

The biggest stir of the feast came when my father noisily pushed back his chair and gave his hand to my mother to help her rise. The hall fell silent as they left together. Everyone was pleased that they seemed to be back on good terms after such a long time apart, though no one else knew of the Lysette and Rosamunde incidents. So I alone was taken aback at my mother's apparent forgiveness, after all that had been said and done.

Some thirty minutes later, I left the Great Hall to empty my bladder. My chambers were next to my mother's, with a shared washroom. As I pulled back the curtain to the washroom, my mother, going out through the other curtain to get to her bedchamber, turned around. She was naked. Then a cough told me that my father was in her bedchamber waiting for her to come back.

I turned and ran.

Back in the Great Hall, I quickly downed two or three cups of wine, ignoring what was going on around me. After the wine started to take effect I began to take more of an interest in my surroundings. Henry was drunkenly boring his neighbours about some recent tournament he had sponsored. Geoffrey had finally begun to get a reaction out of Margaret.

I think she was a little drunk herself, for she had seemed to come alive. I leaned over to whisper in Geoffrey's ear: 'Watch out! The ugly ones are always the most ferocious!'

He grinned wolfishly back at me, and drew his tongue across his teeth in a lascivious way.

I laughed and left them to it. Henry deserves nothing less than to be cuckolded, but he probably will not even notice.

I went to find Hubert Walter. He had anticipated that I would want to catch up with him, for he was waiting outside on the battlements. He was full of praise for the way the day had gone, saying: 'The King and Queen made an unforgettable sight.'

I smiled my acknowledgement and added: 'I just found my mother naked in our washroom. That was an unforgettable sight too. My father was in her room.'

He fell silent as he assessed this information. After a slight pause he replied: 'I am not sure that changes anything. Your mother could never have gone against your father anyway.'

I disagreed: 'I still think she might. I think I may have found out just how far she will go in order to keep him guessing. It is far from the courtly love ideals she keeps on about.'

'I would not worry about that,' Hubert counselled. 'Just be grateful that you have more information than any of your brothers. I take it none of them knows?'

I shook my head.

Hubert might well be right. I am focusing on how my mother could bear to share her bed with my father again, when the real question should be: 'What can I do with this information?'

On my way to bed I passed again through the Great Hall. Geoffrey and Margaret had left the table and were nowhere to be seen. Henry was holding court to three rather unattractive women.

I moved outside to the covered areas. All around

were signs of a general debauchery. I picked my way over bodies, some of which were coupling drunkenly on the floor. Eventually I found Philip, head of my retinue of household knights, and told him to be ready for a dawn departure. He looked aghast, but the resolve on my face quietened him.

We will ride out for training first thing. It will demonstrate my strength when everyone around me is weak.

25 December 1172

Chinon

A good day's training yesterday. My household knights were bleary-eyed and still stinking of wine when we gathered at around six in the morning. A couple of hours of hard riding followed by three hours of sword practice shook them out of their lethargy. We returned about an hour before dusk. My father was up on the battlements. He tipped his hat to me and smiled as we clattered through the main town gate. A small sign of progress.

Today was the usual tedium of a religious feast day. Church early this morning. Geoffrey and I had a hundred sovereigns riding on the length of Gilbert Foliot's sermon. The money passed to Geoffrey at one and a half hours. I had bet on less than an hour and a half. More in hope than in expectation.

I have had virtually no contact with my mother since finding her with my father two days ago. Is she avoiding me? If so, is it out of embarrassment? Or cunning? Or is she plotting with my father to disenfranchise me?

1 January 1173

Chinon

A New Year, and we have set off back to Aquitaine. My mother has spoken barely a word to me this last week for she seems to have been quite taken up with my father. Neither Henry the Young King, nor Geoffrey nor I know what to make of this sudden and unexpected rapprochement.

Even today on the journey she travelled in her wagon with the drapes drawn. Normally I ride alongside, talking. Maybe she was just cold. Maybe it is a sign. Or maybe I am just paranoid.

17 January 1173

Poitou

My mother and I have received another summons from my father. Little has been heard from him in the three weeks since Christmas and his reconciliation with my mother. She is girlishly excited at the prospect, whilst I am overcome with a sense of foreboding. If she continues to be drawn back into my father's sphere, then there is every risk that together they might try to consolidate their inheritance, which would mean that it would all go to Henry.

It is much better for me when my mother is estranged from my father as she feels strong enough in Aquitaine and Poitou to promote me there. My interests definitely lie in having them at each other's throats. Apart from which, it is nauseating to think of them together after my father's behaviour with Lysette and Rosamunde.

We set off at the end of the month. The court will be at Limoges.

28 January 1173

Poitou

I have heard from one of my mother's ladies-in-waiting that Margaret, Henry's wife, may be pregnant. It is only speculation at this stage, but potentially disastrous. The child, if male, would inherit above me.

However, Hubert Walter has pointed out the timing to me. After the events of the Christmas court, it may well be that Geoffrey and not Henry is the father. We shall have to think how to play this. Setting Geoffrey against Henry may well be advantageous, but if I get the timing wrong then I may simply make enemies of them both.

6 February 1173

Limoges

We arrived in Limoges this morning. My father greeted my mother with all of the honour a queen deserves, and she lapped it up. Following the ceremonial progress into town, they immediately retired together to my father's rooms.

I made an excuse to pass by the rooms an hour or so later, and could hear them in peals of laughter. I ran into Geoffrey on the way down the stairs and we repaired to the Great Hall to drink with Hubert Walter.

We sat around gloomily for about an hour. The prospect of Henry lording it above us is about the worst possible outcome for Geoffrey and me.

After three or four cups of wine, Hubert piped up: 'I have an idea.'

We both grunted gloomily. Eventually I mumbled: 'Come on then, let's hear it.'

'Well, I'm not sure how far you would want to go to protect your positions...'

A few moments of silence. Then Geoffrey said: 'Go on.'

Hubert began slowly but gathered confidence as he spoke.

'As you know, the court has been convened in order that Count Raymond of Toulouse can pay homage to your father the King. This is a big, and humiliating, step for the Count. He will be nervous that this signals the end of any independence for him. If we can persuade him to go to your father and reveal that you two princes and Henry, and even the Queen Eleanor have been plotting against your father, then your fears of a joint rule by your father and mother, and a joint inheritance for Henry, will never be realised, as the King will inevitably turn against you, and in particular, the Queen.

'Count Raymond will be happy as your father's control will be diminished. Both of you will benefit from the outcome as your mother and father will almost certainly be estranged.'

Geoffrey and I looked at each other for a full five seconds while our minds raced separately through the possible ramifications. We began slowly to smile at each other. I replied first.

'Our father would be incandescent. He could never trust our mother again. Henry will struggle to persuade my father that he is not involved, as they cannot exchange two words without fighting. It leaves the way open for us all to inherit our separate lands.

'But the downside is that Count Raymond may refuse, and once we have spoken to him, he may well choose to go to the King and tell him of the plan. If the King finds out about this plan we are well and truly sunk. We will have to think hard about how to persuade Raymond to follow us.

'Henry will know that he was not involved and so he may think that we have set him up, which may come back to haunt us. However, he may well not think it through. God knows he doesn't normally think much.

'Our mother will suspect our involvement. But she will not be able to do anything about it as her bridges with our father will have been burned.'

Geoffrey and I were both excited by the plan. We called for more wine and began to work once again through the implications, drinking quickly as we talked. Hubert observed quietly. When Geoffrey left the table for a moment to relieve himself, he moved over to me and murmured in my ear: 'Sire, please do not be tempted to tell the Prince Geoffrey what you know of Margaret's pregnancy. He may try to bring it in to play against Henry the Young King. This will not favour you. And however much you are co-conspirators now, remember that Geoffrey is as much your enemy as Henry.'

I started at this, but even after the effect of a few cups of wine, I recognised the truth in what he was saying, which served to deflate me rather.

Geoffrey came bouncing back in, and although we carried on refining our plan, I sense that he realised that the atmosphere had changed.

It's a shame that I appear to be able to trust a relatively low-born informal adviser rather more than my own flesh and blood. But I fear that the world has always worked that way.

14 February 1173

Limoges

We have spent the past week or so going backwards and forwards with Raymond of Toulouse. Finally he has come to an agreement. Five thousand marks from Geoffrey and five thousand marks from me.

He will see my father tomorrow.

15 February 1173

Limoges

Raymond came back from his audience with my father. He said that the King had been cold, almost aloof, and had shown no emotion on the news that his wife and three of his four legitimate sons had been plotting against him by fomenting discord amongst the leading barons.

Raymond had expected him to fly into one of his customary rages, but he did not. Instead he was perfunctorily dismissed.

At any moment I expected my father to come storming out from his chambers to have us arrested, or to confront us, or to seek an explanation.

But nothing happened. Most odd.

18 February 1173
Limoges

Three days later, and still nothing from my father. He is even still sleeping with my mother. He truly is the consummate tactician, literally keeping his enemies close to him.

Geoffrey is almost wild with the tension; he is becoming uncontrollable. Drunk every night and bedding the most inappropriate women, including the wife of the Castellan of Limoges. He will get a knife in his back if he carries on like this.

22 February 1173
Limoges

Philip, Count of Flanders arrived yesterday. His wife Sarah came too. She was the buxom one from the Christmas court with whom I had mildly flirted, until her teeth had put me off.

The Count's arrival was unexpected, at least to me and Geoffrey. Hubert Walter knew nothing of it either. Has Philip been summoned by my father as part of a dialogue with King Louis?

Although unexpected, I have to say that I was pleased to hear of his arrival, mostly because I have spent a number of pleasurable hours dwelling on the thought of his wife and how she might like to put those terrible teeth to good use.

I saw her before she saw me, for I entered the Great Hall last night by an entrance reserved for our family. I hung back a little, observing her through the gap made as I held back the curtain between the passageway and the Great Hall. She was looking round expectantly. I hoped that it was me that she was waiting for. It was, for I caught her eye across the room as I entered. A brief glance was all that it was, but it was enough.

I kept glancing in her direction during dinner. She was doing the same as, two or three times, our glances connected. I felt almost light-headed after each shared look, my mind working feverishly to identify possible ways in which we could be alone together.

I thought my frustration must be visible as the Count of Flanders pushed back his chair and begged leave from my father to retire. My father airily waved his consent and Sarah also rose. Geoffrey, sitting next to me, nudged me and whispered in my ear: 'Relax. He asked the steward to send up one of the pretty pageboys. I don't think he'll be bothering Sarah tonight.'

My face, when I turned to look at him, must have been a picture. He kindly said: 'I'll get a message to her as to where your rooms are.'

Some ten minutes later, I made my excuses and left. I almost ran back to my rooms. Once there I set about washing myself as best I could, but there was only cold water.

I raced around the room, blowing out and lighting candles to try to get the right level of light in the room.

Finally I lay down to wait, dressed in my nightshirt, but I could settle only for five minutes or so before I had to jump up and pace around the room.

There was no sign of her. Eventually, I must have dozed off, for I woke with a start to hear gentle knocking on the door. I rushed over to the door and pulled it open to see Sarah standing there with her hair up and wearing a dressing gown that fell low across her chest.

She locked eyes with me and gave a slow, knowing smile. She looked down at the rest of me and giggled gently. I followed her gaze and saw my erection clearly straining against my nightshirt. She said: 'I see you've started without me.'

I was mortified, but my shame was quickly forgotten as she pulled open her dressing gown and then lifted it off her shoulders, and advanced towards me, naked.

She leaned up to kiss me, keeping her mouth closed, until I prised it apart with my tongue.

She took hold of my erection with both hands and tugged at it. I must have gasped involuntarily, for she broke from the kiss and whispered in my ear: 'I think we should get the preliminaries out of the way quickly so that we can enjoy ourselves.'

With that, she dropped to her knees, lifted my nightshirt and took me deep into her mouth. After initial misgivings, I decided I might as well surrender to her, and I grabbed her head as I ground myself into her mouth. I came pretty quickly. As soon as I had finished she rose up off her knees and looked me full in the face. It was only after a second or two that I realised that she still had my come in her mouth. She winked at me, then swallowed.

We spent the rest of the night rutting, perhaps three or four times, mostly to her command. Move here, move there, a little bit higher, a little bit lower. I was happy to oblige, as I was learning all the time, part of the education of a prince.

She crept out of my room as the first shafts of dawn cast a reddish glow into my room.

Her parting words were that Count Philip had been drawn here by a mysterious request from my father. It seemed she had mistakenly assumed that I had asked my father to issue the summons in order that I could see her again. Since I had done no such thing, it must be that my father had summoned Philip in reaction to what he had learned from Count Raymond. Maybe he was throwing a decoy.

25 February 1173
Limoges

Sarah has repeated her visit to me every night since the first encounter. She is becoming more and more adventurous each time, as if she has spent each day dreaming up new activities for my bedchamber. An uninterrupted night's sleep was starting to sound alluring.

So, last night, when she arrived late and told me that she had had to 'oblige' Count Philip before slipping out to come to me, I sent her away in a fury. Part of me was genuinely angry, but I was also looking for an excuse not to spend another night with her.

27 February 1173
Limoges

There was news from my father today. He is to leave on a hunting party in two days' time. And he is taking Henry with him. Curious, I thought at first.

Then Hubert pointed out that my father may have picked on Henry as the weakest link in the chain. Like a wolf separating the frailest sheep in the flock he will get Henry alone and either praise him into being indiscreet or he will incite his anger and find out the truth that way. Geoffrey and I are to return with my mother to Brive. I wonder what this portends.

28 February 1173
Limoges

Now Rosamunde has arrived, and she will be travelling with my father. My mother is incandescent. She immediately sent messages to Geoffrey and me to make sure our households are ready to leave at dawn tomorrow. It seems like my father is making his move.

It also transpires, according to Hubert, that Geoffrey has been spending quite a bit of drinking time with Count Philip of Flanders. Hubert thinks that Geoffrey may have told Philip about the liaison between Sarah and me.

Earlier this evening I asked Geoffrey directly whether he had told Philip about Sarah and me. His eyes narrowed and there was a momentary pause, before he replied: 'Not as such.'

'What does that mean?'

'It means that I didn't need to say anything. He knew already.'

'How can that be?'

Almost reluctantly, Geoffrey said: 'Because Sarah told him every last detail. It is part of their deal. He prefers boys, but recognises he has to sleep with her to produce heirs. She can go clscwhcrc provided she is discreet and tells him everything. From the last sexual detail to any pieces of information that he can use. I suppose she is his spy.'

I must have looked horrified as I desperately tried to recall what I had and had not said to her. I don't think I was too candid, although it makes me uncomfortable that Philip knows exactly what happened between us. I said as much to Geoffrey.

He replied: 'You should count yourself lucky. Apparently he normally insists on watching through a peephole or a curtain.'

I blanched at the thought of this. I don't think I shall trust the Flemish again.

3 March 1173

Limoges

My father left for Chinon three days ago with Henry and Rosamunde. Although my mother had originally told Geoffrey and me to be ready to travel on my father's departure, she suddenly changed her mind and told us to stay put. Fortunately, Count Philip and the demanding Sarah have also left. He is a disgusting little man, and she has rather lost her attraction too.

4 March 1173

Limoges

Two messengers arrived this morning, about half an hour apart. The first was from Chinon. Apparently, the royal party arrived safely in Chinon, but father and son had an enormous row at dinner and the King stormed off to find Rosamunde, leaving my brother to his own devices.

It seems that for Henry, this was the straw that broke the camel's back, for he sneaked out of his apartment, found the stables and took off on his horse. For good measure he appears to have stolen my father's favourite horse to use for one of his knights to ride, whose own horse was lame. No one at Chinon seemed to know where Henry and his companions had gone. The messenger had been dispatched to see if they had returned to Limoges. But we have seen neither hide nor hair of them.

The second messenger, from King Louis, brought sensational news. It turns out that Henry had ridden straight to the court of Louis at Paris. The faces of those gathered in the room as the messenger told us this news were revealing. Geoffrey and I were surprised, and rather taken aback by Henry's sudden show of gumption. Hubert, standing beside me, did not seem particularly surprised, as if he had suspected something like this all along. My mother's face was inscrutable, betraying neither shock nor acceptance. Once the messenger had finished, the meeting broke up quickly and we all retired to consider the news.

5 March 1173

Limoges

Geoffrey and I spent last night drinking with Hubert and discussing the possible outcomes from this development. We went round and round in circles, concluding somewhat sadly that it was a shame that we were to be mere spectators at a duel between my father and Henry. We rather admired my father's cunning in splitting Henry off, so that he had only one rebellious son to confront. But equally we, rather grudgingly, admired Henry for his daring in going to Paris and for his impudence in stealing my father's favourite horse. I smile every time I imagine him finding out his horse had gone.

6 March 1173

Limoges

My mother never ceases to amaze me.

Hubert and I were talking again late last night. He went through a list of examples of princely sons rebelling against kings, but he could not think of a single example of a wife of a king, or indeed of any other lesser ruler, rebelling against her husband.

But that is exactly what my mother is now doing.

She came into the hall this morning as Geoffrey, Hubert and I were finishing breakfast. Her exact words to us were: 'It has become clear to me that your father has become contaminated by that whore Rosamunde. It was at my suggestion that Henry the Young King should go to King Louis' court and take up arms against your father. I now want you both to do the same. To go to Paris and be part of an alliance with Louis and Henry against your father. I will remain here and raise an army to support you from amongst the Poitevin Lords. You should go as quickly as you can.'

With that, she turned on her heels and walked out. We were left in a stupefied silence. I was the first to break the spell.

'So, I suppose our plan to stop our mother and father uniting seems to have worked better than expected.'

I laughed nervously, although there was no particular humour in my words.

Geoffrey pushed himself off the bench opposite me, saying: 'Well, I'm off to get ready.' He almost bounced from the room.

I turned to look at Hubert, who was quite pale with shock. I teased him:

'You certainly didn't see that coming, did you?'

He didn't reply at once, but gave me a stare that was a second or two longer than was strictly polite. Then he too rose from the bench and said: 'It seems the decision has been made for you. No need for you to make up your own mind now.'

I was a little shocked by his directness. But he's right. It is exhilarating to be taking on my father at last, but a cynic would say that I am only being so bold because my mother said it was the right thing to do. Not so courageous of me after all.

7 March 1173
Limoges

We leave for Paris in the morning. It's now late and Armande and I have been charging around all day, busy with the preparations. My retinue of twenty household knights has been doubled by my mother granting a further twenty each from her retinue to Geoffrey and me.

She made her entire entourage of knights line up on horseback outside the castle gates, from dawn, shivering in the bitter wind. Once Geoffrey and I got there, we had to march up and down the line inspecting them. We then had to take turns to pick men from her group. It was humiliating for the knights, and nerve-wracking for us, as we had no particular basis on which to inform our decisions.

Geoffrey and I joked conspiratorially about it later. I revealed that I had been choosing knights based on the size of their horses and whether they had my favourite colour, red, on their shields. He laughed and told me he'd been picking the ugly ones, so that he wouldn't have so much competition in Paris.

I admired my mother's generosity, but later Hubert told me she had kept back her fifty favourite knights. We had been choosing from the remainder. Sly rather than generous.

We had a farewell dinner with my mother earlier this evening. I had expected her to share our excitement, but she was businesslike and coldly determined.

Geoffrey was a little annoyed by her aloofness, but I suspect it was nothing more than her being a step ahead of us. She had been skittish and edgy during the past few months as she was unsure where her Christmas reconciliation with my father would lead. Now that it is decided, mostly by the unseen intervention by Geoffrey and me, she has fixed her resolve. I could certainly learn from that.

Her parting gift was to send each of us one of her ladies-in-waiting. They turned up at our respective doors late this evening. I sent mine away. I recognised her as one whom, unknown to my mother, Geoffrey had already been with. I'm not having his cast-offs. Unfortunately, that rules out quite a high proportion of the women at court. Luckily we are moving on to fresh ground.

23 March 1173
Paris

It's been a long journey, punctuated by terrible early spring weather. The roads were virtually impassable in places, particularly around the Loire.

We stayed four nights at Issoudun and five nights at Blois, to shelter from the worst of the rains.

As we approached Paris, the sun at last began to break through the clouds to bathe the city in an ethereal glow, framed in a shallow mist.

We halted a mile from the city gates, to allow the sentries time to fetch whichever dignitary was deemed suitable to meet us. This gave us the chance to don our finest cloaks and armour. I felt a change come over me as I switched horses, mounting Arthur dressed in my armour with the ermine-trimmed red cloak billowing behind me, and holding Excalibur high in my right hand. We had all felt rather low after the harsh conditions of the journey, but now there was a huge collective lift in our morale as we trotted down the sunlit hill towards the city gates.

There, to my astonishment and gratification, was King Louis with a substantial entourage, including, at his right-hand side, my brother Henry. On his left was a young boy, aged about seven or eight, Louis's son and heir, Philip.

We slowed our pace and then stopped completely some fifteen yards from the King. It was my first sight of the man to whom my mother was married all those years ago. He looked impressive, mounted on a great grey charger, and wearing a blue cloak and a small crown on top of his almost white hair. Maybe it was he who originally taught my mother the power of a ceremonial?

A small group of heralds sounded a short fanfare as King Louis dismounted. Geoffrey and I quickly followed suit.

He took a couple of steps towards us, then stopped and gently smiled at me. I moved forward, slowly, and with my head held high and stiff. I stopped in front of him and our eyes locked. I knew that he expected me to kneel, and I knew that I had to.

But I wanted to hold his eyes for just long enough to suggest that maybe I would refuse to kneel. Geoffrey had gone down on one knee almost immediately, but I stayed up until the silence was deep and absolute, and then I stayed up until the first murmuring and shuffling of the crowd started. If I got the timing right, I could achieve my objectives of winning the grateful applause of the assembled crowds, obtaining some grudging sign of respect from King Louis, and establishing myself in his mind as the senior partner out of Geoffrey and me. It was a tense moment, but I relished it.

Just as the crowd's unrest started to grow, and as the King's smile began to look a little forced, I bent my right knee and slowly dropped to kneel before him, all the time keeping my eyes firmly fixed on his. His first expression was one of relief, and almost immediately he caught himself. He then smiled a small nod of acknowledgement to me. My plan had worked.

We remounted and followed our host down through the gates into Paris itself. It is, of course, much larger than any of the other cities in our territories (except London), most of which centre around the castles. Paris has an entirely different atmosphere. There are still plenty of soldiers, as there are in other cities, but in Paris they are swamped by the sheer mass of humanity. As a consequence, the soldiers seem less important. Similarly, the fortifications seem to be less obtrusive. Commerce has the upper hand here. The citizens appear much wealthier too. Thousands of them lined the route into the city, cheering and clapping. They looked prosperous and well dressed, and generally seemed healthier and better fed than the citizens in our towns.

But, whilst the vast size of Paris, almost one hundred thousand people so King Louis told me, generates wealth for its citizens, they clearly have not yet mastered the art of matching the infrastructure to the population size.

The sewers dug down the middle of the road were overflowing and the stench was remarkable, even by the standards we have grown used to. There were rats everywhere. I remarked on the smell to the King, who seemed astonished that I had mentioned it. Perhaps he is accustomed to it. I am not sure I will ever be. I caught Geoffrey's eye shortly after my exchange with King Louis. He knew exactly what I was thinking, and flashed a knowing grin at me. It was all we could to do not to burst out laughing at the absurdity of everyone pretending this terrible smell did not exist.

We eventually arrived at the banks of the Seine, and were taken to our lodgings. King Louis seems to have spared no expense in trying to make us comfortable. No doubt he had heard how notoriously mean my father can be, and he plans to offer a sharp contrast. Hubert reminds me that King Louis has played this trick once before, when receiving Thomas Becket some fifteen years ago and encouraging his delusions of grandeur to such an extent that it ended up in a damaging rift with my father.

The King's son Philip was left with us as we settled into our rooms. He is a bright little fellow, and followed me everywhere as I inspected our lodgings. Clearly he was anxious to please, but he has this annoying habit of standing a pace or so too close. It is slightly unnerving and, even though he is only eight years old, one constantly feels as if one is on the back foot, trying to get slightly away from him. After an hour or two he left us to it, but then reappeared to summon us to a banquet in the Great Hall.

King Louis is clearly fond of ceremonial, as the feast was a magnificent affair. Henry, Geoffrey and I were fêted as the guests of honour and spent a good deal of the time bobbing up and down from our seats as we acknowledged the various toasts. Strangely there were no women at our table. They were seated at a lower level.

As a consequence, Geoffrey looked slightly uncomfortable. It is an interesting weakness of his. He is outstandingly good at talking to women, but he has no feel for how to talk to men, which makes him a poor leader, as he finds it difficult to communicate effectively. The feast was therefore something of an ordeal for him.

24 April 1173
Paris

We have spent the past month getting to know the Paris court and its different customs. As I noted on our first night here the women are kept almost entirely separate from the men. It turns out that women were only at the banquet in our honour. Normally they eat separately.

The absence of women encourages the men to behave badly, particularly when drunk. Three nights ago, for instance, the Duke of Burgundy's younger brother pushed back his chair, belched loudly and announced to the assembled throng that he could not be bothered to go outside. And so he stood on his bench, slowly lifted the front of his raiment, and urinated into an empty vegetable dish.

There was an embarrassed silence as the last drops splattered into the dish and then out again on to the table. After a few seconds, King Louis laughed, giving the cue for everyone else to start laughing. Soon the entire hall was full of men standing on the benches, laughing helplessly as they tried to piss on to the table into the various dishes.

Geoffrey and I looked at one another and raised our eyebrows. We both felt out of sorts in this kind of bawdiness. Simultaneously we both looked round to find Henry. There he was, true to form, standing on the table spraying urine from side to side, laughing uproariously at his own cleverness. To think he is to be our lord and master. I pushed back my chair and left, as did Geoffrey.

The other startling difference between the court here and those of my father is the approach to discipline. For my father, who effectively won his kingdom as a young man through force of arms as much as anything else, military discipline lies at the centre of everything that he does. He even hunts like a soldier, with the objective to provide food for the table. Hunting here is more of an entertainment to be enjoyed simply for its own sake. As a consequence, it is often cancelled in poor weather, something my father would not even begin to understand.

King Louis imposes no discipline, for he clearly did not feel able to slap down the brother of the Duke of Burgundy when he started to piss all over the royal dining hall. All he could do was laugh. However, he does retain all the trappings of kingship, and indeed in some ways is much more successful than my father in presenting a majestic image to the world.

But that is all that he has. He has no power to inspire fear in his subjects. I cannot yet fathom whether that is because his position is weak, or whether it is because he wants to be loved and admired, rather than feared and respected.

I was discussing this last night with Hubert and Geoffrey. I spoke at length about the different styles of kingship and how I thought my father's style was superior. I became quite passionate about it, and as I finished, there was a short silence. Hubert and Geoffrey looked at each other and started to smirk. Their laughter grew as I got more annoyed by their reaction, until eventually even I began to smile, although I still had no idea why they were laughing.

Eventually Geoffrey managed to speak. 'Dear brother, listen to yourself going on and on about how great our father is, and how weak and feeble old King Louis is.'

'Yes,' I retorted. 'What is so funny about that?'

'Well, how the fuck have we ended up at the court of King Louis, having sworn fealty to him, and at war with our own father?'

He is right. But it is no laughing matter. How can we have been so foolish as to pick so weak a king to ally ourselves with? I went to bed cursing my impetuosity.

However, what is done is done, and we will have to see it through.

28 April 1173
Paris

King Louis has been adept at assembling a coalition against my father. There are the three eldest sons: Henry, myself and Geoffrey. Then there is William, King of the Scots, who is able to threaten my father's northern borders. He is an odious man, who smells so bad he must have given up washing since he left his homeland. Truth be told, he is more a cattle thief than a king, but he and his band of savages can provide a nuisance to my father. However, one feels a certain disdain about needing such men in our alliance.

Armande tells me that the servants' quarters are rife with gossip about what he and the other Scots get up to. The rumours are that they spend all night buggering each other. The servants are terrified to go near them, as one night about three weeks ago one of the boy servants was forcibly dragged out and raped in turn by each of the Scots. Then they cut out his tongue, shoved it up his arse and threw him into the cesspit at the back of the kitchens.

The other significant men in our alliance are altogether more noble. The Counts of Boulogne and Blois are here and they, at least, are both distinguished men. Also the Count of Flanders and his wife Sarah.

Initially I did not come across her much, as she has been unwell since our arrival. However, about a week ago she invited me to her rooms 'to discuss a personal matter'.

I talked briefly to Hubert and Geoffrey, who thought it best if I accepted her invitation. She and Philip are unaware that I know that she reports everything back to Philip when he cannot be there himself to watch and listen. As a consequence, I might be able to feed them misinformation, which would be useful to us.

We spent some time thinking about what that misinformation might be. First of all: who was to be the target?

King Louis? If we damaged him, it would merely make our alliance weaker overall. That was no help.

King William of the Scots? None of us could think of any way to reduce the prestige or standing of this pervert. Although people fear him, it is in the way in which one might fear a wild boar. There is no respect in the fear.

This left us with Henry. Although he is our brother, it does not feel as if he is one of us. Damage to him would mean that we would be advantaged, and it would give us both a certain satisfaction.

Now the question was: how to damage him?

Margaret, Henry's wife, is also the daughter of King Louis. Was there some way to drive a wedge between them?

Margaret confirmed about four weeks ago that she is pregnant and is expecting their first child at the end of September. When the news was announced Geoffrey had immediately calculated that he might well be the father of his elder brother's child. Henry, of course, has no inkling of this. His arrogance and self-importance preclude him from even having a passing thought that his wife might look at another man, let alone that she would succumb to his younger (landless) brother, and, becoming pregnant by him, try to pass the child off as Henry's.

If we could plant the seed in his mind that the child in his wife's belly might not be his, then it might prove to be the kindling for a very useful fire.

So, we resolved that I should resume my encounters with Sarah. I feigned reluctance at first, but in truth, I was anxious to see her again, with all of her clever tricks. The serving girls and junior ladies-in-waiting dished up by King Louis are all very well, but there is little of the element of risk that one gets by mixing political intrigue with sex.

So, yesterday, three or four days after her initial invitation, I sent Armande to her lady-in-waiting to inform her that I would be able to grace her with my presence a half hour after dinner in the hall was concluded.

I went up to Sarah's rooms at the appointed hour and knocked firmly on the door. I was actually a few minutes early, and there was a good deal of scuffling and shuffling before a lady's footsteps approached the door on the other side. It is a useful trick of my father's, to turn up slightly earlier than expected. It catches people slightly off guard.

As the door creaked back on its hinges, I began to enter the room, keen to impress on Sarah the extent of my ardour for her, so she might be less cautious and analytical about what I might tell her. Before I could say anything, Sarah spoke to her lady-in-waiting: 'Francine, you may leave now. And please stand guard in the corridor to make sure no one tries to come in. The Prince Richard and I have delicate matters to discuss.'

She smiled at me as she uttered this last sentence.

Francine left the room quickly but not before casting at her mistress a look that she evidently hoped I would not see, as she stood behind me now. Fortunately I caught it in the mirror. She glanced across the room as if to intimate that Sarah should look over to the other side of the room, where the curtains were drawn across an entrance, presumably to her bathroom.

Sarah was very smooth. She came across to me, took both my hands and said:

'My Lord Prince Richard, what a pleasure it is to see you again.'

With beautiful poise, she turned from me, moved towards the curtains and twitched them together in the middle so that they fitted more closely together. Unfortunately for her, the first twitch did not entirely cause the curtains to cover the toes of a man's boots, presumably Philip's, poking out from underneath.

The second twitch of the curtains did the trick, but by the time she turned to face me, I had turned away from her and was looking out of the window at the night sky, so that she would not think that I could possibly have seen.

So, we were to have company on our little adventures tonight. I found the thought quite stimulating. Clearly she did too, now that her fear of discovery had abated. For, as I turned to face her, I found that she had removed her dress so that she was now almost naked.

Her little bush, recently plucked, stood out against her pale flesh, and she wore a kind of bustier that lifted her breasts, but did not cover them, so that I could see her nipples stiffening.

'I thought you called me here to discuss an important matter,' I said as calmly as I could muster. I wanted to make her work for this, so I tried as best as I could to put on a stiff, haughty manner.

It hardly threw her off guard. 'Of course,' she replied, 'I wanted to discuss with you the number of men-at-arms you have in training at any one time and how you go about disciplining them.'

She spoke the word discipline in an overtly sexual tone. At the same time she put her right leg up on a footstool at the end of her bed and gently began to rub herself with her fingers. After a second or two, she took her hand away, brought it to her mouth and licked all the way round the forefinger and middle finger before resuming the rubbing.

I was a little distracted by this and was slow to reply. She encouraged me: 'Tell me, Prince Richard, how do you discipline your men?'

Suddenly I understood the direction she wanted me to go. I decided to tease her a little.

'Well, it depends on the nature of their crime,' I replied.

'What if they had been very bad?'

I swallowed. 'In that case, there is any number of punishments. But my marshal prefers to flog the men. He wakes them in the night, drags them to a central area, usually the hall, and ties them over a table so that they are lying face down with their hands and feet tied to the table legs with leather bands. Then he wakes the other men and bids them to come to the hall to watch.

'Then he strips the clothes from the guilty man with a knife until he is entirely naked. Then he ties a strip of material over the man's eyes, so that he cannot see. Then he selects one of the men from the assembled throng and gives him the whip. He announces the nature of the misdeed and asks the guilty man if he will accept the punishment by one of his brothers. The guilty man always says yes. Then the marshal passes a long whip to one of my men, who whips the man the required number of times.'

I could see that Sarah was getting excited by this, and I decided to embellish the story slightly.

'Then all the men leave, and the guilty man is left on the table for the household staff to find in the morning. Unfortunately, the last time we did this, the Scots got down first in the morning, and buggered the poor man.'

Then a thought came to Sarah. 'I have been very bad too. Will you discipline me?'

I feigned discomfort, to see if I could provoke her into saying anything indiscreet. 'I'm not sure... how bad have you been?'

She began to manoeuvre the footstool to be in front of her. Then she turned to a cabinet beside the bed and pulled out a riding crop. As she did this, she whispered: 'I have been unfaithful to my husband.'

I sighed: 'I know that! Who have you been with, apart from me?'

'Well, the King himself, King Louis. And, of course, your father the King Henry. And then your brother Henry the Young King. And his wife. And your sister Matilda. And...'

I interrupted her with a shocked:

'Stop! You are teasing me.'

She responded playfully. 'Maybe. Maybe not.'

She climbed on to the footstool and kneeled on all fours awaiting her punishment whilst still fingering herself.

I picked up the crop, brought it above my head and lashed it down on her backside. She squealed, almost covering the sound of the groan that escaped from behind the curtain.

Four more times I brought it down on her backside, each time she squealed slightly louder and her hand began to move quickly beneath her.

At the fifth stroke, I said: 'Enough,' and stood back.

Now I tore off my clothes and stood behind her. She leaned back, took hold of my stiff penis and pulled me into her. I began thrusting at her and asked: 'And your husband? Does he still do this to you?'

She froze slightly, but then answered steadily: 'Yes, but he prefers the other hole.'

We soon both came. Or at least I did, and she pretended to.

Afterwards, we lay together on her bed. I was alert and sharp, waiting for the intrigue that was to come.

Sure enough, it did not take long.

'So, have you heard recently from your father?' she asked.

I knew that the French court was rife with rumours that the reason that my father had not yet attacked France was because he was in negotiations with us, his sons, to take us back.

That was an easy question to answer, because it was the truth. 'No, not a word since the day we left Chinon.'

Here was my opportunity to throw in the killer blow:

'It is somewhat fortunate that he has not been in touch. I am not sure what he would make of Henry's wife being pregnant by another man.'

She drew in her breath a little too sharply.

It was out there now. The stone cast into the smooth lake. We all know that there will be ripples. What we do not know is how far the ripples will go.

But Henry is a good friend of Count Philip's, so I do not think it will be long before it all plays out.

Sure enough, Sarah was soon at me again, trying every which way to tease from me the name of the father of the child. I had agreed with Geoffrey and Hubert that I would eventually give in and give her Geoffrey's name. But I didn't, despite her best efforts, because I suddenly felt it might not be sensible to expose Geoffrey to Henry's full wrath. Or not yet, anyway.

Finally, I announced that I had to leave in case her husband came for her. In reality I wanted to get back to tell Geoffrey and Hubert what had happened. I amused myself before leaving by saying that I needed to use her washroom, which of course lay behind the curtain. I had thought that she would jump up urgently and somehow stop me from opening the curtain. But she languidly said: 'Go ahead.'

So I did, and was astonished to find that Philip was not there any more. He must have had a secret exit route. I searched quickly for it with my eyes while pissing noisily into the bucket. But I could not see it.

All in all, it was better that I did not find him there. It would have amused me briefly. But it would have been damaging in the long run to our ability to feed misinformation to the House of Burgundy and beyond.

1 May 1173
Paris

It did not take long.

Today, the court held a May Day feast. It had dawned a beautiful sunny day. For the first time this year I could feel the warmth of the sun against my skin. Everyone seemed to be in a particularly jolly mood. The feast started earlier than normal, and I think the wine, too, was stronger than normal.

After about three or four hours of feasting, the dancing began and the seating arrangements became more fluid.

Henry had been seated at the right hand of King Louis, but he moved to the table occupied by Count Philip. This was not unusual, for the two of them were thick as thieves normally.

I suspect that on Count Philip's side the friendship was born of political calculation. He recognises that Henry will be a useful friend to the House of Burgundy, and that the surest way to achieve Henry's friendship is to flatter him relentlessly.

No doubt Sarah has been useful in this. I now think it is reasonably likely that she has slept with Henry, as she claimed the other night. I can even imagine the scenario. Philip no doubt initially told my brother that Sarah was in love with another man, but that he did not know who the man was. Then, perhaps a week later he would have confessed that it was in fact Henry who was the subject of Sarah's affections, and that after much soul-searching Philip would step aside temporarily to allow them some pleasure.

This way he would bind Henry to him as a friend and future ally. He might also find out some useful intelligence from Henry in the process.

So, there they sat, the two of them, heads together, as if discussing some tremendous secret.

Then, suddenly there was a great roar, followed by a crash. The hall fell instantly silent.

Henry was standing now, having overturned the table at which he and Philip had been sitting. He looked back at Philip then whipped his head round seeking someone out.

For one ghastly moment I thought that all our plans had gone wrong and that he was looking for me. I am ashamed to say that I ducked my head and looked steadily at the floor, while my stomach and throat constricted and I became slightly short of breath. After a few seconds I composed myself and looked up ready for the confrontation.

But it was clear that Henry was not looking for me. He was running across the hall to the area where the ladies were dining. He stood in front of the ladies' High Table and through clenched teeth hissed: 'Princess Margaret, come here now!'

Blushing, she stumbled a little over one of the benches as she made her way round to him, and some of the ladies at her table twittered anxiously. Coming to a halt just in front of him, she tried to speak but no words came out: 'I...' It was as if her throat had dried up.

I was watching Henry closely. His face was very red indeed and the veins in his temples were visibly pulsing. He kept clenching and unclenching his right fist.

The only noise to be heard was the far-off sounds of servants clearing away the plates outside the hall.

I risked a quick glance at King Louis to see what his reaction might be to this incident involving his daughter. He was fixed in his seat, watching developments. But he also cast a sly glance around the hall to gauge how others were reacting.

Finally, Henry began to speak: 'How are you feeling today?'

The Princess replied, obviously surprised at such a civil question: 'I am feeling fine, thank you, My Lord.'

'Is the baby well?'

'I have not yet felt the baby move, My Lord, but I believe that all is well. As soon as I feel the baby move I will let you know.'

At this, Henry's head drooped, as if the strength had been sapped from him.

He took a great heaving breath and forced his head back up.

As he looked up, his right fist snaked out from behind him and crashed heavily into Margaret's mouth. There was an immediate explosion of blood and teeth. Her head snapped back so sharply that at first I thought that Henry had broken her neck. Then Margaret collapsed on to the floor.

It was a strange moment. I would have expected people, including myself, to have rushed to her aid. But we were all waiting to see what Henry would do next.

He roared: 'Why the fuck would you think that I would want to know when the baby moves?' A short pause. 'When the baby is not my fucking baby.'

He stepped towards where she lay on the floor, semi-conscious.

'You stupid, lying, fucking bitch.'

With that, he aimed an almighty kick at her stomach. As the first kick connected, there was an audible gasp as the crowd drew breath. I glanced again at King Louis. Surely now he would intervene to save his daughter? But no, he raised his hand as a sign to his men to stay back.

I looked again at Henry. It was as if the first kick had burst the floodgates. He rained kicks in on her now, accompanied by a low guttural roar. He was almost foaming at the mouth; globules of spit were flying off him.

There was no sound from the Princess, merely the unmistakable sound of Henry's boots kicking her stomach. Eventually he stopped and stood there panting, his hands on his knees as he bent slightly over to catch his breath. From this position he glanced upwards at King Louis, who stared steadily back at him for a few seconds and then looked away. He was not going to do anything. The coward.

Henry raised himself to his full height, as if suddenly remembering that he was a man of royal blood and not some artless peasant who had lost his temper. To his credit he managed to walk in a dignified manner out of the hall. A few of his retinue scurried over to follow him out. He passed Count Philip. They glanced at each other, but Henry did not break stride and Philip did not move to follow him.

As Henry left, the hubbub began. The ladies-in-waiting gathered around Margaret's body lying on the rushes on the floor. Everyone else turned to each other and prattled excitedly about the astonishing scene they had just witnessed. I caught Geoffrey and Hubert by the arms and propelled them subtly but firmly from the hall.

We gathered in my rooms; Geoffrey was the first to speak. 'If it was my baby, he's probably killed it.'

I stared at him. I had not realised that he might think of it in terms of being his baby. And that therefore he might go after Henry himself.

Hubert counselled patience, as ever: 'First of all, let's find out how the Princess is.'

Geoffrey glanced at him, so Hubert added: 'And her baby, of course. Then we must see how King Louis reacts to his daughter being half beaten to death at his own court in front of him and all of his men. I suggest we stick together and have the knights ready for a rapid departure if necessary. In any event, let us not be seen in Henry's rooms, or with his men. King Louis knows of the breach between you. Let's not give him any reason to think there is some sudden family loyalty here.'

I agreed with Hubert, and Geoffrey soon fell into line too.

To tell the truth, I was astonished by the catastrophic violence my brother had unleashed so quickly. Although we had planned for him to find out the truth, and for him to react forcibly, I had not predicted that he would so viciously assault the Princess Margaret in the full view of the court, and that he would in all probability kill the unborn child.

2 May 1173

Paris

The unborn child is indeed dead.

Henry's assault caused the Princess to miscarry the baby this morning. Although badly beaten, she will live.

King Louis has done nothing to move against Henry. He must be embarrassed by his daughter's behaviour and take the view that her husband must be allowed to punish her. But even so, to allow one's daughter to be publicly beaten at one's own court and to allow one's unborn grandchild to be killed… it beggars belief that he can be so weak.

As for the three of us. We are keeping ourselves to ourselves. Only the three of us know who the real father of the child was. And given yesterday's events, perhaps it is best if it remains a secret.

5 June 1173

Paris

Armande has returned after a four-week absence. When he received news of his father's death, I allowed him to return to his home near Périgueux. Not a great deal has happened in the meantime. Count Philip and Sarah left the court shortly after Henry's discovery of Margaret's infidelity. I presume Philip calculated that he could not, for the time being, worm his way further into Henry's affections.

Henry himself has been quiet. As has King Louis. As has my father. It is driving Geoffrey and me to distraction.

We felt as if we were embarking on a great adventure in joining forces with King Louis against my father. But we have seen precious little action. Even when we try to inject some pace into the progress of events by trying to provoke Henry, nothing moves forward. He attacks the Princess Margaret and in doing so brings some dishonour on himself and Princess Margaret and tangentially on her father King Louis. But nothing really changes.

King Louis is mired in the daily rituals of his own court. I believe he knows that his position is weak, but the rituals provide a web in which he is safely cocooned. It is as if the web is preventing him from acting.

Henry is present at every dinner and event, but it seems he is there in body rather than in spirit. He has managed to maintain a forced rumbustiousness in public, but to me there is a vacant look in his eyes. I suspect that the shock of Margaret's infidelity, and his own reaction to it, has punctured his self-belief and confidence.

For probably the first time in his life, something important has gone against him. Previously, he had smarted at perceived slights and fumed at my father's lack of respect for him. But now he has suffered a genuine setback and, rather than rising to the challenge, he seems to be diminished by it. To the extent that he is a rival to Geoffrey and me, it pleases me to see him weakened in this way. On the other hand, after my father, he is the most senior member of our family, and an important part of our alliance against him.

Geoffrey and I are of the opinion that Henry will recover. We will awake one morning to find the confident, swaggering braggart has returned, and we will quickly long for these days of relative calm.

Hubert feels differently. He believes that the rupturing of Henry's confidence in such a dramatic and public way will have had a deeper and more profound effect. He says that confidence can only be built up slowly, layer by layer, and that it will take years to return, and then only if Henry does not allow this crisis to overwhelm him in the meantime.

So, for the time being, Geoffrey and I spend our days training for the fighting that must eventually come. We ride for four or five hours a day either hunting or performing cavalry exercises with our men-at-arms. I believe that our efforts and self-discipline will pay dividends when we do battle for the first time, but we are also reaping the benefits now as our standing in the ranks of our alliance is gradually rising.

I have also been preparing for my first tournament in three weeks' time. My father had previously forbidden us from taking part, presumably on the grounds that it was too dangerous. A month ago, however, Geoffrey and I boldly announced that we would enter King Louis' annual summer tournament, and since then we have had to prepare assiduously.

At first I found it extraordinarily hard to stay mounted when my lance hit the practice target. Gradually I have learned to thrust my lance forward just before the point of impact, so that it hits home with full force, while keeping a slight bend in my arm to allow some cushioning of the impact. On the first day I had four or five painful falls, but with some fifty knights watching each practice session there was no option but to get back on and try again under the full glare of their knowing smirks.

Now that Geoffrey and I have trained so hard and we can manage to gallop through at full speed and hit the practice target accurately each time, we have gained at least a little respect. But I suspect they are still wondering to themselves how we will cope when half a ton of horse flesh is coming at full speed towards us. Indeed, I don't know how we will fare. Sometimes I feel that, if those clowns can do it, then so can I. At other times I am half-hoping, half-dreaming, that my father will ride over the horizon and stop me from participating in this madness.

22 June 1173

Paris

Today was the day of the tournament. Midsummer's Day.

The build-up has been intense, quite unlike anything any of us has seen before.

One hundred carpenters have been brought in to build the stands for the nobility to watch from. The peasants are to be allowed in too, standing on the hillsides of the valley in which the tournament field is set. I had expected perhaps a few hundred spectators. As it turned out, there must have been twenty-five to thirty thousand. It seems that King Louis had sent out announcements telling of the participation of the two Plantagenet princes.

Henry the Young King, styling himself a real king, and therefore above it all, declined to take part. For almost the first time, I thought him wise, for Armande told me that the main attraction for all the spectators and the servants was the tantalising prospect of the high and mighty being tumbled to the ground in so very public a fashion. If the spectators were really lucky, the losers might even be badly injured or killed.

Geoffrey and I were with Hubert in one of the tents set up at the side of the tournament field. We twitched the curtains apart from time to time, amazed that so many people were still flocking in. Our horses, including Arthur, snorted and huffled outside. Inside it was quiet. And tense.

As the most senior rank, I had been drawn to go first against a young novice knight from Lusignan. Geoffrey was to go next, after my bout.

The crescendo of noise outside built slowly as we nervously skittered about inside the tent, making poor jokes and then laughing too much at them, as a relief from the tension. Then suddenly heralds trumpeted the arrival of the King and his party. As the heralds' notes died down, ushers entered the tent to indicate it was time to go.

I crossed myself, smiled at Geoffrey, at Hubert, and went to the exit. I paused briefly on the threshold to check I had everything.

I suddenly realised quite how tense I was. My penis felt tiny, my crotch felt damp, although I had not wet myself, and my buttocks were clenched tight. My armpits suddenly felt as if they were springing water, something my marshal had warned me would happen.

A deep breath, then I marched out of the tent. There was a gathering roar as the crowd saw me, coming to a crescendo as I mounted Arthur and turned him quickly to trot down to the centre of the tournament field. Although I kept my visor up, the rest of my armour cocooned me, so that the noise felt somehow remote.

The knight from Lusignan was trotting towards me from the other side of the field. I could hardly make out his features, as he too was shrouded in armour plating. His horse looked fast, although much smaller than Arthur.

We neared each other, nodded once and turned to face the royal boxes in the stand built to the side of the centre point of the tournament field. King Louis stood, and with his left hand indicated to the Bishop of Paris that he could come forward and begin his prayers. I bowed my head and focused intently on Arthur's ears. I could not hear the Bishop's prayers; all I could hear was the continual thud, thud, thud of my blood beating in my eardrums and the deep rasping of my breath inside my helmet.

The roar of the crowd seemed to indicate that the Bishop had finished his prayers, so we turned and trotted to our respective starting points. My marshal was there with two grooms, who gave Arthur a last drink of water. I lowered my visor and brought Arthur round to face down the five-hundred-yard track.

Halfway down, in the royal stand, I could just make out King Louis rising from his seat to stand. He waved at the two guards holding a great red flag in front of him.

They dropped the flag through ninety degrees and the crowd roared. I lowered the lance in my right arm to face at a forty-five degree angle, and pulled on the reins for Arthur to get moving. We were off.

Arthur was quickly up to full speed and we were flying along. The feeling was exhilarating. At the mark one hundred feet from the centre point, I brought my lance down horizontal to the ground. The other knight, from being a mere speck in the distance, was now becoming much bigger very quickly.

As he came into my sights, I tried to concentrate on two things. Firstly, trying to hold the lance level at a height at which it would catch him at the top of the chest or throat. This was not easy given its weight and the need to hold it slightly forward to lessen the impact. Secondly, I had to try to get forward and up in the saddle so that there was some flex if he should hit me. The flex should absorb some of the impact of the blow. Or that was the theory.

There was a sudden crash, then a great shout from the crowd. My left side took a blow high up, which knocked my left arm loose from the reins. My whole body rocked back in the saddle but I just managed to stop from toppling backwards. My right arm, carrying the lance, had landed with a tremendous thud in the neck of the other knight. There was a ghastly whooshing noise a moment after connection, which must have been the wind being knocked from him. His whole body jerked backwards on the tip of the lance. His horse careered on in a straight line, but his body dropped at an unnatural angle straight to the ground.

As my lance disengaged, I struggled to raise it back up to the level of Arthur's head. I was terrified for a moment that the tip of my lance would become stuck in the ground and I would be catapulted off. I eventually managed to bring it up, and I immediately brought Arthur to a halt.

I turned, acknowledging the cheers of the crowd by raising my lance to the sky. As I trotted back towards the other knight, I could see what a mess he was in. His head was lolling back at a strange angle, and his throat was a bloody pulp. As I came round I could see that his eyes were glassed over.

He was dead.

My throat constricted and I gagged involuntarily inside my helmet.

I lowered my lance, bowed my head to the body of the knight, and then again in the direction of the King, before setting Arthur to trot back towards my tent.

I was dimly aware of the ecstasy of the crowd, but I was too numb to take it in fully. I was shaking quite badly now and I needed to get to my tent and out of public view before anyone noticed. The crowd probably mistook my haste for the ruthless professionalism of a merciless warrior, and seemed to love me all the more for it.

My father once told me, while deciding whether to order a man to be hanged or not, never to underestimate the bloodlust of a mob. He said it was almost always wisest to give in to the bloodlust, however distasteful, because it needed to be satisfied. If it wasn't, it could easily turn to resentment, however illogical that might seem. I seem to have inherited his talent for giving the mob what they want.

I staggered into the tent and collapsed on to one of the beds. Hubert was there and was soon busily organising the two men taking off my armour. Geoffrey had already gone out to his bout. I closed my eyes and the world span as if I was drunk.

'Ten minutes,' said Hubert. 'Ten minutes and you'll recover.'

He was right. The nausea passed and I was soon back on my feet, but the next couple of hours still passed in a blur.

As was customary, the dead knight's armour and horse were brought to me as my spoils of victory. I gave the horse to Hubert and the armour to my marshal. Both seemed delighted initially, but later sheepishly approached to ask if they might swap.

Geoffrey won his first bout, landing a glancing blow on his opponent sufficient to unbalance him from his horse.

My next opponent, who had won his first bout too, then appeared outside our tent, seeking permission from my marshal to enter. After a terse exchange outside, he was eventually allowed in. I nodded at him as he came in, encouraging him to speak.

'My Lord the Prince Richard, I beg permission to forfeit our bout,' he said through gritted teeth. I wondered at first if he had been coerced by one of my entourage into withdrawing, but I suddenly realised it was pain that was causing him to grit his teeth, rather than embarrassment.

I enquired as to the reason. In reply he let his cloak drop down from his neck to reveal his right arm hanging uselessly from his side. It looked to me as if his collarbone was broken.

I was about to grant his wish when he collapsed to the floor, with a loud moan. Hubert summoned our doctor to attend to him, while I went outside to take the measure of the other participants.

I was now through to the final, where I would meet the winner of the bout between Geoffrey and Fulk of Bayonne. I was nervous for Geoffrey, for Fulk was the champion of King Louis's court and had been for seven years. He had never lost a bout and had a reputation for ferocity and malice. He accentuated his reputation by dressing all in black. His horse's livery, too, was black and he carried a plume of black ostrich feathers, given to him by the King, in his gleaming silver helmet. He was a perennial crowd favourite, for his mercilessness as a teak-tough natural born killer contrasted well for them with the preening, prancing dandies of noble and sometimes royal birth.

Certainly, as he and Geoffrey met in the middle of the field, performed a salute to the royal box and turned to trot to their positions, I could sense that the crowd's sympathies lay with Fulk and not with my brother. I was becoming increasingly anxious now for Geoffrey's welfare. I could just make out Henry's head moving in the royal box. I suspect he was quite keen for Fulk at least to win, if not actually to permanently disable or kill Geoffrey.

The flag went down and they were off. From this distance it seemed as if Fulk was twice the size of Geoffrey and was moving much faster. In a few moments it was all over. There was a loud clash of arms, the sound of which reached us a split second after we saw it happen. Geoffrey was off, but he rolled quickly and leapt back on to his feet, dancing towards Fulk as if he wanted to take him on in hand-to-hand combat. I heaved a huge sigh of relief, but the crowd seemed disappointed. I suspect they felt that Geoffrey had dived or taken a tumble rather than going full out for Fulk. From what I knew of Geoffrey, that was perfectly possible, but I was simply glad he had emerged unscathed.

Then it dawned on me that I was now to face Fulk myself. I had briefly been worried about the prospect of a final between me and Geoffrey, but that had swiftly changed to concern for Geoffrey's survival. Now I had to think about my own survival. There was to be a two-hour break while the crowds were entertained with acrobats, clowns, fire-eaters, and gypsies performing horsemanship tricks. Then there was to be bear-baiting. My final with Fulk was billed as the last event. The climax. Or, as I morbidly thought, the end.

I turned and made my way back to the tent. Geoffrey was soon there, full of beans, no doubt with relief at having survived. I smiled at him and cocked my head to one side so that he would know I was asking this question in a friendly manner: 'Did you go for him, or were you ready to come off?'

Geoffrey's eyes hardened a little, as if he were annoyed with me for speaking of what he thought he had brilliantly disguised, but then he flashed me a knowing smile and laughed: 'Dear brother, how could you accuse me of such a thing?'

So he had taken a dive. I smiled back, raising my hand in mock acceptance of his mock denial.

A few minutes later, as we gathered round to collect food from the table, I muttered to Hubert: 'Maybe I should do the same, take a little dive to save my little royal arse?'

He pursed his lips and answered: 'But think of the prize if you actually unseat Fulk. Your fame will be unbounded.'

I looked sharply at him. I had not thought of winning. I had thought only of survival.

'But I cannot unseat him. He's a giant. And he's never lost.'

'But every giant has a weak spot, and I think I've spotted his…'

Hubert stopped, searching my face to see if I wanted him to go on. My eyes must have given me away, because he continued. 'One of the reasons he is able to get so much power into the thrust of his lance is that he lowers it at the thirty-yard mark and brings it back up to chest height at the halfway point. He then follows through and this extra momentum gives him a huge advantage.'

'Yes, I know that,' I said, 'but how can I get round that?'

He studied his feet, as if embarrassed by what he was about to say. 'Well, if you were to hold back your horse just slightly, or even to start a little late, then you might be ten or maybe twenty yards short of the halfway point. And if that were to happen, then he might well miss you entirely as the trajectory of his lance would be all wrong.'

I stared at him for several seconds. He must have mistaken my stare for outrage that he might suggest that I would be capable of so unchivalrous an act, for he started to stammer: 'I'm sorry for even suggesting it...'

But I interrupted him: 'Do you think I could pull it off without anyone thinking I was deliberately holding back?'

'I'm sure you could, especially if just afterwards, I go around saying how amazingly brave you were to carry on with an injured horse...'

He and I both knew there was nothing wrong with Arthur.

'Then, it's just between you and me,' I said in a low voice.

He murmured back: 'Think of the prize, think of the prize.'

He was right; if I could pull this off the news of it would reverberate around Europe. My father will be mad at my impudence in entering the tournament at all, but surely he would be proud if...

Time raced on and before we knew it, I was trotting down the field again towards the great black monster on his great black charger. As we turned to salute the King, my heart had begun to sink again. Surely I could not defeat him? As we wheeled away to trot back to the starting post, he hissed at me: 'Don't you dive as well, boy!'

That made up my mind for me. I gritted my teeth and, turning on the starting line, looked down the field to see my opponent's charger pawing at the ground in its excitement to begin. The King stood up and the red flag fell. I tried to hold Arthur back a second or two, but he was not receptive and was off quicker than I wanted. I pulled at the reins, hissing through my teeth, imploring him to slow down. He relented a little, but I still felt it was all happening too fast. We were too quickly through the two-hundred-yard mark and then the one-hundred-yard mark. I looked up at the great black beast bearing down on us. He seemed to be riding faster than in his bout against Geoffrey, no doubt fuelled by his anger at Geoffrey's perceived cowardice.

I was still straining at the reins, trying to hold Arthur back. He seemed to recognise what I wanted for he slowed very slightly. Before we approached the thirty-yard mark, I lowered my lance, earlier than before for this time I planned impact on my side of the halfway point.

Then, suddenly he was upon me, a good thirty-five feet on my side of the line. His black lance was rising up in front of his mount's galloping hooves. The lance was coming straight at me, straight at me, straight at my chest. Then with a guttural roar he realised he was going to skim over the top of my shoulder and he tried desperately to lower the thrust of his lance. As he did so, he came forward and down in the saddle, bringing his neck forward on to the shimmering silver point of my white lance.

Again, the impact was shattering, almost wrenching my arm from its socket. Again I struggled to raise the lance as it came free, so that again it almost plunged into the ground and catapulted me off. But again I was lucky, just pulling it away from the ground in time.

I halted Arthur, who was whinnying with excitement, and leaned forward to pat his head. I turned to look at Fulk lying motionless on the floor. There was an almost funereal silence among the spectators as they took in the unprecedented sight of their great champion lying in a heap of tangled bones. We could all tell from the way the bones were lying that he was dead.

I approached his body, dismounted and walked slowly towards the knight, now thinking how best to satisfy the crowd. As I got closer, I noticed his feet and hands had begun to twitch. So he was not dead after all. The crowd too had seen this.

To me it was clear what had to be done. He would not live and I had to be strong. I knelt and drew Fulk's sword from its sheath and turned towards the crowd away from the royal box. I raised the sword high into the air and then with two hands brought it down like a dagger into the exposed throat. It clanged on the hard ground underneath his neck. Finally the limbs stopped twitching and I released the sword handle, leaving it shaking slightly in the ground.

I turned to the royal box, and bowed deeply as the crowd began to applaud, first gently and then with increasing fervour until the clapping, cheering and shouting reverberated around the tournament field.

King Louis rose and smiled at me, and the whole court rose with him to applaud. I turned to Arthur, mounted him and trotted slowly back to my tent in a daze. I had just beaten the undefeated champion by stopping him in his tracks in only my second bout. I had had two bouts in my short life and killed my opponent both times. This was the most famous tournament of all and I, a novice only a month ago, was now its champion. I would be famous throughout Europe.

All of this swirled through my mind, but my primary focus was on getting back to the tent without disgracing myself. I was shaking violently now, and was beginning again to gag inside my helmet. I somehow dismounted and as Hubert dragged me inside the tent and pulled off my helmet, I vomited all over the floor. What a great Christian hero, spewing out my guts.

Hubert patted me on the back as I lent over, hands on my knees, trying to get back my breath and wiping away the sick from my mouth. Eventually I stood straight and we embraced, as I began to laugh without restraint. Soon Hubert joined in too. I stood back, my hands on his shoulders, and looked at him, saying: 'Thank you, Hubert, a good plan.'

He smiled graciously. 'Well it took some nerve to pull it off.'

We rested in the tent for an hour or so, before beginning the weary journey back to Paris for the night's feast. I distinctly remember lying on the makeshift bed in the tent, feeling slightly detached and disoriented. Victory was not at all as I had imagined. Instead of wanting to run around with excitement and relief, I just wanted to stop feeling sick.

The ride back to Paris and the evening feast passed in a flurry of congratulations from the courtiers. Some were sincere, some were less so. The sincere ones were thanked humbly, but I tried to provoke the less sincere ones with false modesty.

Henry took my success awfully badly, I am pleased to report. I rather think he might have been hoping that Geoffrey and I might be killed, leaving him to inherit, with only little John as a potential rival. As it is, he is furious that his younger brother is now the proud recipient of this ridiculous adulation within the court, and that over the next few months my reputation will spread across Europe.

I sought to rile him further by organising for Fulk's armour, shield, sword and horse to be brought into the Great Hall with a fanfare halfway through the banquet. Normally, the victor would don the items himself. However, I already have Excalibur and Arthur, which I love, so I suggested that Henry might have them. Poor Henry. It was bad enough to be outshone by his younger brother, but then to be patronised by him as well! To his credit, outwardly he took it well, rejecting my offer with just the right level of amusement and firmness. But inside he must have been seething and he later flashed me a look of pure malevolence and hatred. Hubert, sitting next to me, caught the look.

'Best not to antagonise him needlessly,' he muttered. He's probably right, but it was worth the risk.

I gave Fulk's equipment and horse to Hubert in the end. He has done well out of the tournament, but I think I probably owe him, if not my life, then at least a share of the glory of victory.

He was to do me one more service this evening. A few minutes before I stood to respond to King Louis's congratulatory toast, Hubert took me to one side and said: 'In your speech you might refer to the fact that it is only your first tournament, but that despite this both of your opponents are dead and that you are now the champion of France. You feel it is only right that you retire now to give everyone else a fighting chance.'

I smiled at him. Perfect. My father (and mother) would be mollified, King Louis would be grateful that I was effectively giving him back the rank of being his champion, and best of all, I would not have to go through this terrible ordeal again.

I took Hubert's advice and made the speech he suggested, but everyone seemed to be too drunk to care much one way or another. Henry was not drunk this time. Indeed, I don't think he has been drunk in public since his terrible outburst against the Princess Margaret. He left early, with Margaret, casting dark looks at me as he went.

The feast degenerated in its usual fashion. I was not drinking and tired quickly after the exertions and nervous tension of the day. As I picked my way through the debris, on my way to bed, I paused to survey the scene. I was now champion of this court, where everyone seemed to be drunk or lecherous or oafish. Or all three at the same time. One group of knights were being serviced orally under the table by a band of prostitutes they had brought in for the occasion, while they carried on drinking as if nothing was happening.

I knew that my name and reputation would rise as a result, but, truth be told, being champion of this court was not that great an honour.

29 July 1173
Somewhere in eastern Normandy

The first signs that the phoney war is almost over. It has been almost five months since Geoffrey and I saddled up in Chinon to come to the court of King Louis and there has been no military action since.

Now, however, we are beginning to think that action might be imminent. My role as defined by the King is to lead a war party of one hundred knights, including Geoffrey's contingent but not Henry's. Our objective is to identify the size and strength of my father's forces in eastern Normandy. We are to harry his scouts, pillage his castles and fortifications where possible, and try to make such a nuisance of ourselves that he is tempted into chasing us, whereupon we are to try to lead him towards the forces of Philip, Count of Flanders. A simple plan.

Although I am nominally in charge, King Louis has also provided me with Balardier, a mercenary captain and veteran of a quarter-century's experience. He is a tough warrior, this Balardier. He is not that tall, but he is a bull of a man, with enormous shoulders and a solid mass of muscle at his neck. His face shows not one ounce of fat, but is deeply creased, so that his cheeks puff out like those of a dog. He is deeply tanned and wears his silver hair cropped close to his skull. When he speaks, or rather when he barks, it is with the crisp authority of one who brooks no interference. The deep bass of his voice rumbles right through the person to whom he is talking. He is a hard old nut, and I am sure he does not take kindly to being farmed out to me. He probably despises what he sees in me. A cosseted princeling knight obsessed with chivalric glory, fed a diet of weak opponents in order to build up my confidence and skill and, worst of all, in thrall to my mother rather than standing four-square with my father.

I tested him with this on our first night out of Paris, as we walked together around the camp at dusk, before retiring. He didn't reply at first, but grinned at me in what I imagine he thinks is a disarming way. Even his grin is a fearsome sight. His mouth cracks open slightly, but he has no teeth to speak of, merely a great hunk of yellow gold where his front teeth should be. I conclude that there is not much to be gained from trying to impress Balardier with persuasive arguments. I am going to have to convert him by action in the field.

Pretty quickly, I discovered that Balardier's ideas of our orders and my ideas of how we should proceed are fundamentally different. I imagine that we will proceed around the countryside billeting ourselves politely but firmly on the local nobility, in much the same way as my father's court would proceed around the country. Balardier has very different ideas. As a mercenary captain he is effectively a pirate, but on land. Everything is fair game to him. The treasure and silver plate in the local noble's hall. The valuables from each church we pass. Peasant women, young or old, are bundled into hedges or fields and raped at sword-point. Not by one individual mercenary, but in order of rank by every man in their group. Crops are burned, although they are no use to us. Cattle and pigs are slaughtered, even if we do not need them. Horses are stolen and tethered to the back of our train. The less useful horses have their rear tendons slashed so that they can no longer walk. When one of our knights enquired as to why the horses were left to scream in agony rather than being put out of their misery, old Balardier sneered at the knight's innocent foolishness: 'So that their owners can hear them scream, of course.'

These first ten days have been hard for us knights, with what is for many of us our first full exposure to the horror of modern warfare. It is not the glamorous chivalric ideal of one knight pitted against another, testing each other's strength and skill against the backdrop of an admiring military gallery. What we have seen so far is that an attritional campaign of the type we have been instructed to conduct is a dirty, vicious affair best suited to slaughtermen and tanners rather than to knights and princes.

To the mercenary, the enemy is not another soldier, it is that weeping child there, or this defenceless old crone here, or that tethered horse over there. Every living thing that is not a part of the mercenary squad is a target. What I have learned from them over the last ten days is that brutality is an effective military weapon.

At the beginning of the campaign I was tempted to rush into conflict with Balardier to assert my authority straight away, particularly over this issue of laying waste to everything in our path. But I reasoned to myself that I needed Balardier on our side, that he was probably expecting some kind of a battle over it, and that he would expect to win in the long run as his methods are tried and tested. I thought it best to allow him and his men their head on this and to pick a battle that I could win, in order to establish my authority.

I believe that Balardier must have been a little surprised by my initial attitude. Over the first few days the mercenaries' behaviour became increasingly violent, as if testing the limits of my patience. It culminated in the sack of a nunnery near Évreux. We, the knights, arrived at the nunnery probably an hour or so after the mercenaries, with Balardier at their head. Apparently the nuns had been insufficiently helpful when asked the whereabouts of their treasure. The Mother Superior had had her cowl and nun's habit torn from her and been asked the same question again. She had refused to answer, at which Balardier had taken a hunting knife from his belt and carved off a large chunk of her right breast. Two nuns who rushed forward to protect her were held down by two men each and raped by Balardier's two lieutenants Luc and Bertrand.

This was the scene as we arrived. Balardier stood there, knife glinting in the sunlight, making no attempt to hide what he had been doing. Luc and Bertrand were just standing up, buckling up their leggings. They at least had the grace to look a little shamefaced. I could sense the frisson amongst the knights behind me as we assessed the situation. They were appalled at what lay before them, although not so much out of pity for the poor nuns, as out of fear that God's retribution would surely come to avenge His dutiful servants; they did not want God to mistakenly include them in His retribution.

Silence fell as every man present realised that this was a seminal moment. If we had not come upon the scene, but merely heard about it later then I could have legitimately ignored it. Now, however, both sets of men stood poised waiting to see how their leaders would react.

I was quiet for a few seconds while I thought, hunting feverishly for a solution. Arthur was ambling slowly forward until I pulled him up five feet short of Balardier. He had clearly been assessing his options, eyes darting this way and that, in case I tried to overpower his men with my knights. But my words were not overly aggressive.

'I feel sure that God will be angry with your afternoon's work, Captain Balardier. Perhaps we can now push on in accordance with King Louis' orders.'

My words seemed to deflate the situation, although only because Balardier's men and my knights both thought that I had backed down by choosing not to fight the battle for leadership there and then. But I did have a plan, seared quickly in the heat of those few seconds when all eyes were on me.

Of course, neither Balardier's men nor my knights knew that as we moved off. The mercenaries were noisily exuberant, as if they had won some great victory, whilst my knights muttered dispiritedly amongst themselves. It was a difficult afternoon for me. My men were disappointed in me, and although I thought I had a way to bring the situation round, I could not say anything. Hubert trotted up alongside at one point and muttered: 'Leaders often have to ignore what the ranks are saying.'

I am sure he meant to be helpful, but I could not help feel downcast. My plan had to work.

Once we had made camp, in a clearing in a forest some ten miles from the nunnery, I called together Hubert, Geoffrey and our respective marshals. I quickly outlined my plan and, as I finished, stood back to gauge their reaction. Their stunned silence did not augur well.

Geoffrey was the first to speak.

'You must be fucking mad!'

I had expected that initial response, but was hoping that Hubert would latch on quickly. He did not disappoint me, commenting: 'If we could execute this plan, then the benefits could be huge.'

Thank God for Hubert. Within twenty minutes all four were on board, agreeing to meet at two o'clock in the morning at my tent. I went to find Armande to order him to lend me his monk's cowl and robe. I tried it on, and it was a tight fit around the chest, but my face stayed well hidden in the folds of the cowl.

Supper around the campfire was an uneasy affair. Balardier's men sang raucously and waves of bawdy laughter, partly at our expense, rolled over the gap between their campfire and ours. None of our men reacted, other than to dwell in a kind of mute disappointment.

Geoffrey and I were restless and retired to our tents early. I could not sleep and, once dressed in Armande's cowl and habit, contented myself with sharpening the blades of my knives relentlessly.

Finally, at just before two o'clock, we gathered at the entrance to my tent. After a quick check that everyone knew their part in the venture, we were off, splitting into the pre-agreed groups as we went.

Geoffrey and his marshal were to get Luc, and Hubert and my marshal were to fetch Bertrand. This was the riskiest part of the operation, getting them out of camp without being heard. Fortunately the mercenary camp was quiet as most of them had drunk huge quantities of the red wine I had sent over during dinner.

Armande and I waited in the forest glade we had agreed upon earlier. It was some three hundred yards from camp. With just the two of us there in the forest, it suddenly didn't seem like such a great plan. For three or four minutes we hopped nervously from foot to foot.

Then there was some rustling in the undergrowth and both groups emerged simultaneously into the glade. Luc and Bertrand were tightly gagged and blindfolded, with their hands tied behind their backs. Quickly they were tied against two trees alongside each other, with their arms stretched out behind them.

Just then Hubert signalled urgently to me. He took me to one side and muttered into my ear that we were missing something. I nodded my assent and he and my marshal disappeared for a few minutes, then returned carrying a brazier full of burning coals, with a branding iron perched on top.

These few minutes gave me further pause for thought, but I could not back down now. Signalling to the others to stand behind the tree so that they might not be seen, I stepped forward, my deep cowl disguising my face, and took off Luc's blindfold. He looked terrified at the monkish apparition before him. As I drew my knife and bent to cut his leggings away from his groin he suddenly realised what was happening and desperately tried to thrash around. At the same time, and though it was not in the plan it was a clever touch, Armande began to sing in a low, soft, chant. The moon moved into line, lighting up Luc's features and casting a ghostly pallor over the scene.

By now I had cut away his leggings, and with my heart in my mouth, I grabbed his penis, pulled it clear of his testicles and sliced clean through it with the newly sharpened knife.

The blood came thick and fast. I flung the severed penis into the bushes to my left, seized the red-hot branding iron and twice held the iron to the wound to cauterise it quickly, making the shape of the Cross. The smell of burning flesh was sickly sweet. The blood quickly stopped flowing, but Luc had passed out by now. His blindfold was replaced and he lolled back against the tree.

Now it was Bertrand's turn. I had to move fast, to get it over with, or I would not trust myself to continue. Armande kept up his chanting and Bertrand was dealt with in the same manner as Luc. He, too, fainted as the branding iron was applied.

Once the blindfolds had been checked again, the men were carried back to their camp. Armande and I waited in the forest in silence until Geoffrey and Hubert and the two marshals reappeared. I thanked them quickly and said:

'At least those two got what they deserved for raping nuns. Tomorrow we shall find out how successful we have been.'

With that, we returned to our camp. Unable to sleep, I lay in bed rigid with nervous tension and feeling sick.

The next morning dawned, the camps arose and at first there seemed nothing unusual. However, after breakfast, there was clearly some agitation in the mercenary camp. I retreated to my tent 'for prayers' and feigned disinterest in the commotion. Then after an hour Hubert came in, grinning from ear to ear, to announce: 'We have them, My Lord, we have them.'

Apparently Luc and Bertrand had been discovered still unconscious in their beds well after breakfast was finished. When roused, they babbled incoherent apologies to God for their grievous sins.

Of course the other mercenaries laughed at this and pulled back their blankets to get them out of bed. What they saw stopped them dead in their tracks. The men's penises were both gone, replaced by a large cross burned across their groins. They could not help but see it as the work of an angry and vengeful God. Pretty soon they must have recalled my words of the previous afternoon: 'I feel sure that God will be angry with your afternoon's work, Captain Balardier.'

It was reported that even the ultra-tough warrior Balardier paled when he saw what 'God' had done. The incident has not been mentioned between us, in the six or seven days since it occurred, but the whole command structure in our war party has changed. Not only does Balardier now listen to my orders, but he comes to me to ask permission to do this, that or the other. As a consequence our presence in these hostile lands is less of a burden on the inhabitants. I feel sure that they still do not welcome us with open arms, but at least our action is directed at the property of the nobility rather than at the peasants and their animals and crops. This is crucial for me, as these lands may of course one day be mine. Earning their grudging respect is important to me in a way it that it never could be for the scavenging mercenaries.

It has been an interesting lesson in the exercise of authority and the acquisition of further authority. One does not always have to fight one's battles in a face-to-face confrontation in the manner of a tournament duel. Sometimes it is better to back away from confrontation in order to get a better strike at one's opponent. Given that the vast majority of men have so little education, it is also relatively easy to exploit their superstition or fear of religion to one's own ends. On a larger scale, perhaps, that is why the kings of the last century put an increasing emphasis on their role as God's anointed representatives on Earth. Sometimes the Church connives in this to suit its own ends. At other times it rails against it, again to suit its own ends. For me, the trick is to ride the middle path for as long and as far as I can.

14 August 1173
Portjoie, eastern Normandy

Today was the day. Eventually, after a month or so of ceaseless harrying of the area, my father's forces responded, with a speed, ferocity and cunning that almost caught us out.

We were just emerging from the forest into an area of cultivated land that undulated gently up a rolling hill. We were about three hundred yards from the forest when from over the crest of the hill came the sound of a herald sounding the charge. Within a few seconds, a line of heavily armed cavalrymen swarmed over the brow of the hill. The flag they carried at the apex of the line was instantly recognisable as that of William the Marshal, who, with William de Mandeville, was my father's other leading soldier. They numbered perhaps two hundred men, twice as many horses as us. Furthermore they had caught us completely by surprise and, because of the heat, most of us were wearing only light armour.

I cursed myself for my stupidity in not having sent scouts ahead and for allowing our discipline to slacken so that we were not ready for action. But I had to decide quickly whether to gather my men to me and to try to withstand the charge or whether we should try to make it back to the safety of the trees.

We turned and ran, our horses beneath us sensing the danger and flying towards the woods. I was furious with myself; I could almost hear my father's mockery ringing in my ears as I, the champion of the court of King Louis and the tamer of the wild beast that is Balardier, was forced to turn and scramble for my life in my very first military engagement. It was not an auspicious start.

We made it to the woods by the skin of our teeth.

Only a few stragglers were caught up. Two men, who had been off their horses, had not been able to remount, turn and ride quickly enough. One of them was brutally cut down by the flashing sword of William the Marshal himself. The other slipped to the ground just before the cavalry line reached him. Normally this would not have been a bad tactic. The odds were better than even that he could have slipped unscathed between two oncoming horses. But luck was not with him. He fell right in the line of one of the horses and a ton of horseflesh landed on him. His broken body was carried along for a few of the horse's strides and the jumbled mass of bones was then thrown clear.

I did not know the man's name, but even in the midst of shock and my anger at myself, I could not help but admire the training that must have gone into that horse for it to carry straight on through the man on the ground. It is when a horse stops and starts and changes direction that its rider is unseated, and being unseated in battle almost certainly means death.

The edge of the forest was our refuge. We surged in between the trees and kept going for perhaps four hundred yards before turning and regrouping. William the Marshal called off the charge some fifty yards before his cavalry line hit the edge of the forest. He would have been nervous that the woods would have broken the line that gave his force such impact. He must also have been concerned that we might have laid a trap for him in the woods and that we were trying to lure him into it. As it was, they regrouped and after ten minutes of posturing they set off back in the direction from which they had come. The skirmish was over. We had been fortunate on three counts. Firstly, we had come across them within striking distance of the safety of the forest. Secondly, they had made the mistake of charging too early, giving us just enough time to reach the trees. Thirdly, the fact that they thought we were better than we were meant that they did not pursue us into the forest. A lucky escape indeed. It was a dispirited war party that made camp among the trees tonight.

I am still angry with myself for making such an elementary error. The men will lose faith in me, my father will laugh openly at me, and my hard-won new fame on the tournament field and in subduing Balardier will take a knock. I comfort myself, however, with the knowledge that William the Marshal, wherever he is camped tonight, will also be furious with himself for allowing the charge too early. If he had held his nerve a few moments longer, he could have been marching back to my father's court with me as his prisoner. His stock would have soared ever higher.

On a positive note, facing a charge by Norman horsemen is not something that many survive. In my first engagement I have seen at first hand why the Norman cavalry line has broken so many armies and won so many battles. The discipline and training of the horses mean that the opponent can be facing a two hundred yard wide machine of horse flesh and steel weighing several hundred tons charging at around twenty miles per hour. No wonder it is so effective so often. However, it is only at maximum efficacy when the timing of the charge is exactly right. God knows my men and I practise the actual charge often enough. But timing is everything and I must train myself in getting the timing right.

30 August 1173

Paris

Four days ago we were summoned back to Paris, without having had a further sniff of my father's troops. It is intensely frustrating.

On our return we found that King Louis was being his usual pusillanimous self. His weakness is that he cannot act decisively without the assent of his major nobles, and they will not grant him that assent very often as otherwise he would grow stronger. He is trapped in a vicious circle. It will be interesting to see, when he dies, whether this is a structural problem in the way in which France is ordered, or whether it is a problem of the King's character.

His son Philip, although he is only eight, already seems to have a strength of will about him that his father lacks. He spends a good deal of time in our quarters, and I have grown rather fond of him for his eagerness and willingness to learn. But he can be stubborn too, unyielding until he gets his own way. Given his physical limitations (he is small for his age), he has already learned to be cunning and to play people off against each other. It amuses me, and I trust that our friendship now will stand us in good stead for the future, but I can see that he does not show great favour or deference to anyone in setting out to get what he wants.

He, of course, is certain of his future. He will be king, and king alone. It seems that not only am I to share my father's lands with my three brothers but I will also have to bend the knee to Henry. Although, if he does not produce an heir, and he has already killed one unborn heir, then anything could happen.

3 September 1173

Paris

Henry the Young King is still away with his war party. He had been sent by King Louis with Philip, Count of Flanders to an area two hundred miles north of where we were. I believe that he has endured much of the same frustration as we did, but he was due back two days ago and there is still no sign of him.

We know that they had been laying siege to the castle at Drincourt and that Matthew of Boulogne, younger brother of the Count of Flanders, was hit by a crossbow bolt and died two or three days later. We also know that the Count subsequently called off the siege, but since then we have had no news. King Louis is terribly afraid that no news means that they have been captured and taken to my father.

But he is rather prone to assuming the worst about everything. He wears it like a badge of honour, always telling me that if one expects the worst one can never be disappointed. But I think it is exactly this negative philosophy that makes him so weak and indecisive.

7 September 1173

Paris

Today Henry and his party finally made it back, almost a week after they were expected. Outwardly at least Henry behaved as if he had won some great victory, and rather ostentatiously led the Princess Margaret straight up to his bedchamber like a conquering hero. In fact, both of our expeditions were damp squibs. We failed to provoke my father into anything more than a couple of reflex lashings out. He maintained his discipline and that of his armies well.

The feast this evening was a relatively low-key, almost despondent, affair. King Louis laid on considerable entertainment, with jugglers and fire-eaters, and even a little drama to go with the usual singing. But even this could not raise the collective spirits. I left early to return to my rooms.

What I found there cheered me a little. As I pushed open the door I could see that there was a good deal of candlelight in the room. This was strange as I always have all the candles put out when I leave the room, not out of thrift, as Geoffrey likes to joke, but because I have inherited my father's terror of fire. As I opened the door further I could see that Sarah was back. Her husband, Count Philip of Flanders, had of course returned at the head of the expedition with Henry. I had not known that she was with him. She had her back to me, her hair piled up on top of her head. She was wearing a black fur cloak that ran from her neck down to the ground.

'Good evening,' she murmured as she slowly turned to face me. I saw she was wearing a black mask over her eyes, so that she was completely blindfolded. 'I trust that you are entirely rested, my darling husband.'

I started a little at this, then realised that I was to be playing a role; presumably there was an appreciative audience hidden somewhere in the room. I dared not break the spell by looking round to see who else was there, but I stared straight ahead and she tentatively approached me. I assume that the tentativeness was caused by not being able to see, for as she reached me and felt where I was, she visibly relaxed, although I could have been anyone. Perhaps that was part of the excitement for her.

She raised both arms to her neck to undo the clasp that fastened the cloak. As the cloak fell away to reveal her in the golden candlelight, I gasped a little. She smiled at that, knowing that I had seen that her groin was now completely hairless, and that she had little weals on various parts of her body, presumably where the riding crop had recently been at work. She dropped to her knees, with the blindfold still in place and, rather deftly, lowered my leggings until my penis strained erect. Still, I said nothing.

'Have you missed me, dear husband?' she enquired as she began to lick up the undershaft of my penis. I remained silent.

'I can tell from your silence that you are displeased with me. Let me guess how I can make it up to you.'

She paused, head cocked to one side, as if speculating on a matter of great importance.

'Should I have brought a little help?'

She clicked her fingers and from the bathroom emerged two naked girls. They came up to me, one on either side, and jointly began to undress me while Sarah continued licking my penis. I stood stock still as they set to work fondling, kissing and nipping my arms, my buttocks, my nipples. I was soon beginning to thrust my penis ever so slightly into Sarah's mouth, then I came into her mouth as she clawed, moaning, at my buttocks.

She stood up shortly after and, beckoning the two girls towards her, kissed them both full on the mouth, seemingly transferring a little of my come to each of their mouths. Then they stood in front of me in a line, linked hands and swallowed my come.

At a signal from Sarah, the girls retreated to the bathroom, while Sarah, as she slowly untied her blindfold, said: 'Well, my dear husband, you seem to be at least partly pleased to see me.'

As she finished the sentence, she pulled off the blindfold to find me standing there.

'But you are not my husband,' she gasped in feigned shock. 'And yet I could feel him in the room…'

With that she turned and peered into the gloom behind the candles. A candle rose briefly in the gloom to illuminate the features of Count Philip sitting in the armchair against the wall. He smiled conspiratorially and greeted me: 'Good evening to you, Prince Richard.'

I am not quite sure what the approved court etiquette is for such a situation, so I brazened it out, replying: 'Good evening, Count Philip, I trust you are well. Is my brother Henry the Young King in good heart?'

Sarah and Philip looked at each other and laughed.

'It is Henry whom we wish to talk to you about,' said Philip. 'Do please sit down.'

I gathered my clothes, dressed quickly and sat down, reflecting as I did so that it would be wise not to get too involved with these two. Already things had moved from her telling her husband about me, to him watching whilst hidden in the room, to him now watching in plain sight. If I wasn't careful, he would soon be expecting to take part. I vowed that this would be the last time I would get involved with this strange couple.

I presumed that they wished to share some great revelation that Henry planned to mount a daring raid on my father's court, or that he had entered into some misguided alliance with an inappropriate prince.

But no. It turned out that all that they wanted to tell me was that they had managed to trick Henry into some sexual shenanigans that culminated in him, unknowingly, ejaculating into the mouth of what he thought was a prettily dressed girl, but which Philip and Sarah gleefully revealed to him to be a boy.

As they relayed his story to me, the scales began to fall from my eyes. They were not, as I had imagined, a great princely couple, bending the world to their will with their cunning and sophisticated plans. In fact, they were a pair of low, desperate figures with no ambition for glory and honour. They seemed to change visibly before my eyes; Count Philip now looked like a seedy old man, leaning forward in his chair, with a great belly hanging over his jewelled belt. Sarah, too, now back in her black fur cloak, seemed to metamorphose from the voluptuous sexual animal I had previously taken her for, into a parody of a low-born working woman. To cap it all, she threw back her head and laughed; this now sounded to me like the cackle of an old hag, and as she leaned back her ghastly teeth were revealed in all their glory.

I ushered them out as quickly as possible, together with the two girls still lurking in the bathroom. I called my servants to get ready a bath. They were astonished to be doing this at this late hour, but I had to get clean. I suddenly felt dirty, and used. And I felt stupid for letting myself be used. As I scrubbed myself raw in the bath, I vowed that there would be no more of this nonsense. From now on, I would pursue my ambition by an alliance with those whom I could trust and respect.

10 October 1173

Gisors

We have come to Gisors for a peace conference with my father. We were despondent after the relative failure of the two expeditions to try to draw my father out, and King Louis cannot bring himself to initiate any bold action. So when my father's emissary, William de Mandeville, arrived to invite us to a peace conference we all felt that we should see what he had to offer.

As is the way in negotiations, we immediately began to justify to ourselves why our father would want to accede to our wildest demands. Henry is particularly bad in this respect. He craves real power now, and cannot content himself with the notion of having to wait for things to come to him. As a result we three brothers arrived in Gisors with highly unrealistic expectations.

The conference was established in some fields outside of the town. The three of us attended the parley, with de Mandeville representing my father. Both King Louis and my father remained in their respective camps. It quickly became clear that we were not going to get very far. My father offered us all similar terms. To me, he offered half of the revenues of Aquitaine and control of four castles. Henry and Geoffrey were offered similar arrangements for their lands. In itself, this was quite a generous offer, but it had a condition. He was to retain full control and jurisdiction. In other words, he was prepared to grant us money, but he was not prepared to give us power.

Henry was immediately incandescent, spouting forth about the insult to his position and so on. Geoffrey and I were more circumspect. Henry has of course been lavished with money before, but neither Geoffrey nor I have, so we were less concerned about a struggle for power. We were minded to take what we could get and to leave the struggle for supremacy for another time, or to gradually assume more power in small increments, which would it make it hard for our father to challenge us over any one small step.

King Louis was offered nothing, and that was the real problem. My father was clearly seeking to divide the three of us from King Louis, to whom we all felt some sense of moral commitment. Perhaps my father's real mistake was in pitching his offer at the level he did. If he had pitched it higher, then maybe our moral commitment to King Louis might have been abandoned.

As it was, the conference broke up amicably enough, but without us seeing our father, which I found hard to accept. I know that I am now a fully grown prince, champion of the court of France, but there was still a small part of me that sought the approbation and validation of my father. I did not even know how he had taken the news of my tournament success. I felt the situation keenly, with him in a nearby field and yet refusing to see us. I can understand his discipline in not seeing us while we are in open rebellion against him. Indeed I respect and admire him for it. I just wish it wasn't so.

30 November 1173

Paris

Terrible news.

After the peaceful break-up of the conference at Gisors we came back to Paris, expecting to winter peacefully here and begin a new and more successful campaign in the spring.

But my father, perhaps sensing this, decided to strike before the winter set in fast. He led a group of his Brabançon mercenaries south of Chinon to attack the forces and lands of one of my mother's supporters, Ralph de Faye. These mercenaries are tough old beasts, hewn from the same stock as Balardier, and, given that they had the element of surprise with them, quickly overran the area. They took three castles, and in the last of them at Champigny, they won an unexpected prize.

In exchange for a peaceful and orderly handover of the castle, my father, as was his custom, offered the mercenary soldiers within the castle walls safe passage. He used to do this partly to save time and risk in besieging the castle, partly to protect the fabric of the castle that was about to become his, and partly because once they were outside the castle he usually managed to persuade the mercenaries to join his forces.

In this case, he waited astride his horse as the mercenary inhabitants of the castle filed past. Something unusual and yet familiar about the gait of one of the young soldiers on the far side of the column from him caused him to shout for the column to be halted.

Both sides tensed at the order. The surrendering mercenaries would always have an instinctive fear that the promise of safe passage was an empty promise. But both sides settled as my father dismounted and moved quickly to the young soldier he had spotted. He marched straight up to him and demanded that he remove his helmet. The young soldier, slowly, and with trembling hands, removed the helmet, and there staring back at my father was the beautiful, if soiled, face of his wife and Queen.

My father was exultant. His constant watchfulness, bordering on a kind of paranoia, had paid off in spectacular fashion. According to the reports, he performed a little jig of joy at his good fortune. My mother did not take kindly to this display, and shaking with anger now rather than with fear, she turned and stalked back towards the castle, trying to muster as much dignity as she could whilst dressed in the stinking tabard and light armour of a peasant mercenary.

It transpires that she had been travelling in the area, trying to muster new support and maintain existing support in the rebellion against her husband. She was staying at Champigny with a small entourage of six or seven men-at-arms. They must have had poor information about local developments, for the first they knew of my father's war party being in the area was when they woke to find my father's Brabançon mercenaries camped around the castle walls and his heralds trumpeting his arrival.

However, my mother is never one to submit meekly and while my father's men negotiated with the castellan for the surrender of the castle; she hatched her bold plan to attempt to escape alone disguised as a young mercenary. She summoned the leader of the castle's mercenaries and, with a large bribe, secured his co-operation. She quickly dressed in a spare set of clothes and light armour and scuttled down to join the nervous mercenaries waiting to march out under safe passage. She even went so far as to smear some mud over her skin to enhance her disguise.

It was an audacious plan for any man to attempt. For a woman it was extraordinary, and she very nearly succeeded. If she had, she would have become a legend overnight, and my father would have been humiliated.

But it was not to be. The little fact of my father noticing that one of the soldiers had an unmilitary gait was enough to thwart her plan. On such small chances do great events hang. So, instead of rousing all of our spirits, adding to her own fame and humiliating her enemy, my mother languishes in captivity at my father's pleasure. I wonder what his punishment for her will be?

15 December 1173

Paris

They have finally agreed.

For the past two weeks the court, led by King Louis, has been in a frenzy of inaction. There has been an extraordinary amount of bustling to and fro, and meetings of the various counts and marshals, but nothing has actually happened. Our spirits have dipped and risen so many times as it seems that finally we have a plan, only for King Louis to dash our hopes with yet another display of procrastination and vacillation.

Now, however, it is all agreed. I am to lead a sizeable group down to Poitou to assume my mother's place in command of the fight against my father. I am, of course, Count of Poitou as well as Duke of Aquitaine, but it is Poitou that is really the front line against my father. Aquitaine has always been my mother's land, and my father would not dare venture there at present, although it is nominally in his name.

The size of the group is not really big enough to merit the term army. I will be taking some three hundred knights and a thousand archers together with about five hundred mercenaries led by Balardier. Although I have been negotiating hard over the past two weeks to secure this arrangement, now that the moment is upon us, I feel somewhat fearful of the charge upon me.

As I sat astride Arthur early this morning for an inspection of the troops before a day's training manoeuvres, I was suddenly struck by the awesome responsibility for the lives and well-being of these men now under my sole command. Although I have been a man for some two years, I am still only sixteen. My sole military excursion thus far ended with us turning tail and running for the trees at the first sight of the enemy, having broken the first, unbreakable rule of any military handbook, which is to know where your enemy is at all times.

Although the feeling passed as we moved into the familiar routines of training, it unsettled me enough for me to talk to Hubert about it this evening.

I took a stroll with him around the city walls and, as the Cathedral of St Denis came into view, I said: 'Now that the moment is at hand, I am not sure that I am fit to lead this group of men. You remember the difficulties of the summer's expedition, and getting caught out by William the Marshal. I think we need more experience at the helm.'

He glanced at me, a little surprised and, I suspect, anxious to see whether I was serious or whether I was just fishing for some reassuring words. Something he saw in me told him that I meant what I said.

He thought for a while before replying: 'I believe that it is all a question of bluff. You and I may know that nothing is a substitute for real battle experience, but the men under your command simply do not see it. The men-at-arms on horseback see your triumph over Fulk at the summer tournament as a sign that you are favoured by God.

'You not only have a one hundred per cent winning record in the duel. You also have a one hundred per cent kill record. You and I know the background to that and how nervous and sick you were. But they never saw any of that. They need someone to respect as a leader, because it makes them feel better about their chances of survival. And you fit the bill for the men-at-arms.

'As for the mercenaries, they do not understand honour and glory. They are like wild dogs. They understand only two things. The first is iron discipline, and Balardier gives them that. The second is that, because they have no power to reason or think for themselves, they are terrified of anything unfamiliar or strange, and they saw the punishment meted out by God to Luc and Bertrand and they saw that you predicted God's wrath. So they will follow you anywhere.

'As for the archers; they have heard the stories from the other two groups and that will have some effect on them. But archers are always something of a breed apart, listening to their own captains and lieutenants. Like all soldiers, as long as they are fed and watered regularly, they are reasonably happy.'

I considered Hubert's words and then said: 'So, what you're saying is that my authority is derived from two incidents that are basically lies?'

Hubert smiled. 'Well, yes, if you choose to put it like that. But what is the alternative? You are clearly a better choice than Henry the Young King or Geoffrey or Count Philip or King Louis himself.'

I had to agree with him. My crisis of self-confidence would have to be tempered by the fact that the alternatives were so much worse. I had no choice. I just had to rise to the challenge.

Each day would be a trial of getting over my nerves. I would have to act without showing a single moment of fear or hesitation. I had done this in a small way before, in meetings with my father, in the tournament, and in the showdown with Balardier, and I found it exhausting, mentally and physically. To do it on the road with no respite will be a true test of my inner strength. It will be a baptism by fire.

15 January 1174
Saintes

We set off from Paris some three weeks ago, on the day after Christmas, and our journey to Saintes took roughly ten days. It was another arduous journey, bitingly cold and with treacherous conditions underfoot. But the greatest worry was the provisioning of the men. Food and wood for fires are always in short supply at this time of year, so we had set out with what we thought were plenty of provisions for five to six days' travel.

But the journey took longer than expected and the weather was harsher than usual. The prey in the forests seemed to sense our coming, so the archers were having difficulty in killing enough deer and boar for the men to eat. More importantly the cold was so intense that our axes simply would not go into the frozen bark of the trees, so we were short of firewood. In the end we had to resort to pillaging further and further afield, making our forces dangerously overstretched.

But we made it to Saintes in the end and the city elders were delighted to see us, not least when they learned of my plans to move against La Rochelle, the great port city and the biggest local rival to Saintes' markets. The soldiers were happy too, to be warm and fed after the difficulties of the march. At Hubert's suggestion, I went around making sure that the men were all comfortably settled before retiring to my own quarters. A simple ruse to inspire loyalty from the men, but he tells me that it is effective, and I can see the logic in it, even when I was desperate to get to my quarters and have a hot bath.

Tomorrow, we move to La Rochelle. The leaders of Saintes tell me that La Rochelle will be an easy target. It is the port that controls the vast majority of trade with England and as such it is hugely valuable to my father, and therefore by extension to me, both in terms of its revenues but also its psychological importance.

Hubert keeps nagging at me that we should not necessarily take the words of the leaders of Saintes at face value. They have a vested interest in La Rochelle being brought down a peg or two, but I am confident he is wrong in this. I am the Count of Poitou, and La Rochelle is therefore mine, and tomorrow I will be outside its gates with nearly two thousand men to enforce my claim. I am sure they will give me no trouble.

18 January 1174

Saintes

I was wrong. La Rochelle caused me no end of trouble.

We arrived outside the city at about noon on a glorious winter's day, with snow crisp and even under a bright blue sky.

As we approached, I could hear the sounds of alarms being raised and I could see peasants scurrying with their animals from the fields back into the city. Then, as we got closer, I could see that the gates had been closed against us. My heart sank a little at this, with a sense of foreboding about how this might turn out. But I was quickly into my stride, sending a small party of men-at-arms to hammer on the gates and demand that they be opened in the name of the Prince Richard, Duke of Aquitaine and Count of Poitou.

But clearly the townspeople had made their choice. They preferred to side with my father, who is stationed at Poitiers, than with me. I should have guessed that they would, for their livelihoods depend on selling their wine to England, which is still controlled by my father.

They signalled their choice by hooting with laughter at the loud demands made by my men banging on the city gates. Then some oaf threw the contents of his slop bucket over the wall at my men, and soon the guards all along the walls were doing the same thing. My men turned and retreated. As their leader approached me, I could see that he was bursting with indignation at the humiliation. I too was furious, and frustrated by the fact that we had none of the tools of siege warfare with us. We had assumed that our sudden appearance at the gate would be enough to get us in. It wasn't and we had failed.

We spent the rest of the afternoon examining the length and breadth of the city walls, searching for weaknesses. There appeared to be none. La Rochelle was well fortified indeed; the long-standing enmity between La Rochelle and Saintes meant that the city was well prepared for any threat.

My first instinct was to set the sappers to work digging tunnels to undermine the walls, but when I summoned the captain of the sappers, he blanched at the prospect of digging into the hard frosty ground. The other possibility was to attack by sea, but our reconnaissance scouts came back with the information that all of the local vessels had been taken inside the harbour as we approached. Furthermore the citizens had hauled into place a massive chain across the harbour entrance, which made it impossible to bring a ship in.

We were thwarted, but there was a moment of humour at the end of the meeting I held with Hubert and Geoffrey. We had pondered the various options for an hour or so, going back and forth, certain that one flash of inspiration would solve our problems. Eventually Hubert ran through the possibilities one last time. As he finished speaking, Geoffrey and I looked at each other and simultaneously mimicked King Louis's voice: 'I just know that no good will ever come from campaigning in winter.'

We burst out laughing at this absurd ending to our grand plan.

So we marched back to Saintes with a surprising spring in our step, disappointed not to have found La Rochelle open to us, but relieved to be returning to the unexpected warmth and food and wine of Saintes. On our return I contented myself with supervising the takeover of part of the cathedral for use as an arms depot.

27 January 1174

Taillebourg

Things have gone badly awry. I am not quite sure how to make sense of it all but I will try.

Since the debacle outside the gates of La Rochelle, we stayed within the immediate environs of Saintes training the men and spending the evening dreaming up elaborate plans for attacking the city as soon as winter thaws a little.

Last night was much the same as any other in the past fortnight. An early meal, no wine and to bed promptly at nine o'clock.

I awoke with a start at about midnight, judging by the wick of the night candle on my bedside table. I had been having a terrible nightmare. My father had been hunting me through a dark forest. He was dressed in full battle chain mail, but was hunting me with his spear as if I were a wild boar. I stumbled over a tree root, but got up briefly and ran on, before stumbling again as another tree root rose out of the damp ground to catch me by wrapping itself around my left foot. As I lay trapped on the ground, I looked up to my father dismounting his horse to come and stand over me, with his spear ready to throw at me. He paused briefly before striking to lift his visor. When he did so, I could see blood gushing in jets from both his nostrils. It was at this moment in my dream that I realised I was dreaming and I woke with a start. In retrospect maybe this dream was, in fact, a premonition.

It took me ages to calm myself and fall back to sleep. So much so, that when I was awoken again at about five in the morning, I thought it must still be a part of my dream.

But this time it was not a nightmare, although it took me a few minutes to acknowledge it fully. The captain of the town guard was battering at my door, imploring me to wake. He was shouting but there seemed to be a general hue and cry in the corridors behind him, so it was difficult to understand what he was shouting about.

I pulled open the door, drew him by the arm into the room and tried to get him to calm down. He was an impressive figure normally and the men had come to respect him for his quiet and unassuming competence. But now he was in a dreadful state.

Eventually I managed to get some sense out of him, and he said: 'King Henry has come. His men are inside the town and they have opened the river gates to allow the rest of his men into the town.'

The news hit me like a great stone had been swung into the pit of my stomach. I had thought my father was celebrating Whitsun at Poitiers. How could he possibly already be here, some hundred and fifty miles away? And how did he get in?

These were questions that were going to have to wait; we had to choose straight away to fight or to retreat. I dashed downstairs and across to the cathedral bell tower, shouting to the captain of the guard to raise Geoffrey and Hubert and to get them to meet me at the top of the bell tower.

When I got to the top, panting with the effort of running up all one hundred and seventy-eight steps (Geoffrey had been making the men run up and down them last week), I knew immediately that the game was up. My father's men had indeed taken the smaller of the city's two gates, down by the river, and they had opened them to the mounted horsemen who were now entering the city. With the advantage of surprise on their side, there was no chance that we could muster our resources in time to mount an effective counter-attack. What we had to do now was to salvage what we could. And find the bastard who had betrayed us and sneaked my father's advance guard into the city.

But first things first. I started down the stone steps of the bell tower, almost running into Geoffrey and Hubert on the way up. I signalled to them to turn round and as we reached the bottom and ran full tilt across the cloisters towards the halls where the men were barracked, I explained what we had to do. We had five minutes to rouse the men, get them ready and out of the city's other gates, before the hordes of my father's men were upon us.

We just about made it. Early on I decided we had to abandon the huge cache of weapons in the cathedral. There was simply no time to recover them. As the men formed up and began trotting down towards the main city gates, we could hear the sounds of my father's men getting ever closer.

The citizens of Saintes were, not surprisingly, in an utter state of panic. Last night when they had gone to bed all was relatively peaceful and there was a reasonable sized force inside the city walls, dedicated to the defence of the city, and there was no enemy within one hundred miles. When they were shaken from their sleep by the noise of battle, they suddenly realised that not only was the enemy not very far away at all, but it was inside the gates. Still worse, the brave force dedicated to their protection was turning tail and running, leaving them and their families and their property to the depredations of the incoming army.

As we rushed down the streets, the faces of terror of those to be left behind were appalling to behold. I felt a great wave of guilt wash over me, but then as I caught sight of my father's men at the end of the lane, I refocused on the need to get out.

We thundered down the narrow lanes on horseback, sending anything in our path flying as we crashed through. Shortly we came to the city gates, now open and with our men pouring out. This was the moment of truth. Would my father have set an ambush to cover us leaving via the main gates? Did he have enough men both to attack the city by the river gates and to cover the main gates? We would soon find out as we pressed forward. It is amazing how silent a few thousand men can be when they are retreating. When these same men are attacking they make the most fearful racket.

Those were tense moments as we made the first four or five hundred yards out of the city gates. But there was no one there. My father must have come with relatively few soldiers in order to have moved so quickly. While this meant that there was no ambush to fight our way through, it also meant that he had been able to take the city with far fewer men than we had had inside it.

As we settled into a gentler pace, anger rose inside me. Once again, my early attempts at military leadership were failing. If only we had had more men on the guard; if only we had had more scouts outside the town. We had tried to take La Rochelle in midwinter and because we had failed we assumed that taking a city in midwinter could not be done. But my father had shown me that it could be done, and with fewer men than I had at my disposal. Presumably he had bribed or blackmailed or bullied his way in. None of these three tactics had occurred to us as we stood outside La Rochelle. They came naturally to him. We were going to have to be more cunning in future.

We made for Taillebourg, the castle of Geoffrey de Rancon, who is one of the senior men in Geoffrey's party. Morale was low as we trudged towards the relatively small castle in the hour or so just before dawn when everyone is at their lowest ebb anyway. For the men there was some relief at having escaped, but their initial euphoria was short-lived as they realised that they had lost a good deal of their possessions and that we were likely to be pursued by my father's troops anyway.

As for me, the indignity was almost intolerable. The fears I had expressed at the outset about my capabilities seem to be well founded. But, as dawn began to break and as Taillebourg came slowly into view, so our spirits lifted somewhat. Taillebourg is small but incredibly well constructed. It has the reputation of being impregnable, so let us see if I can hold on to this castle.

We shuffled into town, and again I went about making sure that the men were settled before retiring to meet Hubert and Geoffrey. We have lost all of the army stores, which remain in the cathedral at Saintes. Of our three hundred knights we have lost about sixty. Of the thousand archers we have lost four hundred. Surprisingly, Balardier's five hundred mercenaries have stayed with us. I would have thought that they would have been the first to defect to my father. Perhaps the incident with Luc and Bertrand has had more influence than I thought.

The diminution of our forces is not too bad, but being chased out of town in our nightshirts is not exactly the glory of which we have all been dreaming.

There is now a long gap in the legible diaries. Up until this point Richard has been reasonably scrupulous in keeping the diaries since he was instructed to start, some twenty-one months ago.

We assume that he continued with his record, but the diaries covering the next period have disintegrated as a result of water damage and are irrecoverable.

The legible part of the diary resumes in 1183, nine years later.

The gap is frustrating, because this intervening period was crucial to Richard's development. The rebellious, sex-obsessed teenager we see chased away from Saintes in his nightshirt slowly becomes a man to fear and respect. After the fiasco at Saintes and the retreat to Taillebourg, Richard was safe for a while in its impregnable fortress, as his father turned his attention northwards to force Henry the Young King and King Louis to capitulate. He then turned southwards again to focus on Richard, who nimbly stayed just out of range, perhaps having learned the painful lesson taught to him at Saintes.

Eventually, however, Richard submitted, throwing himself down before his father who lifted him up to grant him the symbolic Kiss of Peace. At the Treaty of Mont Louis Richard ended up accepting rather less than he had been offered a year earlier at the abortive peace conference of Gisors.

However, his father seems to have been impressed by his conduct, for Richard was sent to Aquitaine to try to pacify the region's plethora of rebellious lords. With his mother Eleanor still a prisoner, Richard appears to have learned quickly to use his father's power and resources. He recorded his actions in letters to his father, which were then recorded in Roger of Howden's book on the life of Henry II. There is a litany of castles successfully captured and subsequently razed to the ground to demonstrate the King's power, and Richard slowly began to build for himself an unrivalled reputation in the science of siege warfare.

His reputation was sealed by the events of May 1179, when Richard, as a twenty-one-year-old, captured the fortress at Taillebourg. Undoubtedly he was aided by the fact that he had taken refuge there himself five years earlier, when fleeing from his father after the capture of Saintes. The fact that his father turned away from Taillebourg demonstrated what everybody knew, that Taillebourg, perched on a rock above the River Charente, was unassailable.

But Richard had clearly matured since his humiliation outside La Rochelle, for this time he managed to lure out the enemy from its supposedly invulnerable position. He put his camp temptingly close to the walls of the fortress, and then set about simultaneously bombarding the one wall of the fortress that was not sheer rock face, and ravaging the surrounding vineyards and properties. The frustration borne of these twin pressures was too much; the defenders sallied forth to attack Richard's camp. This was, of course, a trap, and Richard's counter-attack narrowly saw him and his men capture the fortress's gates after hours of hand-to-hand fighting, where Richard threw himself into the thick of the action. The capture of Taillebourg was seen as a master stroke, and Richard was hailed as a conquering hero when he took the news himself to his father in England.

Now fully restored to his father's good favour, Richard was the undisputed lord of his territories. He was able to exert his ducal rights to an extent previously unknown in the area, and a large rebellion of lords discontented by Richard's new power was successfully put down in the summer of 1182 with the help of King Henry II, Henry the Young King and Prince Geoffrey. This was the apotheosis of Plantagenet power. Three sons working together to their father's directives made an instrument of government without parallel in Europe.

But it was not to last. The second half of 1183 saw Henry the Young King again confronting his father over his inheritance. The trouble was fomented by Philip, now King of France following the death of King Louis in 1180. Henry had three choices to make. He could dutifully support his father until such time as he inherited. He could go on a pilgrimage to Jerusalem, as he threatened many times. Or he could listen to the entreaties of Richard's disaffected vassals and join them against his brother and his father. There was much vacillating between the various options but by the time the diaries start again on 6 February 1183, the situation was now clear. Henry and Geoffrey were in alliance with King Philip of France and such rebellious local lords as they could find against Richard and his father.

Richard was now twenty-five years old, and at the height of his physical powers. According to contemporary chroniclers he had developed into a giant of a man, a head taller than average, handsome, if slightly arrogant in appearance, with blond shoulder-length hair. He remained unmarried, although technically he had been betrothed for twenty years to Alice, daughter of King Louis and sister to the current French king, Philip. He had never met Alice, as she had remained a ward of his father throughout her childhood and she was secreted at Alnwick Castle in Northumberland for most of her life.

The diaries open with Richard downcast at the perilous state of affairs in which he finds himself.

6 February 1183

Vouvant, near Poitiers

I am deeply frustrated that just a year after we, as a family, had seemed united and invincible, we now find ourselves split once again.

All of my hard work over the past five or six years in slowly reducing the rebellious lords and counts of Aquitaine comes to nothing as the extraordinary self-absorption of my eldest brother once again dominates our lives. It was not enough for him that I should pay him homage at Christmas time. It was not enough for him that I should hand over the castle of Clairvaux. But he had to go and ally himself with the very people whom I have spent half of my life pacifying. The same people who this time last year were in despair because we, united as a family, had crushed them, have now joined forces with Henry the Young King and Geoffrey.

In fact, I am almost angrier with Geoffrey than I am with Henry. At least Henry cannot help himself; we all know, and have known for years, that he is by turns weak, vain, self-opinionated and greedy. But Geoffrey has been my friend and confidant throughout most of our formative years. For a third son, he has been treated extraordinarily generously by my father, who granted Brittany as his inheritance. It is only slightly less generous an inheritance than mine of Aquitaine. Maybe I have not been as solicitous of him as I might have been over the past few years. Maybe he is jealous now that I bask in our father's affections and now that my military reputation is second to none. Maybe he seeks to enhance his own reputation by taking me on.

Whatever his motivation, this is something I shall neither forgive nor forget. Maybe he has been badly advised, but we are all old enough now to take our own counsel. If I prevail, there will not be much mercy shown.

However, the likelihood of me prevailing does not seem very high at present. My father is still in Normandy, yet ranged against me outside Limoges are the assembled armies of my brothers together with their considerable forces of knights and the other men-at-arms, numbering perhaps four thousand in total.

They are joined by their Brabançon mercenaries under the command of William Arnald and another group of mercenaries under the command of William's uncle Raymond le Brun. All of these men are augmented by the local troops led by Count Aimar of Limoges. There are perhaps ten thousand men in total against the one thousand five hundred that I currently have in addition to Balardier's mercenary force of almost one thousand. So we are outnumbered four to one. We do not even have the element of surprise on our side, as they know exactly where we are. It is indeed looking bleak.

I have tried to keep my spirits up in front of the men, but truth be told I think that they are well aware of the situation. I have noticed some of them falling slightly quieter than usual when I enter a room, fearful of provoking me into a rage. I have had two or three outbursts today. Am I simply imagining their reaction, imagining that they are falling silent when I pass? I think they know that my rages are borne of frustration rather than aimed at them, but nevertheless I must try to appear calmer. Fighting men are like horses and dogs; they can sense fear and they react skittishly to it.

In some ways keeping this diary and reviewing the events of the day helps me to see how others see me.

Today goes down as a bad day. Tomorrow I shall be bold once more.

10 February 1183
Vouvant, near Poitiers

I am indeed back to being bold. Some might say foolhardy.

The plan is as follows: since we are hugely outnumbered our only possible advantage can be the element of surprise. We are going to attack them before they can come and crush us.

However, they know exactly where we are. Geoffrey, in particular, has learned, like me, that accurate information from scouts is worth many hundreds of fighting men. Like me, he will have a system of regular reports and he will instantly be on the alert if a scout does not show up at his rendezvous at the prescribed hour. So simply eliminating his scouts will not be the answer.

The answer is to move quicker than his scouts can report back. This will not be easy. The scouts generally have lighter, faster horses and are trained to catnap while riding. We will be on heavy chargers, in full armour, and we will have to take a change of horses with us. It is about ninety miles from here to Limoges, so it will be two days and a night of hard riding, with no breaks. I have selected seventy-five of the fittest knights.

It is strange how the announcement that there is a plan, however foolhardy, lifts the men's morale. It is the not knowing, and the hanging around, that they cannot stand.

14 February 1183

Aixe

I had guessed that Geoffrey would be using the same system for his scouts as I had developed for mine. There is usually a rotation system in teams of ten or twelve. One man would be detailed to watch our movements for six hours or so. At the end of this period, usually six in the morning, noon, six in the afternoon and midnight, he would be replaced by another scout and he would ride back to his master to report on developments. In this way Geoffrey would be getting reports every six hours provided by the fastest means possible, a single rider on a fast horse travelling alone. If the scouts did not show up at the predetermined time, then Geoffrey would know that something was wrong.

I assumed that Geoffrey was using this system, as we had spent several months together refining it in the campaigns of 1182. We had thought it foolproof. As a consequence, if I could somehow circumvent it, then I would be in a position to give him a nasty surprise.

We set off at seven in the morning, seventy-five men and one hundred and fifty horses moving as fast as it is possible for such a group to move. I had anticipated that the previous scout would have left to make his report at six. The replacement scout could not leave until midday as his replacement would not be arriving until then. I could almost picture this anonymous man's agony as he tried to decide whether to follow us or to wait for his replacement. The correct response would have been to follow us, but soldiers are not trained to think. They are trained to blindly follow orders, and particularly so with the scouting system, which relies on consistency of application for its success.

We changed horses every four hours, not stopping for lunch and only resting for an hour at dusk, so that the men could get some hot food inside them for the night ride. By the time of the dusk break, the men were beginning to complain. I shared some of their gripes: I was saddle-sore, my thighs were chafing and my fingers were frozen, despite my ermine-lined gloves.

But the hot meal buoyed us for the long night ahead, and our spirits were further lifted when soon after setting off, Balardier, at the front of group, spotted a lone horseman a few hundred yards ahead. He was carrying no visible markings to identify his master, and yet he was riding an expensive and fast horse.

Without checking with me at the back of the line, Balardier ordered one of the archers to bring him down, after the horseman refused Balardier's repeated shouts for him to halt. The archer duly got him on the third attempt, right in the middle of his back. He slumped forward in his saddle for perhaps ten or twenty strides, then slowly toppled from his horse, to a great cheer from our men. His right heel was caught in the stirrup so that his body was dragged along for several yards until the horse came to a complete halt.

Balardier reached the man first, but waited to turn him face up until I arrived. I dismounted and nodded to Balardier who flicked the body over. I recognised the face at once, he was one of Geoffrey's men. It must therefore have been his six o'clock scout whom we had caught up. I thought at first that this was a great stroke of good fortune because it would feed Geoffrey misinformation, but I quickly realised that catching the messenger made no difference at all to Geoffrey's knowledge.

What I really needed to do was to intercept the next messenger. I cursed my stupidity in not having grasped this earlier, and set five knights to the task of ambushing the next man to come.

The men seemed buoyed up by the kill. It is as well they had something to cheer them; we were still less than a third of the way through our journey. I noticed that Balardier was helping himself to the dead messenger's purse. The archer who had brought down the messenger stepped forward to claim his rightful share of the purse, but Balardier fixed him with such a baleful glare that he quickly scuttled back to his ranks. Balardier and I have worked together well now for almost ten years, but he still sometimes shocks me with his heartlessness.

He has brought his son Mercardier along on this venture. He is much the same age as me, but physically he could not be more different. He is short and bull-necked, like his father, and with the same immense strength. He copies his father's cropped hairstyle and has the same dark leathery skin. But we have got along well in the one or two conversations we have had. I was surprised not to have come across him before, but Armande has told me that he has been apprenticed to another mercenary captain. It was only on the death of this other captain that Mercardier returned to his father's troop.

Given the history of discord between my father and his sons, it will be interesting to see how long it is before tensions emerge between Mercardier and Balardier.

We pushed on through the night, some of the men falling asleep in the saddle before being jolted awake by the relentless bumping of travelling at high speed on horseback. The worst hour, as always, was the hour or so before dawn when everything seems so much worse. When I was very small, I remember Hodierna telling her son Alexander Neckam and me that the hour before dawn was 'the time when God sleeps and Satan dances'. The image remains with me vividly.

As dawn came, I ordered a brief halt, again to allow hot food to cheer the men up. It was at this breakfast that I first noticed the manifest strain between Mercardier and Balardier. I am not sure what the specific cause was, but it was clear to all that it may not be good to have father and son working alongside each other.

As we continued after breakfast, Mercardier hung back at the rear of his father's troop, presumably to be as far away from his father as possible. As I was at the head of my knights, we naturally fell into step alongside each other.

He is a fine horseman, and his strength is something to behold. I know that people stare at me, not just because of my birth, but also because of my physical frame, but I could not help but stare at Mercardier. His muscles look as if they are fit to burst through his skin. He is bright too, and almost immediately there sparked a connection between us. Born worlds apart, we somehow hit it off as we talked breathlessly on the long day's run. Of course, his father Balardier is clever too, but too often his innate intelligence is focused on the here and now, and not on the wider picture, and it comes across as a low, furtive, animal cunning. In Mercardier, his intelligence is on an altogether higher plane. I will keep an eye on him; he may turn out to be useful.

This spark with Mercardier was the highlight of what was otherwise a desperately gruelling and dispiriting day. I sometimes forget how lucky I am; my unusual physique gives me additional powers of endurance, and my expensive horses and fine quality clothing give me a further advantage over the other horsemen. So although I was tired as we closed on Limoges, I was nowhere near the end of my limits. So I was surprised to find, as we made camp for the night, quite how low the men's spirits were. I ordered that each man should have an extra allowance of brandy, and this seemed to cheer them a little. As the men enjoyed this bounty, a scout arrived with news.

Viscount Aimar was at a small village called Gorre about ten miles west of Limoges. He was camped outside the church and had given the village priest twenty-four hours to yield up the church without force. Aimar is notorious for doing this. He professes to be a virtuous Christian, but when it comes down to the day-to-day practicalities of keeping a large group of fighting men together for a protracted period of time with no visible enemy, then he too succumbs to the temptations of an easy target. The silver and gold of the church at Gorre is well known for its opulence and the mercenaries of William Arnald under Viscount Aimar would have been thirsting to get their hands on it.

I know what Aimar would have been thinking. If God really wanted the church to keep its famous treasure, then He would have twenty-four hours to give some sign of His desires.

I felt some empathy with Aimar's position. There is, after all, a certain logic to it. But equally, the notion of waiting on God's favour, which never comes clearly, means that delay will always disrupt momentum.

Aimar's delay gave us a huge opportunity, as they did not know we were here. I had planned to allow the men a few hours' sleep only, and then to push on through the night. But now I recalculated quickly. We were only some twenty-five miles away, and Aimar was due to have his showdown at the church at noon the next day. If we aimed to arrive there shortly before noon, we would need to set off at about eight in the morning, which meant the men could have a full night's rest.

I gave the order to strike a full camp, with the men to be woken at dawn. There was to be no leakage of the information. It was just for the commanders. I wanted the men to rest, not to skitter about edgily all night.

I had a quick conference with Balardier, who came without Mercardier. We agreed to leave speedily at eight o'clock, and to form up three miles from Gorre to establish a plan. I walked around the camp before retiring. The men were sound asleep, no doubt exhausted by two days and a night of riding. Normally it is never silent in a soldiers' camp at night, but that night it was the stillest I could remember. I soon entered my tent and fell fast asleep as the moment my head hit my makeshift pillow.

Dawn came and men were moving stiffly around the camp. If they were anything like me, their heads were still thick with sleep, their limbs felt heavy and their skin was sore from chafing. Not ideal conditions under which to take on a force almost five times our size, but at least we had rested. And we had the element of surprise. Or at least we did as we set off. Would we keep the element of surprise right up until the last moment, to extract every ounce of value from it?

The morning's ride passed in a blur, and we were soon forming up in a glade just over a mile from Gorre. We paused to allow the horses a feed and some water. Mercardier sidled up to me and suggested that I give the order for the horses' hooves to be muffled with cloth, to dampen the noise of our impending arrival, thus giving us time to get closer. I thought it a brilliant idea and gave the order straight away. This must have been an old mercenary trick, taught to Mercardier by his mentor. As the order was passed down the line, I saw Balardier's head jerk up as he heard the command. He looked over and saw Mercardier at my side. A look of uncertainty crossed Balardier's face. Maybe he recognised instinctively that the old lion was about to be replaced by the younger one.

The moment passed, and Balardier gave the orders to line up in his usual brutish fashion. We waited for the scouts to return, and when they did they brought us good news. Aimar's men and William Arnald's mercenaries were slowly drifting into Gorre, apparently unaware of our presence. There were not even any guards; they had been stood down at dawn.

It was at that moment that I knew we were going to succeed. The depression of the last three or four months lifted like a veil at the altar. I addressed the group of troop captains who were gathered around me.

'We have ridden so hard over the last two days and nights that we are in danger of forgetting that we are on the verge of achieving something quite remarkable. The men ranged before us are formidable and there are four times as many of them as there are of us. But they don't know what is about to hit them, and if we stay focused then untold wealth and glory can be ours. Remember, hammer them with utmost force at the beginning. If the momentum is sufficient then we will win. But leave Aimar and the church's treasure for me.'

With that, I dismissed them and turned to find Mercardier and Hubert at my side. I mounted Arthur and shortly thereafter we set off, trotting in almost complete silence up through the wooded hills. At the summit, I saw for myself the picture laid out before us. The sleepy town of Gorre in the valley below was encircled by the camps of Aimar's followers. In the camps there was no sign of urgency or caution. The stage was set.

I gave the signal and we advanced down the other side of the hill at a slow trot. I could feel my heart pounding as I closed the visor on my helmet. With about twenty yards of woodland left, I gave the order to charge so that we were at full speed as we came out into the two hundred yards of clear ground between us and the first of Aimar's men.

The next hour passed in a frenzy of bloodletting and screaming. I knew from the moment that we hit their lines that we were going to be successful. My major concern was that we did not get carried away. But, typically, I then ignored my own concern for the first quarter of an hour or so. I must have cut down maybe a dozen men in those first few minutes. In truth, it was easy work as they were all running for their horses and weapons, but I remember one particularly good strike where I took a knight's head clean off as he struggled to draw his sword from its scabbard. The severed head bounced along the road in front of me, the face with a mask of fear and surprise.

This curious sight brought me to my senses, and I made my way to the high ground on the other side of the bridge to get a better view of the overall situation. What I saw was carnage. We were now half an hour into the mayhem and any hope the enemy might have had of salvaging their position was long gone. Now they were fighting only to try to flee. But our men, marshalled by Balardier, were expertly manoeuvring them into positions from which there was no escape. Small group by small group, they were throwing down their weapons and surrendering. My men were corralling the captured men into a pig enclosure just by the entrance to the bridge. There were about five hundred men there already, with their numbers swelling every minute.

I looked further afield, and just caught sight of a group of horsemen from enemy ranks breaking free and making a run for the hills. I was sure I saw the livery of Viscount Aimar of Limoges amongst them. I swivelled and barked orders to Mercardier and Hubert and three other knights to follow me.

We hared across the bridge in pursuit, but they were disappearing into the trees by the time we crossed on to the open land. Mercardier and Hubert pulled up their horses slightly as we approached the treeline. I knew that if I stopped to consult them they would try to persuade me not to go into the woods, with the risk of ambush. I desperately wanted to crown our victory with Aimar's capture: he would be immensely valuable. So I pressed on, heedless of the danger. To their credit, Mercardier and Hubert pressed on too, once they had seen what my intentions were.

Once in the woods, I began to have second thoughts. The chances of capturing Aimar, with the head start he had, were slim. The chances of one of us being separated from the others were increasing the further we went on. Reluctantly I pulled Arthur up, and gave the signal to turn back.

As the horses walked back through the woods, Hubert and Mercardier began to tot up the ransom we would get for the knights we had captured. Mercardier mentioned that his former troop of mercenaries was fighting under William Arnald for the enemy. I was pleased by this. Presumably, as mercenaries, they would come straight over to our side. Our numbers and wealth were both about to increase substantially.

As we crossed the bridge back into the town, things appeared to be going very much our way. The number of men now corralled in the enclosure had grown significantly. The fire and smoke rising from the area where their tents had been suggested that the operation of clearing through the enemy's ranks was progressing smoothly.

I then saw that there was smoke rising from the church. I frowned. Had someone deliberately flouted my explicit orders not to ransack the church? I wheeled Arthur round and set off in the direction of the church, with Hubert and Mercardier in pursuit.

As we approached I saw that the church had indeed been attacked, but it was not immediately clear whether it was Aimar's men or mine who were responsible.

Then the door opened, and Balardier peered out. By chance we were behind a couple of elm trees as we trotted up, so he failed to spot us approaching. I almost shouted out to let him know we were there but some sixth sense stopped me. He obviously judged the coast to be clear, for he soon emerged carrying a large, heavy sack. My immediate thought that it contained the gold and silver treasure of the church was confirmed when we watched Balardier approach one of his troop, a boy on horseback, and hand over the sack while giving him instructions. As Balardier patted the boy's horse on the rump as if to say goodbye, I made my presence known with a great roar: 'What the fuck is going on here?'

Balardier jumped like a scalded cat and stammered out a few incoherent words. I roared again: 'Silence!'

I addressed the boy on horseback: 'What were the instructions just given to you?'

He looked terrified, glancing from me to Balardier and back again. He tried the easy way out: 'I'm not sure what he said, sire.'

I jumped down from Arthur and stalked across to the boy. I yanked the sack from his side and dropped it on the ground, then with one swipe of my sword I cut it open. The gold and silver plate clattered on to the hard earth.

My first instinct was to look at Balardier, but I knew that what happened next could be critical. I stood staring at the treasure for a full ten seconds, willing myself not to look up. My mind raced. I was strong enough and secure enough to discipline Balardier now. But if I did, I ran the risk that I might lose him altogether, either because he might resist and be killed or because he would accept his punishment but then slope off to join the enemy.

If I was going to punish him I had to be prepared to punish him properly, by death. I jibbed at this, our accumulated experiences together telling me that I would not be able to go through with it.

I sighed and looked up and across at Balardier. Just as I was about to speak, the decision was taken from my hands, for Balardier pre-empted me, saying: 'Sire, I know it looks as if I was taking this treasure as booty, but I found it inside the church already in the sack and I was simply arranging for it to be taken into safe custody.'

I understood at once; he was offering me a way out. He knew that I would not believe his story, but he also knew that I could pretend to believe him and we could all carry on as before.

I was torn. On the one hand I was furious and wanted to assert my authority once and for all. On the other hand I felt I could not afford to lose my attack dog. I was inclined to let it go, but again someone interrupted to take the initiative from me. This time it was Mercardier. Perhaps he sensed his chance. 'Sire, you could check with the boy. He would be able to tell you where Balardier instructed him to go.'

Both Balardier and I turned to face Mercardier. My face was one of incredulity. How could Mercardier not see that this was his father's one chance of escape? Then I realised Mercardier knew exactly what he was doing; he knew he was cutting off his father's one remaining option. Balardier knew it too. His face was thunderous, and the full extent of his murderous wrath could be measured by the veins bulging in his neck and temples.

I turned to the boy. I noticed he had pissed himself and drops of urine were gently hanging from his stirrups before dropping softly to the ground. But a mighty roar caused me to turn back, to find that Balardier had launched himself at Mercardier.

Mercardier clutched desperately at his reins to try to hold on as his horse reared up, but the weight of Balardier hanging off him eventually caused him to fall to earth with a great clatter. The horse panicked and made off, trampling on both men in its haste to get away.

The two men on the ground were now fighting for all they were worth. The intensity of the hatred between them was astonishing even to me, who had lived alongside the venomous Balardier for so long.

Hubert looked at me as if to question whether we should intervene, but I mouthed a silent no. It was better to let them get this out of the way; otherwise the enmity would only resurface later.

The dogfight wore on in a frenzy of kicking, biting and scratching, until simultaneously they both decided that this was not getting them anywhere. They scrabbled free and quickly drew daggers from their belts as they rose into crouching positions.

At this stage, I thought the fight would now be Balardier's, for I had never seen anyone as quick with a blade at close quarters. Mercardier had lost his chance to take advantage of his youth and superior strength in the hand-to-hand fighting. But I was taken aback as Mercardier quickly showed that he was no slouch, dancing easily clear of Balardier's feints and thrusts. It appeared he had decided that keeping out of range and trying to tire the older man was his best option.

Balardier kept on coming forward, but Mercardier now began to counterpunch cleverly, drawing his father further and further forward to try to unbalance him. And at the third or fourth attempt he succeeded. Balardier lunged, Mercardier feinted back and then ducked forward to pull Balardier's leading leg out and away from under him. He twisted his father's body round in the same movement so that he fell on his back, looking up into the face of his son, who now held his knife to his throat.

Balardier looked stunned at first; he had not been bested like this for many years. Quickly his expression turned to one of resignation, tinged, it seemed to me, with a touch of pride at his son's performance. I fully expected Mercardier to rise and, having proved his point, to pull his father to his feet. We would all then carry on, with the balance of power having shifted in his favour, but with no blood spilled.

But Mercardier kneeled forward to whisper something in his father's ear. Balardier's eyes widened in terror as Mercardier slowly and very, very deliberately drew the knife across his father's throat. A pool of blood began to swell and then to race across the stony ground.

I was stunned.

I had spent nearly ten years in almost constant contact with this man. In some ways, he had been my mentor, tutoring me, although unconsciously, in the relentless ruthlessness required to keep control of large numbers of fighting men, who, if truth were told, were often little more than vicious pack dogs.

We had never become close. The difference in rank and birth precluded real friendship; but a kind of kinship borne of shared hardship might have been possible, although it never really developed. Nevertheless I was shocked to see him lying there, his lifeblood draining slowly out beside him. I had thought of him as invincible in his dark and brutal way. And now he was gone.

Mercardier had walked over to retrieve his horse, which had bolted when Balardier attacked. He looped the reins over his left arm and stood staring straight ahead in the manner of an ordinary trooper waiting for instructions. I stared at him to try to provoke some kind of acknowledgement, but none was forthcoming.

I looked at Hubert and issued my orders: 'Have Balardier buried here in the grounds of the church he tried to rob. Bury him with his head facing the church tower so that he is eternally reminded of his crime against God and against me.'

Hubert acknowledged my orders and wheeled his horse away to carry them out.

'And make sure the treasure stays safely in the church,' I shouted after him.

I nodded cursorily to Mercardier, who now mounted his horse and followed me silently as I made my way back into the village to take charge there.

Our success at Gorre was astonishing and even my father would be proud of this victory. But I felt curiously deflated by Balardier's death. I was hugely impressed by Mercardier, but something about his emotionless demeanour had worried me. I had grown used to his father's consistent greed and callousness; now it looked like I would have to learn to deal with a more complex character. And I did not relish the prospect.

I turned to Mercardier. 'You take charge of cleaning up this lot. I'll take a small party and head towards Limoges to see if I can find Aimar.'

Mercardier nodded, clearly in two minds. He was pleased with the responsibility, but he was reluctant to leave my side.

I met up with Hubert and we set off, returning some five hours later having found that Aimar was back in Limoges with Geoffrey and that together they were already hard at work fortifying the citadel of St Martial, at the heart of Limoges.

In my absence Mercardier had moved the bulk of our men to Aixe, up on the River Vienne and nearer to Limoges. He had left behind a group of men to supervise the digging of burial pits for the mounds of corpses that had been stacked up at the riverbank. I noticed amongst the dead some men wearing the colours of Mercardier's former mercenary troop. I questioned one of the men digging: 'How did these men come to die? They were mercenaries and they had surrendered. Why did they not simply declare for us and they would have joined our ranks?'

One of the men piped up: 'They tried to, sire, but they were not permitted. Mercardier said that we could not accept troops who might turn against us in the future. They begged for their lives, but he ordered all their throats to be slit. The screaming was terrible, sire.'

'Mercardier ordered this?'

I turned and set off for Aixe, with Hubert close on my heels. As we rode he worked hard to try to calm me down. What he said made some sense. I had hitherto followed my father's policy of immediately recruiting defeated mercenaries, on the basis that it was better to have them on our side than on the enemy's. But controlling and disciplining new groups of mercenaries was always difficult. Perhaps Mercardier was right. Executing them at least absolved us of the responsibility of feeding them and keeping them warm at a time when we were going to need to be at our quickest and strongest.

The digger had also told us that Mercardier had taken all of the captured knights with him. I hoped he had started the process of ransoming them. We had to make sure that they, too, did not become a burden, and, God knows, we could do with the money now that I have left all that treasure behind at Gorre.

As we approached Aixe I was impressed by Mercardier's organisation in such a short space of time. Tents had already been erected, fires were burning, pots were boiling and pigs were roasting. But as we rode further through the camp I began to hear the terrible sounds of agonised screaming. My heart sank. After the butchery at Gorre, what was Mercardier up to now?

I soon found out. Mercardier had taken the captured knights and lined them up in a square surrounded by armed guards. He had started by establishing through questioning which knights had sufficient family resources such that a ransom was likely to be paid to release them. In truth one can normally tell by the quality of a knight's armour, sword and horse whether his family is likely to be able to afford a ransom, but it is always worth asking the question as a knight might well have been stripped of much of his wealth by the time I see him.

This time it had emerged that twenty of the knights had previously fought for me, but had gone over to Aimar last autumn. They had announced this as a matter of pride, as if they would receive better treatment on account of their prior allegiance. Indeed, under some codes of engagement, they might have had their claims recognised. Unfortunately for them, Mercardier was not a great respecter of codes of chivalric conduct. It seems that he was more concerned with basic military discipline and loyalty.

He had lead the leader of the group, a squire called Norbert, out from the square and taken him to a burning brazier full of red-hot coals. He had told him to kneel and when Norbert had refused to bow his knee to a mere mercenary, Mercardier had drawn his sword and sliced into the man's right Achilles tendon. As he fell forward, Mercardier had caught Norbert's hair and yanked back his head. With his other hand, he had reached towards the burning brazier, pulled out the glowing poker and with two short, firm jabs had plunged it into Norbert's eyes.

It was at this point that I arrived to the searing smell of recently burnt flesh and the desperate cries as Norbert writhed on the floor. I trotted slowly up to Mercardier and looked at him questioningly as he took Arthur's bridle while I dismounted.

The captured knights had begun to whisper urgently amongst themselves, no doubt relieved that I had arrived to restore the normal rules of engagement.

I held a hurried conference with Mercardier and Hubert. Mercardier kept it plain and simple: 'Sire, these men have betrayed you once. They will not be worth much as they are, so we will get little, if any, ransom for them. We cannot afford to keep them prisoner for long, as supplies are limited. If you release them they will be back fighting against us in a few weeks or months. And if you do not punish them for their leaving you before, then what is to keep your existing knights with you?'

Hubert looked at me. In his eyes I could read that he agreed with Mercardier, but that he was reluctant to endorse such a fundamental break with tradition. For years, knights have fought, safe in the knowledge that they could throw down their weapons at any time and surrender and be reasonably certain of being ransomed or released. It is the code we have all grown up with. As a result knights have become quite canny at changing sides at the slightest shift in the prevailing wind. What Mercardier had done was to challenge the assumptions under which knights operate.

Maybe it was the fatigue. Maybe it was the cold and the hunger. Maybe it really did come to me as a revelation that we needed to be firmer with our knights, to forge a tighter bond. Or maybe I did not have the stomach for a confrontation with Mercardier today.

I stepped back from our conference and addressed both Mercardier and Hubert loudly so that the whole square could hear: 'Take those who have betrayed me by leaving my service and gouge out their eyes with the poker. Then take them to the river and drown them.

'For the rest of you, those who can be, will be ransomed in the normal way. Those of you who do not have family to pay a ransom, you can choose: either you join Mercardier's troop in my service, or you will be drowned in the river as well.'

With that I turned and stalked towards the tent with my banner fluttering above it in the breeze.

While I have been dictating the events of the day to Armande, we have endured the screams of men being dragged to an excruciating death. I have been counting them while relating the events of the past few days. Eleven men have been blinded. I presume they have now been drowned too. I suspect the others have all taken up the option to join Mercardier's troop.

Now that is done, I am going to bed.

17 March 1183

Outside Limoges

It is now some six weeks since the great ride across from Vouvant to Poitiers. My father arrived with his forces two weeks after the routing of Aimar at Gorre. He was thrilled with the stories of the night-time ride and the way we sprang such a surprise on Aimar.

I know that one of my faults is a desperate need to please my father. I am slightly ashamed by it, for such a juvenile sentiment is unbecoming of a Christian prince. But sometimes I revel in his enthusiasm for hearing the stories of my deeds; it is a kind of validation.

But after a sixth consecutive night of my father asking detailed questions about the event, I began to wonder if his fascination is not so much born of pride in his son, but is more an indication of his ageing and his desire to relive some of his youth through me. Perhaps he is beginning to sense his mortality, which may be important in determining the succession. He is fifty-three years old now, and more than three decades of constant travelling on horseback appear to be taking their toll.

I admit to a conflict of emotions on this subject. My father getting older, and therefore nearing death, means that I will, at some point, be the sole ruler of what are considered to be my lands, which I cannot deny is an exciting prospect. But, as his son, I naturally feel that I want my father to live as long as possible.

Either way, there is not too much point in brooding over the true nature or motivation of my feelings. The fact is that it is happening: he is getting older, and less dominant. I must just position myself as best I can.

We have been camped here outside Limoges for almost four weeks. Geoffrey and Aimar have taken refuge in the city and fortified the citadel at St Martial effectively.

My father has taken charge of the siege but he is not being particularly dynamic in his tactics. I have chosen to hold back, rather than to confront him again. In truth, there is not much that I would have done differently: I would simply have been much bolder and more forceful. Perhaps it is the consciousness of his own mortality that is making him more cautious. So, when trying to persuade Aimar's mercenaries to join us he offers them half the rate that I would. When he sends sappers in to try to undermine the walls of the citadel, he sends in twelve men. I would have sent in forty. Small things, perhaps. But he is beginning to look indecisive, and that is dangerous in the leader of a fighting force. Half the time, the trick is making a decision quickly, rather than making the right decision.

This gradual realisation of my father's mortality came to a head yesterday. He was out with a small party of about a dozen men. They were trotting around the city, observing it from various points, discussing options for attacking the city or for drawing out its occupants.

Suddenly a watchman sounded the alarm inside the city, the gates were opened and fifty or so knights charged out at my father's small band of horsemen. Backed up against the river, they had no choice but to face head-on the rapidly advancing knights. My father's royal standard was clearly held aloft by his standard-bearer, but still the men came on.

My father and his men stood firm, which must have taken some nerve. Finally the first wave of men hit them, although my father and his men had not drawn their weapons. The knight to the left of my father was speared in the chest, carried from his horse and tossed like a limp doll, dead, to the ground.

Gradually the men from the city halted their attack, bemused by the non-combative behaviour of their quarry. Then a great cry went up: 'It's the King... it's the King.'

They looked around in some confusion, trying to find a leader to tell them what to do. Either there was no leader there, or no one was prepared to come forward and identify himself as the man who had attacked the person of his own King. So they melted backwards, retreating like spring ice on a frozen river, until they were about thirty yards away, when they turned and ran to the temporary safety of the city.

My father was incandescent with fury when he returned to camp: 'How dare they attack their own King? I'll have them all skinned alive and roasted till their eyes burst. How could my own son send out his men to kill me?'

In fact, my father had shown remarkable bravery and foresight in facing down his attackers. If he had drawn his weapon, he would almost certainly have been killed.

I cannot work out if it was the sheer hubris of the attack that so upset my father, or whether it was the realisation of how close he had come to being killed that induced a sort of shock, which led in turn to his ensuing fury.

A few hours later, towards dusk, a party bearing the banners of my brothers Henry and Geoffrey appeared under a flag of truce at the main gates to our camp. My father made them wait half an hour before receiving them in the main tent. I stood at his right-hand side as they filed in.

Henry entered first, followed by Geoffrey. Count Aimar had come, but my father had ruled that only his two sons were to be granted admittance. Their attendant lords were to wait outside. No doubt Count Aimar would be out there somewhere, seething at this humiliation.

Henry looked at me as he came in and gave an almost imperceptible nod. Geoffrey could not bring himself to look at me. He would have known how badly I would have taken his betrayal of me. He thought that by staring fixedly at the floor in front of him he could somehow ignore me, but if he had looked at me and shrugged as if to say: 'Sorry, but this is all a game and this is what suited me best,' then I would probably have forgiven him. But ignoring me served only to inflame me further.

My brothers went down on one knee before the King, their heads bowed. My father, from his great wooden chair, grunted his grudging approval that they had bent the knee to him. But he gave no sign that they might rise. After about twenty seconds Henry lifted his eyes to check what my father was doing, and that he had not simply forgotten to release them from their bow.

Poor stupid Henry. He has no understanding of other people. He caught my eye and I helped him out by shaking my head and glancing in my father's direction to indicate that he should not move. I could sense momentary uncertainty as to whether he should trust me, but then he bowed his head once more.

My father heaved himself out of his chair and began to pace up and down in front of my two kneeling brothers. I allowed myself a surreptitious smile. He was about to explode at them. I was going to enjoy their discomfiture.

But, unwisely, Henry chose to speak first, no doubt thinking that an early apology would somehow defuse the situation: 'Sire, I must apologise for the reckless and ill-disciplined behaviour of a small number of the troops of Count Aimar of Limoges…'

That was as far as he got before my father bellowed at the top of his voice: 'What the fuck do you mean "reckless and ill-disciplined"? It's not like they were late for parade or they got drunk and got back after curfew. They tried to fucking kill me. Me. Their sovereign King. And you roll up here, happy as a fucking puppy, with a great smirk on your face to say sorry as if it was some playground rough and tumble. You think you can just say sorry and that will be it, you miserable fucking toads. I wish you had never been born, you useless pair of fucking cunts. Get out of my sight, both of you.'

I sighed inwardly. It was almost over too soon. There are few better sights than your enemy being humiliated, and it is especially pleasing when it happens to your brothers.

Henry got to his feet and, summoning as much dignity as he could muster, inclined his head slightly in the direction of my father before turning to leave the tent. Geoffrey scuttled after him.

A moment or two later I followed them to see if I could catch a word with them but they were already mounting up and riding off. I laughed to myself as I went back in. This would be water off a duck's back to Geoffrey. But to Henry this humiliation would cut right to the very core of his being. It would be the first thing he thought of in the morning and the last thing he would think of at night.

I pity him. How can he be so sensitive to real or imagined humiliations against himself and yet be so insensitive to how his behaviour is perceived by other people?

I fear the answer must be that he is simply not very intelligent. Or, at least not very cunning, because he certainly did not struggle when studying Latin and philosophy, mathematics and theology. However, being learned and being shrewd are not the same thing.

I was careful not to smirk when I went back into the tent. My father may be getting older, and his powers may be on the wane, but he is still a formidable foe and, for the time being at least, he is on my side. Or rather, I am on his side.

31 March 1183

Outside Limoges

The last two weeks have been spent in an endless toing and froing between our camp here outside Limoges and the camp of Henry the Young King and Geoffrey inside the city. It is an absurd situation, laughable if it were not so serious. The constant back and forth has been all about the nature and scale of the apology that my brothers are to give my father.

Never mind that they are in open rebellion against him. Never mind that their men have devastated his lands. Never mind that they plot against him at every turn. That is all ignored. He wants an apology and suitable penance for being charged outside the gates of Limoges, which in the great scheme of things was not such an unreasonable or unlikely event. We are at war, for God's sake.

I suppose that my father does not see it as war. To him it is just a family quarrel, to be played out within a framework of rules based on the chivalric codes. Those codes generally mean that we, the great and the good, can greatly reduce the risk of death for ourselves, whilst ignoring the fear and suffering of everyone else along the way. Breaking those rules seems to him to be a more heinous offence than taking up arms against your own father.

I wonder if the mental strain of thirty-odd years of sole rule is finally taking its toll. In the early days he had my mother, and to a lesser extent Becket, to keep him grounded. Now that he has killed Becket and locked up my mother, he has no one to keep him sane. Other than me. But he does not take counsel from me. I am sure he is proud of my achievements, such as they are, and I am sure that he has great hopes for me, but, for the moment at least, he would never think to take my advice. And I would not think to offer it.

The outcome of these negotiations is that Henry and Geoffrey have handed over fifteen of the men who charged against my father. This afternoon we had to sit outside in our ceremonial chairs in the weak spring sunshine and watch as my father meted out his punishment.

I think it was almost certainly the most uncomfortable experience of my life.

In his madness, my father remembered the first words he had said in his initial rage against the men. So we had to sit and watch fifteen good men, who had done nothing wrong other than to serve their masters faithfully and well, be skinned alive.

It took six men to hold down each of the men while the three butchers did their work with their long carving knives. The first three men were unconscious after just a few minutes, but the other men had to watch and wait their turn.

I stared fixedly ahead through the hour-long process, tuning out the sounds of the screaming.

Then it got worse, if that were possible. My father ordered the men to be spit-roasted while still alive until, as he had promised in his fury, their eyeballs burst from the heat of the fire and shot out their bloody contents to hiss in the embers.

I was sickened by the whole affair. I was not the only one to feel like this: all around me knights were retching on to the ground. But mostly I was sickened by the fact that no one in that whole ghastly ensemble wanted this to happen, only my deranged father. He sat there in his great wooden chair staring fixedly ahead. None of us, not even the supposed great Princes of Christendom like me, sitting alongside my father, or my brothers watching from inside the city walls, did a single thing to stop it happening. Shame on us. Shame on all of us.

14 April 1183

Outside Limoges

Another two weeks of intense frustration have passed. Henry and Geoffrey have done a good job of fortifying the citadel, and my father's tentative steps to undermine their position have got us nowhere. He seems quite happy with the status quo, as if his honour has been satisfied by the grisly retribution he visited on the men who dared to charge him. I am fuming quietly, while outwardly showing self-discipline in adopting a subservient role to him. It is hard when I am used to being in sole command, but I have no option.

I had an interesting visit from a priest yesterday afternoon.

Hubert arranged it. The priest, Benedict, is one of those itinerant preachers who move about the countryside living on the charity of the locals and promising them plenary indulgences in return. Hubert came across him preaching in a nearby village and fell into conversation with him. Hubert had been impressed with the man's air of calm certainty and the modesty of his claims. He asked around and found that the priest had something of a local reputation as a seer. He knows that I am not fond of those who claim visionary powers, believing most of them to be charlatans. So for him to bring this one to me meant that he was unusually impressed.

The priest came into my tent in the early afternoon. He is tall, but with stooping shoulders so that he is not quite as imposing as he might otherwise be. He is not that old to judge from his relatively unlined skin, but his shock of white hair and his stoop make him look older than he probably is. He carries himself well, hinting perhaps at a noble birth.

He spoke in a low and gentle voice, so that I had to lean forward to catch everything he said. It is an effective trick, and one that I have been using recently. I find that it establishes my authority much more effectively than constantly shouting instructions.

He began by telling me a little of his background. He is indeed nobly born, the third son of a minor county family in the Limousin. As the third son he was sent to a Dominican monastery at the age of eight and remained there as a novitiate until his sixteenth birthday. He was due to become a monk, but was expelled for 'being too friendly' (his words) with the concubine of the abbot.

He wandered here and there, staying several months in various monasteries and abbeys, before his great revelation. Benedict claims to have been visited by the Virgin Mary in his dreams and to have been given visionary powers. From that moment forth, he began to be able to predict events of significance. I have heard many such stories before and I generally retain a healthy scepticism. For instance, it was curious that his stories always seemed to revolve around the fortunes of noble or wealthy families.

I quizzed him on this: 'Why does the Virgin Mary only seem to concern herself with the rich? The Bible would seem to tell us that she would be at least as interested in the poor as in the rich.'

His response was as calm and measured as the manner in which he related his stories: 'I profess my humble ignorance on the matter, sire. I have tried many times to have dreams on request, but it never works. The dreams come to me. I cannot summon them. I relate them and about a month later they come to pass.' He raised his hands in an expression of genuine puzzlement.

I was still in two minds. His stories of the events he had predicted, such as the master of a well-known family falling from a horse while out riding alone, such as a much-wanted heir to a great estate being stillborn, such as a great vineyard near Bordeaux suddenly being overrun by a plague of caterpillars, all these stories were told with such a quiet assurance that it was almost impossible not to believe his tales.

The only discordant note came at the end when he knelt to kiss my ring. I noticed that the roots of his white hair were dark.

I quizzed Hubert about it later: 'Why do you think Benedict had white hair, but the roots of his hair were dark?'

Hubert had noticed it too, but he had no explanation. Eventually he suggested, tongue in cheek: 'Maybe it is God's way of marking him out as special?'

It has been bothering me all day. I am always unsettled by things I cannot understand.

Armande has just come up with a possible explanation, as I stand here dictating to him. He says that he has heard that it is common in the Pyrenees for older women to use potions to colour their hair back to its original shade, once their hair starts to go grey. As their hair grows so the greyness begins to show at the roots. Armande suggests that maybe Benedict was doing this process in reverse to make himself look older and therefore wiser than he really was. The dark roots were, in fact, his darker, younger hair coming through.

I think he must be right. We shall find out in the morning.

15 April 1183

Outside Limoges

I caught Benedict just before lunch as he passed near my pavilion. 'Brother Benedict, I should like a word with you about your hair,' I told him.

He looked relieved to have the chance to speak to me. This was not what I had expected. I was rather pleased with myself for having worked out his little subterfuge, and had fully expected him to blush and skulk guiltily into my pavilion.

It was he who opened the conversation, most irregular in the presence of a prince. 'Sire, I am mighty grateful to see you. I had another of my dreams last night and I must...'

'Quiet,' I roared, irritated by his rudeness in not waiting for me to speak. 'I noticed yesterday that your white hair has dark roots. Is it true that this is because you use a potion to dye it?'

He looked at me quizzically, as if he could not understand why I would ask such a question. With a slight shake of the head he replied: 'Of course I do, sire. I am twenty-six years old. I have enough trouble convincing folk of the truth of my dreams, without them wondering why a young man has been entrusted with them rather than some wizened old man who fits their idea of what someone with special powers should look like.'

He seemed to think that this was sufficient justification of his deception, but I was not so sure that the casual but deliberate lie that this implied could be so easily dismissed.

I urged Benedict to continue with a wave of my hand.

'Sire, as I was saying, I had another of my dreams last night, and it concerns your brother, Henry the Young King. I have had a vision that he will come to an untimely and unfortunate end, and soon.' He looked around the pavilion, checking that no one else was present in the gloomy recesses of its tented folds.

I was shocked. I realised after three or four seconds that I was staring at him with my mouth agape. I gathered myself with a nervous laugh, and said: 'You are joking, Brother Benedict?'

'No, sire, I am not joking. I had an extraordinarily vivid dream in which the Young King is poisoned by drinking contaminated wine. Its effect is felt only slowly, so it is not clear to anyone that he has been poisoned at all. They think he has been overcome by some mystery illness, and despite the best efforts of his doctors, nothing that they try will halt or even slow down its progress. Eventually he succumbs.'

There was a long silence. I was running through a number of scenarios in my mind, and then I caught myself. Here I was taking at face value the word of someone who not five minutes ago was telling me that he dyed his hair in order to make his audience more receptive to believing his 'dreams'. Now here he was confidently predicting the death of my older brother and my father's heir, and I was on the verge of believing him. It was the classic move of the trickster: to draw someone in by telling him what he wants to hear.

I turned to face him. 'How am I supposed to believe in your dream, Brother Benedict, when you have just confessed to me that you dye your hair in order to deceive people? I want you to retire to your tent while Hubert Walter makes further enquiries. Do you understand?'

He stared defiantly at me for a second or two, but then seemed to remember his place, and nodded before turning to go.

I set Hubert to work to find out more about this mysterious Brother Benedict, whilst I began to consider all the possible ramifications if he were to be proved right.

19 April 1183

Outside Limoges

What a disaster.

I had better begin at the beginning.

This morning Hubert interrupted me during cavalry drill. I knew immediately that something was seriously amiss. Firstly, Hubert knows not to interrupt cavalry drill for any minor matter. Secondly, he was ashen white. Thirdly, he was running. Men of his rank do not run.

Panting from the exertion, he said: 'Sire, I must speak with you on a matter of great urgency. In private.'

I dismounted and took him to the side of the drill field. I urged him to speak. 'Come on, spit it out! It can't be that bad.'

He began, breathlessly: 'I have been making further enquiries about Brother Benedict. You remember that new group of mercenaries that arrived last night? Well, it turns out that it contains some men who have recently joined up from the Bordeaux region. They have been telling me of a white-haired preacher who could tell the future through the revelations of his dreams. Apparently, he predicted the arrival of caterpillars to destroy the communal vineyard, and when they actually arrived he revelled in the glory of it for a fortnight. Then suddenly he disappeared. It turns out that one of the itinerant merchants passing through the town had recognised him, which is why Benedict had fled.

'This merchant recognised Benedict as the man who had predicted the death of the Count of Auvergne. When the Count fell from his horse after it reared unexpectedly whilst descending a rocky path, Benedict had made a great song and dance about the accuracy of his prediction. But it transpired that Benedict had been spotted hiding in the undergrowth near where the Count died, and when the Count's horse was examined it was found to have an arrowhead lodged in its rump. The family came to the conclusion that Benedict had fired an arrow at the horse to make it rear up and throw the Count down the stony hill. He had then tried to retrieve the arrow to cover his tracks, but the arrowhead broke off in his hand. However, before the Count's family could catch Benedict he had disappeared.

'When the vine growers of Bordeaux heard this from the merchant they rushed to find Benedict, but again he had already fled, this time in such a hurry that he left his possessions behind. Amongst his things they found a jar containing exactly those caterpillars that had suddenly arrived to decimate their crops. He must have made his prediction, and then set the caterpillars loose to spread amongst the vines. The growers were livid but could find no trace of Benedict.'

I studied the ground at my feet, suddenly sick to the stomach. I tried to think of some flaw in what Hubert had just told me: 'And the stillborn baby?'

'I haven't got any information on that one, sire. Before you ask, I've checked his tent. He's gone.'

We fell into silence. A host of thoughts crowded into my mind.

Had Benedict really gone to Henry's camp to poison him so as to ensure his vision would come true?

Or would he have realised that we would be on to him, and fled in some other direction?

If I sent men after him to Henry's camp, would Henry believe my messengers?

If I did nothing and Benedict poisoned Henry, then I would have been complicit in the murder of my own brother. God would never forgive me. Nor, I am sure, would my father, if he were ever to find out.

Hubert and I quickly determined that the best course of action was to send messengers straight away to Henry. We had to get him to take the threat seriously, if it wasn't already too late. I summoned Sir Guy Strathbourne, who knows Henry well. I explained the urgency of the task. He was to take three men and to proceed under a flag of truce to the city walls. I impressed on him the critical importance of getting through and seeing Henry.

They set off about six hours ago. There was a delay at the city gates while they waited for Henry's authorisation that they should be admitted. Eventually the word came, and I watched from our lines about half a mile away as they trotted through the gates. Since then, there has been no news. We can only wait.

The best outcome is that Benedict decided to disappear entirely and went nowhere near the city or my brother.

Any other outcome is likely to spell disaster in one way or another.

20 April 1183

Outside Limoges

Nothing today. No news at all. I have been pacing up and down all day. I cannot stand it when situations are completely out of my control. I know my advisers and staff have suffered today from my consequent ill temper.

22 April 1183

Outside Limoges

It has turned out as badly as it possibly could have done.

Sir Guy Strathbourne returned early this morning, with his three men. They were unharmed but I could tell from their demeanour that things had not gone well. I greeted him outside my pavilion and invited him in. I sat and waited, feeling like a prisoner on trial awaiting the verdict.

As soon as Sir Guy began to speak, I knew that we were in trouble:

'Sire, I regret to inform you that I was not successful.'

I tried to focus on his words, rather than to let my mind race away.

'After the long wait at the gates, which I believe you saw, we were finally taken inside. I had thought that we might see the Young King immediately, but, despite my protestations, we were left in the outer courtyard until late in the evening.'

I cursed Henry for his stupidity. His inflated vanity and sense of self-importance would have been behind his decision to try to humiliate Sir Guy.

'Eventually we were told that we would not see the Young King that night. We were told to sleep in the stables with the horses. The next day was the same. We were kept without food or water in the stable yard all day.'

Even I, who have known Henry all my life, was taken aback by the pettiness of the gesture.

'Eventually, on the next day we were granted an audience. Henry was at his most difficult, shall we say.'

I smiled wryly at Sir Guy's understatement: Henry will still be seething at my father's humiliation of him over the charge outside the city walls.

Sir Guy continued: 'When we entered the hall, Henry greeted me as follows: "Well, well, well. If it isn't the perfidious Sir Guy Strathbourne come to see me, skulking in with his tail between his legs. What is it that I can do for you, Sir Guy?"'

'I bristled slightly, sire, but I conveyed the message that you asked me to, saying: "I have been commanded by My Lord the Prince Richard to come to warn you of a potential threat against your life. It comes from an itinerant preacher named Brother Benedict." I knew immediately that the man had been there, sire, because the whole hall fell silent. You could almost hear the creaking in people's necks as they turned towards Henry seated on his great wooden chair, keen to see how he would react. He seemed slightly startled at first, his face coloured and his voice rose a little in pitch as he bade me to continue.

'I told him: "My Lord the Prince Richard has discovered that this man has a history of trickery and chicanery. He has been unmasked as a scoundrel, and your brother implores you to have nothing to do with this man." At this, to my surprise, after a short pause, Henry began to laugh and to clap his hands together ironically, saying: "Oh, that's brilliant! My brother, the great soldier the Prince Richard, sees the priest defect to my side and he sends you here to undermine him. Well, let me tell you, Sir Guy, that Brother Benedict is an honourable man of God. He was so disgusted by the vile and inhuman punishment meted out to fifteen of my men outside these city walls, that he decided that the only path open to him was to abandon your lord, the Prince Richard, and to join my ranks, where he will find himself treated with dignity and honour."

'To be honest, sire, I was a little nonplussed by this turn of events. Clearly Brother Benedict is a cunning fellow. I did however ask: "Might I enquire as to the whereabouts of Brother Benedict now?" Henry replied: "You might well enquire, Sir Guy, but I am not inclined to tell you."

'The Young King looked very pleased with himself, sire, but after a short pause he continued: "However, I will tell you that he is no longer here. As soon as you came to the city gates, I sent him on an errand to the King of France's camp. I thought you might have been sent here to kill him, so I kept you waiting long enough to give him time to escape. Frankly, I am surprised that a fine knight such as you, Sir Guy, should stoop to performing squalid murderous errands for my brother the Prince Richard. Perhaps it is as Brother Benedict suggests, and you have all become dissolute under my father's tired leadership. If you wish to preserve your honour, Sir Guy, perhaps you should follow Brother Benedict's noble example and join us here."

'The whole hall laughed in appreciation of their master's supposed wit. I replied as best I could, sire: "Please listen to the heartfelt entreaties of your brother the Prince Richard, who genuinely fears that this man, Brother Benedict, means you harm…" But I was cut off by the Young King. He grimaced as he stood, clutching his right side, and said: "You have been given a cordial hearing, Sir Guy, as is required under the flag of truce. But I am tiring of you. Please go now!"

'His last three words were slightly strangled as he seemed to suffer a stab of pain and sat down heavily. His attendants swarmed around him as we were escorted out on to our horses and out of the city gates. I am sorry, sire, but I have failed.'

Sir Guy stood before me, head bowed. I made a faint attempt to console him, but I could not find the right words so I lapsed into silence.

It is worse than I thought. Brother Benedict has been into the city, gained my brother's confidence and has now fled again. The question is: did he get a chance to poison Henry?

The fact that my brother was last seen clutching his side and moaning in pain does not bode well.

25 April 1183

Outside Limoges

Hubert and I have been holed up in my pavilion, waiting for news. Every time one of the scouts arrives, Hubert dashes to the entrance to speak directly with him. But for three days we have heard nothing of interest.

The scouts must think it odd. Normally we are avid for news of the slightest changes in the training or manoeuvres of our enemy, anything that might expose their weakness and provide us with an advantage. Then, suddenly we are interested only in the personal movements of Henry the Young King. Has he been seen outside his bedchamber? Has his chamber pot been used? Is he looking pale and wan?

My father appears distracted by his digestion. He ate some old pork a couple of days ago, and has been suffering terrible stomach cramps ever since. It is his own fault; he never pays much attention to his hygiene. Anyway the discomfort has distracted him from the task of winkling out Henry and Geoffrey from the citadel.

17 May 1183

Outside Limoges

If Henry the Young King is ill, then he is doing a fine job of disguising it. He has not been seen himself, but his men have sallied forth from the city a couple of times and had quite some success on each occasion, partly because neither my father nor I really have our hearts set on this siege.

My father has been ill with one bug after another. It started with that pork, and then led on to influenza that seemed to last an age. The doctors were bleeding him four times a day, so it is no wonder that he was weak.

He originally had plans to raise the siege and to move on but I think that I have dissuaded him from that idea. We cannot give my brothers the satisfaction.

Meanwhile I have been worrying about the noxious Brother Benedict, who seems to have vanished off the face of the Earth. None of our spies at the court of King Philip have seen hide nor hair of him. I now suspect that Henry was lying when he said that he had sent him there. But since Henry has not been seen in public for a while it is difficult to know.

25 May 1183

Outside Limoges

Disaster.

One of Henry's men defected to our side today. This in itself is normally a good sign. The first man to leave a city under siege is normally followed by another, and then another and so on, until a small trickle becomes a stream and then a flood. But today any elation at the first sign of the city's collapse was immediately doused by the news he brought with him.

Henry has been ill. Gravely ill. And worse, the defector tells us that he has been nursed by a team lead by Brother Benedict, who has now pronounced that my brother's fate must be left in God's hands as he can do no more.

When the troubadours sing about a man's heart sinking, I have never really known what they mean. Until now. As the words came from the man's lips I felt my insides subside through my stomach, and I almost gasped for breath:

'You do not speak seriously.'

It was clear that the man was indeed serious. My father was there, as were William de Mandeville and Hubert. We must have had very different emotions running through our minds. No doubt my father was worried for his eldest son, notwithstanding that he was at war with him.

For William de Mandeville, the news was perhaps not so unwelcome. He had always had a poor relationship with Henry and he must have expected to lose all rank and privilege under my brother, when the time came.

As for me, my first instinct was still one of family loyalty: I wanted my brother to survive. But I surprised myself by how quickly my mind shifted to considering the ramifications if he did not.

But before long, my father jolted me from my thoughts, by dropping to his knees and raising his hands in prayer. His first mumbles were indistinct, but gradually it became clear that he was reciting the Lord's Prayer. I followed suit, as then did de Mandeville and Hubert. My father lead us three times through the prayer, then abruptly rose to his feet, turned to me and nodded. His eyes were full of tears, pleading.

In one instant my view changed. The man revered throughout Europe as the strongest king since Charlemagne. The man who would brook no opposition to his word as law.

The man who would make war with impunity on his own family and who would imprison his own wife for ten years. This same man was transformed in an instant into an ordinary supplicant begging at the altar for the life of his eldest son.

For all his wilful cruelty, for all his unyielding fierceness, for all his crass obstinacy, I felt a surge of compassion. I took a step towards him and after a brief pause embraced him. To my surprise he clung to me, as he shuddered. After a few moments he released me, looked at the floor and turned to walk out. William de Mandeville followed in his wake.

I was left feeling numb and fended off Hubert's rather half-hearted attempts to engage me. Not knowing what to do with myself, I eventually made for the makeshift chapel in a pavilion near mine. In all my years of dutifully attending religious services because it is expected of me, this was the first time that I felt voluntarily drawn to seek spiritual solace. I entered the gloom of the chapel slightly unsure as to what to do, so I sat down on one of the pews and stared straight ahead. A couple of times I vaguely sensed a priest approaching, presumably to see if he could help in some way. But I sat staring fixedly at the candles burning on the altar and my eyes gradually lost focus as I entered a kind of trance. I must have been there for two or three hours, before I swam back into consciousness.

What was I thinking about all of that time? It is hard to recall exactly.

In truth, the conversation with God, such as it was, related more to giving my parents comfort than to any special pleading for the life of Henry. I suppose I assumed that what will be will be in respect of him.

When I hear others speak of having communicated with God in some way, I have always understood it to be in a direct, quite human, way, as if it were a conversation. For me it was different; I came away from the chapel suffused with a sense of peace and serenity, but there was no sense of having had a 'conversation' with God.

But it did give me great comfort, and that was most unexpected.

11 June 1183

Outside Limoges

After two more weeks of clinging to life, Henry the Young King died early this morning. A monk from the monastery at Grandmont came straight from the city gates to see my father, sent by Geoffrey. I moved to my father's pavilion, next to mine, as I saw the monk approaching. I suppose that I knew what was coming. It seems that everyone else did too, for there were a large number of senior nobles and knights crowded in there with us.

Although we had been expecting this outcome, the announcement still came as a shock. My father gasped and stepped back, one hand feeling for the arm of his wooden chair, into which he slumped heavily. I must confess that I had already planned my reaction. I stood to the right-hand side of my father's chair and, bowing my head in prayer, stayed silent for a moment. Then I began in what I imagined to be a strong clear voice to lead everybody through the Lord's Prayer. It worked, this subtle assumption of leadership, as everyone lowered their heads and began to pray with me.

Although I admit premeditation in my actions, there was also an element of genuine religiosity in them too, stemming from the time I have been spending in the chapel recently.

My father and I undoubtedly felt a sense of guilt at what had befallen Henry. We were at war with him when he died, which must be especially hard for my father. I think his guilt at the situation deepened as Henry's condition deteriorated. My father and I had sent numerous messages to Henry pleading that we might be allowed to come and see him. But, typically, he rebuffed our approaches with disdain. I suspect that he thought he was going to recover but by the time he realised he was, in fact, going to die, it was too late to change his mind and summon us.

For my part, I also feel additional guilt over the role of Brother Benedict in my brother's death. I believe I did all that I could to warn Henry, but, as Hubert has pointed out, if I really was comfortable with the whole episode, then I would have told my father about it. As it stands, he knows nothing about Brother Benedict's part in this, and it is probably best to keep it that way for now.

14 June 1183

Outside Limoges

Today was the funeral of Henry the Young King.

We held an open-air service halfway between our camp and the fortifications outside Limoges. My brother's body is then to be taken north for burial.

It is said that one should not speak ill of the dead, but I find it difficult to lie and to speak well of my brother. It is also said that blood is thicker than water, and this may indeed be true, for, despite our personal animosity, and despite the fact that my own interests will be greatly served by his death, I was genuinely desperate for Henry to recover.

He was a man who was to inherit a host of titles and estates and immense wealth, but who could not once acknowledge his good fortune and smile at the world. He set everyone on edge, eventually. But no one would have known this from his funeral, at which he was lauded as the finest Christian Prince since Roland and the great hope for European chivalry.

Bertran de Born delivered a eulogy. Bertran has been a thorn in my side ever since I can remember. He won great fame as a very young man at my mother's court, and is now probably the most renowned troubadour in Europe. I will concede that his verses are pretty and clever, but I have always found them to be little more than that. They are showy for their own sake, seeking to demonstrate the author's cleverness rather than to convey his passion. Perhaps I am biased by Bertran's appearance and demeanour. He dresses and carries himself like a peacock, and his mannerisms, which he cultivates assiduously, are effeminate. Bafflingly, this seems to make him very popular with the ladies of the court. I am always slightly ill at ease with him, and feel clumsy and awkward by comparison.

His eulogy, delivered from the makeshift pulpit, was typically fulsome:

Youth stands sorrowful,

No man rejoices in these bitter days.

For Cruel Death, that mortal warrior,

Has harshly taken from us the finest of knights.

After an hour or so of such sentiments, I began to wonder if anyone else was feeling as cynical as me. I looked around. Everyone seemed intent on their prayers, with their heads piously bowed as they kneeled. Perhaps it was only me, after all.

At the end of the funeral, Henry's men exited first in silence and made their way back to Limoges. We all stood respectfully as these men, until three days ago our sworn enemies, made their way peacefully through our ranks. Geoffrey's men went with them, although Geoffrey himself stayed behind to speak with my father. I do not know what they spoke about.

As soon as we could leave, I summoned for my horse and, together with a small party of four men, went for a long, fast but aimless ride. I just needed to get away from the cloying hypocrisy of it all.

My father went alone, as planned, to perform the last lonely task. Henry's eyes, brains and entrails were buried in a gravesite at the monastery of Grandmont, lowered into the ground in a small oak casket. The rest of his body is to be taken to Rouen Cathedral for burial.

I have only just returned and the camp is quiet, although it is still quite early.

24 June 1183

Limoges

We gave the enemy five days' grace before resuming the siege, this time with a proper sense of urgency and purpose.

My father seems to have recovered his former grim sense of determination. His apathy has gone. It is as if the death of his son and primary heir has breathed new life into him. He probably feels that he needs to reassert himself if he is to establish his inheritance properly.

We have not spoken about the inheritance; I am just assuming that I will step into the role previously designated for Henry, but nothing explicit has been said. I am anxious to keep Aquitaine, having spent the best part of nine years fighting to secure it. Furthermore, it is an inheritance from my mother and not my father, although I suspect that he does not see it exactly that way.

I have resolved not to mention the matter myself, but simply to get on with the task in hand.

We did that successfully today, completing the job that our sappers began six days ago. They had tunnelled well beneath the city gates, and then brought the tunnel back towards our positions outside the city walls, so that there were effectively two tunnels underneath the gates. They had reported back that conditions were perfect for them. There was no rock to speak of, and the soil was not too sandy, which can often be a problem. Furthermore it has not rained for three weeks so the earth was well dried out.

The sappers withdrew their men from the tunnels and reported to me that they were ready to go as planned. I consulted my father and he gave me the authority to proceed.

Mercardier had the men all lined up in readiness as we lit the first fires at the far end of the tunnels. The wood down there was very dry and must have burned well for after only twenty minutes the timbers holding up the tunnels began to give way and collapse the earth underneath the city gates.

A great cheer went up at this first collapse, and soon there were other cheers as the fortifications themselves began to shift and crumble. It was important that we held on until the right moment to attack, but it was difficult to hold the men back. When the last part of the front ramparts to the right of the gates came crashing down, I gave the order to Mercardier to proceed.

The men surged forward, releasing the frustration of four months of enforced idleness. Normally I would have been at the forefront of the action, as bloodthirsty as the rest of them. However, today I hung back, wanting to direct operations from the back of the battlefield. I wanted to get this operation over with quickly, with no mistakes. I was keen to quit this place altogether after the events of the past few weeks, but I also hoped to impress my father with my control and discipline so that he would trust me as his nominated replacement.

All went to plan and we took control of the walls quickly. The city's defendants were feeble; no doubt they were demoralised by the death of their leader Henry. A number of them had fallen to their deaths as the ramparts collapsed, and the remainder had failed to get adequate replacements into position, so our men barely had any need of their scaling ladders. They just clambered over the rocky debris into the city through the settling dust, and did not really encounter any significant resistance until trying to take the citadel into which Count Aimar had retreated.

His resistance was short-lived, however. We had only just wheeled the mangonels and other weapons into position when his heralds sounded the call for a truce. I had expected as much. We were fighting in the city in which he had been born and raised. He had little incentive to fight on in a lost cause and see it destroyed. To be honest, I was a little surprised that he had not capitulated straight away after Henry's death. I suspect that honour and pride had driven him on.

We signalled an agreement to the truce, but I stayed at the rear and sent Mercardier forward to the parley. I had given him instructions that if we were going to spare the city then we needed to agree terms immediately, for the men were anxious to put the city to the sword and commence the looting.

It was Count Aimar who led their delegation. He accepted our terms readily enough. He was to cease all of his support to the other rebels in the area immediately. He was to leave the citadel at Limoges and we would have it razed to the ground so that he could not use it against us again. He was to pay us a forfeit of ten thousand pounds (deferred for three years), and he was to provide his two eldest sons and his daughter as hostages for his good behaviour.

The capitulation was complete. But I felt no sense of euphoria that the long siege was over. Neither did my father when I took him the news in his pavilion. In fact, I am not sure that he entirely registered the news at first. Although he has been reinvigorated recently, he seemed to slip into a kind of stupor as I broke the news. He simply stared past me from his wooden chair. It was only as I turned to leave that I knew that my words had sunk in, when he said: 'And what is to happen to the Prince Geoffrey?'

He should have known perfectly well what the answer would be, as we have discussed it several times recently. But I patiently replied: 'He has agreed to submit himself to your mercy with no conditions.'

My father looked pleased, as if this piece of information was a surprise to him.

Upon surrender, Geoffrey came almost straight away to our camp, and was taken immediately to see my father. I escorted him into the pavilion, where he threw himself dramatically at my father's feet, with loud protestations of apology and pleas for forgiveness. It was all rather embarrassing. For him. I enjoyed it, however.

Unfortunately, my father cut the scene short much earlier than he needed to, and stood up in order to lean over and pull Geoffrey gently to his feet. He took Geoffrey's face

in both of his strong hands and murmured: 'My son, my son.'
He leaned back and brushed the hair out of Geoffrey's eyes,
so that they could see each other better. 'Do not let us quarrel
like this again. I have lost one son this way. Do not let me lose
another.' And then he leaned forward and clasped Geoffrey to
him, saying: 'You are everything in the world to me.'

I have to say that I bridled a little at this. After all,
Geoffrey has actually been at war with us. I have stood
steadfastly by my father's side against my two brothers, only
to be rewarded by this overt display of affection for Geoffrey.

As Hubert pointed out this evening, maybe my father
feels guilty over Henry's death and has transferred some of
that guilt into blaming me. Hubert says it will pass and my
father will become more rational once he is no longer grieving.
We shall see.

After a few seconds my father pulled back from
Geoffrey and said: 'However, you do need to be punished for
your sins in taking up arms against me.'

He said this with a sigh, followed by a short pause, as
if he were only now thinking about what punishment to set.
Then he made up his mind and said: 'I have determined that
you will forfeit your castles in Brittany to me. You may keep
your lands and the revenues from the land, but you must hand
over your castles to my control immediately. I think there are
seven castles...'

My father looked up at the roof of his pavilion as he
tried to remember how many castles there were in Geoffrey's
dominions.

'Actually there are six, My Lord,' Geoffrey volunteered.

My father paused a moment, then realised that he was
correct.

'Do you accept these terms, my son?'

'Willingly, My Lord,' Geoffrey replied.

He dropped to one knee and took my father's right
hand to kiss his ring. When he had done so my father stooped
to raise him up and give him the Kiss of Peace. Then they

turned and left the pavilion together, my father's right arm draped loosely over Geoffrey's left shoulder.

I was livid. How could he let Geoffrey off so lightly? How could he ignore me in the decision about Geoffrey's punishment?

I spent the rest of the day training the troops furiously. They must have gathered that something was up as I kept them out there for two hours longer than normal and I was harsh in my treatment of them.

My father and Geoffrey spent the rest of the day together and then dined alone with each other. It was as if my father was making a point.

6 July 1183

Hautefort

Finally something good has happened after four months of frustration, delay and misunderstanding. In fact, ever since my father arrived in the south to 'take charge' of the war with my brothers things have gone from bad to worse.

First of all, in conceding the command to my father I lost my usual drive and energy so that the war lost all direction, even after the brilliant start with my two-day dash across country to Aixe.

Then the Brother Benedict affair made me lose confidence in my own judgement. I should have followed my initial instincts and dismissed him as a charlatan. Instead I listened to him, albeit briefly, and lost control of events. Then Henry died, and now my father seems to be acting as if Geoffrey is his preferred heir, rather than me, his ally and oldest surviving son.

Maybe things will improve now that my father has left. He departed ten days ago for Poitou, and took Geoffrey with him. It is sickening: he is behaving like a love-struck adolescent around my brother. I was glad when they left.

Geoffrey was due to travel on to Brittany from Poitou, but the way my father is behaving he might not let him go once they get to Poitou.

After they left, I decided that it was time to reassert my authority in the area. At least that is what I call it. Reasserting my authority as the Duke of Aquitaine over my rebellious vassals, which sounds noble and just.

Hubert, I know, calls it 'taking it out on the poor Lords of Aquitaine'. Somehow this sounds less noble and just.

Today we stormed the castle of Hautefort and took control of it. In fact, I stand here in the grandest bedroom dictating to the faithful Armande. It has always been thought that Hautefort could not be taken. Indeed, my father had said as much as he left. Perhaps he said it deliberately to challenge me.

He had given the castle back to Bertran de Born after Henry's funeral as a reward for his 'eloquent' eulogy. No doubt, he had expected Bertran to come to heel and swear allegiance to me. Much to my father's annoyance and to everybody's surprise, Bertran had accepted the gift, but once ensconced in the castle, refused all commands to swear allegiance. Presumably he was confident that the castle could not be taken and that I would soon lose patience and move on.

He miscalculated. This was the perfect opportunity for me to vent my frustration and demonstrate to the world that I am still a force in my own right.

Bertran's younger brother Constantine has been fighting alongside my father and me for the past six months. He and Bertran are supposed to share the castle, according to the custom that has been prevalent here for centuries. But they do not get on, and have been fighting over the inheritance for two years.

Now was Constantine's chance to shine and he took it with both hands. He is very different to his brother. He is tall and tough, and looks as if he has spent a lifetime outside fighting wild beasts, whereas Bertran looks like he has just emerged from a ladies' dressmaker.

Constantine's intimate knowledge of the terrain was a great advantage for us, and he was convinced that he knew how to exploit the weakness of the castle. I have to say that at first hearing I was not too keen on his plan, which involved climbing at a forty-five-degree angle up through a sewage pipe. The bottom of the pipe comes out into a ditch at the foot of the steep hill on which Hautefort is built, but the bottom of the pipe is shielded from the castle by a rocky overhang.

So we could enter the pipe unseen, and provided we could climb up through the tunnel we would emerge in a cellar underneath the kitchens. Constantine was confident that the tunnel would be undefended as he was sure that he was the only person who knew of its existence. He claimed it had not been used for thirty or forty years, and he had only come across it by chance as a young boy when playing hide and seek with his brother. He had never told Bertran about it.

I was sceptical. Firstly, how could he be sure that nobody else knew of the tunnel? Secondly, even if he were right, how did we know that the tunnel was still intact and had not disintegrated over the years? Thirdly, what would we find at the top of the tunnel? If there were men stationed there, they would slaughter our men as soon as they emerged from the tunnel.

But Constantine was so sure that I eventually agreed to go along with his plan. Mercardier had been equally sceptical, but once I had acceded to it, he seemed to lose his reservations, or at least he decided to hide them.

Constantine was to lead the way with six of his own men-at-arms. I was to follow with Mercardier and a further thirty knights. Everyone tried to dissuade me from going myself, and normally I would have bowed to their pressure, but I was so fired up by the events of the last few months that I was really spoiling for a fight. I did not want to miss this opportunity.

We set off at dawn this morning. Afonso of Aragon led a frontal attack on the front gate, designed to distract the enemy and to reduce the chances of the castle's defenders seeing us gather at the bottom of the hill. We could hear the sounds of intermittent skirmishing as Afonso tried to bring up a battering ram within range of the main castle gate, an almost impossible task. The hoots of derision from the defenders as they saw his men drop back time and again could be heard clearly down in our little corner.

Constantine managed to make good progress up the pipe with his six men-at-arms. We struggled a little behind him. Not only were we more heavily armed and therefore slower, but we also found it more difficult to gain and keep footholds as the men ahead took what grip there was. Besides which we were somewhat overcome by the smell. The tunnel might not have been in use for forty years as a sewage pipe, but it smelled as if it had been in use until yesterday by a large contingent of diseased men with rampaging diarrhoea. The tunnel was perhaps five feet wide and at such an angle that at any one time the floor of the tunnel was only inches from one's face. Furthermore the men above loosened the debris so that one was crawling along with forty-year-old shit raining down from above.

I judged it to be about halfway along, when I bumped into the man ahead of me who had stopped. Constantine in the lead had heard a noise from above, in the kitchen cellar. He was desperately trying to get the men to be quiet, but it took a while to silence men clanking along the tunnel in almost full armour, bumping into each other as they stopped, and complaining all the while about the smell and the compacted shit.

Eventually however, all was quiet.

We were still for about a minute, and I rested there in an extremely uncomfortable position on all fours, blocked in by men ahead of me and behind me, in a tunnel built for a completely different purpose. I think my mind must have begun to play tricks on me as I imagined that the walls were beginning, imperceptibly, to close in on me. My breathing was becoming shallow and laboured and I could feel and hear my heart pumping at an abnormally high rate. I had not felt anything like this since the tournament challenge with Fulk ten years ago. But on that occasion, I had simply been in fear of him. This time I was in fear of the tunnel around me. My heightened senses thought they could hear the earth beginning to slip and slide, and my vision started to fail. How had I ended up here? I realised that I was about to faint.

Fortunately, just at that moment Constantine must have pushed open the hatch at the top of the tunnel and the light flooded in. This revived me, for we were now scrabbling upwards as quickly as possible. The top of the tunnel was undefended, but we had to get as many men up there as quickly as possible to protect the entrance and let the other men come up.

Constantine and his six men were there, poised for action with swords and daggers drawn as I came up through the opening, exhausted, and pulled myself over the edge on to the hard, cold stone. I paused to catch my breath as the others emerged behind me. Soon we were all there. All with weapons drawn. And all slightly euphoric at having escaped from that foul tunnel with our lives. We were about to spring a monumental surprise on the castle's defenders.

Then Constantine motioned for silence and said: 'Remember that this castle is my family home. The people who live and work here are my people. I do not want them harmed or my property damaged. They will probably surrender when they see that we are inside the gates and that I am here. So make sure you accept their surrender. No rape, no pillage. Understood? Anyone who disobeys this command will to answer to me.'

The men shuffled uneasily. This was not what they had expected. They had risked their lives coming up the tunnel and they were about to risk them again going out into the castle. They wanted their fair reward for their risk.

I added: 'Constantine is right. This is his ancestral home and the defenders are his people. We would never have been in a position to take it if he had not known of the secret tunnel. However, I will share my first year's revenue from this castle equally amongst you, provided that you keep to Constantine's terms.'

This seemed to assuage them. I was angry with Constantine for waiting until now to dictate terms, but I would deal with that later by getting my money back from Bertran.

We burst into the courtyard, with an almighty roar.

I was gratified by the look of sheer astonishment on the faces of the defenders as we raced around the castle perimeter securing the position. Constantine had been right. They surrendered more easily than one would normally expect, for they knew they would get good treatment at Constantine's hands, which made them less inclined to fight.

After twenty minutes, the keep door opened and Bertran de Born emerged, dressed as flamboyantly as usual. He threw down his sword in that effeminate manner of his and announced his surrender. His arrogance, even when he had been humiliated, provoked me, and I barked at him: 'So you would defy your lord and master, would you? You snivelling bitch. Get over here and get down on your knees.'

He obliged, shocked by my outburst. He sank to his knees and put his hands out to take my right hand to kiss my ring. I let him kiss my ring, but as he took his head away I placed both my hands firmly on the top of his head, forcing him down into the mud. With him crouched there on all fours, with his face and hair in the mud and shit, I leaned over and hissed loudly in his ear so that everyone could hear: 'Don't you ever disobey my commands again! Or I will come back and slit your throat. Now don't move until I say so.'

I gave his head one last push down into the mud and turned to stalk off to the castle gates. They opened as I approached to find the cheering ranks of my men on the other side.

Afonso of Aragon, at the head of his men, beamed at the sight of Bertran de Born still crouched with his head bowed in the filth. He has long been Bertran's enemy, ever since Bertran seduced his wife and then boasted about it in his famous poem 'Eu m'escondisc, domna'.

I marched past them out of the castle and down to our camp, and changed out of my clothes, stinking from the ordeal in the tunnel. I returned some eight hours later, ready for the feast prepared in the castle's Great Hall, to find Bertran still bent double in the centre of the castle square. I had completely forgotten about him.

I ordered him to rise, but as he tried to get to his feet he stumbled and fell flat on his face unable to stand at first after spending so long with his knees bent double. He was a shameful sight, as he hobbled away, his fine clothes and hair covered in dirt. Normally I would not be so cruel as to enjoy the humiliation but on this occasion I could not help but smile.

In some of his poems he has been calling me Richard 'Oc e Non'[1]*, saying that I cannot decide whether to be a friend or foe to my father.

Well, he can shove his words up his perfumed arse now. Along with whatever else he shoves up there.

24 August 1183

Hautefort

How very curious.

I have not heard from my father for seven or eight weeks. Then today I receive a message from him that contains nothing but an instruction that Hubert Walter is to make his way to my father's court to take up a position in his administration as one of the Barons of the Exchequer. In itself the instruction is not such a surprise. Hubert has after all spent a good deal of time being trained for exactly such a role by his uncle, Ranulf de Glanville. But over the past few years Hubert has become an indispensable part of my retinue and my day-to-day life. I am not sure that my father had particularly noticed Hubert before, so it is odd that he would send for him in such a peremptory manner. There must be something else behind it.

Hubert left this evening. He is already missed.

1   * Roughly translated as Richard 'Yes and No'.

17 September 1183

Uzerche

A further message from my father arrived today. I am to attend to him at a Michaelmas court at Rouen. I have twelve days to get there, which means I have to leave imminently.

The message contained no other information. No congratulations on my work in subduing the remaining rebellious lords of Aquitaine. No news of his plans for any changes in the inheritance.

I presume he is instructing Hubert not to communicate with me, or he is somehow intercepting his messages, as I have heard nothing. I had hoped that Hubert would be able to keep me apprised of developments at my father's court, but my father seems to have foreseen that and put a stop to it.

If only we had had more time to plan before Hubert's departure, then we could have developed a proper scheme for communicating.

29 September 1183 – Michaelmas

Rouen

We arrived late last night after a foul journey.

The harvest has been late this year, so our journey was made through fields where the harvest was either being brought in or where it had just been brought in. The crop dust got into my eyes and nose causing my whole face to puff up. I react like this every year and it is one of the reasons why I had chosen to stay in Uzerche, in order to avoid the dry harvesting areas.

Where the harvest had already been brought in, the fields have been set alight as part of the annual scourging of the soil. In addition to the hay fever, the smoke getting into my eyes has been almost unbearable.

Never again will I cross France at this time of year.

I have arrived at court looking as if I have some kind of strange sickness. I looked in the mirror after washing when we arrived and I barely recognised myself. The whites of my eyes are bloodshot and the area around my eyes is inflamed. My nose is bright red, and raw at the end from constant rubbing and it has swollen dramatically. I know that it will pass once the dust has settled, but it is unpleasant to see people recoiling as they look at me.

I spent most of today closeted in my rooms. I cursed myself for worrying about what other people might say about my appearance, but I know people modify their behaviour based on what image one projects. So, for the sake of one or two days, it is best to lie low and recover.

Hubert has been my sole visitor. He has been effectively frozen out of the circle of information here at Rouen and he seemed rather despondent. I had to smile to myself. When Hubert was summoned to my father's court, I think he was secretly pleased: he thought that he was being recognised for his talent. He was a little deflated to find that he had been summoned to court and then ignored, just to spite me.

Given that Hubert knows nothing and that I have spent all day holed up in my rooms, we are still in our splendid bubble of ignorance. We will see what tomorrow brings. Will my father finally appoint me as his heir?

30 September 1183

Rouen

So now we know what it was all about.

My unspeakable brother, the Prince Geoffrey of Brittany, has surpassed even himself with his cunning and duplicity. He is pure evil.

But at least I now understand why my father has spoken barely a word to me since the death of Henry.

It all began at a conference called by my father for noon. A messenger brought the summons shortly after breakfast. I was to attend alone. There were to be no advisers present. This was unusual, but given the import of what I hoped we would be discussing, I assumed that it was justified.

I walked up to my father's rooms at the appointed hour. I had been pacing up and down in my own rooms for an hour or so, and I was as nervous as I could remember ever being.

I knocked on the door, a firm confident rap. There was a short pause before I heard my father's voice calling: 'Enter!'

I pushed the door and went in. My father was there, seated in his favourite wooden chair. As usual, he had positioned it in front of the window so that his expression would be difficult to make out against the bright sunlight streaming in from outside. There was a familiar figure standing to his right. It was Geoffrey. It was difficult to make out his countenance but his silhouette stood confidently against the backdrop of the window.

I walked forward, still sure at this stage that everything would go well. I knelt before my father and kissed the proffered ring. I stood, took a pace back and greeted them both emolliently: 'Father, I bring good news from Aquitaine. You will already have heard about the capture of Hautefort. Since then, all of the rebellious lords have submitted and accepted the King's Peace. I have personally taken homage from all of the main families and, in particular, I have brought the Count of Périgord to heel, which, you will be pleased to know, has been a very lucrative exercise.'

I inclined my head towards my brother. 'Brother Geoffrey, I am delighted to see you restored to your rightful place at our father's side. I trust that we can set aside our differences in the interests of our family?'

My brother studied his boots and made no reply. There was an uncomfortably long silence, and I began to realise that something was afoot. I rocked backwards slightly on my heels and took a slow, deep breath.

Then suddenly my father moved swiftly out of his chair and swivelled on his heel to face out of the window with his back to me. Then, finally, he spoke. It sounded as if he were making a superhuman effort to remain calm. 'What was your involvement with this itinerant monk, Brother Benedict?'

My heart sank. I knew I should have told my father at the time about Brother Benedict. Now it was all going to come out. I must have reddened slightly with embarrassment. My father could see this. 'Aha, so you do not deny it?'

I stumbled a little in my reply. 'There is nothing to deny, My Lord. Brother Benedict came to my attention and I dismissed him as a cheap vagabond and a charlatan after I interviewed him about his supposed dreams.'

My father stood there as if expecting me to carry on. I added: 'And I sent Sir Guy Strathbourne to warn my brother Henry the Young King about this man and his tricks.'

My father looked at Geoffrey enquiringly. He responded by shrugging his shoulders as if to say: 'I told you so.'

My mind raced as I tried to work out what was going on.

'My Lord, perhaps I should have told you about this man, but frankly, you had been unwell for a good number of days and you are normally sceptical of men of this type...'

My voice trailed off.

My father heaved a great sigh, as if trying to get his emotions under control. Then he spoke. 'It has been alleged that you saw this man Brother Benedict behind my back. You listened to his stories of dreams, describing events that then happened to take place a month or so later. It turns out that the reason these events happened is because he caused them to happen, rather than because he had any great ability to predict the future.'

My father paused and gulped, as if unable to go on. I was wondering why he was reacting in this manner. But it soon became clear as he gathered himself to continue. 'After the death of Henry the Young King...' – he paused to cross himself – 'Brother Benedict confessed to Geoffrey that he had poisoned the Young King over the course of the month or so that he was treating him, and that he had done so on your orders.'

I gasped as if someone had punched me in the stomach. I could not understand.

My father went on: 'You callously sent Sir Guy Strathbourne supposedly to warn your brother of the danger posed by Brother Benedict, when you had yourself arranged the whole scheme. And you did all this while serving under my command. You caused your brother's death and you have made me complicit in it. God will have His righteous vengeance for this.'

I reeled backwards. How could he possibly have come to this conclusion? Elements of the story were true, but the important part was just plain wrong. I stammered: 'But it's just not true. I tried to warn the Young King that Brother Benedict was a fraud. Ask Sir Guy Strathbourne...' I realised how weak my words sounded.

My father smiled bitterly and replied: 'We did and he confirmed that he was part of the plot.'

Another sickening punch.

'Well, ask him again. It is just not true,' I pleaded.

My father shook his head. 'He is dead. He died shortly after revealing the truth.'

It then started to become clear.

'Who was in charge of the torture?' I demanded.

'The Prince Geoffrey,' my father conceded.

'And who was it who took the confession of Brother Benedict? And was that a confession obtained under torture too?'

My father looked at Geoffrey but it did not seem likely that he would change his mind about why his eldest son had died. No doubt he and Geoffrey had run through all my possible defences to the charge before the meeting. Then Geoffrey spoke for the first time. He remained stony-faced.

'I have three witnesses to each interrogation. They will swear under oath as to what they heard.'

'Of course they bloody would,' I cursed.

I needed time to think, but I needed to buy that time. I took a deep breath and addressed my father: 'Sire, you must believe me when I say that I had nothing to do with Henry's death. I have only ever been a humble and loyal servant to you and you must believe me. I beg you to allow me to retire to my rooms to consider this allegation and assemble evidence to prove to you that I was not involved.'

Geoffrey made as if to protest, but my father nodded his assent. He seemed exhausted by the confrontation.

I turned and hurried out of the room.

My mind was racing as I stumbled blindly back to my rooms and ordered Hubert Walter to be brought to me.

Why would Brother Benedict have thought to accuse me of having plotted my brother's murder? What motive would he have? How would he expect to gain from it? Was it some kind of mad revenge against me for not having believed him about his visions? Or was he just plain mad and bent on fomenting trouble wherever he could?

Similarly, how could Sir Guy Strathbourne have 'confessed' to being part of the plot? Even under torture he would surely not have admitted to that. He was a man of great strength and integrity. After all, these qualities were why I had chosen him to go to Henry in the first place, because his reputation was such that Henry would take him at his word.

There were so many possibilities that my mind was in turmoil. I needed to slow down and think my way through it.

There was a knock at the door, and shortly afterwards Hubert entered. He knew from the urgency of the summons that something was amiss.

I quickly apprised him of events, and even as I did so, I could see the truth hardening and becoming fast in the shifting sands of Geoffrey's treachery. As I spoke, almost mechanically at times, my mind was racing ahead examining my thesis and testing it against the facts.

When I finished my account, Hubert held up a hand as if to ask for a few moments to assimilate all that I had told him. I waited impatiently for him to give me some signal that he was ready. He had been studying the ground in front of him but now he looked up and turned slightly towards me. I launched into my analysis.

'I have been thinking about this. It must be Geoffrey who is behind all this. I reckon that, as soon as he knew that Henry was dying, he would have started to think about how the hell he was going to get out of the hole that he had dug for himself. He was at war with his father in alliance with a brother who would shortly be dead.

'That left him terribly exposed, particularly as I am now our father's elder son and would therefore naturally expect to replace Henry as the King's heir. When he was third in line behind Henry and myself Geoffrey was in a reasonably comfortable position as he knew that my father would need to balance us all equally, particularly since Henry was so extraordinarily ineffective as a leader. But with me as the heir apparent, my father would probably choose to grant me all of his powers, especially since I already control Aquitaine. And where would that leave Geoffrey?

'So he hatched this plan to pass off Henry's death as a premeditated murder conceived and executed by me. Even if my father did not entirely believe the story it would plant enough seeds of doubt in his mind to prevent him from making me his sole heir.

'So he must have tortured and then killed, in front of "reliable" witnesses naturally, first Brother Benedict and then Sir Guy Strathbourne.'

I shook my head incredulously as I finished, my voice tailing off in astonishment at my own conclusion. My little brother, the one who for years was my best friend and confidant, the one who has always been the most light-hearted and gay of all of us, was plotting to have me discredited as the murderer of my own brother.

In order to further his own story and thus his own interests he would torture and murder two people. One of them, Brother Benedict, probably deserved nothing less, but Sir Guy was an innocent, good man caught up unwittingly in Geoffrey's machinations.

Hubert looked aghast. He, too, had spent a lot of time with the Prince Geoffrey and he was probably as shocked as I was by the way that the worm had turned. Over the next half an hour, we pored over my thesis, testing it against various different questions, but we could not fault it. We drifted to a halt.

The next question was what to do about it. I suddenly realised that my life might be in danger if my father really believed all Geoffrey's story. He might be forced to bring me to trial.

I suspected that there was already some element of doubt in his mind about Geoffrey's allegation, for he had allowed me to retreat to my rooms to prepare my defence. But if Geoffrey's accusation was to become public then my father would have no choice but to act decisively against me. Geoffrey would have known this, but my father must have forbidden him from speaking to anyone else about his charge. The stakes were high and Geoffrey must have been tempted to let his version of the story slip out. The fact that it had not must mean that my father had proscribed him from discussing it under threat of severe penalties if Geoffrey did not comply. Curiously this gave me some further comfort that my father had not entirely believed Geoffrey's story.

But frustratingly I cannot prove my innocence. I can provide Hubert and others as witnesses to my version of events. This should be sufficient to ensure that considerable doubt is thrown on Geoffrey's version, and to save me from a guilty verdict if it comes to it, but it will not be enough to restore me to a position of trust with my father. Just as Geoffrey has no doubt planned.

2 October 1183

Rouen

I could not dictate my diary yesterday as Armande, my precious scribe, had been taken away at night to be questioned by my father. It is probably just as well that he was not here, as the entry would have been filled with bile and hatred for my arrogant, cunning brother Geoffrey, with rage at my father for not taking my word at face value, and with incredulity at the way in which events have overtaken me.

I had a headache the entire day, which I attributed to nervous tension. I was in and out of my father's chambers all day. My first appearance was to make a speech renouncing all that Geoffrey had said and reiterating that I had tried to warn Henry about the danger posed by Brother Benedict. All the time there was the malign, brooding presence of Geoffrey standing at my father's side. I can hardly bear the irony of Geoffrey acting, with my father, as interrogator, judge and presumably executioner, when it is all his scheming that has brought about this farce.

They listened to my first impassioned address and then, relatively politely, asked me to leave while they considered matters. Then they summoned me back in to ask me some pointed questions, which I answered, and then we repeated the whole process several times. Once or twice I confess to fingering the dagger on my belt as my fury at Geoffrey threatened to boil over, particularly when he was dismissing me from the room.

Eventually they ran out of questions. My father called for Armande to be brought before him. Given that Armande had originally been a gift from my father I suppose that I should have felt some nervousness that he might betray me. However, after eleven years together I felt comfortable that he would tell my father the truth, and that he had not been got at by Geoffrey. My father tried to catch him out a couple of times, but without success. I suspect his heart was not really in it by this stage.

So I was dismissed for the final time. I was to return the next day, when I would find out my fate. Strangely, in spite of the strain and the uncertainty, I slept well.

And so to this morning.

I woke feeling rested and confident and was summoned to my father's quarters at ten o'clock.

As I went through the by now familiar routine of knocking, waiting for a reply and then entering, I reflected that perhaps my confidence was borne of the fact that if they were planning a dramatic punishment, they would surely have acted last night. The fact that I was here unscathed in the morning must mean that my father was not entirely convinced of my guilt.

Geoffrey was there at my father's right-hand side, of course, but there was another figure at his left, hidden in the shadows. I could not make him out easily at first but then I saw it was my youngest brother, John. He must now be sixteen years old, but I have not seen him for four or five years.

My father looked up as I came in. My easy confidence on entering vanished as he immediately looked away again.

He took a deep breath, pulled himself up out of his great wooden chair and turned to walk behind it. Then he turned again to look at me, leaning on the back of the chair for support with my two brothers standing at his side. After a short pause he began: 'You have been charged with a great crime, namely that of conspiring to cause the death of Henry the Young King. God bless and keep his soul.'

I noticed that he used the word 'death' rather than 'murder'. Perhaps it was a good sign.

'There are two key witnesses to events. Unfortunately, they are both dead. It would have been much better if they had been kept alive and I had been able to question them myself.'

At this, Geoffrey shifted uncomfortably. My father had found the weak point in his plan. If Geoffrey had been so convinced that Brother Benedict and Sir Guy Strathbourne had been telling the truth, why then had he found it necessary to kill the two witnesses after their 'confessions'?

My father continued: 'However, it is true that there were witnesses to the interrogation of these two men, and that their stories are reasonably consistent. Furthermore, the fact that you did not tell me about Brother Benedict even when you believed him to be a danger to Henry the Young King does make me question your motives. Why would you keep it a secret if your motives in dealing with him were entirely pure?'

There was no real answer to this question. I had not deliberately kept it secret from my father. Rather, I had simply not told him. There was a difference, although I accept that the distinction could be considered arcane. I had no choice but to keep quiet.

My father continued: 'My conclusion from this whole sorry affair has to be that there is doubt that you deliberately engineered the death of your brother, partly because the witnesses are now dead and partly, frankly, because I want to believe that you had nothing to do with it. Certainly your character and behaviour to date suggest that you would not have done such a thing.'

I breathed a tentative sigh of relief.

'However, it is clear to me that you could have done a great deal more to avoid the death of your brother, and it may well be that the evidence that your brother Geoffrey has so painstakingly collated is true. I simply cannot know.

'But, the fact remains, even if you are not guilty you are certainly partially culpable. Therefore, although you are to inherit the lands that were once Henry the Young King's, you must not benefit unduly from your culpability. I am stripping you of your lands in Aquitaine.'

I gasped. I had not foreseen this. Aquitaine is my home. It is where I grew up. It is the wealthiest province in Europe. It is the source of all of my wealth and, more importantly, the source of all of my soldiers. And what is more I inherited it from my mother and not from my father. My father was seeking to emasculate me as a ruler, in much the same way as he had emasculated Henry by giving him titles but no real power.

As I took this in, my father went on: 'The new Duke of Aquitaine will pay you homage as his overlord, as you paid homage to Henry the Young King. But you will not return to Aquitaine unless at the specific invitation of the new Duke. You will relinquish control of all of your castles there and your revenues will pass directly to the new Duke. Do you understand?'

I was dumbfounded. I could not think of anything to say, other than to ask the obvious question: 'And who will be the new Duke?'

Everyone in the room was expecting the answer to be the Prince Geoffrey, whose manoeuvrings had brought about this crisis, after all. He stood there preening himself, waiting for the answer that would surely come, the reward for his scheming and treachery.

But the answer, when it came, was entirely unexpected.

'The Prince John will be the new Duke of Aquitaine.'

I let out a short laugh of astonishment, but quickly reined it in. I glanced around to see how the others were taking this announcement.

Geoffrey looked shocked. It was clearly an entirely unexpected outcome for him. Disappointment was etched on his face. His hard work in seeking to destroy me had been successful, and he had taken a grave risk in setting me up in the way that he had. But he was not to be the one picking up the prize.

John looked no less amazed, in the way that a small child might look when told that he is being given an unexpected treat. No doubt he was dreaming of the power and glory that would come his way as the new Duke of Aquitaine.

My father looked smug, which I found surprising. Then I realised: John was to be Duke of Aquitaine, but my father was to wield the real power and control its revenues and men. Despite being its nominal overlord he had never really controlled Aquitaine because it had come to him when he married my mother, and she and then I had effectively controlled it. Now, just when I have spent years bringing it to heel, he seeks to take it from me. No wonder he looked self-satisfied. No wonder he was eager to believe Geoffrey and to find me culpable for Henry's death.

How could I not have seen this coming? I had underestimated my father, thinking that his powers were declining, but he has comprehensively outmanoeuvred both the Prince Geoffrey and me.

I said nothing but turned and left the room. Nobody moved to stop me.

This is a disaster.

It is all very well in theory being nominated as my father's successor, replacing Henry, but in practice it will mean not just one backward step, but several. I will have greater titles and the succession will in theory be secure, but I will have no real land, no real income and no real soldiers. And I will lose Aquitaine, my home. The efforts I have made in the past nine years to bring it back to some semblance of order will all have been in vain. I cannot let this happen.

Again we come to a break in the diaries. Again water damage confounds us. Why could the carpenter who manufactured Berengaria's coffin not have used just a little more care? We would know so much more. But I suppose we should be grateful for what has survived.

This time there is a shorter break: a gap of some five and a half years. It was a period almost entirely taken up with continuing the sibling feuding described so candidly in the earlier surviving volume.

Richard rode away from Rouen on the day after his diary entry describing the scene at which his father King Henry II outmanoeuvred all three of his sons by announcing that John would take over Aquitaine.

One can imagine Richard's feelings. He had spent the previous nine years fighting to secure the duchy against his own rebellious vassals. Now that he was finally successful, he was to give up the duchy. In exchange for what?

When he reached Poitou, some two days later, Richard sent back a message to his father. The message was short. Richard would not relinquish Aquitaine under any circumstances.

Given that he had spent a good part of the previous nine years cementing his relationship with his father and campaigning with him, this was a major fissure. If Henry had calculated that Richard would meekly give way on Aquitaine in order to reach for the greater prize of being Henry's undisputed heir, then he severely underestimated Richard's attachment to Aquitaine, which he saw as his ancestral home.

For a few months Richard was left to his own devices. Presumably he spent the time in preparing his defences.

Henry, meanwhile, had to contend with the demands of the French King Philip that Henry return to him the lands that had been given as dowry when Philip's sister Margaret had married Henry the Young King. Now that he was dead, Philip wanted the lands back.

Eventually this was settled. Henry was to pay Margaret a pension and the lands were to be transferred to whichever of his sons was to be married to Philip's other sister Alice. The language of the diplomatic exchanges here is interesting. Richard had technically been betrothed to Alice since 1169. Now Henry was allowing for the possibility that he might prefer her to be married to one of his other sons. It would be fascinating to have Richard's thoughts on this development at this stage, but Alice does have a more central role in the diaries later.

Henry spent the rest of the winter trying to persuade Richard to accept his proposed course of action, with no success. Frustrated, he changed course and gave permission for John, now seventeen, to raise an army and try to take Aquitaine by force. Even now, over eight hundred years later, the idea is so ridiculous as to be laughable.

Of course John got nowhere. He allied himself with Geoffrey and together they carried out a few minor raids in the region of Poitou. Richard's response was to launch one of his by now trademark lightning raids on Geoffrey's lands in Brittany. Henry quickly realised that he was not going to get anywhere by taking on Richard on the battlefield, either with or without his other two sons. He had to think of another plan.

As ever with Henry, when challenged with a difficult problem, he came up with a solution. And it was ingenious in its own way.

He summoned John and Geoffrey to his Christmas court in London in December 1184. He knew that he could count on their attendance. But something altogether different was required to persuade Richard to attend. Henry played his trump card. He released his wife, Eleanor of Aquitaine, from her captivity and invited her to attend court. When she accepted, Richard *could hardly refuse. He was, by all accounts, the closest of all the children to his mother, and furthermore his rights in Aquitaine were derived through her.*

So Richard was present at this court, but somehow it seems not to have all gone Henry's way. The records are sketchy but it appears that Richard left the court early. Certainly by Easter 1185 it seems he was back in Aquitaine preparing for war with his father. Henry was in the process of preparing an army to march against Richard, when he appears to have changed his mind. He summoned Eleanor to him once more at his camp in Normandy and pleaded with her to bring Richard to heel. She agreed but her terms were onerous. She was to be restored to all of her rights in Aquitaine. The restitution was to be full, final and irrevocable. In turn Richard would lay down his arms and command his castellans to obey Henry.

Although nominally Richard suffered a slight loss of face at this, in reality the victory was his. With his mother restored to her rights to the duchy, he was now the racing certainty to succeed her. Perhaps Henry was settling for an easy life.

Certainly, by the time Easter came around again in 1186, Richard looked to be firmly ensconced as the heir apparent. At a peace conference with Philip of France, Richard was once again nominated by his father as the son to be betrothed to Alice of France. Shortly afterwards, Geoffrey headed to Paris to seek Philip's aid in scheming against his father and his brother.

Richard, meanwhile, spent the next year and a half engaging in a tremendously successful campaign against Count Raymond VI of Toulouse. The line of Toulouse had long been a thorn in the side of Angevin ambition in the area, and with his father's full support Richard was able to reduce the Count to begging for help from Philip of France. Philip was not able to offer any support and by August 1186 Richard's victory seemed assured.

But then, just as Richard seemed likely to inherit the bulk of his father's empire without further incident, there occurred one of those random unexpected events that turn the world upside down.

The Prince Geoffrey was attending a tournament in Paris. He was there purely as a spectator, for in common with Richard he had forsworn taking part in tournaments since their first tournament together in Paris. He had walked round from the main grandstand erected for dignitaries to the tent where one of his men was preparing for participation in the tournament. By all accounts he had had a fair amount to drink and it appears that he simply wanted to go and wish his man well. Whatever his purpose, as he rounded the corner he stumbled and fell directly in the path of a horse that had just bolted after its saddle was pulled too tight. The horse's right fore hoof struck him clean in the side of the temple. He was dead before he hit the ground.

Henry II must have wondered what he had done wrong. Three of his five sons were now dead. Maybe Becket's dying curse really was upon him.

For Richard the political situation was set fair even more clearly than before. One by one his rivals were disappearing.

We know from his earlier diaries that he had been extraordinarily close to the Prince Geoffrey, but that they had gradually become estranged by their competing interests. Indeed they had been at war for much of the period preceding Geoffrey's death. What were Richard's feelings on his death? Perhaps we can guess from Richard's later generous provisions for Geoffrey's son, Arthur of Brittany, that he felt a sense of loss in a way that he did not feel on the death of his brother Henry.

Geoffrey's death gave King Philip of France the excuse he had been looking for. He demanded his feudal right as overlord of Brittany to custody of Geoffrey's two infant daughters and threatened to invade Normandy if his demands were not met. A truce was agreed until January of the following year, 1187, but it was clear to all parties that this was a short-term agreement. Richard and his father busied themselves with the preparations for war, seemingly acting as one unified command.

The war started in June 1187, when Philip invaded Berry. Richard managed to hang on to the castle of Châteauroux long enough to allow his father time to relieve him with the main Angevin army. But Philip could not withdraw entirely without losing face so the two armies drew themselves up for battle.

A full-scale battle was an extremely rare phenomenon at this time, especially when kings were involved. Battles were too risky; too much depended on chance. Henry II, a noted warrior king, never fought a full-scale battle in his life. Neither did Richard, perhaps the most famous warrior in history. They both made and maintained their reputations in siege warfare and skirmishing raids.

Not surprisingly, therefore, both sides were reluctant to commit to battle. Instead they camped opposite one another, posturing for all that they were worth, whilst teams of negotiators scuttled backwards and forwards. There are no detailed records of what transpired during these negotiations. What we do know is that Henry and Philip agreed a further truce and agreed to part their armies. What is remarkable is that when the armies broke up, Richard went to Paris with Philip rather than maintaining what had seemed to be an increasingly solid relationship with his father.

Conceivably it was some tricky plot or subplot by Henry and Richard to confuse or beguile Philip. But it seems more likely that Henry and Richard simply fell out during the course of the negotiations, and that Richard determined that his best interests were served by allying with Philip, at least for a time.

The stand-off continued in a desultory fashion over the course of the next year and a half. If this stand-off seems strange to us now, given the stakes involved, then one has to factor in the effect of the news that was emanating from the Holy Land.

The First Crusade, some eighty years earlier, had been, from a Western Christian viewpoint, a glorious success, capturing the Holy Land and establishing the Kingdom of Jerusalem. The Second Crusade, on which Richard's mother Eleanor had fallen out with her first husband, King Louis of France, was much less of a success, and in its aftermath the Kingdom of Jerusalem had been progressively weakened by a combination of insufficient resources, internal feuding and the rise of Saladin to unify the Saracen forces. This deterioration culminated in the Battle of Hattin in July 1187, at which King Guy of Jerusalem, against all advice, committed his troops to a battle against vastly superior numbers. The Christian forces were annihilated. Those who were not killed in battle were captured and executed shortly afterwards. The victorious Muslims advanced on Jerusalem itself and took it with ease.

The full scale of the disaster began to filter through to Western Europe in the late summer and early autumn of 1187. The effect of this news cannot be overestimated. At every social level men were encouraged to take the Cross to begin a new Crusade to recapture the Holy Land. On offer was the chance for glory, adventure and, of course, eternal salvation. One of the great figures of the Catholic Church, St Bernard of Clairvaux, was the most eloquent advocate of crusading; he proposed a fantastic bargain:

> *O mighty soldier, o man of war, at last you have a cause for which you can fight without endangering your soul: a cause in which to win is glorious and for which to die is but gain. Are you a shrewd businessman quick to see the profits of this world? If you are, I can offer you a bargain, which you cannot afford*

to miss. Take the sign of the Cross. At once you will have the indulgence for all the sins which you confess with a contrite heart. The Cross is cheap and if you wear it with humility, you will find that you have obtained the Kingdom of Heaven.

Crusading zeal reached fever pitch and Richard was, typically, the first European Prince to take the Cross, which he did at Tours in the late autumn of 1187. No doubt this was one of the sources of his subsequent conflict with his father. Richard was eager to be on his way and yet both Henry and, to a lesser extent, Philip, delayed and prevaricated, keen to settle their affairs in Europe before departing into the unknown.

By the early summer of 1189, when the extant diaries resume, Richard was in a state of open rebellion against his father, in a loose alliance with Philip. What is more he had his tiring, dying father on the run. Even Le Mans, the city where Henry II was born, opened its gates for Richard. Victory was now assured.

28 June 1189

Ballon

After the breathless excitement of having my father in full retreat, and the key moment of Le Mans falling to me, I was today suddenly brought up short. Twice. It was not some grand divine revelation, telling me that I ought to be a loyal son once more. Although, even as I dictate these words, I have to reconsider. Perhaps it was, after all, a way for God to tell me something. Relating the story may help me to decide.

I set out from Le Mans this morning with five hundred knights. Yesterday there had been the usual carousing, drunkenness and mayhem that accompany the taking of a city, even when it is on agreed terms. I had left the men to it, as is now my custom, and was paying court to Charlotte, the third daughter of the Count of Le Mans. My days of drinking competitively with the men are over. I prefer to settle down with a few friends, or, sometimes, as on this occasion, to be alone with a lady.

Charlotte is a lady of rare enchantment. Her figure is delightful, yet she keeps it well disguised. I first encountered her last summer, when I was passing through on the way to Aquitaine. I was intrigued by this quiet, demure girl who seemed to have her head almost permanently bowed, as if deliberately to obscure her beauty. When she raised her head to look at me, it was as if dawn had broken in an instant, as I basked in the warmth of her gaze. She was gorgeous. Unfortunately, she was also unusually virtuous. I extended my stay by first two and then three days, but she remained steadfast. Her manner towards me was not exactly frosty, but just ever so slightly disdainful, as if I were a favourite dog who had farted at the wrong time. In the end, I had to leave, but I sought out her company before I left and told her that I would be back. Frustratingly, she just nodded dismissively as if to say: 'Yes, yes, now run along.'

So the fall of Le Mans was a double source of excitement for me. As soon as I was shown to my quarters in the castle, I began to enquire as to her whereabouts. It did not take long for the servants to track her down. She was in the Great Hall. I went downstairs myself to see her, rather than summon her to me. I thought it might help my cause.

When I first saw her, she almost took my breath away. She looked and saw me, and smiled. I swooned like a young girl who has unexpectedly been given her first horse. I eagerly made my way over to her, but my conversational skills abandoned me as I blushed and stammered and talked nonsense. Despite this, however, she seemed to be won over and I was surprised when, shortly after dinner, I left the table, stopped by her chair and stooped to whisper in her ear an invitation to my rooms, and she replied with an unequivocal nod.

I hurried to my rooms for a quick wash. As I waited nervously for her, I reflected that I had not been this anxious about a woman for a long, long time. The diet of average but eager women that has been served up to me has diminished rather than nourished my appetite for sex or love or romance. This felt different. I felt excited and, for the first time in an age, slightly insecure.

Shortly, there was a rap at the door. Firm and confident. Not soft and timid, as I might have expected. I opened the door and there she stood, beautiful in a green dress, with her chestnut hair flowing over her shoulders. She moved towards me confidently, so I stepped aside quickly to welcome her into the room. She seemed much more assertive than I remembered from our brief encounters of a year ago.

I offered her a glass of wine, which she accepted, and she sat on the couch and crossed her legs. She drank from the goblet a little too eagerly, I thought, as I made desultory attempts at conversation. Enquiries as to the well-being of her family were difficult to deliver sincerely when we both knew that they were now dependent on my favour.

I tried a different tack instead, another old gambit. I asked her to come to the window to tell me a little about what could be seen outside. She complied meekly, recognising the invitation for the device that it was, and accepting it readily enough. As she stood there at the window in the gathering dusk, she pointed out the bands of peasants drunkenly weaving their way home as they streamed from the city gates. I had performed my usual trick of declaring free beer and wine for the peasantry for the day. It cost little relative to the goodwill and, more importantly, good intelligence that it generated.

I moved up behind her as she giggled at a couple of men, clearly known to her, who stumbled and fell. There was a slight intake of breath as my arms encircled her waist, and I nuzzled into her neck. But she gamely carried on describing the scene outside: 'There goes Roger Fitzwilliam. He appears to be with young Molly Taylor... and he was only married three months ago to Frances, the gatekeeper's daughter...'

My hands moved up to cup her breasts, and I could feel her chest begin to rise a little with each breath. I untied the sash at her back that gathered the dress together. As the sash came away, so the dress was loosened and my hands came back round on to her firm, full breasts. Still she faced away and still she chattered on. I cannot recall now the names of all the peasants she described, but the shocked prurience with which she described the scene below contrasted amusingly with the scene playing out in the room.

I was hard now, and pressed myself a little against her rump to let her know. She acknowledged it with a gentle push against me, talking all the while of Thomas, the mill-owner's bastard son. I stepped back and undid the buttons down the back of her dress. Her conversation continued, pausing only slightly as I let the dress fall away entirely. She was a splendid sight there, framed by the stone arch of the window with a backdrop of the setting sun, naked except for her shoes.

I removed my clothes and stepped towards her, but she did not turn to face me, nor did she stop her descriptions, even as I ran my hands over her buttocks, her breasts and through her hair as I kissed the base of her neck. The only acknowledgement she gave was an occasional slight catch in her breath. I carried on caressing her for a minute or two, and

I could feel her pressing back more firmly into me, as she giggled at something Mary the carter's daughter was up to.

Finally she leaned forward to rest her arms on the window frame to give herself a little purchase. As she wriggled her bottom against my erection, I figured that now was the time and I guided myself slowly in from behind. She was wet now and her descriptions continued, but now with the occasional grunt as we thrust at each other. The pitch of her voice rose as we approached a climax, but she never stopped talking.

As I slumped, spent, against her back and, with her arms on the window frame holding us both up, she whispered: 'And there, in the courtyard below, is my father. Staring straight up at this window.'

This startled me, but Charlotte seemed remarkably unconcerned, although she did finally stop her descriptions.

She stayed the night in my rooms, which is not something I normally allow, but I was intrigued by her manner, which remained slightly brusque and detached, even during three further bouts of lovemaking.

Something in her manner nagged away at me. She was so different from the shy beauty who had charmed me last summer and who has occasionally wandered across my dreams and thoughts in the year since. In the end I raised it with her, as we lay side by side, slowly recovering our breath. 'You seem different to last summer, when you rebuffed me so consistently and firmly. What is it that has changed?'

There was a long pause. 'I've fallen in love,' she replied eventually.

I confess I started a little at this. Given her consistent rejection of me last summer and her matter of fact attitude of today, I was surprised to hear that she was in love with me. I muttered something like: 'I'm sorry, I had no idea.'

She said nothing. I was not sure what to say, so I stumbled on: 'Was it today that you first realised this?'

There was a sniff from the darkness beside me. 'His name is Sir Ralph Percy.'

It was only then that I saw what a fool I had been. I blushed scarlet there in the darkness embarrassed at my easy assumption that it was me whom she was in love with. How arrogant, how conceited, how thoughtless.

She explained: 'My father gave his permission for us to marry last month, but when he heard of your approach he insisted that we put off the wedding. He is keen for me to become your mistress, as he feels that it may bind you to him.'

'And what of Sir Ralph Percy?' I enquired. 'What does he think of all this?'

She paused, clearly thinking carefully about what to say, before continuing: 'As you can imagine, he is a fiercely jealous man...' Her voice tailed off.

'So he wants to kill me,' I finished her sentence for her.

'No, no, not at all. Or, at least, not any more. He did at first, but now he has calmed down. My father and I made him promise, and my father gave me permission to lie with him before my wedding day, so that at least it was he who would have my virginity.'

It was all becoming a little clearer. Charlotte's change of heart from last summer, her brusqueness and practical approach to the business of love – plainly she was not a virgin – her punishing her father by letting him see her at the window with me. The Count's plan to win my favour demanded the sacrifice of his daughter's love and her virtue. And I, the tough soldier, the noble Prince, the wise ruler, had fallen for the plan, unable to see past the end of my nose.

I was furious with myself for being taken in, and that is the reason that we set off so early this morning from Le Mans, when we might have been expected to stay a few days. I was not angry with Charlotte; she was a relatively innocent pawn, but I felt sorry that our sex would probably ruin her chances of happiness with Sir Ralph Percy, for his jealousy would destroy them. I also felt foolish that I had assumed that she was in love with me. My pride was punctured, for the first time that day.

As we rode hard, away from the city towards the north, I was determined to carry on harassing my father. I know he is ill, but I have seen enough fluctuations in his health to dismiss this as just another setback, even if it is not just another of his staged contrivances. I was determined that we would soon see an end to the erraticism and madness that have characterised his behaviour over the last couple of years. As the Greek tragedian says:

'Whom the gods would destroy, they first make mad.'

Towards lunchtime we caught sight of his men on the hills in the distance. The ground is dusty after several weeks without rain, so we could see quite clearly the plumes of dust as we set out to catch them. They did not notice us for an hour or so, when suddenly there was a great commotion and they began to hurry forward. But we had set a good pace and continued to gain steadily. I began to formulate plans for what we would do with the prisoners, for what my first words to my father would be. I should have known better.

We crested the largest hill at almost a full gallop, with me at the head of the men. My eyes were full of the dust thrown up by the retreating horses ahead, so it was not until it was too late that I saw what was happening. Through the dust clouds I could just make out five knights charging back down the track towards us. The foremost looked familiar. It was William the Marshal, my father's champion, making a last desperate attempt to slow us down and thus protect his master, my father the King.

I gasped and almost choked in panic. I was not in full armour; I did not even have a helmet on. I had only a sword whereas the men bearing down on me were fully armed and carrying battle lances. At the centre was William the Marshal, about fifty yards away now, and closing fast. I tried to move either left or right but the horses flying along beside me prevented me from veering off course. I scrabbled to draw my sword, but the press of horses from my right gave me no room.

As I galloped towards inevitable death, unable to turn either right or left, unable to draw my weapon and with no armour and no shield, my predominant thought was not fear of death, but merely of what a waste it would be, that I had worked so hard and battled so long only to be deprived by casual carelessness. I had dreamed for so long of glory, of a new age of kingship unsullied by the madness of my father's last years. And now it was all to come to naught, here on a dusty track in the middle of nowhere. I cried out, not in fear, but in furious feral frustration.

William the Marshal was ten yards away now and his lance with its point sharpened for battle was arrowing towards me at chest height. I closed my eyes and began to mutter the Lord's Prayer, seeking God's forgiveness for my sins of pride, lust, avarice and most of all for my sins against my father. In the last few seconds, I suddenly saw my father's recent madness as a test of my faith and loyalty, a test set by God. If it was, then I had conspicuously failed it, and an inglorious, wasteful death was to be my punishment.

'Our Father, who art in Heaven, hallowed be Thy name, Thy Kingdom come,

Thy will be done—'

That is as far as I got.

I remember seeing William the Marshal's horse about two yards away and wondering why his lance suddenly dipped. Then I was tumbling after a great impact and then, suddenly, darkness.

I woke with blurred vision to find a bright light boring through my eyes into my head, which was throbbing ferociously. I could see nothing else. I could hear a babble of voices around me, but I could not make out what anyone was saying, or indeed what language they were speaking. I closed my eyes again, not knowing if I were in Heaven or Hell.

Then I gagged and turned my head quickly to vomit on the floor, which seemed to spark me back into life. The bright lights dimmed, and everything came slowly into focus, while gradually the babble of voices subsided. I could make out the anxious faces of Hubert Walter and others standing in a circle around me. William the Marshal was there too.

I got to my knees, then staggered slowly to my feet, clutching at Hubert for support. I spat on the ground a couple of times and turned to face William the Marshal, attempting to recover some dignity from the situation. I said: 'By God's legs, Marshal, I was unarmed...'

He paused, and looked at the ground before looking up at me and replying evenly: 'The Devil may kill you, but I will not. That is why I lowered my lance and took your horse and not you.'

My men around me reacted at this, reaching to their sides for their swords, but I raised my right arm to indicate that they should stay their hands. I bowed to William the Marshal and then turned away. He left, mounting up quickly and riding off with his four men.

I whispered to Hubert: 'Get me away from here, look at my hands.'

He glanced down and understood immediately. My hands were shaking and I could not allow the men to see me in this condition. He shouted instructions to the men to turn about. The chase for my father was off. He commandeered one of the knight's horses for me, and I mounted up, feeling desperately sick and disoriented.

Hubert put it down to the shock of the fall and the bang to my head. But I felt it was something more. It was as if I had not realised before that I had a great glass shell around me protecting me. Now that glass shell was shattered, firstly by the episode with Charlotte, and secondly by William the Marshal sparing my life. I had thought that I was in control of events, that I was master of my own destiny. But these two people had punctured that belief.

Perhaps God had sent them to bring me back down to earth. Or perhaps it was just two chance events on the same day.

Either way, I have changed my mind. I will reconcile with my mad, bad father and honour him dutifully for the rest of his days, whatever the cost.

4 July 1189

Ballon

My change of heart has angered King Philip. He had thought we had my father at our mercy and he cannot understand why I have suddenly taken my foot off the old man's throat. I have not tried to explain myself to him, but I have made sure that he is treated well in today's accord.

We all met today here at Ballon to sign the terms we have agreed over the last few days.

My father is to pay twenty thousand marks in compensation for the various technical infractions of the last few years. He refused this at first, but consented once I agreed to pay the fine for him. I need him to be able to die with his kingdom intact and his affairs settled. In order to do that, I had to bring Philip to heel, so paying the fine seems a small price.

I have finally agreed to marry Philip's sister Alice, when I return from the Holy Land. She has been my father's ward for twenty years, and some say she has been his concubine there these last ten years. However, I have closed my ears to this innuendo in order to satisfy my father.

The Crusade to rescue Jerusalem and the Holy Land will commence in Lent next year, in eight months' time. There will be no further delay.

The treaty is harsh on me. I have to pay the twenty thousand marks, although nominally it comes from my father. I have to marry Alice, whose reputation is cast into doubt, and I have to wait a further eight months before the great Crusade can begin. But these are all small penances to bring peace to my father.

When we met this afternoon, I was shocked by his deterioration. The strong ruddy features have melted into a grey brittleness. We met on horseback and I think he had rather hoped to be able to remain on horseback throughout.

But we had to dismount to grant each other the Kiss of Peace. I had to avert my eyes so that I would not see his shame as he dismounted inelegantly with the help of four men. He shuffled towards Philip and me, and I felt a deep sense of dread as I recognised that he was now near death.

I consoled myself that at least I was reconciling myself with him before it was too late. Prompted by the events of only a few days ago when first Charlotte unwittingly exposed my pride and then William the Marshal punctured that pride, I had conceded much to reach this point of reconciliation.

I thought my father would be pleased at my change of heart and all that I had given up for him so it was in confident mood that I stepped forward to embrace him. We kissed three times as is the custom, but as we made to separate, he clutched at me and pulled me towards him. I recoiled a little as he smells very bad now. The canker of his illness is eating away at him. But I allowed him to pull me to him and I leaned forward to hear what I thought would be some grateful words about our reconciliation.

Instead he hissed: 'God grant that I may not die until I have had my revenge on you.'

With that, he shuffled away.

At first I was astonished, then angry, then finally I simply felt sad that my efforts and my change of heart had come too late.

We parted shortly afterwards, and I watched his horse bear him away towards his camp, the King slumped over in the saddle, overcome with the exhaustion of the meeting. I know it was the last time that I will see him alive.

8 July 1189

Fontevraud Abbey

I came to the abbey here late last night, with only four horsemen accompanying me.

I had received word two evenings ago that my father had died at Chinon and that his body was to be brought to the abbey, so I rode directly here, arriving some two hours after dark.

The party with my father's body had not yet arrived. The abbot was expecting them in the early morning, so I ate and then retired alone to the abbey church to pray for my father's soul.

It was a long, silent night. At some points, I knelt in prayer, as I felt I should. I started with the conventional prayers for my father's soul, but my thoughts inevitably spiralled off into memories, dreams, half-remembered incidents and emotions.

He had been a giant of a man in his achievements, single-handedly carving out vast lands to make himself the most powerful man outside the Holy Roman Empire. Admittedly, he had some luck in his timing and in his marriage, but sheer force of personality and determination were the crucial ingredients in his success.

His decline in the last ten years has been painful to behold for all those who loved and honoured him. His physical deterioration detracted from his previous aura of invincibility, but it was his increasing madness that really destroyed him. At first he used the initial signs of it as part of his games in setting one son against the other. But now, looking back, I think that the deaths of first Henry the Young King and then Geoffrey accelerated his degeneration to such an extent that his lucid moments came less and less frequently.

It was only a few days ago that I recognised the need to try to bring him peace before he died. The incidents with Charlotte and William Marshal were the warnings, but they came too late. I will remember his last words to me forever: 'God grant that I may not die until I have had my revenge on you.'

Maybe he will be waiting for me in the afterlife. If so, I wonder if death will cure his madness. When he is in Heaven, will he be the young, vital man who carved out a great empire? Or will he be the frail, grey old man hissing venom into my ear?

I must ask a bishop about this. I want to know that I will see him again, that he will finally be proud of me, and that I can once again be proud of him.

Eventually the doors to the church creaked open behind me, and I could hear the shuffling, reluctant approach of the abbot. I felt his hand on my shoulder, and I heaved myself up from my knees. I moved to the aisle, took a deep breath, crossed myself in front of the altar and followed the old man out of the church.

Even now, a few hours later, I can remember the feeling of dread at the prospect of seeing my father's body, as I made my way blinking out of the gloom into the early morning sunlight. The abbot led me across the courtyard into the hall where my father had been laid out.

From a distance, I could see his body, hands clasped together on his chest in the traditional position of penitent prayer. I moved to the side of his body and looked down on his face. He seemed curiously peaceful, which was a shock. I suppose I had expected his final breaths to be taken in the wrath that dominated his later years. I drew some comfort from this as I knelt again to pray by his side.

To tell the truth, my prayers were perfunctory. I felt that I had done my thinking and praying in the night-time hours I had just spent alone in the church and I was emotionally exhausted. But, aware of the need to keep up appearances, I managed to make myself stay there for half an hour.

Then I rose to look at my father one more time. He looked peaceful still. I leaned over to kiss his forehead. His skin was cold and clammy to the touch, unpleasant but not unexpected.

What was unexpected, what shocked me deeply, and made my heart miss a beat, was that as I looked down at him for the last time, a thick trickle of blood emerged from his nose and dripped slowly down his left cheek. I jumped, but forced myself to look back. It was as if the peaceful countenance that he had when I came in had gone. His face seemed contorted by the wrath that I had expected.

Was it my kiss to his forehead that had caused this change? I was confused. I touched his hand to make sure he was dead, and it was indeed cold and lifeless.

This must be his final deed, his promised act of vengeance, his final victory. So I forced myself to walk slowly away, one step at a time. As I pushed open the door of the hall, the light flooded in and my fear evaporated.

Had I imagined the whole thing in my exhaustion? Armande thinks not. He tells me that the servants' quarters are rife with stories of how my father's blood had started to run again, to boil with fury, at the sight of me.

I cannot get out of my head the image of the blood running from his nose. I hope it will disappear when we bury him tomorrow. Or maybe it is his final poisonous gift to me.

10 July 1189

Fontevraud Abbey

We buried him yesterday, but the image of the blood running from his nose continues to invade my thoughts. I can abide the image when there are others around but I find it deeply unsettling when I am alone. As a consequence, I have not slept well.

I have thought about asking the abbot to supply a local girl, not for sex, but to keep me company at night. But how ridiculous to ask a churchman to procure me a woman when I am supposed to be in mourning, in order to cover up the fact that I am scared to be alone.

I decided to face last night on my own, and I did, starting at every noise, every rustle, and waking often from fitful sleep. I am exhausted, but I made it through the night. I feel more proud of that than of any of my deeds of valour on the field of battle.

The funeral went well enough. I had given instructions that my father's men should be treated with dignity and respect. I suspect that those who remained with him till the last were nervous that I would demean them, or strip them of the lands and favour granted by my father. But that is far from my intention. I admire the fact that their allegiance to my father was recently tested to the limit, but that they remained loyal. Those are the kind of men I need on my side. So I picked the two most prominent amongst them, William the Marshal and Baldwin of Béthune, and I rewarded them handsomely, in full view of everyone.

William the Marshal is to marry Isabel de Clare, a noted beauty, but, more importantly, the heiress to the vastly wealthy Lordship of Striguil in the Welsh Marches, to the County of Pembroke in Wales, and to the Lordship of Leinster in Ireland. Baldwin has had to make do with the promise of the next rich widow who comes into my gift. Both seemed immensely pleased and relieved. In fact, William has already left for Dieppe to get to London to marry the girl. He was in such haste that I suspect that he is worried I will change my mind. In fact, he was in such a hurry that reports have come back that he fell off the gangplank when boarding the ship at Dieppe, and got a thorough soaking!

Although some onlookers may be surprised, rewarding the best of my former enemies and binding them tightly to me serves notice to all that the place of the brightest, the best and the most able is at my court rather than anywhere else.

22 July 1189

Gisors

Today I received my comeuppance for laughing so heartily at the reports of William the Marshal's soaking at Dieppe.

It has been a busy time since leaving Fontevraud. A couple of days in Tours, securing the fortification there, and then three interminable days in Rouen, receiving homage from what seemed to be every man and his dog.

Finally, all the men were seen and we could move on to Gisors, towards a conference with King Philip. It was as we rode out towards the meeting point with King Philip that it happened.

We were about to cross a wooden bridge three miles out of Gisors. I remember thinking as we approached that it looked new, and I wondered if the tolls ended up with me or with King Philip. I made a mental note to ask the Castellan at Gisors to find out when I returned tonight. Just as I approached the middle of the bridge there was a loud crack. The next thing I knew, I was looking up at a clear, blue sky with people scurrying anxiously around me. I was soaking wet. Clearly I had been dumped in the river as the bridge collapsed.

I began to laugh at the incongruity of it all, and after a few seconds, the men began to join in until soon the whole troop was reduced to helpless, puerile hilarity.

As the laughter began to die down, I became aware that the back of my head was throbbing, so I touched it and saw that my hand was covered with blood. The laughter ceased in an instant, or at least I think it did, for everything went dark.

I woke to find that I had been moved into a makeshift tent. My head felt as if a blacksmith was trapped in there, pounding and pounding at his anvil in an effort to get out. I had been stripped and changed, for I was now dry. As I opened my eyes and lifted my head, there was a low murmur of approval around the tent. No doubt my men were pleased to see that their provider was good for a little while longer.

Hubert came to my side and I asked: 'How long have I been out?'

'Three hours, sire, and you need to rest.'

I shook my head and instantly regretted it, as it seemed to spur the little blacksmith to even greater efforts to smash his way out.

'Have you sent word to King Philip?' I asked Hubert.

'No, sire. We did not want to until we knew what…'

His voice tailed off. I smiled at him: 'You mean, until you knew whether I would live?'

I sat up, grimacing as my head thudded, swung my legs over the side of the stretcher, and got to my feet. A great wave of nausea washed through me, and I think I must have visibly blanched, judging from the faces of those around me.

'Right, let's get going,' I muttered, walking through the entrance to the tent to my men outside.

My father once told me that my men will have to believe in two things: my invincibility and my infallibility. The fact that I am invincible will make them follow me anywhere and give them the confidence that is often the key determinant between success and failure when fighting breaks out. The fact that I am infallible means that I can maintain tight discipline amongst fierce and unruly men. My word must be law.

An incident such as this, even though it was an accident, could make me seem vulnerable. I had to snuff out that suggestion as quickly as possible, whatever the personal cost to me.

And so, with the blood still seeping from the gash, with the little blacksmith pounding away inside my head with his heaviest tools, with nausea coming over me, I set off to meet the King of France.

The meeting passed in a bit of a haze. The details of our agreement had all been worked out beforehand by the court officials, for which I was most grateful. Given my condition, I did not want to have to be quick on my feet in negotiations with Philip.

He was to give back the land he had taken from my father, I was to pay him four thousand marks, and I had to confirm my agreement to marry his sister Alice. In return he would not dispute my entitlement to my father's lands.

The agreement to marry Alice was the most difficult one to swallow. I can no longer ignore the prevailing view that she was my father's mistress for ten years. I cannot possibly marry her, partly out of pride in not wanting my father's cast-offs, partly because I know that God would not bless the children of such a union, and partly because I fear that my father's dying curse on me will somehow be realised through her.

But I have plenty of time to figure out a way of getting myself out of that particular commitment. It may well be that once we are on crusade and Philip and I are brothers in arms, he will willingly release me.

And so we march onwards to England, to claim my kingdom and all of its magnificent riches.

13 August 1189

Portsmouth

The day dawned on a beautifully calm sea, but as we approached Portsmouth towards midday, the wind suddenly began to get up and the sea, from being as flat as a Flanders' field, began to swell into waves some six feet high.

The ship's captain made a bad joke about the tide turning with the ascent of the new King. I cannot quite recall what he said, but I do remember his sudden alarm when I turned a baleful glare on him. I had not meant to, but clearly I had struck fear into him, when I had simply been staring into the middle distance, focused on the task ahead. I smiled slightly at his discomfiture. I generally try not to revel in my power, for that way lies the madness that consumed my father. But sometimes it amuses me in a small way.

I had sent Hubert ahead of me to make the necessary preparations. His first task was to release my mother from her imprisonment at Winchester. After discussion with her, he had identified what he thought would be a successful way to strike a clear break with the past. As soon as our ship docked, I moved ashore into a pavilion set up on a pier. There, he quickly briefed me on the plan.

He and my mother had determined that the chief foci of resentment towards the end of my father's reign were Stephen of Tours and Ranulf de Glanville. Stephen of Tours had been one of my father's most ruthless ministers in exploiting the new and improved methods of tax raising, and he was well known for having enriched himself hugely. In general, I have been reluctant to turn on my father's men when they can be useful to me. There are few who can truly inspire their men and they are valuable to me. Men such as Stephen of Tours, however, who is little more than a scheming, venal bookkeeper, are two a penny, and can be found under virtually every stone I could care to turn over.

He was brought into the pavilion, and he looked in a sorry state already. Chains in front of him bound his hands, and his legs were also chained together, with just enough give to allow him to shuffle forward and make the beginnings of a bow to me.

I turned to one of my stewards and demanded that more chains be brought. If we were going to go to the effort of humiliating this man in order to make a symbolic statement, then we had to make that statement as loud and as explicit as possible. It was no good to us if the crowd thirty yards away could see only a bedraggled figure following us. They had to see that he was loaded down with chains. By the time my stewards had finished with him they would barely be able to make out the man beneath all the chains.

Now, of course, he needed a cart to travel in, so there was a delay while a humble cart was found.

Then, just as the crowds began to sound restless, we set off. There was a murmur of excitement as the flaps of the royal pavilion were folded back, and then, as I emerged on horseback, wearing the great red cloak designed by my mother and carrying my sword in my right hand, there was an almighty rolling cheer.

It was a powerful sensation, and as I sat there, smiling alternately to the left and the right, I reflected that I was one of very few men in this world – alongside the Emperor Frederick Barbarossa and King Philip of France – to have experienced this feeling, of thousands upon thousands of men cheering me because I represent hope and change and leadership.

I know that clever churchmen advocate this type of parade and pomp. They are very much in support of increasing the mystique of the Crown, but I am not sure whether they genuinely believe that this ceremonial aspect of kingship will really increase the power of the Crown, or whether they have invented it in order to make us, the Kings and Emperors, feel good and therefore willing to support the Church.

I suspect it is the latter, as the symbolism of the ceremonial is too subtle for the masses to grasp. As my father used to say, no ruler should ever underestimate the stupidity of the masses. Like a herd of cattle, they are easily led most of the time, but once the cattle stampede out of control, it is extraordinarily difficult to bring them back into line, even when it is in their own interest. The trick is to never lose control.

That is what this parade was all about: demonstrating that there is a new master; that the old master is dead; that the causes for any discontent with the old master have gone. And that there is a bright new future.

Stephen of Tours, clanking along in his cart, wreathed in chains, was the poor unfortunate chosen to be the symbol of this break with the past, and I could hear the crowd's cheers for me turn to boos and jeers as he was processed a minute or so behind me.

I congratulate my mother; she certainly knows how to play to the crowd. Or maybe she too knows the intoxicating effect that all this adulation can have, like one of those drugs from the East. I must be careful not to become possessed by it, for its heady potency may have been one of the causes of my father's madness.

The procession ended at Portsmouth Castle, and Hubert, presumably on my mother's instructions, had laid out a great feast in the courtyard. The mid-afternoon heat was by now quite intense, and I was pleased to get into the relative cool of the stone castle and take off the heavy red cloak of state.

I went to my rooms and found a bath already drawn for me. I stepped into it eagerly, keen to get clean after the long journey and the two nights aboard ship. I know that some of my men laugh behind my back at my obsession with cleanliness. They think one bath a month is a little suspect; they would be shocked to know that I sometimes have as many as two a week. I sank back in the water and closed my eyes, promising myself just a short rest before heading back down to start taking the homage of the great men of the land.

After a couple of minutes I heard the door creak open. I assumed it must be Hubert, for there were two guards outside and they are normally understanding of instructions to allow no one else entry. I muttered with my eyes still shut: 'Well done. I thought it went excellently today. Loading down Stephen of Tours with those chains was a master stroke...'

I waited for a second, expecting a reply, but none came. I opened my eyes to see where Hubert had got to.

Instead, I was greeted with the sight of a woman standing before me. She was an extraordinary spectacle. Her long blonde hair was piled high on her head in tightly braided tresses. Her face was beautiful, with smoky blue eyes, and sharp cheekbones framing a petite nose. She had bright red lips and from her mouth dangled a key on a leather tress. She wore no clothes, and her breasts were perfectly shaped. Moving my eyes down across her flat stomach, I came to the most remarkable sight of all, which made me sit up in my bath, sloshing the water on to the floor.

For she was wearing a set of silver chains around her groin. The chains came together, just below her pudenda, into a shining silver padlock. Then I understood. This must be what a chastity belt looks like.

I stood up in the bath, and the beauty opposite me had the good grace to blush, as I caught her glancing down at my penis while the water cascaded off me.

She took the key from her mouth with her right hand and then spoke, which was a surprise. Ladies who are not of royal rank are usually required to wait until they are spoken to.

'My Lord Richard, it is an honour to meet you, some fourteen years after we first became betrothed.'

My mouth dropped open. This was the Princess Alice, my betrothed, the sister of King Philip of France, and the ward of my father for twenty years. Now she was standing here wearing nothing but a chastity belt.

'Sadly, I understand that France's enemies have been circulating rumours that my chastity was compromised by your father. It is not true, and I stand here before you now, naked, so that you may know the truth. I wear the belt as a symbol of my virtue.'

Her voice tailed off. Her speech was over, and she was now clearly at a loss as to what to expect from me. My eyes ran up and down her body. I moved towards her and she flinched slightly as I reached out. But it was only to take the key from her hand. I knelt in front of her and inserted the key into the lock. It turned smoothly, and I gently unlinked the silver chains and let them drop to the floor.

I smiled to myself and looked at the ground. What is the prescribed etiquette when presented with a naked beauty bound in silver chains, to whom you have been engaged for fourteen years, but whom you have never met?

Alice and I both looked up from the floor, equally embarrassed, it seemed, and unsure what to do next. I felt sorry for her, being led to a man's rooms by the Queen Eleanor, her father's former wife, and now her future mother-in-law, and then being sent unclothed into the room to confront the new King of England, and her future husband.

It was Alice who took the initiative, however. She stepped forward, took both my hands in hers and raised herself up on tiptoe and kissed me. It was no light brush on the cheek. It was forceful and, it seemed to me, practised in the way she pushed her tongue into my mouth. I was just beginning to recover from my surprise, when she let go of my hands, reached between us and began to play with my penis.

This was no shy virgin, I thought, as she dropped to her knees, pushed her hair out of her eyes and took me into her mouth, deep into the back of her throat.

There was a momentary frisson as the thought crossed my mind that the man who had taken her virginity and taught her these tricks was in fact my father. The father who had placed a dying curse on me.

How attached had Alice become to my father? Was she now a part of his plans to avenge himself?

Such thoughts, rather than putting me off, served only to excite me further. Normally on a first encounter, I would withdraw gracefully before coming, so that I might service the lady. But on this occasion, as I tried to withdraw, she clamped on tighter and put her hands behind my buttocks, so that I could not move.

I abandoned myself to the moment, thrilled by the combination of her beauty, her desire and by the uncertainty of her purpose. As I came into her mouth, she kept going as if my orgasm made no difference so the come must have gone straight down her throat. She only began to slow and stop once my thrusting ceased.

What on earth am I to do now? I cannot possibly marry this woman, for despite her nobility and her beauty she is now seriously compromised. Not simply because she is no virgin, but because her lover was my father, and I have no intention of letting him reach from beyond the grave to wreak his revenge on me through her.

I have sworn, only last week, to King Philip of France that I will marry her. Under normal circumstances, I could employ any number of diplomatic devices to delay and prevaricate. But in eight months' time, we will be on crusade together, brothers-in-arms, which will make it doubly difficult.

This was all for the future, however. Alice dragged me back to the present, staring up at me with her smoky eyes.

She raised herself up from her knees, walked over to where the silver chains had been discarded, picked them up and walked back towards me, smiling provocatively. She looped one chain over my head, allowing it to drop around my neck. Then she pulled me to the bed like a dog on a leash.

I was a little perturbed. She could easily have strangled me if she chose, but I went along with it. Perhaps the risk excited me.

She pushed me back on the bed and started to tie me to it with the chains, so that I lay there spreadeagled, anchored by each arm and each leg to the corners of the bed. My penis was beginning to revive as she finished tying off the last of the four chains. She noticed and seemed to look pleased with me, as if she were a young mother smiling at a child who has done something clever.

However, such thoughts were swiftly banished as she disappeared from the bed to return a few seconds later, holding my dagger in her right hand. My heart stopped. So she was after all my father's creature, sent to dispatch me as a cruel retribution.

I closed my eyes and strained against the chains, but that only bound them more tightly. The frustration was intense; just as I was coming into the full bloom of my life, it was to be snatched away, not gloriously on some battlefield in the pursuit of Christian glory, but sordidly, in a borrowed bedroom, at the hand of my father's whore.

I opened my eyes again and my writhing stopped. Alice crouched above me, knife in hand, whilst a slow smile played across her lips.

I dared to wonder, maybe she was not about to kill me, maybe she was simply some kind of bizarre fantasist, trained by the hand of my father.

She brought the point of the knife down so that its sharp tip rested on my breastbone, then she drew the knife straight down my body, pressing just a little too firmly for comfort. I cursed my obsessive habit of sharpening my knife and my sword, as she pressed a little too hard, and drew a faint line of blood as the knife passed over my stomach and down to my navel.

'Oops,' she said, as she saw the line of blood, perhaps four inches long, and she leaned down to lick it off. She straightened up as the knife carried on downwards, lifting off my stomach to run down the underside of my erect penis and down the centre line of my scrotum where she brought it to a halt.

She looked at me quizzically, as if running over something in her mind. She played the knife up and down in slow movements all along my scrotum, while she stared down at my groin. Then she slowly raised her head up towards me, as if she had decided something.

Our eyes met and locked. She smiled at the fear in my eyes and in one swift movement flung the dagger away from the bed, grabbed my stiff penis and guided herself to a sitting position on it, deep, deep inside her.

Then she began to grind herself rhythmically on me, closing her eyes and clutching her arms to her head. She cried out in a frenzy of orgasmic delight. It was as if she had pleasured herself on me, rather than as if I had played any part in it.

I thrust desultorily away for a moment or two, but then for the first time faked as if I had come. I was still hard, but having been in fear for my life, I had no enthusiasm for this.

After a few moments, she disentangled herself from me, and without a word stalked over to the door, where she knelt to pick up the cloak, which had been left there. She turned, looked at me with a blank expression that told me nothing, and left the room.

I breathed a sigh of relief. I had survived: my father's curse had not got me yet. My relief turned to laughter when I realised I would have to call the guards to rescue me, trapped as I was, naked and tied by silver chains to the bed.

13 September 1189
Westminster

Today I was crowned King of England.

Although I already hold large tracts of land and innumerable grand titles, the title of King has an intoxicating power.

Over the past hundred years or so my forebears have tried to accentuate this, both through the mystique and ceremonial of the Church, and also through increasing formality at court.

The notion that Kings rule by divine right as God's representative on Earth is difficult. What is there in me that can live up to the weight of divine majesty? How can a mortal man, albeit of royal blood, but with the sins and weaknesses of the flesh, be considered semi-divine?

But it is easy to fall into believing it. In the ceremony at Westminster Abbey today, I certainly came close to believing it, as I stood there in front of the assembled throng, stripped to the waist in only my breeches, whilst Baldwin, Archbishop of Canterbury, anointed my chest, head and hands with holy oil. He then turned to the congregation and proclaimed me king.

Caught up in the enthusiasm of it all, I felt a great sense of power wash over me, as if I really am the 'chosen one', equipped with all the resources of a great kingdom, to lead a Christian army in pursuit of the grandest of holy tasks, the recovery of Jerusalem and the rest of the Holy Land.

I know deep inside that the notion of me being the 'chosen one' is absurd, and that for me to really believe it is the start of descent into the type of madness that eventually claimed my father. But sometimes, for a while, it is wonderful to relax and sink into unthinking acceptance.

20 September 1189

Westminster

After the splendour and the glory of the coronation I have been brought soundly back to earth.

The business of trying to prepare for the Crusade is a grind of relentless money raising. I am determined that when we leave, we will do so as the best-equipped army there has ever been. That is my first responsibility as leader of the Crusade.

Unfortunately this conflicts with my responsibility as leader of the people, as it is those people who will have to fund the army. I have set about this in what I consider to be the fairest way. My father had already raised large sums through last year's Saladin tithe,[2]* so I cannot use that option again so soon. And the Pope's recent promise of freedom from the Saladin tithe for those who take the Cross has not helped, as many families seem to be sending their fourth, fifth or sixth sons on the Crusade simply so that the rest of the family can avoid the Saladin tithe.

However, the change of regime has offered me the opportunity to raise more money by selling off the offices of sheriff, justiciar, castellan and so on. I had originally hoped that by conducting an auction for the various royal offices in each county I could achieve two objectives, as the money would flow to my treasury and the office holders would largely change, thus providing a clear break from my father's regime. Regrettably, it seems that my father's office holders were so successful in lining their own pockets that they are always the highest bidders, which is not what I wanted at all.

Then William Longchamps came up with a shrewd plan. If I fined the existing sheriffs large sums for misconduct, then not only would this bring in extra revenues, but it would also mean that they would not be able to afford to pay the sums they bid in the auction. Making the fines public would demonstrate to the second bidder how much money can be made out of the office, which would in turn encourage them to pay the amount bid by the current holder. And, of course, it means that the offices change hands to men who now owe their advancement to me. This will be important during my absence on the Crusade.

---

2   *The Saladin tithe was a tax of a tenth of all revenues and moveable property levied to assist the Crusade. Those who went on Crusade were exempt from the tax.

Armande looks up from his desk and tells me that all but seven of the thirty-one sheriffdoms have changed hands, so not only have we got roughly twice the amount of funds we hoped for, but the kingdom is also in the hands of my men.

So that is the sordid business of money dealt with. More important is the issue of power, and how to deal with my younger brother John and my bastard half-brother Geoffrey whilst I am away. It would be easier if I had an heir already, but of course there is no time to marry, conceive and bear children before we depart. So that will have to wait. It is also complicated by the fact that I am engaged to someone whom I cannot possibly marry.

Geoffrey was relatively easy to deal with. He is five years older than me, and because he is illegitimate, he remained loyal to my father as his Chancellor throughout the various troubles. But I believe that his so-called loyalty was really a reflection of the fact that he had nowhere else to go, unlike the rest of us who had our own lands and titles. But I know that he still harbours ambitions.

He was elected Bishop of Lincoln years ago, when he was about twenty, but he was never actually ordained into the Church, managing to delay it by saying that he needed to study on account of his youth. After several years, the Pope insisted that he be consecrated, but Geoffrey resigned rather than become a priest. He claims, sanctimoniously, that he does not feel suited to the life of the Church, citing his interest in warfare, hunting and women. But this is a charade. Everyone knows that such interests are no bar to a successful career in the Church. His real reason is that if he were ordained a priest, then he would have to give up forever any hope of secular office, including that of King.

My brother Henry once told me that he had been dining with Geoffrey the Bastard when Geoffrey, a little drunk, put a golden bowl upside down on his head and asked Henry whether he thought that a crown suited him. I had scoffed at this, but Henry reminded me that our great-grandfather William the Conqueror had started off life as William the Bastard.

I have always found Geoffrey extremely personable. He is bright and sharp, with a familiar manner of talking that makes one feel comfortable and at ease. He is definitely my father's son, with his strong nose, and from his mother's side he has much darker skin and hair than us, the legitimate children. It is an attractive mix to women.

Given his loyalty to my father, and his intelligent nature, I was tempted to take him into my own circle at court. But something in his manner tells me that he is not entirely to be trusted. So, three months ago, I ordered the canons of York to elect Geoffrey the Bastard as Archbishop of York. By all accounts he was livid at first. But apparently he is obeying my instructions and is on his way here to Westminster to be ordained in three days' time. I know that this disappoints Hubert Walter. He had hopes of the archbishopric himself, but it could not be. Three days ago I made him Bishop of Salisbury instead.

John is another matter, and not so easily dealt with. He is twenty-two years old now, ten years younger than me. We should be natural allies as we are completely different in character and therefore have no rivalry in warfare. He is, of course, my heir, but he cannot resist plotting against me. It is as if he has some sort of compulsion that makes him do it, even when it is so clearly against his own interests.

John is the complete opposite of Geoffrey the Bastard. Geoffrey is open whereas John is devious. Geoffrey puts you at ease whereas John makes you feel uncomfortable. Geoffrey is dark and handsome, whereas John is attractive in a feminine way.

I suspect, although I have no hard evidence to support it, that John has a streak of cruelty running through him. I do not deny that I am capable of being cruel. Indeed, to be a successful leader of fighting men, one needs an element of cruelty to enforce the strict discipline required. I suspect that John enjoys his cruelty, however. There are rumours of how he treats his wife and mistresses that beggar belief.

The reason that I dwell on the shortcomings of my younger brother is because I know that the right political decision would be to force John to come on crusade with me. As the old saying goes, it is good to keep your friends close and your enemies closer.

However, the plain fact is that John repulses me to such an extent that I cannot possibly take him with me. I cannot stand even to be in the same room as him for more than five minutes. His position as my brother and my heir would dictate that we should spend a good deal of time together, and I simply cannot stand that prospect. So, despite knowing that it is probably the wrong decision, I am going to leave him behind.

I have appointed Hugh du Puiset as Chief Justiciar and William Longchamps as Chancellor to deal with the practical running of the kingdom, but this is only by way of counterbalancing John, who will be the highest-ranking man in the kingdom in my absence.

I am under no illusions that it is a perfect solution. Perhaps John has played me; perhaps he deliberately set out to ensure that I would not want him on crusade with me. If so, he is a better plotter than I have given him credit for, but I suspect that he is not that sophisticated or disciplined. I believe that he sets me on edge simply because of who he is, not because of some clever scheme of his. But I may be wrong.

In any event, I have given him the counties of Cornwall, Devon, Dorset and Somerset on the grounds that they are the furthest-flung of my dominions and therefore the most difficult to reach. They are wealthy counties, I am told, so he cannot complain on that account, but it will take him ten days to a fortnight to get there and back each time from London. I have also not given him control of the castles in those counties, which will remain with me. I am not sure that this is a real advantage to me, given that I will be away for at least two years, but it gives me some satisfaction to inconvenience him.

I have also given him the counties of Nottingham and Derby. There are stories of a band of outlaws in Sherwood Forest, led by a man named Robin of Sherwood. I am not sure if the stories are true, but if they are then the county of

Nottingham may well give John more problems than he needs.

And so, my plans for England are laid. I know that I can justify them to myself, but in my heart of hearts I know that they are borne of political necessity. I trust I will not live to regret them.

13 October 1189

Godstow Abbey

My mother is a strangely vindictive woman.

We are passing through Oxfordshire and have been offered lodgings here by the abbot. Over dinner he told me the story of what became of Rosamunde Clifford, my father's mistress. Not content with having destroyed Rosamunde's relationship with my father, my mother took things a stage further. It is said, the abbot whispered to me, that Rosamunde was killed whilst in her bath, at my mother's command.

I had dismissed Rosamunde from my mind years ago, but this assertion did startle me. I know that my mother is capable of a great many things, but murder? But the more I think about it, the more I think she probably was responsible for Rosamunde's death. She knew that my father's interest in his mistress was extinguished, so she was more or less free to act.

Rosamunde came up in conversation because it happens that she is buried here at Godstow Abbey. The abbot told me that my mother, or, as he calls her, 'the great Queen Eleanor', had recently ordered a new stone for Rosamunde's tomb. It arrived two weeks after my father's death. He invited me to have a look at it, so after our meal we went by torchlight into the main church where my father had had Rosamunde entombed. There on her tomb stood the new stone ordered by my mother. It read:

> This tomb doth here enclose the world's most beauteous Rose,
> Rose smelling sweet erewhile, now naught but odour vile.

I almost laughed out loud. My mother is relentless, but this was special even by her standards. She harbours a grudge like no one I have ever known.

The next volume begins on the eve of the departure of the Third Crusade, eight months after Richard's last entry. With the benefit of the perspective of over eight hundred years, we can see that things have moved on hugely in those few months. However, Richard, with every day of delay before departure, was becoming more and more impatient.

It did not help his mood that Frederick Barbarossa, the great Holy Roman Emperor, had left a year earlier in May 1189 from Regensburg in Bavaria. He was taking the overland route, making slow but steady progress, and at Easter 1190 he crossed the Bosphorus and was now in Asia Minor, beginning to make his way to the Holy Land.

Barbarossa's progress piled the pressure on Richard and Philip of France. Their departure was delayed first until March 1190, and then until June, after Philip's wife, Isabella of Hainault, died in childbirth.

Richard spent the time touring his dominions, preparing them for his absence, which he recognised was likely to be lengthy. At a family conference in March 1190, he appears to have changed the arrangements he had recently made for John and Geoffrey the Bastard, for he secured from them both an oath not to enter England for the next three years. We do not know the thinking that lay behind this change of plan.

Richard also spent time preparing the fleet that was to carry him, his men and his horses to the Holy Land. The regulations he issued to govern the behaviour of his men make interesting reading. He issued this ordinance from Chinon in Anjou in June:

> *Richard, by the grace of God, King of England, Duke of Normandy and Aquitaine and Count of Anjou, to all his men who are about to journey to Jerusalem by sea – health!*

Know that with the common counsel of approved men we have had the following regulations drawn up:

Whoever on-board ship shall slay another is himself to be cast into the sea lashed to the dead man; if he have slain him ashore he is to be buried in the same way.

If anyone be proved by worthy witnesses to have drawn a knife for the purpose of striking another, or to have wounded another so as to draw blood, let him lose his fist; but if he strike another with his hand and draw no blood, let him be dipped three times in the sea.

If anyone cast reproach or bad word against another, or invoke God's malison on him, let him for every offence pay a pound of silver.

Let a convicted thief be shorn like a prizefighter, after which, let boiling pitch be poured on his head and a feather pillow be shaken over it so as to make him a laughing stock. Then let him be put ashore at the first land where the ships touch.

Witness myself at Chinon.

Richard's English fleet had left Dartmouth without him on 20 March and took forty-eight days to reach Lisbon, a distance of approximately one thousand miles. One wonders if Richard's ordinance cited above was prompted by events at Lisbon, where the Crusaders ran amok. The main flotilla of sixty-three ships was forced to wait for the arrival of a further thirty ships. During the enforced delay the Crusaders worked themselves up into a religious frenzy and this erupted in an orgy of violence against Lisbon's Jewish and Muslim populations. The King of Portugal was furious and threw a large number of the Crusaders into makeshift prisons, causing Richard further delay whilst he negotiated for their release.

Meanwhile, Richard moved down overland into the most southerly of his dominions, intending to shore up their defences against their southern neighbours. He aimed to do this by negotiating an alliance with the King of Aragon, Afonso II, and the King of Navarre, Sancho VI. These two, he reasoned, would provide a useful counterbalance to Richard's old enemy, the Count of Toulouse.

The diaries resume with Richard in Bordeaux.

4 June 1190

Bordeaux

It is just as the poets and troubadours describe.

A great physical shock to the body, yet no one and nothing has touched me.

I can think of nothing else. My mind trips over itself as thoughts run away on their own course. My stomach seems permanently knotted. My armpits are damp with sweat even in the evening's cool air. My whole upper body is stiff with tension, which will not dissipate even as I lie here and dictate these words to Armande.

He has heard my thoughts along these lines before, of course, but then it was just sexual tension.

This time it is more. Even though I met her only for the first time this morning. Even though I barely know her. Even though it is entirely unsuitable. This time it is different.

To start at the beginning. I was standing against the wall in the corridor outside my rooms here in the castle at Bordeaux. I was waiting for Hubert who had just returned to his room next door to mine to fetch something. I was talking to him through the open doorway, leaning back against the wall. Then I heard someone walking purposefully down the corridor. As the figure turned the corner and came into view, I swear that the sun burst through the window at the end of the corridor, throwing a shaft of glorious light on to the face of the person approaching, a young woman.

She stopped in the shaft of light, perhaps dazzled by it compared to the gloom of the corridor. The effect was extraordinary. Framed by the darkness of the corridor the sunbeams illuminated a simply beautiful face. Her blonde hair was unusually short, cut at the neck rather than flowing down her back. Her face was broad, with sculpted cheekbones and a wide, sensuous mouth. When her bright blue eyes looked into mine I was transfixed. At that moment my world changed forever.

I am not sure how long we stood there, staring at each other, in perfect stillness. It was only when Hubert coughed gently that I realised that we must have been standing there a while. He announced: 'My Lord, may I present the Princess Berengaria, daughter of King Sancho VI of Navarre. My Lady, may I present Richard, King of England, Duke of Normandy and Aquitaine and Count of Anjou.'

As Hubert uttered my name, her head shot round towards him. Clearly she had not known who I was, and her cheeks reddened.

I made a fool of myself with some dreadful joke about never knowing when you might find a king loitering in a darkened corridor. She laughed politely, but I felt an idiot before her grace and beauty.

I had thought that she might turn and disappear down the corridor, but when Hubert suggested that I walk her down to the Great Hall, she accepted the invitation decorously, holding out her right arm for me to hold in the formal Southern fashion.

She spoke quietly to me as we made our way: 'I must apologise for being lost. I was looking for my brother's rooms, but I became very confused and must have wandered down the wrong passage.'

I coughed nervously and replied: 'But I am very happy to have met you as I did. Perhaps it was God's will.'

I immediately wished I had not said this. 'Sorry, I am not some kind of religious zealot. It's just that...' I tailed off.

She smiled at me. A radiant, forgiving smile that promised laughter and fun and yet, at the same time, understanding.

She giggled gently to herself, then said:

'My father always says that it is a curious world. If you spend your life talking to God, then you are a great example to your fellow man and you are to be greatly admired. If, however, you claim that God talks back to you, then most educated men will think you have gone mad.'

I stopped and turned towards her and smiled. We held the gaze for just a few seconds, but it was enough. I was hooked like a fish.

The rest of the day passed in something of a daze. I delivered Berengaria to the Great Hall, was excessively polite to King Sancho, her father, and remained longer than was diplomatically necessary.

Sancho must have guessed what was afoot as he later made a great play at dinner of ensuring that Berengaria was seated next to me. During dinner I talked exclusively to Berengaria of things I had never shared with anyone before, and she listened patiently and compassionately. The nature of my relationship with my father before his death. His dying curse on me, and the blood running from his nose. My admiration for my mother together with my incredulity at both her resolve and her malice. My mixed feelings for my brothers, my guilt over whether I had in fact been responsible for the death of Henry. It seemed perfectly natural to hold nothing back.

From her side too flowed the intimacy of truth. Her genuine love and esteem for her father who has greatly strengthened his little mountain kingdom. Her grief over the death of her mother who died seven years ago. Her concern that her brother is not up to the task of succeeding her father. Her worry that the poor of her kingdom seem to derive little benefit from the increased prosperity her father has brought.

I dared to ask why she was not married. She replied simply: 'My father loves me too much. He wants me to marry for love, and not for political purposes. He and my brother row about it all the time. He used to argue with my mother about it too before she died.

'And what do you think about that?'

She looked down at her hands folded in her lap and said: 'I respect my father's wishes.'

I probed further: 'And what happens if you never find love?'

She looked up at me, smiled and replied: 'What will be, will be.'

I could not speak. I looked out into the Great Hall over the tables set out below and my eyes lost their focus. I knew then that this was what the troubadours call love, that it had finally come to me, and that I, like all men before me, was powerless in its path.

After a few minutes my eyes swam back into focus. Once more I was the confident leader of men. I pushed back my chair, scraping it loudly as I did so, so that everyone turned to look. I bowed deeply before the Princess Berengaria and as I put her hand to my mouth to kiss it goodnight, I whispered to her: 'I rather think your wait might be over.'

She smiled tentatively at first and then with a warmth that made my heart want to burst. I had to force myself, the great Crusade leader, not to dance from joy out of the hall.

I called Hubert to my rooms. He entered holding both hands out in front of him, palms outwards, as if he were trying to slow an oncoming horse, and said: 'I know what you're going to say, My Lord, but it can't be done.'

'How do you know what I want to talk about?' I demanded.

He thought for a minute and then decided that plain speaking was his best course of action. 'Well, sire, might I venture that you have taken a shine to the Princess Berengaria?'

I nodded, and replied: 'There may be something in that, Hubert.'

He sighed and said: 'It is my responsibility, sire, to remind you of your obligation to the Princess Alice. Besides the solemn nature of your promise...' He paused while I smiled and had the good grace to smile himself before continuing: 'Besides the solemn nature of your promise, the King of France will not wear the disgrace of his sister being cast aside by you. His honour and dignity could not countenance it. And

I would remind you that you are shortly to depart on crusade together.'

'Yes, yes, yes. I know all of that, Hubert,' I replied. 'It will all be very well for King Philip to stand on his pride and talk about the disgrace to his honour, but what about the disgrace to my honour, to have a woman like that as my wife? A woman who allows herself to become mistress to my father, and who then seeks to play tricks on me by simultaneously appearing as a demure virgin bound in chastity chains whilst also being such a woman of the world in the bedroom that she leaves me tied up in chains for the guards to find.

'Did you know, Hubert, when you stand there sanctimoniously telling me that I must marry this woman for the sake of honour, that when I stood there with my cock in her mouth I was genuinely fearful that she might bite it off? And then, she tied me up and toyed with my balls with a sharpened dagger and drew blood. And this is the woman you expect me to marry out of honour! Don't be so fucking ridiculous.'

I had made myself seem angrier than I really was, in order to support my argument, but clearly Hubert had had no idea of what had occurred between me and the Princess Alice, for he stood there open-mouthed.

I took the opportunity to land another blow: 'And besides… I am in love.'

He took one look at my face and saw I was serious.

It was diverting to imagine the conflicting arguments running through his mind as he struggled with what to say next. Eventually he sighed in exasperation, and raised his hands in mock surrender. I thought he had given up completely, but he said: 'I don't suppose that you and the Princess Berengaria could just…'

His words petered out.

I did not blame him for trying; after all he genuinely believes he is acting in my best interests. But I decided to amuse myself by feigning outrage: 'Do you mean to suggest that I should do anything dishonourable to the Princess Berengaria? Do you?'

Hubert held his hands up over his head as if he thought I might actually hit him. The joke had gone far enough. It was time to get down to the serious business of planning how to deal with the situation.

My mind is made up. The Princess Berengaria shall be my wife.

8 June 1190

Bordeaux

We have received disturbing news from England.

At my coronation in England last summer, there was an incident at the celebratory feast when some Jews tried to enter the Banqueting Hall in order to present their coronation gifts to me. For some reason, a fight broke out and a number of the Jews were killed. The trouble then spread to the City of London, where a number of Jewish houses were burnt down. I was furious; the Jews are under my royal protection. I gave orders that the fact of my protection should be promulgated throughout the kingdom. This action seemed to have worked; there have been sporadic outbursts of violence but nothing too serious. Until now.

The news has taken a long time to reach me. About ten weeks ago in York an argument flared up between a Jewish moneylender and a local merchant about whether or not a loan had been repaid. Somehow this argument escalated into violence, and a mob soon formed.

About one hundred and fifty Jews managed to escape the mob and take refuge in the castle at York. Unfortunately there was a fanatical hermit in town who kept stoking the mob, reminding them that the Jews were the descendants of those who had clamoured for the death of Jesus Christ, and promising the mob that loot from the Jews could be used to go on crusade without fear of divine punishment.

Eventually the Jews realised that they could not hold out inside the castle. About one hundred of the men came out on to the walls and slit the throats of their wives and children before committing suicide themselves. The fifty or so who remained agreed to accept Christian baptism and were promised by the hermit that they would be spared. However, they were massacred by the mob at the hermit's urging, as soon as they came out of the castle gates.

The ringleaders will have to pay substantial fines of course, but we need the Jews, particularly when we are raising such large sums.

12 June 1190

Bordeaux

My mother has not taken well to my marriage plans.

She arrived yesterday unexpectedly. I am not sure how she knew of my plans; maybe she has spies in my court. Regardless of how she knew, she was not best pleased. It was an uncomfortable interview, and reminded me of some of those awkward conversations with my father, punctuated by long silences.

She appealed to my sense of honour. I had given my solemn oath to marry the Princess Alice.

She appealed to my sense of family duty. It was my responsibility to make a marriage with someone of sufficient rank.

She appealed to my sense of Christian duty. I was putting the Crusade at risk with my selfishness.

She appealed to my sense of breeding. She conceded that the Princess Berengaria has certain physical charms, but alleged that the peasant mountain blood would eventually surface if we had children.

She appealed to my sense of filial loyalty. Surely I could not expose her to such embarrassment?

I made no reply to any of her accusations. I sat in the great wooden chair I inherited from my father, whilst she paced around the room, becoming more agitated with each new accusation until she finally came to a halt in front of me.

I had been sitting forward with my arms on my knees, head down. I raised my head to look at her and spoke for the first time: 'But I love her.'

She stared at me for a long time. Then she nodded gravely and said: 'In that case, I will help you all I can.'

A tear rolled down her left cheek and she smiled at me. Then she turned and left the room.

An extraordinary woman.

15 June 1190

Bordeaux

It is only eleven days since I first encountered the Princess Berengaria, and yet I cannot imagine what life was like before I met her. It is not just that she is exquisite. It is as if she actually glows with an inner warmth and beauty.

Only she could get away with having her hair cut short, rather than growing it long like all other women. Only she could get away with wearing a lowish-cut neck on her dress, whereas all other women are wearing necklines up to their throats. Only she could be a Spanish Princess who is blonde and blue-eyed, when all other Spaniards of my acquaintance have dark hair and brown eyes.

But her loveliness is not the end of it. Our minds seem perfectly suited and our characters complement each other. Naturally, I am impatient and intolerant where she is patient and kind, and I can sense that my behaviour is gradually being modified by her example.

I spend nearly all day with her (and the chaperone provided by her father). Negotiations for our marriage are being conducted by Hubert on my side and the Princess Berengaria's brother Sancho on the other. They are progressing well, the only stumbling block being my betrothal to the Princess Alice.

We wander through the city like lovers, hand in hand, whispering conspiratorially to each other. We must make an amusing sight for the citizens of Bordeaux, something for them to gossip about in the taverns.

But our liaison ends at dinner time. I will not take her to bed before we are married. We have not discussed it, but I would not want it any other way. She is so beautiful, pure and just.

25 June 1190

Tours

I left Bordeaux three days ago, and we arrived here in Tours early this morning.

Leaving Berengaria in Bordeaux was hard. I had to maintain a dignified poise as we rode away from Bordeaux, but inside I felt like I was leaving part of me behind.

It is some consolation that we have made good progress on the negotiations with King Sancho. He has consented to the marriage but he understands that this must remain secret until I have dealt with the situation regarding the Princess Alice. I have decided that I can only raise it with Philip once we are on our way to the Holy Land. To do so before we have left will give him the opportunity to delay further, or worse, to pull out altogether.

It has been agreed that, when the time comes, my mother will accompany Berengaria to join me. I think that this is the part of the whole arrangement that frightens Berengaria the most.

So I felt confident that all was going well until the ceremony this afternoon in the cathedral to mark the beginning of the Crusade and to pray for its success and the health of the Crusaders.

As part of the ceremony every man and woman who has taken the Cross is given a staff, the attribute of the penitent pilgrim. Naturally I received mine first, and as I was standing there waiting for all the others to be presented, I began leaning on it as I daydreamed about Berengaria.

That will teach me to moon about like a lovesick youth, because the next thing I knew, there was a loud crack and I found myself lying on the floor staring at the vaulted ceiling of the cathedral. The staff had snapped in two. Then I started to laugh, which must have broken the tension for soon everyone was laughing.

I carried the top half of the staff with me as I left the cathedral, strangely buoyant considering that some might interpret it as a terrible omen for the staff to break beneath my weight.

2 July 1190

Vézelay

I met with Philip today here at Vézelay and we attended church together.

We chose this small hilltop town for its symbolic significance. As the preacher reminded us from the pulpit, it was in a field outside Vézelay where St Bernard of Clairvaux first preached a call to arms for the last Crusade, forty-odd years ago. When St Bernard had finished speaking, the crowd enlisted in their thousands. They ran out of cloth from which to make the crosses, and St Bernard had to give up his own clothes to be cut up to make more. This was an example to inspire us, said today's preacher, a powerful and moving speaker, and I felt again some of the zeal I had first felt when taking up the Cross. I feel shamefaced that my complaints about the delay to our departure have soured my enthusiasm.

When Philip and I left the church arm in arm to signal our unity, there was a loud cheer from the throngs of soldiers outside. If only this concord could last, I thought to myself, knowing the harm I will be inflicting on it when I bring up the small matter of my marriage intentions.

Nevertheless, today has been about delivering a show of unity, and we did that with our performance at the church and in signing the treaty whereby the spoils of war will be divided equally between us. I had a slight sense of dread as I placed my mark on this document, that this was a terrible hostage to fortune.

But, as my father always used to say: 'A signed treaty is a good basis from which to start negotiating.' He never took much heed of the treaties he had signed. We shall see how this treaty will fare.

15 July 1190

Lyons

We departed Vézelay in good spirits, Philip and I setting out together on horseback at the head of our respective armies.

Philip's army is smaller than mine. He has perhaps seven hundred knights and fifteen hundred squires. Using my usual formula of about nine men for every knight he must have about seven thousand five hundred men on the move. People tend only to talk of knights when discussing the relative size of an army, but there are a vast number of support men who must also be fed and watered: men-at-arms, sappers, artillerymen, bowmen, bowyers, fletchers, packhorse and cart drivers, blacksmiths, cooks and, of course, priests. And that is just the men. There are the women too: laundry women and prostitutes. And then there are the pilgrims, for whom we must also provide.

It is clear from our march south to Lyons that Philip is not as experienced in supplying large groups of men as I am. He insisted, against my better judgement, on us travelling together when the countryside around us can clearly not support his army as well as my army of nine thousand five hundred men. I use a rough guide of three pounds of food and four pints of water per day per man. That is before the horses, which each need about twelve pounds of fodder and twenty pints of water per day.

Even at harvest time, this would place too great a strain on available resources, so I have now persuaded Philip that our two armies should take different routes. It is not a very auspicious beginning, and I think that Philip's pride is smarting from the realisation that he should have listened to me in the first place.

Soon after his army left, heading for Genoa, we had a setback. The wooden bridge over the Rhône collapsed with about one hundred men on it. Incredibly, given that none of them could swim, only two were drowned. We must give thanks that it has been a long, hot summer and the river is drier than usual. Mercardier organised for some fishermen's boats to be lashed together to form a temporary bridge so that the rest of the men could cross.

I have heard whispers that it is my father's dying curse that brought this mishap upon us. This constant desire to see every bad event as the fulfilment of some prophecy or curse makes me angry. I do not believe that it is in keeping with Christian doctrine to believe in the power of curses and prophecy, so I have instructed the clergy to preach against this kind of superstition. However, I gather that this has been unpopular with the clergy, many of whom are themselves poorly educated and with little true grasp of the religion they profess to preach. They are as superstitious as their congregations.

How else can I rid myself of this talk of a curse on me?

2 August 1190

Marseilles

Despite the problems with the English fleet in Lisbon, I had at least expected them to have arrived here by now.

It should be about thirty days by sea from Lisbon to Marseilles, and the fleet was supposed to have left Lisbon on the 1st of July. When we marched over the top of the hills that dominate Marseilles we had a marvellous view of the port, framed by the cathedral and its close on one side and by the great Abbey of St Victor on the other. I fully expected to see the one hundred ships of the English fleet at anchor waiting for us. But there was no sign of any of my ships. I am deeply disappointed after all the preparatory work I have put in.

When we reached the port, there was a message waiting that had come on a fishing boat from Barcelona after being carried by horse across Portugal and Spain. It was from Robert de Sable, the commander of the fleet. The fleet had left Lisbon only on the 26th of July, three weeks later than planned. I cursed. It would only now be coming around the Straits of Gibraltar.

Perhaps I have made a mistake in assembling my own fleet. Perhaps I should have followed Philip's example and simply hired one; he has hired the Genoese fleet to transport all of his men. The problem with that is the age-old conundrum one faces with any mercenary: how can one trust a man whose loyalty is bought with gold? What happens when the gold runs out? I think I still prefer to trust our fate to men whose loyalty is sworn to me rather than bought by me.

Armande smiles ironically at Mercardier, who is in my tent as I dictate these words. Mercardier is, of course, the greatest mercenary in Europe. He could command a higher price than he receives from me, but he chooses to stay as my most trusted soldier. He laughs and quotes his father Balardier to me: 'About the only useful thing that Balardier taught me was an old Jewish saying: "Gold will never get rusty".'

I think it is Mercardier's way of asking for a pay rise. I assure him that there will be plenty of plunder in the days, weeks and months ahead.

7 August 1190
Marseilles

I visited the Abbey of St Victor this afternoon to see its famous relics. It is a splendid building with a rich and thriving community of Benedictine monks, about one hundred, I am told.

It also contains within the Abbey church one of the ribs of St Lawrence the Martyr, the jawbone of St Lazarus and the rods that were used to scourge Our Lord. I kissed each of these in turn, in front of a large group of our men whom I had made sure were there to witness this. I am not sure myself that any particular benefit is to be derived from kissing these old bones, but if the men see me do it it might help to lift the superstition about the curse on me.

It will also help if our numbers are reduced to a more manageable size, so we have determined to split my forces into two. One, led by Archbishop Baldwin of Canterbury and Ranulf de Glanville, will go directly by ship to Tyre in the Holy Land. At this time of year, it should take about thirty-five to forty days by sea. We can hire ships from the Pisans for this purpose. I will remain with my own company and will travel on southwards to Sicily and wait for my fleet to catch up.

I have also decided to send Hubert with them. This is a wrench, as, over the years, he has been my constant companion, but I feel strongly that I need someone in the other contingent who knows me well and is able to articulate what my views would be in any given situation. He is to be my proxy. I am conscious that Ranulf de Glanville is his uncle and that there is some danger therefore that Hubert will be unduly influenced by him but he is here listening as I dictate this, so he is, at least, aware of the danger.

I am very much aware that I also need to settle the matter with Philip regarding my betrothal to the Princess Alice. And, of course, I must do this quickly so that I may send for Berengaria and my mother.

8 August 1190

Marseilles

I wish to express my yearning for Berengaria, but do not know where to start.

I suppose the first place is doubt. Does she really love me? Will it last, this surging passion? Did I imagine the whole thing? Or, if I did not imagine it, did I project on to a harmless flirtation and mild attraction something much, much stronger, and fool myself that it is really the true love of which the poets write?

My mood goes up and down as I veer from one extreme to another. It is like that child's game with the petals of a daisy: 'She loves me, she loves me not.'

The stakes, however, are a little higher than the plucking of a daisy. Arguably, the future of the Crusade and of my kingdom and Philip's are all at risk.

Whenever a letter arrives from her, my heart sings, and I rush to open it. Today I received one where she had had a love poem from Catullus carefully transcribed. I will read it:

> Let us live, my Lesbia, let us love,
> And all the words of the old, and so moral,
> May they be worth less than nothing to us!
> Suns may set and suns may rise again,
> But when our brief light has set,
> Night is one everlasting sleep.
> Give me a thousand kisses, a hundred more,
> Another thousand and another hundred,
> And, when we have counted up the many thousands,
> Confuse them so as not to know them all,
> So that no enemy may cast an evil eye,
> By knowing that there were so many kisses.

I was so touched that she had found this poem that so accurately describes the two of us, wrapped up in ourselves, daring to defy a disapproving world because the love we seek is everlasting, and should not be compromised by the temporary hurdle of political expediency.

I long to see her again.

21 September 1190

Messina, Sicily

Armande has been unwell recently, so it has been six weeks since my last entry.

What an instructive time we have had. We moved from Marseilles to Genoa by hired boat and visited Philip who was laid low there with illness.

When I had moved on to Portofino, he sent a message asking for the loan of five galleys. I had only three spare, which I offered him, but for some reason he was most offended by this. I suspect that this Crusade may see its fair share of arguments, misunderstandings and grudges arising out of simple poor communication.

We sailed slowly down the coast of Italy and even put ashore at the mouth of the Tiber. But I did not go ashore for an audience with the Pope. I am still angry with him for charging me one thousand five hundred marks simply to ratify the appointment of William Longchamps as the legate for England. There is a good joke going about that the Pope preaches only the Gospel according to the Mark (of Silver).

I spent ten days in Naples and then a fascinating five days in Salerno, where I was able to indulge my interest in medicine, since Salerno is the main school of medicine in Western Europe. It was founded by the Tunisian Muslim Constantine the African, who translated the great Arabic medical treatises into Latin.

I know that a lot of medicine stems from superstition and ignorance, and indeed my old teacher John of Salisbury was particularly scathing about it. I still have a letter he wrote to me eleven years ago, just before his death, which I was able to find in my correspondence chest. Here is an excerpt that perfectly encapsulates his irascible wit:

> Often students who cannot succeed at philosophy go to Salerno or Montpellier, where they study medicine, and then their careers suddenly take off.

> They ostentatiously quote Hippocrates and Galen, pronounce mysterious words, and have aphorisms ready to cover all cases. They use arcane words as thunderbolts with which to stun the minds of their clients.

> They follow two precepts above all:

> First, do not waste time by practising medicine where people are poor.
> Second, make sure you collect your fee while the patient is still in pain.

The principal of the school spent a good deal of time explaining to me the current theories of medicine, which I understand to be as follows:

In essence there are four main parts to the human body: the brain, which is served by nerves; the heart, served by arteries; the liver, served by veins; and the genitals, served by spermatic ducts.

There are also four main components or humours: blood, hot and moist like air; phlegm, cold and moist like water; red bile, hot and dry like fire; and black bile, cold and dry like earth.

So, depending on which humour dominates there are four temperaments: sanguine; phlegmatic; choleric; and melancholic.

In order to achieve good health, one needs to have a balance of these humours. The best way to understand if one has that balance is for a doctor to inspect one's urine. The doctor duly did, and, thankfully, pronounced me healthy for my age. So at least I will be facing the rigours of this Crusade in good health, whatever else may come my way.

I must record an adventure that happened to me near Mileto in Calabria, as we were making our way south to Messina.

I was out riding on my own. Having been unable to sleep, I had decided to get up early and go for a good gallop. It was beautiful countryside around Mileto, and I found myself going on and on, until I was a good way from the camp.

I had stopped at a stream to allow my horse a chance to drink and to rest in the shade. There was a hamlet on the other side of the stream, and I could hear the telltale screech of a hungry hawk coming from the vicinity. I had to investigate. I miss my hawks; they are with the blasted fleet, which seems fated never to catch up with me.

So I waded across the stream and set off towards the houses.

When I found the hawk it was in a terrible state, tied by a thin chain to an old post in the yard behind one of the hovels. It had clearly once been a beautiful bird, but it was bedraggled now. I was outraged. How dare they treat this bird so poorly? And what were peasants doing with a hawk anyway, when only noblemen, at the very least, may own and fly hawks?

I went towards the bird, holding my hand up higher than the perch on which it sat, so that it would automatically hop on to my hand. He did so, and settled there comfortably. But there was still the small matter of the chain. I drew my sword and severed it with one swipe. As the chain snapped, I turned with the hawk to leave.

There, facing me, was an enormous, and very ugly, peasant. He had frizzy, unkempt hair and his face was contorted and red with rage. He opened his mouth to reveal one solitary stump of a tooth, and started shouting at me in a dialect that I had no chance of understanding.

I ignored him and moved to go past him, taking the hawk with me. I presume that he had no idea of my status, for he blocked my path. I stopped to give him a chance to desist. He did not. Indeed, two of what can only have been his brothers appeared behind him. When he drew his knife from his belt I knew I was going to have to fight to get out of this situation.

I was still not unduly perturbed. I drew my sword, confident that this action would cause them to retreat, which it did a little. In fact, the peasant with the knife turned, but found his path blocked by his brothers. I had to do something, so I struck him on the arse with the flat of my sword. To my astonishment, the blade promptly snapped in two. It was not my battle sword, but nevertheless there must have been a flaw in the metal for it to snap in this way. Either that, or the peasant must have had an arse made of steel.

The three peasants stared at the broken sword and then at each other in wonder. I was off like a hare, whilst the hawk took flight.

I can declare that the King of England, Duke of Normandy and Aquitaine and Count of Anjou has no rivals in the Christian world when it comes to running for his life. Whereas before, I had picked my way gingerly around the faeces and rotting food on the path, now I charged straight through, slowing only to pull over random objects to slow the progress of the oncoming peasants. By the time I reached the stream I was twenty or thirty yards ahead. I had to slow down through the stream to make sure I did not fall, for that would have spelt disaster. As I got to my horse, the peasants were just lumbering through the water. I was fumbling desperately to untie my horse's reins, but finally they came free from the branch round which I had looped them. I pulled myself up and we were off. The peasants were perhaps only five yards away.

I held my hand aloft for the hawk, and believe it or not, he came! He must have been well trained before he fell into the clutches of these peasants. The fact that it came to me only served to goad them further and they were clearly shouting the most blood-curdling, albeit unintelligible, obscenities as I cantered off.

I had a close escape. Perhaps God is with me after all, despite what some people say.

22 September 1190
Messina, Sicily

Although we had already been camped outside Messina, today I made my grand entrance into the city. I know Philip arrived here last week, and I thought it might do the spirits of both of our armies good if I made a spectacle of my arrival, remembering my mother's teaching.

All of our galleys were marshalled into the small harbour, with trumpets blaring, with polished shields glittering in the autumn sunshine, and with myself standing proud and resplendent in my red cloak of England. I was on a raised platform built specially on the *Esneca Regis*[3]* to enable the men to see me.

However, I knew that something was amiss as soon as I disembarked and saw Philip's face. He was furious that my grand entrance had overshadowed his. I seem to have offended him yet again. He announced abruptly that he would be leaving for the Holy Land this afternoon, and there ensued a great scurrying about as his sailors and men made their hasty preparations. They set off at four o'clock but by about seven they were already back. Apparently the wind had changed and they were forced to return. Poor Philip. Indignity after indignity.

On reflection, perhaps my ostentatious entrance was not such a good idea. It may have been appropriate in front of

---

3   *The Esneca Regis was Richard's own ship.

my own subjects, but would be unlikely to be well received by a rival monarch. I have made an error of judgement.

28 September 1190

Messina, Sicily

It has been time to lay down the law.

My younger sister Joanna, who is eight years younger than me, was married at the age of twelve to William II, King of Sicily. Eleven years after the marriage, they remained childless when William died last year. There was a little whiff of scandal about his death, as he was found asphyxiated in a room full of his favourite slave girls from the Barbary Coast. It was officially described as an accident, but many people had sufficient motive to desire him dead. Including my own sister.

William was succeeded by his bastard cousin, Tancred of Lecce. Tancred was supported by most Sicilian nobles, for the alternative was a German ruler. I have not yet met Tancred, but by all accounts he is freakishly ugly. The citizens of Messina tell me that he looks like a monkey with a crown on his head.

He also disgraced my sister by imprisoning her under house arrest and by withholding the dower that was due to her as William's widow. I sent ambassadors to Palermo as soon as we landed and they returned today, with Joanna, who looks in remarkably good health despite her treatment.

Philip seems to have taken a shine to her, in fact, which is interesting, as he will be searching for a new bride after Isabella's death earlier this year.

But I haven't finished with the little monkey Tancred yet. He may have returned Joanna, but he still owes her the dower, and he also owes me the large legacy that William left to my father in his will specifically for the purpose of the Crusade.

4 October 1190

Messina, Sicily

Today the citizens of Messina paid the price for their greed. Over the past few days, the locals have been raising the price of food and drink. I know that the presence of so many soldiers must inevitably push up demand, but these Greeks have been profiteering. Fights have broken out inside and outside the city walls, and the situation was now highly volatile.

I had been feeling vulnerable with all of our supplies still in store on the ships at anchor. There were any number of ways in which our access to these stores could be curtailed. So I took over the monastery at St Saviour's and we have begun to store our supplies there. Naturally this has required an armed guard and I understand that this had set some of the local population on edge.

The populace is an interesting mix. Huge numbers of Normans have settled here in the last century or so, bringing their particular kind of pugnacious brutality to the region. Despite their bellicosity, they live relatively harmoniously alongside the Greeks who had already settled here and alongside the Arabs who are more recent arrivals. It is the only place I know of in Western Christendom where three different races live together in reasonable peace, and it is interesting to see the cultural exchange this brings. For instance, Christian women have taken to wearing veils when they go outdoors.

I invited Philip and the leading citizens of Messina to a conference in my pavilion this morning to discuss the supply issues. It looks like we will be here for the winter, as the winds have now changed, and in the current state of tension spring seems a long way off.

The citizens arrived early and were duly deferential, uncomfortable with the presence of two large armies: one inside the city and one outside.

Philip was late. Two hours late. And then he wafted in without apology as if nothing had happened. I managed to control my annoyance as I called the meeting to order: 'Gentlemen, we are gathered to discuss—'

There was a great shout and commotion from outside. We all went quickly to the entrance to the pavilion and one of the men outside told me that the pavilion of Hugh de Lusignan had been attacked by the Greeks. I sighed; this was the spark that was going to ignite the simmering tension. All around me men were rushing to arms. I turned back into the tent. Despite all the disorder, Philip was still sitting at the conference table, with one leg casually folded over the other, studying his fingernails in a distracted fashion. He looked up and smiled at me: 'I presume the conference is over?'

I nodded, confused by his nonchalance. He got to his feet and then moved to the entrance, where his household guard waited for him. He stopped just before leaving and remarked over his shoulder: 'Who could have guessed that this would happen?'

I did not have time to stop and think about his comment, but called for my armour and hurried off to lead my men towards the town. This attack was the final straw. Now, we would take the town by force.

It was easier than I expected. The gates to the city were firmly shut by the time we got there. I could just make out Philip disappearing with his guard into the fortifications well off to the side. Clearly he was just going to watch and see what developed.

By chance, I had had Mercardier reconnoitre the city defences two or three days ago, just as a precaution. I summoned him and asked his opinion. He told me: 'Give me ten men, sire, and I will get those gates opened for you.'

I did not ask any questions, just nodded my assent and he scurried off to collect his ten men.

Meanwhile, the main body of my men were setting themselves up for a pointless charge at the city gates. They have been itching for some proper fighting, whipped up into a frenzy by the hysteria of the preachers. Now they want to take it out on people who should really be our allies. But, once the mob has the bloodlust, it is wise to give it something, otherwise it turns its frustration on authority.

I resolved to let them make their pointless charge, even if it cost lives, perhaps many lives. They had to learn the hard way. So I remained in the background whilst various barons organised the charge. It was difficult to watch them make their mistakes, but this lesson in how not to besiege a city may be useful in the battles to come.

Sure enough, when the men charged the gate, their makeshift battering ram came to a shuddering halt on the stout gates. Then the men were left there exposed to the Greek Fire[4]* raining down on their heads, and to the arrows of the defenders on the city walls. I can still see them now, staggering back towards our lines, perhaps forty or fifty men, on fire and with arrows sticking out of them like porcupines. All but one of them fell before they reached our lines. I could hear and see the men around him retching at the horrific state of the sole survivor.

I stepped forward as he fell to his knees in front of me, his agonised face pleading with me to end his pain. I drew my sword and with one fierce swoop took off his head. The blood from his neck spattered my legs as it pumped from his body. It was an act of kindness to him, but it stilled the army at my back. I turned to face them and roared:

'Now listen to me, your commander and your King. If anyone, ever, dares to move without my express command again, I will punish him with death, and God will punish him with eternal damnation. Do you understand?'

No one dared to speak.

'Do you fucking understand?'

There was a sort of low rumble of embarrassed assent, and a shuffling of feet. It was enough. I had made my point.

---

4   *Burning liquid, a Byzantine incendiary weapon usually used in naval battles.

I turned away from the main body of men and scoured the city walls for any signs of where Mercardier might have got to.

The defences of a city normally include some kind of secret passage to allow the citizens inside to send messengers to the outside world for help. Sometimes they use tunnels, sometimes they use concealed passages, or sometimes sections of wall, which can be moved. Normally, of course, a besieging army does not have the luxury of having spent two or three days examining the city from the inside. But as Mercardier had, I knew that he would find a way in. We just had to be ready to take advantage.

I ordered the cavalry to the front. Not the heavy chargers, but the lighter, nimbler horses. The men looked at me as if I were mad. What would horses do against the solid stone of the walls and the dense wood of the city gates? But, sure enough, after twenty minutes, there was a commotion inside the city walls. We could see nothing at first, but then suddenly on the top wall above the gates two of the city defenders were unceremoniously toppled over the edge. I could tell even from a distance that their throats had been cut. They were dead long before they crumpled on the ground. Mercardier was inside the city, and throwing the bodies over the wall was his signal that we should be ready to charge.

As soon as the gates began to open, I gave the order to charge. I was positioned in the middle of the front line. By the time we were twenty yards from the gates they were fully open. But Mercardier was having a tough time. A second wave of defenders had fallen upon his little band, outraged at the ease with which the defences had been breached. Two of his men were busy working away at the wheels that controlled the gate. The rest of his men were defending them. One of them looked up at the sound of hooves. It was a mistake. A sword punched through his ribcage and his startled eyes stared down at the blood vomiting from his mouth. One moment's distraction had cost him his life.

But we were in time to save the rest of them, the defenders scattering and fleeing before our mounted men. I caught up with Mercardier, who was wiping his blade clean on the shirt of a young man who lay dead at his feet.

'Well done,' I grunted.

Mercardier smiled with the satisfaction of a job well done.

'Thank you, sire. The preacher Peter of Rouen told me last night that this town could not be taken by force. I told him that I could take it quicker than he could say matins. Seems I was right!'

I laughed, and wheeled away. Mercardier is the ultimate soldier to have on one's side.

As I turned I caught a glimpse of Philip's men observing the scene in the city from high up in their fortified lodgings. They had not lifted a finger to help. Still, at least they would miss out on the plunder.

I made my way back to camp. I find the whole business of sacking a town extremely dispiriting. The violence against anyone who stands in the soldier's way, the rape of women and even young girls and boys, and the senseless, wanton destruction of property depress me greatly. I want no part of it, but as it is the soldiers' payback for risking their lives and suffering the privations of warfare I cannot stop it.

As I reached our camp, I turned to see my banners being hoisted above the city. No doubt the ugly little monkey Tancred will want to come to terms now.

5 October 1190

Messina, Sicily

Philip is outrageous. He came to see me late last night, after I had retired. I often go to bed early if there has been fighting during the day. I think that the nervous tension of the responsibility of command takes its toll, and when it is all over, I suffer crushing headaches. Little pinpricks of white light dance before my eyes, and any bright light sends me scurrying for darkness.

So I was not best pleased to be woken. I came out of my sleeping quarters to find Philip warming his hands at the fire in the centre of my pavilion. It was a cold night for this early in the autumn.

My manner was terse: 'Yes?'

Philip stiffened slightly at my tone, but answered: 'Your Majesty, I have come to complain that you have broken the terms of our agreement at Vézelay that we would share the treasures of war equally between us.'

I was puzzled, then the fog began to lift. He was complaining that my banners flying above the city meant that all treasure would accrue to me. I responded stoutly: 'But you did not participate in the military action. In fact you actively avoided it.'

'Nevertheless, I must insist on my rights...'

There was a silence as we stared at each other, me now boiling over with rage, he cool with icy determination.

I gave way. Technically he was correct, although outside the spirit of our agreement. But, more importantly, we could not be seen to have a split in the leadership of the Crusade. Everyone knew it was my men who had taken the city. To toss him some of the loot would be a magnanimous gesture.

'Philip, Your Majesty,' I bowed in mock surrender, 'you are perfectly correct. I suggest that we hoist the banners of the Hospitallers and Templars and they may hold the city on behalf of us both.'

Philip thought for a moment, then nodded his assent and left. I thought I detected a hint of smugness about him as he did so.

This morning one of my informers came to tell me that Philip planned the whole attack, to demonstrate to his men that a fox like him could outwit a lion like me. It was his men who were behind the attack on Hugh de Lusignan's lodgings, knowing that it would be enough to tip over the unstable situation. His men then retired to their quarters, watched us take the city with some significant losses, and then sauntered out to collect their half of the city's treasure when it was all over.

No wonder Philip had been so arrogant at this morning's conference. I am furious at being outwitted, but I can grudgingly admire Philip's strategy.

8 October 1190

Messina, Sicily

We are getting used to the prospect of spending the next five or six months here. Quite how we are going to get through it, confined as we are in this small town on this small island, God only knows. Perhaps it is one of His tests.

I have sworn to myself that patience will have to be my watchword. Partly because it is a quality that Berengaria emphasises in her letters: 'Be patient, my love, and we shall soon be together.' Partly, because if I am not patient, and do not bide my time, then there is no chance that Philip will agree to my withdrawing from the promise to marry the Princess Alice.

Tancred settled the day after we took Messina. He paid twenty thousand ounces of gold to settle Joanna's dower. After some gentle pressure, she has consented to using these funds in support of the Crusade. I have also agreed that Arthur of Brittany, the son of my dead brother Geoffrey, should marry Tancred's daughter. Tancred granted me a further twenty thousand ounces of gold in respect of this. A satisfying day's work.

Today I met Tancred for the first time. He is almost exactly as they describe. He is bizarrely small; he comes up to about my navel. His chin sticks out almost further than his nose, and to accentuate this he has an underbite. His skin is deeply marked by what must either have been the worst case of adolescent acne ever known, or by some kind of pox. His nose is crumpled over to the left, and his eyes bulge from their sockets, as if he is permanently startled. In addition he has a limp and a lisp.

The purpose of the meeting was to bring some order to life for the next few months. We have fixed the price of bread at one penny a loaf, fixed the price of wine and instructed that no merchant may make a profit of more than ten per cent on each deal.

We also have had to do something about gambling. Fights have broken out over arguments about whether gambling debts fall under the Crusader's exemption from his debts. We decided that it was only debts from before the Crusade began that are to be forgiven. Any debts incurred since the start of the Crusade must be honoured.

We have also banned soldiers and sailors from gambling, unless their officers are present to ensure fair play. Knights and clergy can place for up to twenty shillings a day. Kings can gamble as much as they like.

We have also established a group of well-respected senior men as a committee to administer the Army Fund, which looks after the possessions of those who die on crusade. Half of their possessions will go towards the Crusade, half will go back to their families.

Now we must hunker down for the winter.

17 November 1190

Messina, Sicily

To get the men through this winter of delay we need to receive regular good news. This month's instalment was actually instigated by Hubert Walter, as Bishop of Salisbury, over a year ago at around the time of my coronation in England.

The new Abbot of Glastonbury, at Hubert's urging, began a fresh search for the grave of King Arthur. There had been a terrible fire at Glastonbury Abbey six years ago, and in the process of rebuilding the masons had unearthed two ancient stone pyramids. Now, according to the legend, Arthur was buried between two stone pyramids. So the abbot put up screens around the site to keep out trophy hunters and grave robbers, and set about digging.

When they were about eight feet down they came across a Celtic cross bearing the legend in Gaelic: 'Here lies King Arthur and his second wife, Queen Guinevere.'

Understandably excited, they resumed digging, carrying on through the night by torchlight. But there was nothing there. They were on the point of giving up when, finally, eight feet further down they came across a great oak coffin. The abbot was summoned from his bed, and he came scurrying through the cold early morning fog, to stand at the side of the deep pit and utter a few words of prayer.

Gradually the lid of the coffin was eased off and the abbot was able to see in. At one end of the coffin lay the bones of a lady, with long golden hair still attached to the skull. At the other end, lay the bones of an enormous man. The abbot described the eye sockets alone as being nearly the size of a man's palm.

Slowly and carefully the bones were removed, but Guinevere's famous blonde locks turned to dust as soon as they were touched, and no trace of them remained.

The abbot described all of this in a letter that reached me today. He added that half of the bones are to be kept at Glastonbury and half have been locked in a specially constructed chest, and have been sent with the letter to join us on crusade.

I stood before the men this morning with my foot on the chest, and read them the letter from the abbot. Their reaction was extraordinary. Tough old soldiers had tears running down their faces. That the great King Arthur of legend should join us in our quest brought an almost indescribable surge of pride. With that surge came the affirmation of the righteousness of the cause of the Crusade.

I finished reading the abbot's last lines: 'I praise God that He has delivered what remains of the great King Arthur to you, the King Richard, his successor on earth.'

The roar of the men could be heard for miles. After half a minute or so, I held up my hand for silence, and said: 'Let us pray.'

The men fell silent while I recited the Lord's Prayer.

As the amen sounded, I turned in my great red cloak and went into my pavilion, leaving the chest with the relics of Arthur and Guinevere for the men to file past and bow their heads in homage.

It all went perfectly; the men will be quiet and happy for a while now. I have not enquired too closely into the veracity of the story and the abbot's letter. Perhaps it is best that Hubert Walter is not here, for I do not think I could resist asking him, and I do not think that I really want to know the answer.

2 December 1190

Messina, Sicily

I miss her.

A dull ache in my guts nags at me, gnaws at me. When will she be here? When will she be mine?

I have determined to wait until Christmas has passed before raising with Philip the subject of my engagement to Alice. I have resolved to see Christmas as the summit of the hill of boredom that we are climbing. Once Christmas is past, we are coasting down the other side of the hill towards our departure, and towards Berengaria and the sunny warmth she represents.

15 December 1190

Messina, Sicily

I am not sure that in my entire life I have ever been stuck in one place for so long.

It would be bad enough to be cooped up here on my own. But I have three and a half thousand men here who feel exactly the same. And Philip has more.

It is a wonder we have not killed each other, just for something to do.

19 December 1190

Messina, Sicily

A few days ago I sent for a man called Joachim of Fiore. One of the preachers mentioned his teachings in the daily sermon and I was told that Joachim lives not far away, in Calabria, just the other side of the straits. I thought a bit of theological argument might lift my spirits. That is a sure sign of how bored I have become.

He arrived today and my initial scepticism has vanished. So has my boredom. I found him fascinating.

He is old now, about fifty-five, I would say, with the slightly frail look of an older man. He has a great frizz of white hair and a beard to match. He was dressed in what had clearly once been the habit of a Cistercian monk, but was now little more than rags. He was thin, almost painfully so, but he refused all offers of food or drink.

He told me a little of his life story. He had served as a young man at the court of the Regent to King William II of Sicily when the King was but a boy. Subsequently he had gone on pilgrimage to the Holy Land and experienced a dramatic spiritual conversion in Jerusalem. Upon his return he lived for a number of years as a hermit in Calabria, sustained by the charity of his neighbours and the nearby Cistercian monastery. One of the monks was so impressed with Joachim's devotion that he persuaded him into the monastery as a lay brother, and it was here that he produced his seminal work, dictating, often through the night, to three scribes provided on a rota by the monastery.

He described his theories to me in great detail, and I was captivated, although I did not understand some of the finer points of his theology, which required a more intimate knowledge of the Bible than I can boast.

He started with his division of world history into three parts. Fist came the Age of the Father, which occurred during the time of the Old Testament. Then came the Age of the Son, which is the time of the New Testament until now. Yet to come is the Age of the Spirit. This will be the culmination of history, when God is in the hearts of all good men. The Empire and the Church will wither away and be replaced by a community of saints who have no need of wealth, of property, or of work. It will be a new epoch of Peace and Concord.

According to Joachim, this third age of history is only seventy years away. His complicated calculations conclude that the Age of the Spirit will begin in 1260. The Book of Revelation (verses 11:3 and 12:6) confirms it, according to him. Interestingly, he also identifies Saladin as the sixth of the seven great persecutors of the Church in the second age.

He predicted that Saladin will be driven out of the Kingdom of Jerusalem and will be killed. The infidels will be slaughtered and Christians will return to rule the Holy Land. Then he turned to me, laid his hands on my shoulders and boomed: 'And God has decreed that all these things will be done through this great Crusade. Persevere in this blessed enterprise that you have begun and He will give you victory over your enemies and glorify your name for evermore.'

I could see that such inspiring words gave heart to the men in my pavilion.

20 December 1190

Messina, Sicily

I could not sleep last night, tossing and turning Joachim of Fiore's words over and over. Something was nagging at me.

Then I remembered Berengaria, putting me at ease within moments of our first meeting, had reported her father's views about anyone who claims that God speaks to them. He thought them mad. I smiled in fond remembrance of her, and at my unusually easy acceptance of Joachim's nonsense. The confinement here in Messina is beginning to affect my judgement.

20 January 1191

Messina, Sicily

The peace and calm will soon be over. After the pleasantries of Christmas, when Philip came to dine in my wooden castle, Mategriffon, which we have built outside the town, I judged it best to allow a couple of weeks to pass.

But now I have sent a letter to Philip demanding that he consents to the abandonment of my commitment to marry the Princess Alice on the grounds of her having been my father's mistress.

He must have been expecting it, but it will still hit his pride hard. Alice and I have been betrothed for more than twenty years.

I wait to see how he reacts.

15 February 1191

Messina, Sicily

Philip's reaction has been predictable. A lot of toing and froing: we must have exchanged letters over a dozen times. A lot of posturing: Philip feigning outrage at my slur upon his sister's good name, me feigning outrage that he expects me to marry my father's mistress. A lot of technical legal argument: the betrothal is governed by at least eight different treaties. A lot of arguments about canon law: does the Church actually allow a man to marry a woman who has slept with his father?

Philip has to go through the motions of defending the Princess's honour. I am sure that he could not really give a fig for it, but he senses that he will lose political face if he gives in. I don't know why this is so important to him. I am his chief rival, and yet he knows that for me this is a personal not a political matter. The only other ruler of any consequence is the Emperor Frederick Barbarossa, and he is already halfway to the Holy Land. Philip sees giving in as a sign of weakness, but I think he is virtually the only one who thinks that.

In the meantime, Berengaria is coming ever nearer within my grasp, physically, as well as metaphorically. My mother arrived in Navarre to collect her last September, just as I was travelling down the Italian coast to Messina. Together they left Navarre shortly afterwards. It is a long and arduous journey for a man to undertake; for two women it is extraordinary, especially as my mother is now sixty-eight years old. First of all they had to get through the lower Pyrenees, as winter was beginning to set in, then across Toulouse and Provence to face the Alps in midwinter. They are travelling in open carriages where possible, and in litters where the roads or paths are too damaged. I had urged them both to think about waiting until the spring, when crossing the Mediterranean by boat would once again become possible. I argued this without any great passion, for I was desperate to be reunited with Berengaria, but there was some sense in it. However, Berengaria insisted on travelling now and my mother acquiesced, much to my surprise.

My mother has been a dominant figure in the politics of the last fifty years and she should by rights be dead set against this marriage, as she made clear in her initial argument with me. But Berengaria has spent a lot of time alone with her on their journey and in her latest letter she tells me that my mother is very supportive, won over by the strength of our love.

My mother has been through two loveless marriages. One ended in a disgraceful divorce, and one ended with her imprisoned for years by her increasingly disturbed husband. She has seen three sons die, one in childhood, two in early adulthood, and, as she has said to Berengaria, she wants for once to give love a chance. My tears dripped on to the vellum when I read this. Sometimes people we think we know well can surprise us.

Now Berengaria and my mother are just over the Straits of Messina. They will have to wait until I send for them, once Philip has finally acquiesced.

29 March 1191
Messina, Sicily

It is done. Signed, sealed and delivered in the treaty signed here today. I am to pay Philip ten thousand marks, and he is to renounce the Princess Alice's claims upon me. I feel as if the sun has come out after a particularly dark day.

I have sent the *Esneca Regis* for Berengaria and my mother. They should arrive tomorrow.

30 March 1191
Messina, Sicily

Philip skulked off this morning, heading for Acre in the Holy Land, a journey of probably twenty-five to thirty days. I knew that his men had been making preparations to leave. No doubt he delayed the signing of the treaty until he was ready to depart straight afterwards.

It is a relief to see him go; we are back to our normal positions of not trusting each other and each searching the other for the tiniest sign of weakness. I fear this has done nothing for the prospects of a successful Crusade, but it was ever thus. The Crusades of 1096 and 1147 suffered from the same problem of mistrust between the leaders.

I watched Philip's ships leave, whilst out on a morning ride. I dismounted on the top of a hill overlooking the port and the sea behind, and I scoured the horizon for signs of the *Esneca Regis*. Unlike the others in our fleet this ship has sixty oars, so that it can easily enter and exit the harbour at speed and under control. It is not so fast in the open sea, as it has only one square sail from one single mast, but for manoeuvrability it has no rival.

And then I saw it. I watched for a few minutes as the ship made steady progress towards the entrance to the harbour. Once I was sure it was the *Esneca Regis*, I fell to my knees and said a brief prayer of thanks. As an offering of gratitude, I renewed my Crusader vow. I was on my own and spoke out loud, so that God could be sure of my intentions. I swore not to rest until Jerusalem and the Holy Land are once again in Christian hands.

Then I remounted and turned down the hill towards the city. My horse could sense my excitement and we fair flew down the paths. As we approached our camp, the men were gathering to cheer me on. They know what a battle it has been to secure Berengaria.

I pulled up outside my pavilion. I have chosen to stay here rather than to lodge in the wooden castle we have built. I have a morbid fear of fire in wooden structures, and in any event Mategriffon is currently being dismantled so that we may take it with us to the Holy Land.

I rushed inside the pavilion and began to get changed. New clothes had been prepared for the occasion, but I would still wear the great red cloak of state over the top. I was nervous, I knew, chattering uncharacteristically to the servants getting everything ready.

Eventually, I was ready and I moved outside.

What I saw outside astonished me. The men had gathered and formed a guard of honour that seemed to lead all the way down to the port. Unusually there was no arrangement of rank, suggesting that this was a spur-of-the-moment display of support. I was deeply moved and I set off down the path formed by the guard. As I passed, each man muttered or shouted: 'God bless you, sire,' or 'Good luck, sire.' I tried to look each man in the eye as I passed, to acknowledge them. I have never seen or felt anything like the solidarity expressed by this apparently spontaneous gesture.

And so, down to the dock. A small pavilion had been set up dockside with my father's great wooden chair for me to rest in whilst we waited for the arrival of the ship. I sat down, but not for long: I was too agitated.

Then, after perhaps quarter of an hour, the *Esneca Regis* drew up to the dock. The oarsmen raised their oars, as they came alongside, and the men on the dock scurried to secure her.

I could not see either Berengaria or my mother. They must have been below the canopy set up amidships. Then I saw my mother's head as she mounted the steps to the edge of the ship. She stopped at the top, smiled at me a moment, and then descended the steps on the landward side, down towards the wharf.

And then I saw the top of Berengaria's head as she emerged from the ship. First, her hair, shining like gold in the morning sun. Then her eyes, dazzling blue as the clearest sea, and catching mine immediately. Then her mouth, upon which played the hint of a smile. And then, the rest of her, dressed in a splendid ivory gown. She was like a celestial vision, shimmering with beauty.

The silence was, just for a second or two, total. Then one of the men in the crowd cheered, and the others picked it up until the whole harbour was reverberating to the sounds of men cheering their new Queen. Berengaria stood dignified, poised on the top step, seemingly waiting for something. Then I realised that she was waiting for me to come to her. I walked towards the ship, ascended the steps and at the top knelt with a full bow as I took her hand and said: 'My Lady, welcome to Sicily.'

I kissed her hand and then moved to stand beside her, as we stood together acknowledging the applause of the crowd. I allowed myself one short sideways look at her. She did the same. As our eyes met, my heart surged.

She gently took my left hand and squeezed it slightly. This small gesture was a breach of courtly protocol, but it was all I needed. The men loved it and cheered all the more loudly. In front of the jubilant men, my mother beamed at us.

Much of the rest of the day was spent with Berengaria. Once I had greeted my mother properly and I had shown them to their respective quarters, my mother retired, leaving us alone. I will not recount here all the trivialities of what lovers discuss when reunited after a long absence. Suffice it to say, this has been the happiest day of my life. The only blot on the horizon is that we cannot be married straight away as it is Lent, when no marriages are allowed to take place. So we shall be married, appropriately enough, in the Holy Land.

11 April 1191

At sea, one day out of Messina

At last we have left Messina. Through the descent into winter in November and December, and through the cold months of January and February, I felt confined and locked in, partly because we were trapped on an island, and partly because we had nothing to do. But as March came, bringing with it the prospect of a reunion with Berengaria, so my spirits lifted.

The eleven days between her arrival and our departure passed in a flash. I am not sure that I could recall precisely what we did from one day to the next, just that I thanked God every day for my luck in finding her.

We set off from Messina, with just over two hundred ships. Berengaria and I could not travel together, of course, but fortunately Berengaria and my sister Joanna have formed an instant bond, as if they have known each other for years. So Berengaria has pleasant company in what is to her a new and entirely foreign court. My mother left only three days after arriving in Messina. She needed to get back to my lands to ensure good order, particularly as the campaigning season is almost upon us, and that normally stirs some of my vassals into restiveness.

We left yesterday aiming to rendezvous at Crete after seven days. The ship carrying Berengaria and Joanna has stayed close to mine thus far, as I want to make sure that they do not fall into the hands of pirates. There are a lot around at this time of year, hungry for victims after the lean months of winter, when there is no shipping to speak of. We are an attractive target, loaded down with treasure and coin for paying the men and for supplies. Our sheer size should afford us some protection, but it is best for our treasure and my prospective Queen to stay close to the centre of the fleet.

17 April 1191

Crete

What a terrible storm we have come through.

It blew up on the third day out of Messina, almost halfway between Sicily and Crete. Ironically, it was Good Friday, although there was not much good about this particular Friday. The captain of my ship coped extraordinarily well. The *Esneca Regis* performs well in rough seas, and we quickly became the focus of the fleet, holding it together despite the storm. I ordered a brazier to be lit and kept burning on deck so that the other ships would know where we were. It was extremely difficult to keep the fire alight in the teeth of the storm but somehow the men managed it.

The bad news is that we are missing twenty-five ships or about one-eighth of the fleet. And amongst these twenty-five ships is the one carrying Berengaria and Joanna. Everyone keeps telling me that they will arrive at any moment, but I cannot rest until their ship is sighted.

24 April 1191

Rhodes

I am quite frantic now.

I have divided the fleet up into fifteen groups of three ships, which I sent out from Crete to scour the surrounding sea. I have brought the remaining one hundred and thirty ships here to Rhodes, where I wait for news. Everyone knows the importance of finding these ships and bringing me the news in Rhodes. I have promised great rewards to anyone bringing Berengaria and Joanna to me alive.

I spent the whole of last night in prayer at the cathedral here. I was convinced that if I spent eight hours straight in prayer on my knees for their safe deliverance, then by morning they would be found. Morning came and no sign of them. My faith is being tested.

28 April 1191

Rhodes

Still no news. I am desperate. I am not sure that I have slept or eaten at all in these past fourteen days, but I suppose that I must have done.

1 May 1191

At sea, one day out of Rhodes

They have been found, praise God! The news was brought to me yesterday evening. We left Rhodes three hours later, once my captain had been able to gather his crew together from the various taverns in which they were scattered. The other ships will have to catch up as best they can.

Joanna and Berengaria's ship lost its way during the Good Friday storm and, as a consequence, missed Crete entirely and ended up nearly foundering on the coast of Cyprus. Two ships were shipwrecked, including that of Roger Malcael, my seal-bearer. He was drowned and his body was washed up on the shore. With luck the Great Seal of England was still on a chain around his neck, so that was recovered.

The other ships, including that of Berengaria and Joanna, are safely anchored off Limassol on the Cypriot coast. It will take us four or five days to get to them. God preserve them until we arrive.

6 May 1191

Off Limassol, Cyprus

I was up before dawn this morning, talking with the slightly startled junior officer who had been left in charge of the tiller. It is strange how rank seems to lose some of its importance late at night or early in the morning. He was moaning that it was his fourth consecutive night watch. I am not sure that in the cold light of day he would have been quite so voluble in his criticism.

I forgave him, though, as we soon spied the mast of Berengaria's ship through the early tendrils of the breaking dawn. I roused the entire crew with my roar of delight, and I was soon running around the decks, urging the men to their oars, so that we might draw up alongside the anchored ship.

Half an hour later we were there, and I was scaling a rope ladder thrown from the side of the tall ship. Both crews were watching and cheering me on. I clambered inelegantly on to the deck and there, luminescent in her beauty, stood Berengaria. This time, for this reunion, there was no protocol. I ran to her and drew her into a great bear hug. She laughed with delight and surprise in my ear. I whispered with fierce urgency: 'I cannot lose you. You are everything to me.'

We stood there in our embrace for ages.

Later, I learned that the storm had not been the only danger facing Joanna and Berengaria. The ruler of Cyprus, Isaac Comnenus, had heard of her arrival on his shores and had moved up to Limassol. He had been trying to tempt Joanna and Berengaria ashore offering fresh provisions and safe passage. Wisely, they had turned his offers down, preferring to rely on my arrival.

He is a strange fellow, Isaac Comnenus. He was not much more than a pirate himself, originally. Although born nobly into the Byzantine imperial family, his was a minor branch and he was of no real consequence until about five years ago when he hatched and executed an ingenious plan. He forged documents from the imperial family in Constantinople, purporting to appoint him as the new governor of Cyprus. He arrived on the island bearing these documents, and was promptly installed as the ruler by virtue of the fact that all of the fortresses and treasuries were placed in his hands. He then revealed himself, declaring himself Emperor and declaring Cyprus to be independent of the Byzantine Empire. I have to admire his audacity. By a simple trick, executed brilliantly, he won an island famed for its highly valuable cypress trees, and for its vineyards.

But, in order to defend himself against the Byzantine Empire, Isaac Comnenus had made an alliance with Saladin that is highly detrimental to the Crusade, as Cyprus could be a vital staging post to the Holy Land. From the top of its hills, I am told, one can see the hills of the Holy Land.

Isaac has taken prisoner some of our men who washed up alive from the wreck of the two ships and claimed all the goods that were on board. I have sent a message demanding their immediate return. How he reacts will determine if his rule of Cyprus lasts more than the five years he has managed so far.

7 May 1191
Aboard Berengaria's ship, off Cyprus

Given the fright we have had, I determined after last night's diary entry that I will not leave Berengaria's side again.

So, in breach of all protocol and precedent, we spent the night together on an improvised bed, hurriedly thrown together from available materials. We were chaste. We can wait. But I spent the night holding her tight. At one stage, she whispered to me that I was squashing her, so I loosened my grip a little, but still her closeness kept me erect all night.

10 May 1191

Limassol, Cyprus

I had given Isaac Comnenus twenty-four hours to release the hostages he had taken and the stores he had usurped. His response had played into my hands. If he had conceded, then I might have found it difficult to justify taking the island. I would have had to construct an uneasy truce with him but would then always be wondering whether Cyprus would be a support to us in the Holy Land, or a thorn in our side.

But he had shown no sign of capitulating to me. Instead he was busy building barricades on the beach at Limassol to defend the town against us. He must have stripped the whole town bare, given the extent of the barricades. But it was a hopeless task given the size of the beach.

I called Mercardier over from his ship and we ran through the options until we settled on the one that seemed the most obvious: a full-frontal assault on the beach, with covering fire provided by our English archers. They would go in the second line of rowing boats and loop arrows over the top of our front line on to the waiting Cypriot forces. I would lead the first line. All knights would have to forfeit their usual mail, as it would be too heavy in the water.

To a certain extent, I was counting on Isaac's Cypriot troops not being wholly loyal to their leader, given that he had obtained the throne by deception and was notorious for his exactions upon his new people. Our men, by contrast, were raring to go. Their enforced confinement, first on the island of Sicily through the winter, and then in the inhospitable bowels of the ships, meant that they were now itching to fight.

Whilst on board ship with nothing to do, I have been rereading *De Re Militari* by Vegetius. The advice he gives is the distillation of six hundred years' worth of expertise in the Roman armies. The words that strike a particular chord with regard to our current situation are these: 'To encourage the enemy's soldiers to desert is of especial service, for an adversary is hurt more by desertion than by slaughter.'

The plan worked perfectly. One hundred yards from the beach I gave the orders for the archers to let loose. The muted twangs as the bows released their arrows behind us were followed ten seconds later by anguished cries of surprise and pain from the shoreline. Even by the time that the first of our boats ran aground on the beach, I could see some of the Cypriot soldiers abandoning their positions and running. This just incited our men further, who roared as they jumped from the rowboats into the water up to their waist and then waded ashore. I was first amongst them, keen to set a good example.

The assault was a complete success. The Cypriot soldiers fled before us, and we caught only the stragglers, who were taken prisoner rather than being butchered; they may be valuable as bargaining chips later. We marched into Limassol, where we received a very cordial welcome. I ordered the ships at anchor to be left with skeleton crews, and everybody else to come ashore.

We had an enormous feast tonight, the town being full of meat and corn and wine. Isaac camped some five miles away, and declared his intention of giving us battle tomorrow.

Mercardier and I had different plans for Isaac. It is never a good strategy to let your opponents dictate the terms of how and when you meet, so we thought we might give him a little surprise. While the feast carried on in the city we had all the horses disembarked under cover of darkness. The sounds from the feast no doubt lulled Isaac into a false sense of security, for when Mercardier and I surrounded his camp one hour before dawn with five hundred fully mounted cavalrymen, the surprise was total.

Isaac managed to escape by mounting up and riding away still in his nightshirt, with the laughter of my knights ringing in his ears. Mercardier looked at me as if to ask if we should pursue him. I said no. Watching Isaac being chased out of camp in his nightshirt brought back memories of my humiliation all those years ago at Saintes. Isaac had already left me his treasure, his armour and his banner. If I caught him now, he would have nothing left to give me. If I catch him again in two weeks' time, perhaps the prize will be greater as he will have replenished his treasure chests and his horses.

The remaining Cypriot nobles came and gave homage. We took temporary hostages for good behaviour, but I suspect we will be able to release them after a week or so.

I returned triumphant to Limassol to find Berengaria and Joanna taking charge of the castle. I came across them in what is evidently to be our bedchamber. I dismissed the servants and turned to Berengaria, took her hands in mine and said: 'My dear sweet Berengaria, I could just about bear the long absence we endured whilst I was in Sicily because I knew that you were on your way to me. But I could not endure the last two weeks since the great storm, because I had no idea what had happened to you. Finding you again has convinced me that God means us to be together. We must be married now. In this place. At this time.'

Berengaria smiled her agreement and embraced me while Joanna left the room, brushing away a tear.

As I dictate this some hours later, the wedding has been fixed for the day after tomorrow. Thank the Lord.

13 May 1191
Limassol, Cyprus

So yesterday was the day I have longed for. It started inauspiciously with a sudden spring storm in the early morning. The rain was so heavy that some leaked through the roof and temporarily flooded the chapel floor. Berengaria and Joanna took personal charge of the mopping up operation, while I made a morning tour of Limassol, collecting the good wishes of the men.

I also met briefly with the two Lusignan brothers. One of their nephews, Hugh, is already under my command. The elder of the two Lusignans, Guy, had the title King of Jerusalem until he lost his kingdom to Saladin at the Battle of Hattin.

I have heard that Philip, now safely arrived in Acre, is manoeuvring to have his preferred candidate, Conrad of Montferrat, recognised as King of Jerusalem in place of Guy. The Lusignans caught me in a good mood, and, rather on impulse, I agreed to support Guy, more to spite Philip than anything else. I hope that I will not regret the decision.

Then, it was time to get ready. The various tailors of my household had been beavering away for two days and nights. They had made a rose samite tunic, a gown of embroidered gold cloth and a cream silk sash. They also have made a rose cap to match the tunic, but I refused, despite their protestations, to wear it. It makes me look ridiculous.

The Chapel of St George, inside the castle walls, was already full to overflowing when I arrived. The weather was now glorious, and the sun shone dazzlingly through the stained glass. Everybody was dressed in their finery; it even looked as if some of my knights might have bathed for the occasion.

And so I moved to the front of the chapel to await the arrival of the bride. It was a nervous time, even for a king. We had had to overcome so many obstacles to reach this point. My engagement to the Princess Alice, Philip's determination to hold me to that commitment, the initial hostility of my mother, the reluctance of King Sancho VI to part with his daughter, particularly to someone imminently leaving on crusade. Then there were the physical challenges. Berengaria's journey through winter across Europe, and the recent great storm that scattered our fleet. All these had been overcome to bring us to this moment, and yet I was still nervous.

Then Berengaria arrived, with Joanna at her side. She glowed with beauty, dressed in a cream gown adorned with hundreds of little pearls and she beamed at me as she walked slowly down the aisle towards me.

I can barely recall the service. Apart from our vows, I really remember only the bad breath of John d'Evreux, the presiding Bishop, who stood much too close for comfort. I also remember smiling to myself in wonder as my beautiful Spanish princess was crowned Queen of England in a small port on Cyprus by a Norman Bishop.

After the service, we held a short reception in the Great Hall of the castle. And then it was time for bed. The entire group of guests traipsed up the stone staircase to stand outside the door of our bedchamber. The tradition is that the door is left ajar, so that the crowd may hear, if not see, all that goes on. But I shut the door firmly. Berengaria and I were to be alone.

There was none of the awkwardness between us that I believe is so common amongst newly-weds, and which causes so much ribaldry and amusement when the experiences are later regaled in the tavern, or in the army tent, or on a dull night watch.

Berengaria had dismissed her maids, and so it was I who fumbled with the delicate buttons on her gown, it was I who drew the gown from her shoulders, it was I who let her gown drop to the floor as she stood entirely naked, and perfectly formed, before me. She had no fear, no embarrassment, just an absolute confidence in my love for her.

I was a little overawed, and was only jolted into action by her coming forward to help remove my clothes. Soon they were off, and we stood naked opposite each other, holding each other's hands loosely.

Then I lifted my hands either side of her head, took her face in my hands and stooped to kiss her. The slow, lingering kiss was exquisite in its tenderness.

I stroked her back gently and then her buttocks before moving my hands round the front, between us, to stroke her stomach.

My mouth sank from her mouth to nuzzle first at her neck and then at each of her smooth breasts in turn, her nipples coming hard in my mouth.

My hands moved lower now to caress her vagina: I could feel that she was already damp.

Then she gently pulled me backwards towards the bed, leaning up to whisper in my ear:

'Take me now, then we can dispense with the crowd.'

I looked at her to check that she was indeed happy, then she lay back on the bed. I positioned myself on all fours above her and took my straining penis in my hand to guide it to the right place. She put her hand across her mouth in anticipation of the impending pain. A stifled cry from her and I was in, moving slowly and rhythmically. The worst over, her hand came away from her mouth to caress my back.

As soon as I met Berengaria I had abstained from other women, so this was the first time I had made love for almost a year. So there was never any chance that I was going to last long, despite being as slow and gentle as I could. As I came, Berengaria clutched at my back, as if willing me deeper inside her. I collapsed on top of her panting and heaving. She chuckled beneath me, and asked for permission to breathe.

I hoisted myself up on my elbows, looked down into those magnificent blue eyes and said: 'You are everything to me, Berengaria. Everything. I will never let you go.'

She smiled, and answered: 'Go on, you had better give them the sheet.'

We both moved to inspect the sheet. Three or four spots of blood. That would keep the crowd happy. I tore the sheet from the bed and stalked across the room, opened the door a crack and flung it out, before slamming the door shut.

I made my way back across the room, kissed Berengaria and said: 'Now, where were we?'

There was a little cheer from outside as the sheet was displayed to the crowd. We both laughed, before kissing again.

17 May 1190

Limassol, Cyprus

Isaac Comnenus came to our camp yesterday, ostensibly to wish me well in my marriage, but partly, no doubt, to see if he could negotiate terms with me.

I was still in bed when he arrived, and I instructed that he be made to wait. I wanted a little time to think. I needed to make the terms of my proposed settlement so onerous that he would have no choice but to reject them. Otherwise, if I did settle with him, and we moved on to the Holy Land, leaving Isaac Comnenus behind, then he would no doubt immediately revoke all of his promises and ally himself again with Saladin. Then, he could really be a thorn in our side.

In fact, as I thought, it gradually became clear to me that I needed Cyprus to secure our supply line to the Holy Land. Taking it as mine could prove to be a tactical master stroke. It might take three or four weeks, and Philip will no doubt be angry at the delay, but it might well prove invaluable.

Resolved, I sent a message to Isaac outlining my terms. I had pitched it at a level that I thought he would find unacceptable but still worth negotiating.

Clearly, however, I pitched it wrong, as shortly after lunch he left our camp. He must have calculated that I would hurry on to the Holy Land and he could recover his position once we have left. Well, he has miscalculated. I am going to take this island. And then I am going to keep it. It will be his wedding gift to me.

1 June 1191
Limassol, Cyprus

What a wonderful feeling it is when everything goes according to plan.

I wonder if God really is with me now, first, in finding and then, against the odds, in marrying Berengaria, then in granting me this rich island, an unexpected bonus indeed.

The plan was simple. I allocated half of our men to Guy de Lusignan. He was to pursue Isaac on land. The rest of the men were boarded on to the galleys. I took half of these galleys and, together with Berengaria and Joanna, sailed clockwise around the island. The other galleys were given to the command of Robert of Thornham, who was to sail anticlockwise around the island.

For a fighting man it was the perfect honeymoon. Warm, sunny days with a light breeze, sufficient to ensure steady progress. Clear, starry nights to sit on deck and drink wine and dream of the glory to come in the Holy Land. A comfortable stateroom for nights of pleasure. And if that were not enough, every so often we would anchor, disembark some horses and go hunting, either for wild boar, or occasionally in pursuit of Isaac's scouts who tracked us around the island.

Each major town surrendered to us readily enough. I was pleased by this but I had to feign disappointment at the lack of fighting opportunity. The men were keen for further action. I was happy enough to be cruising around the island, collecting levies and oaths of obedience, confident that the fighting in the Holy Land would soon be more than enough.

We had a lot of fun when the two halves of the fleet met at sea halfway round the island. In a burst of goodwill, I ordered ships to stand steady about half a mile off the coast at Akanthou. The wine butts were unlocked and everyone on board was given a goblet of my wine and I climbed up to the halfway point of the mast of the *Esneca Regis* so that all the men could see me clearly. Then I shouted myself hoarse, straining my voice so that all the men could hear me leading them in a toast to the success of the Crusade. What a moment to savour, standing there on the rigging, sixty-five feet above the deck, looking down on my enormous fleet holding my mighty army, on a brilliant, clear day in the eastern Mediterranean, with a sparkling sea reflecting the beauty of my new and loving wife staring up at me in admiration. As my voice trailed off, I thought to myself: 'Surely nothing will ever surpass this day?'

After eight days we sailed back into the harbour at Limassol. Robert of Thornham was already there with his ships, as was Guy de Lusignan with the ground forces. Although we had effectively captured the entire island, meeting only token, sporadic opposition, there was still no sign of Isaac Comnenus. Guy was fairly sure that he had holed up in one of the three great castles in the northern mountains.

This was a setback; he could easily hide out almost indefinitely there. I could not afford to spend weeks in a siege, or in starving him out. If we left, he would simply emerge blinking into the sunlight and be able to resume his rule.

I spent a night cursing my presumption that God's favour was with us. The nobles are not too concerned with Cyprus, but I am. I have come to conquer and then hold the Holy Land, not just to conquer it and then leave it undefended and undefendable. And in order to hold the Holy Land in the longer term, we are going to need Cyprus.

Berengaria and I had our first cross words that night. She is convinced that God is smiling down on our endeavours and that the Crusade will be some kind of easy procession. I know from fifteen years of campaigning that God's favour (or plain simple luck, as I prefer to call it) only comes with hard work, training, good planning and constant vigilance. She chastised me for my pessimism. I snapped back something about the loneliness of leadership, and I could see that I hurt her.

Then, in the morning, perfectly timed to prove her right and me wrong, we had the most enormous piece of luck. Kyrenia, a small town on the northern coast, surrendered to a small group of our knights. Amongst those captured was Isaac Comnenus's daughter, Theodora, who is apparently the apple of his eye. She was brought directly to our camp outside Limassol.

I gave her to the custody of Joanna and Berengaria, and dispatched a small troop to the north of the island to let Isaac know that we now had Theodora.

The instructions to the captain of the troop were clear. Isaac was to surrender unconditionally or his daughter would suffer the consequences. He would be treated in a manner befitting a man of his rank. This last part was slightly ambiguous as he was born as a man of relatively low rank and had usurped his way to his current status.

It took only three days for the captain to locate Isaac and persuade him to surrender. The captain reported to me that the whole process had been relatively straightforward, as Isaac had capitulated almost immediately. His only request, which the captain had granted, had been that he should not be put in irons, as this would remind him too much of his days of imprisonment after the war in Cilicia, when he had spent five years in captivity.

I dismissed this as a matter of small importance but when I mentioned it to Berengaria later that evening, she drew herself up in that haughty manner that comes so naturally to princesses and said: 'Do you mean to say that this man remains unshackled? This man, who has stolen an entire island kingdom, who has raped and pillaged his way across the island like some Viking marauder, who has had the temerity to try to take your wife and your sister hostage, is to be allowed to be treated like a member of a royal family? I think not!'

I tried to explain to her that the captain had only been doing what he thought was right, and that he had given my word that Isaac would not be put in irons. I could not very well go back on my word and now have him shackled. In any event there was nowhere for him to escape to. We controlled the whole island.

However, I could tell, even as I was speaking, that this was not going to be enough to mollify my determined wife. She paced up and down for a while, as I watched, amused, waiting for her next line of attack. She knew that on the issue of hostage and peace negotiations my word has to be my bond, even if my word is given by an emissary or an ambassador on my behalf. Otherwise I would have no leverage the next time I am negotiating a truce, or the occupation of a castle or the exchange of hostages.

But then an idea came to her: 'Your captain assured Isaac Comnenus that he would not be put in irons. Is that right?'

I nodded.

'In that case, we could legitimately put him in a set of silver chains.'

I laughed out loud. Of course we could. And to indulge my wife, that is exactly what we did.

Isaac Comnenus was apoplectic, by all accounts, but it amused all of us greatly and it gave me a new insight into the character of my wife. She is not a woman to be crossed lightly, it appears. It is said, after all, that a man ends up marrying a woman like his mother.

We will spend the next few days in making ready for our departure. I have already extracted a fifty per cent capital levy from the Cypriot nobles in return for confirming all of their titles and privileges, so our coffers have swelled somewhat. Robert of Thornham and Richard de Canville are to stay here with a small garrison to enforce our rule. I have also instructed that all Cypriots have to shave off their beards; from now on they have to look like Western Christians rather than Muslims. When she heard of this, Berengaria innocently enquired if this order to shave off beards included the women.

These weeks in Cyprus have been the happiest of my life: marriage to a woman I adore, the easy and quick conquest of a rich and strategically important island, the defeat of a treacherous enemy. And now we move on to the Holy Land. Will our luck hold?

5 June 1191

At sea, off Famagusta, Cyprus

Now that we are within striking distance of the Holy Land, I have been mulling over how best to deal with the tricky political situation.

From the other side of Europe I was confident that the mess would somehow resolve itself of its own volition, and given the difficulties of getting here, I have not had time to focus on the very real problems now facing us.

Berengaria and Joanna made me try to explain the situation to them earlier today, and whilst explaining it to them I began to see that some of the problems might well prove to be intractable.

The best place to start is with Guy de Lusignan, King of Jerusalem.

Guy journeyed out here some twelve years ago, after my mother banished him and three of his brothers for ambushing and killing their overlord, Patrick of Salisbury, as he was returning from pilgrimage.

After arriving out here, through one means and another, he had inveigled his way into the court circles of the Kingdom of Jerusalem and had ended up marrying Sibylla. Sibylla was the sister of Baldwin IV, King of Jerusalem at the time, so Guy was immediately elevated into the highest rank of the Jerusalem hierarchy.

When Baldwin IV died six years ago from leprosy, his young son Baldwin V became king but he died within the year. The stage was now set for Guy. Following much political intrigue Sibylla was crowned Queen of Jerusalem in 1186, but in order to garner the support of the rival faction in the Haute Cour[5*] she agreed with them that she would renounce Guy as her husband and would select a suitable new husband at some point in the future. With this agreement in place she was crowned Queen.

However, she soon astonished the Haute Cour, and the rest of the watching world, by choosing as her new husband the very same man she had renounced: Guy de Lusignan. They remarried almost immediately and shortly afterwards Guy was crowned as King of Jerusalem.

If Guy had proved to be an effective leader from the outset, this might have been the end of the saga, but his military

---

5   *The High Court, the feudal council of the Kingdom of Jerusalem.

and strategic failures, culminating in the disastrous defeat at Hattin, threw open the whole question of leadership. Guy was one of the few nobles captured by Saladin at Hattin to be spared. Saladin mercilessly butchered the rest. His particular venom was reserved for the Templars and the Hospitallers, the warrior monks, who were slaughtered to a man.

Guy was kept by Saladin as a prisoner in Damascus, whilst Saladin moved on to take Jerusalem, which offered only token resistance now that all of its fighting men had been killed at Hattin. It was, in fact, Sibylla who surrendered the city to Saladin, who gave her safe passage in return.

Saladin eventually released Guy a year later, in June 1188, and he was reunited with Sibylla. He sought sanctuary at Tyre, the only city to have held out against Saladin's army, under the exemplary leadership of Conrad of Montferrat. It was a clever move by Saladin. If Guy had been killed or had remained as a prisoner then undoubtedly Conrad would have emerged as the undisputed leader of the Christian presence in the Holy Land. And Saladin already knew from his own failure to capture Tyre, that Conrad was an energetic and effective commander. By releasing Guy, Saladin was muddying the waters and opening the way for further intrigue and infighting amongst the remaining Christians. It was a brilliant move. He is, I think, an opponent to be respected and feared.

The promised infighting broke out soon enough. Guy and Sibylla were denied access to Tyre by Conrad, so Guy found himself in the humiliating position of being a king without a kingdom. He camped outside the walls at Tyre for months, slowly increasing his number of knights and other fighting men as men began to arrive from Europe in advance of the Crusade. By the summer of 1189, two years ago, he felt he had enough men to make his move. And it was a bold move.

He headed south to Acre and began to lay siege to the Saracen-held city. At first this looked like yet another one of Guy's poor errors of judgement. So far he had lost his ancestral lands in Poitou through bad decisions, and then he had lost the entire kingdom he had gained through his marriage by giving

Saladin battle in a situation where he could only lose. The move to Acre looked like a last, desperate, almost suicidally stupid throw of the dice from a man known far and wide for his gambling.

Yet, somehow it worked. He set up camp outside the city on the hill of Turon. Although he could not take the city, he set up his defences well and Saladin was unable to dislodge him. As each month went by a few more reinforcements would arrive in advance of the main Crusade. Eventually Guy had enough men to be able to blockade Acre by land. The only provisions its inhabitants could obtain now had to be brought in by ship. Gradually the inhabitants began to run out of supplies. Saladin redoubled his efforts to relieve the city but to no avail. Slowly and miraculously the tide looked as if it was beginning to turn in Guy's favour. If he was not in a position to defeat Saladin and take the city, at least he had tied down Saladin and provided a base for the Crusade proper to begin. The stalemate at Acre, which has lasted for about a year, is in many ways a success for Guy.

Unfortunately for Guy, however, about nine months ago, just as things were beginning to improve for him, his wife Sibylla and his two daughters died from a disease that spread quickly through the camp. His claim to the kingdom, which had been at best tenuous, now looked distinctly weak.

Given his improved performance as leader, with his bold march on Acre, Guy might have expected to have held on to power. But Conrad of Montferrat was a capable and ambitious rival for the throne, as he demonstrated with a manoeuvre that was daring in its conception and consummate in its execution. He seized Isabella, Sibylla's younger sister, from her tent in the camp outside Acre and set about making her his wife, so that he too might have a claim on the kingdom. There were two problems to overcome.

The first was that he was already married. In fact, the gossips say that he was possessed of two wives. Having been in the East for so long he has succumbed to eastern ways, it seems. The second problem was that Isabella was also already married, to a man named Humphrey of Toron.

But these were small impediments to a man such as Conrad. Although I have not met him yet, I suspect that if circumstances were different I would rather like him, with his dynamism and his certainty. From his actions he sounds rather like Mercardier.

Conrad has managed to dispose of his wife or wives. No one is quite sure how, and it seems most men of his rank or below are too scared to enquire too closely. I shall make a point of asking him directly when I do finally meet him.

Getting rid of Isabella's husband was little trickier. He tried to have the marriage annulled by Baldwin, Archbishop of Canterbury, who had arrived in the Holy Land with Hubert. However, Baldwin refused so Conrad turned to the Archbishop of Pisa. It never ceases to amaze me how even senior churchmen can be bought and sold like cattle. In exchange for the grant of certain commercial rights to the Pisan fleet, the Archbishop annulled the marriage, and on the 24th of November last year Conrad was married to Isabella. They promptly returned to his home city of Tyre.

Since Philip arrived in the Holy Land, he has taken up the cause of Conrad as King of Jerusalem. No doubt he did this precisely because he knew that Guy's family had been vassals to my family, which is why Guy had come to see me in Cyprus and, by that accident of timing of catching me on my wedding day, had secured my support. I am loath to say it, but I suspect that if Hubert had been around to counsel me, I might well have acted differently. In fact, Hubert would probably have ensured that Guy had not gained access to me in private at all. I have rather missed Hubert and I am looking forward to having him at my side again when we arrive in Acre.

So there we have it. Not only has the Kingdom of Jerusalem been all but lost after eighty or so years of successful existence, but what remains of it is being squabbled over like hungry dogs fighting for scraps outside a tavern kitchen.

However, hopes are high that we can achieve military success. The problem will be ensuring a more permanent solution.

6 June 1191

Outside Tyre

I had thought that Conrad of Montferrat would be here in Tyre, but it transpires that he has rejoined the Christian forces encamped outside Acre. No doubt he feels that he will be best served by being near his benefactor Philip.

He has left instructions that we are not to be granted access to his city. I and ten supporters can enter and spend the night there in his apartments, but the bulk of the men are to remain outside. I bristled at the impertinence of him leaving instructions for me, and for a while I toyed with the idea of taking the city by force. However, eventually I relented. Firstly, taking the city would delay us further, and everything at Acre hinges on our arrival. Secondly it might provoke Philip and Conrad unnecessarily. We have enough on our plates without making the feuding worse. So I gave instructions to set up a light camp outside the walls. We will spend the night here and move on to Acre by ship. But we will camp with the men. I will not enter Tyre under conditions set by another man.

7 June 1191

At sea, between Tyre and Acre

After all my bristling outrage, it seems that Conrad's impertinence in leaving instructions for us may have turned out for the best.

It had promised to be a night spent in angry contemplation of the various ways in which I would wreak my revenge on Conrad for his insult. At heart, I could understand his position – he did not want my armies running amok in his city in his absence, even for one night – but this did not make the insult any less stinging. I understand myself well enough to know that, in the absence of anything else to do, I would work myself into a rage over this. It seems my wife has learned quickly too. Foreseeing that this was going to happen she decided to distract me.

As the sun was low in the sky, perhaps an hour before dusk, Berengaria came to my side as I was issuing loud instructions for the setting up of the camp. I did not want too much work to be done. We needed to be off early in the morning. She slipped her hand into mine and drew me down so that she could whisper in my ear: 'It is our first night in the Holy Land. Perhaps we should explore it together.'

She led me to the back of my pavilion where my horse was saddled and ready to go. The saddlebags were bulging too. It looked as if she had prepared some sort of feast to take with us. I looked around for escorts. I would normally expect to ride out with at least eight men, but there was no sign of an escort in the buzz of activity around us. She leaned in to my side and said: 'I thought we should go alone?'

I was hesitant at first. To ride out into unknown lands with no scouts and no escort was the height of folly. We had no idea what or who was out there. And the Saracens are notorious for targeting the leaders of their enemies, figuring that a headless enemy is a less dangerous enemy. I have been warned many times that I must be more cautious of my personal safety than is necessary in my kingdom. But the thrill of our arrival in the Holy Land made me cast caution to the wind. I whistled my horse over, and heaved myself up before leaning down to help Berengaria up into the saddle behind me.

As we rode out of camp, with Berengaria clinging to me from behind, we were both breathless with excitement. As we careered away from the nascent camp we both began to scream into the onrushing wind with a sense of liberation. We galloped across the dusty plain away from the city walls and towards the low hills, perhaps two miles away. As we began to climb the gentle undulations of the hills, I brought the horse into a settled walk. The land began to become more green and lush and a gentle coolness settled over us after the heat of the day. There did not seem to be any sign of enemy scouts. After an hour, we reached the top of the hill, and emerged from the thick woods into a little clearing at the top of the hill, like a tonsured monk's head.

In the middle of the clearing stood two enormous slabs of stone, pointing up towards the sky like those I have been told about at Stonehenge in England. In between them, on its side, lay another narrow slab of stone, perhaps two and a half feet wide. The horse walked up to this stone, whinnying gently, and then nuzzled his head against the stone as if drawing great comfort from it.

Berengaria and I dismounted, and looked in awe at the spectacular view laid out before us. The city of Tyre lay down below, and beyond that the Mediterranean Sea shimmered in the golden glory of sunset. We sat on the flat narrow stone that had caused our mount to behave so strangely, and in the last of the warm rays of the sun we feasted on Berengaria's supplies. It was a perfect moment, one I tried to fix in my mind so that I can draw strength from it later.

After we had eaten in companionable silence, I got up to fetch a second goatskin of wine from the saddlebag. As I sat down again, Berengaria broke the silence, smiling at me: 'Of course you know what this stone is, don't you?'

I looked at her blankly, with no idea of what she was talking about.

'It's a fertility stone. Any couple who makes love on it will be blessed with child. That's why the horse was behaving so oddly; the stone is supposed to have magical powers.'

I snorted, perhaps rather too loudly expressing my disbelief of old pagan practices. Berengaria rushed on: 'Apparently this stone never fails…'

I was beginning to understand. Berengaria had known about this stone before we even set off, and had lured me here. I could have been cross with her. After all, whoever had told her about the existence of this stone might well have been part of a plan to ambush me. But the look of fragile innocence on her face doused my anger. She knows I now need to produce a male heir, so she feels it is her duty to conceive as soon as possible.

The last of the sun had now gone and was replaced by bright moonlight. We could see quite well in the clearing, but the woods around seemed dark and menacing. In the distance the sea glittered silver. It was as if we were on a stage illuminated especially for our purpose.

Berengaria got to her feet and held out her hand to pull me up to stand with her. She led me over to where the flat stone met the taller of the upright stones and pushed me gently back against the stone. She leaned up and whispered gently into my ear: 'Tonight you must follow my instructions… now lean back against the stone and close your eyes.'

There was no point in worrying about ambushes now, I thought. I might as well surrender myself to Berengaria and just hope that all would be well. For someone like me, accustomed to control and power, surrendering oneself to the whim of another is not easy. However, it felt intoxicating to be giving myself up to Berengaria on this special night.

I leaned back and closed my eyes. I could feel Berengaria slowly undressing me. Soon I was naked, feeling the stone under my back, still warm from the day's heat.

There was a short hiatus while I could hear Berengaria undressing. I half-opened my eyes to catch a quick look around. The clearing was still bathed in moonlight. The trees at the side still looked full of potential dangers.

Berengaria's voice ordered: 'Keep your eyes closed!'

I surrendered. No more thinking about the enemy scouts who might be lurking in those trees. What would they make of the enemy King who travels all this way with a huge army, only to abandon it to go and frolic naked in the woods? No more thinking about my own scouts who might well have been sent to follow us at a discreet distance to ensure our safety. What stories would they have tomorrow for the rest of the soldiers?

I closed my eyes and kept them shut.

I could feel Berengaria press her naked body against me, her head resting on my chest. Then she began kissing my chest all over. Light feathery kisses that just fluttered above the hair on my chest. She moved to first one side and then the other, now licking at my nipples, her tongue causing them to come erect. Then she bit slowly and gently on each in turn.

Then she moved lower to place her fluttery kisses on my stomach. I could feel my penis now rising up towards her, but she ignored it for a while longer, preferring to continue kissing my stomach. Then slowly, finally, she knelt down before me. My penis must have been quivering visibly before her.

Still she chose not to touch it. Instead she ran her hands round my buttocks, again with a light, feathery touch, then she moved them round to cup my balls, her fingers gently playing with the most sensitive of areas. Her delicate touch combined with the very slightest of breezes to make the sensation almost unbearably intense.

Then, finally, I could feel her tongue very softly licking in circles around the head of my penis. Her hand then pinned my penis back against my stomach as she leaned down and under and licked from its very base, very slowly and deliberately, all the way to the top. I lost count of how many times she repeated this in the delicious agony of it all.

My hands were pressing down hard now on the stone behind me, and the muscles in my arms and torso were locked tight whilst my legs were arching back to give me purchase against the stone. I was desperate to come but I was also desperate not to come. Berengaria was licking me so tantalisingly that coming seemed both far away and imminent all at the same time.

Finally, she released me, rising from her knees to place her face against my chest. Then she whispered gently: 'Now kneel before me and keep your eyes closed.'

I sank to my knees obediently, keeping my eyes closed as instructed. My face was now at a level just above her groin. I nuzzled my face forward into her stomach. She took a grasp of my shoulder with her left hand and in one graceful movement hooked her right leg up and over my left shoulder, so that her crotch was now right in my face.

'Now lick me,' she commanded, in a voice devoid of all nervousness or uncertainty. My virgin bride had turned quickly into a woman who knew her own mind and how to express her wishes.

I nuzzled down further into her crotch, finding her wet and open to the first touch. I licked up and down her vagina and then further and further back as she in her turn began to arch her back and moan. I slipped first one finger, then two fingers up into her vagina and the moaning intensified.

Then as I continued licking at her vagina, my nose rubbing up at her clitoris, I slid one wet finger up to press against her anus. I rested there a second, uncertain of the reaction, but she seemed to like it, pushing herself down on to my finger, so I gently pushed it in. As I did so, Berengaria writhed in pleasure, clutching at my shoulders as she ground her clitoris into my nose, her vagina against my bristly chin and her anus down on to my finger. She cried out loudly as she came in three or four waves, shuddering violently against me. I continued licking at her, but as she subsided she pushed me away from her crotch saying breathlessly: 'No more, no more.'

I opened my eyes and looked up at her. She stood above me stretching with her arms folded behind her neck, her magnificent breasts framed against the moonlight above. What a sight of perfect womanhood to behold.

And then she looked down at me, smiled and crouched to lie with her back on the stone. It was wide enough to support her back and shoulders but her legs dropped down on either side of the stone to rest lightly on the ground. I dropped down to sit on the stone between her legs with my legs also on either side of the stone, resting gently on the ground. My penis rose between us, but I tugged it downwards to enter her from my sitting position.

She mouthed something at me, but I could not quite hear, so I leaned forward to catch what she said the second time: 'Now close your eyes, fuck me really hard and give me a baby.'

It is a curious thing, but I began now to believe in the power of this stone. There was something about the relative position of the man and the woman that made penetration seem much deeper than normal. Perhaps it was this that had generated the myth about its powers of fertility.

As we made love and I approached climax I suddenly knew with utter certainty that this was to be it. This was to be the moment in which life was to be created, the moment in which I would beget a male heir and in which Berengaria could cast aside the unspoken fear of barrenness.

What a perfect moment in which to create my son. Naked and alone together beneath a moonlit sky. Against the backdrop of a silver sea. Basking in the glory of the Lord's favour. In the Holy Land at last.

Our son who will be born from this union will be truly blessed.

11 June 1191
The Crusader Camp, outside Acre

Just as I was finishing dictating the last entry to Armande, I was summoned to the deck of the *Esneca Regis*. The lookouts had spotted a huge ship making for Acre. It appeared to be hanging back a little as if reluctant to come too close to us.

I dispatched a galleyman, Peter des Barres, in a rowboat to enquire as to who was on board, as it was displaying no flags on any of its three masts.

The answer came back that it was a relief ship belonging to the King of France. I was perplexed. Given what we know about Philip, who is notoriously short of money, would he really have commissioned such a large and clearly well-equipped relief vessel? And if he had, he would have made sure that everyone would know that this splendid ship belonged to him, surely?

Puzzled, I turned back to go down to my cabin. Perhaps Philip was finally beginning to learn that not every action needs to be shouted from the rooftops. But as I turned away one of the junior galleymen called out: 'Sire, I saw that ship being loaded in Beirut. It has all sorts of provisions for the relief of the Saracen garrison in Acre, and it has six or seven hundred Saracen fighting men on board—'

Before he could get any further, the boy was felled by a swipe across the face from Peter des Barres, who shouted: 'Silence, boy! Do you not know that you may not address your King unless you are asked to?'

The boy lay on the floor, wiped his hand across his bloody mouth and looked down in surprise at the amount of blood running from his nose and mouth. Peter des Barres then addressed me: 'I am sorry for the impudence of my man, Your Majesty. When I approached the ship all of the men were clean-shaven and could not therefore have been Muslims. Also they had pigs running about on the deck and we all know that Muslims do not eat pork. So they must be French, as they say.'

I was about to turn away when the boy on the floor piped up again: 'They have all shaved off their beards so as to trick us. And the pigs are just a ruse. I swear that the ship is full of men and supplies for the relief of Acre.'

As he finished he cowered expecting another swipe from des Barres, but none came. Des Barres turned to face me with a look that suggested that he knew he had been duped. The boy continued: 'They even have sackfuls of poisonous snakes on board that they plan to release into the Crusader camps outside the walls of Acre.'

Somehow this settled it. The sheer improbability of the story convinced me that it must be true. No one would make up something like that.

I gave the order for another boat to be sent to make further enquiries. This time it came back with a different story. The men were apparently Genoese and were on their way to Tyre.

The contradiction between the two stories persuaded me that something was wrong. I ordered all the galleys to turn and encircle the great ship. If it turned out to be friendly then no great harm could come from being extra careful.

But it quickly became clear that the boy had been right. As our galleys drew up to the tall sides of the vessel, missiles and darts began to rain down on our ships. There could be no mistaking their hostile intent. However, the sides of the ship were so high that there was no effective way for our men to try to board, particularly as the ship was now making good speed.

I summoned Peter des Barres, who was clearly anxious to make up for his earlier mistake, and asked: 'How are we going to get aboard? I want all of the supplies on that ship.'

He thought for a moment, then he summoned a small group of what appeared to be his crack team. He barked at them in Italian. They listened attentively then ran to the side of the galley and dived head first into the swirling sea below. I stood open-mouthed in astonishment. They were like water rats making for the stern of the great ship. I have never seen such able swimmers.

Des Barres turned back to me and explained: 'Their job is to foul the ship's rudder with ropes. If it works, it will stop the ship in its tracks and leave us with an easier target.'

And it did work. To an extent. The ship was slowed and finally our men could clamber up the sides. However, the sheer number of fighting men aboard the great ship meant that we could not get sufficient men on board in order to fight effectively. Our men got as far as the gunwales but were then tossed back into the sea, butchered by the knives and swords of the Saracen fighting men.

After a few minutes our men began to despair at the situation. We were not going to get anywhere pursuing an all-out assault. I could feel their surreptitious glances turning towards me, looking to me for leadership. I admit I began to panic a little inside. I am the undisputed master of warfare on land. It is second nature to me. I do not even have to think about it very hard. But this warfare at sea is different. I have no experience of it and I felt out of my depth. What should we do now?

Then the answer came to me. Perhaps I was being too greedy, wanting to capture all of the men aboard and take the ship and all of its precious cargo. That was an objective defined by a man used to fighting on land and used to capturing castles and cities, which either belong to oneself or to one's enemy. At sea there is an alternative, a less ambitious objective. To deny the enemy his supplies. I decided to be less greedy.

I turned to Peter des Barres and said: 'Give the order to turn all the galleys in towards the ship. On my order we will ram the ship with the iron beaks at the front of each galley.'

His face lit up, as did those of the men around him. There would not be so much treasure to take as bounty but at least the slaughter of his good men would stop. He ran off to give the orders.

It took half an hour for the order to be passed from galley to galley, and for each galley to turn slowly so that, rather than lying abreast the ship, the galleys bobbed in the waves with their prows pointing straight at its hull. I made my way to the prow of the *Esneca Regis* and clambered over the sails on the deck to stand right on the figurehead, so that everyone could see me.

I lifted my right arm in the air. The oars at the side of each galley were raised in unison. As I dropped my arm to my side, the oars plunged into the water. They had about one hundred yards to build up some speed before crashing into the great ship. The oars ploughed through the water at a furious rate, carving up great spumes of spray until the sea around the ship was foaming white. Then came the first crash. The first galley was about twenty yards ahead of the others for some reason. Either it must have started earlier or it must have generated extra speed from some freak wave. However, it rebounded from the side of the ship causing no apparent damage. When they saw there was no damage a great roar rose up from the Saracen soldiers on board. I sincerely hoped the ship was not so robust as to be able to resist all forty galleys.

Then the next wave of galleys hit the ship. Four of them at once. There was a tremendous crash and then a great tearing of timber as the galleys came away from the ship. Three of them had torn holes in its side, and because the galleys were so low in the water the ship was now taking on water. There was a mighty roar from our side now as the men realised that the plan was going to work. The next galleys crashed into the ship with much the same effect. They then rowed back to the starting point to give themselves another run at their target. But by the time they got there again the ship was already much lower in the water. It was not long before much of it was submerged.

The Saracen soldiers began jumping into the sea, looking desperately before they jumped for some piece of floating wood to which they could cling. Clearly none of them could swim.

I turned away, knowing that the next ten minutes would see utter carnage as the enemy were either drowned or butchered by our galleymen. I wanted to make sure that Berengaria and Joanna did not witness the slaughter. I rushed them below decks from where they had been standing on the main deck, brushing aside their protestations.

Through the window of our staterooms at the rear of the *Esneca Regis* we could now see quite clearly the city of Acre, smoke rising from its ramparts. Outside the city, on the hill, we could see the Crusader camp and beyond that the massed ranks of Saladin's armies. The Crusader camp seemed to be in a state of agitation. I wondered aloud why that might be, and Berengaria provided the answer: 'If we can pick them out on land then they must be able to see us too. They must have known that the great ship was coming to relieve Acre, and now we have dealt with it.'

I smiled a little at her use of the word 'we', as if she herself had been in the middle of the hand-to-hand fighting. But she is a formidable woman, my wife. I suspect she would be fighting, given half a chance.

'I wonder what King Philip will make of it?' she continued. 'He has been here for three months and achieved nothing. Then you arrive, and within minutes of coming into view of the Crusader camp you despatch a thousand Saracens to the bottom of the sea.'

She was right. King Philip was not best pleased to see me carry on from where we had left off in Sicily. He disguised his feelings reasonably well in public, coming down to the shore to envelop me in a great hug as I stepped from the small boats bringing us ashore. The roar of the men watching was something to behold, but I could still hear the bitterness in his voice as he formally welcomed me to the Crusader camp and announced that there would be a night of celebration to mark the occasion.

I was as gracious and as modest as I can be, but it did not seem to lift his mood. Berengaria pointed out to me later that grace and modesty are not my strongest suits, and that he may well have interpreted my remarks as being ironic, which would have exacerbated the situation. She might be right, but I have determined to press on regardless. There are enough obstacles in our path without me always worrying about Philip's sensitivities.

When the men had disembarked all of the equipment from the galleys, I gave them permission to participate in the celebrations. I had a quick meal and then summoned the engineers to my quarters so that I could be briefed on the state of the siege.

Philip remained with me at first, but after a couple of hours he decided that he had had enough and left. Somewhat awkwardly, the siege engineers and other fighting men were very keen to obtain my view on the state of affairs and none of their questions were directed to Philip. But after all, I am the one with experience of siege warfare, whilst he has virtually none. Nevertheless, he may well have felt that his pride and his dignity were further punctured by the evening's meeting.

5 July 1191
The Crusader Camp, outside Acre

I finally arrive in the Holy Land only to fall seriously ill for the first time in my life. So ill, that at one stage I thought I would die. I spent almost a week in the throes of a dangerously high fever, and when that abated I was left so weak that I could not eat. It was all that I could do to drink enough ale to stay alive.

When at last I began to feel a little better and I sat up for the first time in a fortnight, I noticed that my hair had begun to fall out in great clumps. I summoned an orderly and commanded him to bring me a mirror. I looked like an older, weaker man. I could not allow the men, or indeed Berengaria, to see me like this.

I called for the barber and ordered him to shave my head. As I sat, drained, while he shaved my head with his sharpest blade, I looked down at the golden hair lying on the floor around me. I decided that this must be some sort of a sign, a symbolic rebirth as a man capable of tackling the holy task of taking back God's land. This illness had been one of God's challenges. I could almost feel the strength flowing back into me as my hair cascaded to the floor. When the barber had finished and he brought me the mirror to show me his work, I gasped.

The man staring back at me was not the handsome prince who had arrived in triumph in the Holy Land just three weeks ago. In front of me was a man who looked leaner, harder and fiercer. In some ways I looked older. The loss of weight meant that the lines on my face were more pronounced. There was now a little sagging around my jowls, the skin was not quite as taut as it had been. However, my shaved head also made me look more defined, more determined, more focused.

I called for my clothes and when I was washed and dressed, I summoned Berengaria. She had been kept from me for fear of contagion whilst I was ill. I think that she was so relieved to see me that she hardly even noticed the change in my appearance. She clung to me, sobbing into my chest. There was no need for words. I understood. She had been terrified that after all that we had been through, I was suddenly to be snatched from her. Through the past couple of weeks she would have been stoic in her demeanour, giving no hint in front of anyone else of the worry, the fear that would have been preying on her. Now that the fear was over, and now that it was just the two of us, she could finally let go her anxiety in great heaving sobs.

But then she spoke and I realised that my diagnosis had been partly wrong. She was not simply relieved that I had recovered. She is pregnant! She is expecting our child. The fertility stone outside Tyre has worked its magic.

When she sensed my excitement Berengaria tried to calm me a little, saying: 'It's still early days. I was due two weeks ago and I'm never late. But it's still too soon; something could go wrong.'

But I was exultant. A son. An heir. The first duty of any king will be discharged with the birth of my son.

Again Berengaria sounded a note of caution: 'It might be a girl...'

I paused. Yes, of course it could be a girl. But that is not what I had felt at the moment of conception on that stone on the hill outside Tyre. I had just known then that it would be a boy. And, even if it is a girl, then the next one will be a boy.

Despite my illness and the doctors counselling caution, I feel full of energy. I will throw myself into this siege and capture Acre and restore it to God as a small token of gratitude for his munificence in granting me a son.

6 July 1191

The Crusader Camp, outside Acre

While I was unwell almost nothing has happened.

Philip has been ill too, apparently, or, as Hubert has pointed out, maybe he saw it simply as an opportunity to lie low for a while. He would not have wanted to be thrust into the glare of attention as the leader of a siege when he has no experience of siege warfare, risking further humiliation. I have no interest in his humiliation so I am glad that his illness, whether real or feigned, coincided with mine.

Now that I am well I can take charge again.

The siege has not advanced in my absence. Our catapults have continued to pound the walls of the city, but they rebuild the walls as fast as we can knock them down. We have good catapults and slings, but finding stones and rocks of the right size to hurl at the walls is no easy task after a year and a half of the siege. They have all been used up. I have offered two gold pieces to any man who can bring me a stone worthy of our great catapults. I did this at the suggestion of Hubert who reminded me of how, at the siege of Jerusalem, almost one hundred years ago, Raymond of St Giles famously offered a penny for every three stones thrown into the ditch. When the ditch was full he was able to roll his Machina across the ditch and up to the city walls.

This morning we had a stone of a perfect size and weight and amidst much anticipation it was hurled right over the walls and into the city market. Our spies tell us that it killed twelve people, which was a cause for great celebration amongst the men who operate our catapults.

During my illness the ghastly Philip, Count of Flanders has died and two of his catapults have now passed to me. Fortunately he had left his wife Sarah behind in Flanders to govern in his absence, so I have not had to endure any uncomfortable meetings with her. I am not sure that I would particularly enjoy explaining our past history to Berengaria.

So, above ground the siege has not been going too well.

Below ground the news is not much better. I had expected my sappers to have had much more success in my absence than they have had to date. It is partly because the Saracens seem to have developed some new, and quite effective, defensive tactics.

Normally my men start by building a defensive shelter as close as possible to the walls of the city. The shelter should be strong enough to defend against stones from catapults, against battering ram charges in a sally from the city gates and against the dreaded Greek Fire.

Under the cover afforded by this shelter they then begin to dig tunnels towards the walls. We have brought a group of a hundred men from Wales for this very purpose. According to Mercardier, the Welsh make the best tunnellers.

Once the tunnel is under the walls they set fire to the wood supports within the tunnel, hoping that when the supports give way, the tunnel will collapse and bring down the walls with it. Needless to say, it is an inexact science and it fails as often as it works. Often they will need to dig and set fire to five or six tunnels before they have any luck. But if one has the luxury of time then one will get there in the end.

However, the Saracens have figured out an effective counter to this tactic. They have started digging tunnels from their end in the hope of coming across our tunnels and engaging in hand-to-hand combat underground. I think our sturdy Welsh friends were a little surprised the first time this happened. There they were, merrily digging away, thinking that they were entirely safe from the Saracens, when suddenly the walls gave way and there were ten Saracen soldiers armed to the teeth and ready for battle. My little Welshmen scurried away back up the tunnels screaming for all they were worth. Not all of them made it. Six were cut down by the Saracens and their bodies were dragged up and dangled over the ramparts in a show of defiance.

The Welshmen were somewhat truculent after this, moaning that they had not signed up to be in the front line and that they required protection if they were going to continue digging. They asked for an armed knight to protect each digger, otherwise they were going to set off home. They are a militant lot, the Welsh.

I pointed out that their efforts had not been particularly successful thus far, and that they were not really in a position to try to strike bargains with me. I assigned one knight to guard every six diggers. They could take it or leave it. If they left my offer, I would seal up the tunnels at our end and they would have to dig their way out through the Saracen-held city. Not surprisingly they took the offer, although not with especially good grace, and their progress has slowed noticeably.

7 July 1191

The Crusader Camp, outside Acre

When my sister Joanna had been married to King William II of Sicily, she had inherited two Egyptian slaves whom she had kept in her service even after William's disreputable death. They had come with her and with us through Cyprus and now to Acre. I had assumed, as had everybody else, that they were Christians, but it now turns out that they must have been Saracen all along, for today they defected to Saladin's camp.

It is not a particularly significant loss in itself, but it has made us all feel rather uncomfortable, in addition to the constant threat of robbery and kidnapping. It is said that Saladin has hired large bands of robbers and thieves and brought them here from his cities to prey on us.

We are all on edge, so I feel we need to seize the initiative. Tomorrow we will go properly on to the offensive.

8 July 1191

The Crusader Camp, Outside Acre

So close and yet so far. My three-pronged attack nearly finished off the siege.

We started early this morning with a massive bombardment of the city walls. I finally managed to get all of the captains of the catapults to target the same stretch. One would have thought this would have been an obvious thing to do, but in the eighteen months of this siege they have never previously agreed on the best part of the wall to attack. It has taken my arrival to break the impasse.

It was a fearsome sight to see the walls being pounded every thirty seconds or so by huge rocks. My offer of two gold pieces per man seems to have worked well in improving our stock of rocks to hurl at the enemy. There were great plumes of smoke and dust rising from the walls as they suffered under the barrage.

The whining Welshmen had also been hard at it for the last two days and nights, building four tunnels under the same segment of the walls. The wooden beams supporting the tunnels were set alight just before dawn this morning. They take three or four hours to burn completely through and to start collapsing, so if we were to have any luck with this strategy it would probably come two or three hours into the attack. It is impossible to judge whether any advantage will be gained from tunnelling work. One just has to hope for the best.

The third phase of the attack was to bring up close to the city walls a series of circleias. Under these mobile shelters we can hide our crossbowmen, to shield them from the Greek Fire thrown down from the walls, or in some cases catapulted in earthenware jars from inside the walls. The circleias also offer some protection from the arrows of the Saracen archers. I myself went forward under the cover of one of these and had a little sport with a crossbow, not because I have any great skill with a crossbow, but rather to set an example to the men. I found it difficult in my weakened state to wind in the crossbow effectively, but I still managed to catch two Saracen archers on the walls.

I was there for about an hour before deciding that I would be better placed further back so that I could see more clearly and issue more effective instructions. As I was walking back to our lines, out of range of the Saracen archers now, there was a tremendous, deep rumble from the earth. I turned to see that one of our tunnels beneath the city walls had given way in just the manner we had hoped. Not only had the earth beneath given way but the wall was visibly crumbling into the hole. This was our chance. I broke into a run back to camp, urging my escort of men-at-arms to keep up with me.

As I ran, shouting orders for our men to saddle up and ride into the breach, I was dumbfounded to see that the French contingent of our army were still breakfasting outside their tents. They were entirely unprepared. I was furious and screamed insults at them as I hurtled past.

Our men-at-arms were geared up and ready to go. They were simply waiting on my instruction. I ran towards my horse, waiting for me at the head of our men, and vaulted into the saddle.

The visor of my helmet was still up, and I wheeled Arthur round to face the men before letting out a mighty roar, slamming my visor down and charging off towards the city walls. I brought the horse to a halt a hundred yards from the walls, and waved the men past me and on to the crumbling walls. They needed no encouragement and charged past to clamber up the rubble now strewn everywhere.

They must have posed a fearsome sight to the city's defendants. I was confident of victory; I could not conceive that the city's inhabitants would be numerous enough or strong enough to resist our men, fresh and strong and desperate for God's approbation.

But I had underestimated the Saracens. Their leaders, Mestoc and Caracois, had clearly prepared well for the inevitable moment when the walls would collapse. Our men were met by a volley of arrows and crossbow bolts. Those who survived this still had twenty or thirty yards to go to get to the first line of Saracens, and then they had to get through a line of small earthenware pots of Greek Fire being hurled by hand. I saw plenty of our men peeling away from the assault trying vainly to beat out the flames from the oil sticking to their armour. I grimaced; their injuries would be horrific.

To succeed in taking the city we had to get inside. And to get inside we had to get through the opening quickly before it was sealed up again. Our men knew this and ploughed on. Probably seven out of ten made it to the Saracen lines and could engage for the first time in the kind of hand-to-hand fighting they relished. If only we'd had greater numbers, we could have pushed even harder at this gap. But the French were still nowhere to be seen.

A small group of Austrians appeared at my side five minutes after our main charge. I urged them forward but they refused to take my command, preferring to wait for their leader, Duke Leopold. He eventually appeared thirty minutes later, when I first began to realise that the momentum of the fighting was swinging against us. I took my frustration out on him, enquiring rudely as to why he had only now deigned to join us, and instructing him to give the command to get his men forward into battle.

But, instead of pushing his men forward, he turned and headed back towards the camp, taking his men with him. I could not believe what I was seeing, and screamed at his departing back that he and all of his men were the worst kind of cowards. It was all I could do to stop myself chasing after him and forcing him to return.

In retrospect, my insults were probably excessive. He had taken a look at the unfolding situation and probably decided that throwing his small band of men into the fray was not going to make that much difference. Given the limited number of his men, he could not afford to lose many.

I turned my attention back to the battle in front of me, its progress still ebbing and flowing. We would suddenly make inroads on the left and I would think that we were soon to break through their lines entirely, only for there to be a sudden surge from their side and our men would be thrown back again. At one stage the arrival of a hundred Pisans looked like it might tip the balance in our favour, but they too were eventually repulsed.

I cursed the French, throwing glances over my shoulder from time to time to see if they were coming, but there was no sign of them.

Finally I raised my right arm to signal the retreat. It was time to accept that we had failed. If we had had just a couple of hundred more men we could have broken through, but the Austrians and the French had let me down. Although I had taken it out on Duke Leopold, in truth I did not particularly blame him. He had taken a decision, probably the right one, for his men. But the French, led by Philip, I could not forgive so easily.

I stormed back to camp, determined to have it out with Philip. I dismounted quickly and threw the reins to the steward standing guard outside Philip's pavilion. I pulled back the curtain that acted as the entrance. His honour guard of ten men stood there blocking the way into Philip's private quarters.

'I would speak with your King,' I thundered.

The curtains separated and Duke Hugh of Burgundy emerged, looking, it must be said, a little nervous. He stammered: 'His Majesty remains indisposed, sire. A relapse in the illness that you both suffered. Perhaps I could take him some message?'

I choked with frustration as I understood: Philip had set this up. He intended to see from a distance how the battle was going. Then he would decide whether to commit his men. If things were going well they would come and join us and thus participate fully in the spoils that the city had to offer. If success looked more marginal then he would hold back and feign a recurrence of his illness. He could then claim that he would have loved to commit to battle but that his men would not go forward without him at the helm. In that way he was not tainted by defeat, and yet my reputation would suffer.

I turned and left Philip's pavilion, kicking the ground as I went. A terrible day. Men's lives wasted. Failure in front of the entire army. A fracture with the Austrians and the French. The day had started so promisingly. By lunchtime it had turned to disaster.

I made my way back to my pavilion. There stood Berengaria, radiant and exquisite. Was it my imagination or was her stomach already starting to swell? My anger and frustration dissolved almost immediately. She gently pointed out to me that it was not quite the disaster I imagined. The important thing was that the city walls had now been breached for the first time. Although we had not entered the city this was in itself enormous progress. The army had been here for nigh on eighteen months and achieved virtually nothing. And although Philip had tricked me, it was a fairly obvious stratagem that would be easily seen through by the court of army opinion.

Furthermore, although the Saracens had fought fiercely and well, they must know that their eventual capitulation is inevitable. Their best hope now is for a negotiated truce.

I started to calm down. She was right. I have become so used to easy victories over the past few months that I have forgotten that progress is normally a series of steps forward interspersed with some steps back. Since our marriage everything has gone so smoothly that I had forgotten that setbacks are a normal part of life. I did, however, experience a shiver of unease as I pondered this. I hope my luck has not changed. Or maybe God's favour is no longer shining quite so brightly on me? That initial shiver of unease turned into a feeling of slight nausea.

I took myself off to the small private chapel we have established at the rear of our pavilion, to pray for God's continued kindness.

9 July 1191

The Crusader Camp, outside Acre

My beloved Berengaria was right, again.

Although I had returned furious at being repulsed from the city walls, furious at Duke Leopold for his refusal to join our charge, and furious at King Philip for his deviousness, it appears that the rest of the army was less bitter about our failure.

As Berengaria had predicted, the general consensus, as reported to me, was that this first breach of the walls in over eighteen months represented great progress. There was a certain amount of resentment at Duke Leopold for his failure to engage with the enemy when he might have made all the difference. But the real bile was reserved for King Philip, who was being roundly derided for cowardice, certainly by the factions of the army not directly under his patronage. Even those who were loyal to him seemed somewhat shamefaced by his actions.

These reports buoyed me up. Perhaps the situation was not as bleak as I had thought on my initial return. But Berengaria still counselled caution, saying: 'Philip will be livid that his stratagem has been exposed and that he is the laughing stock of the army. He is a vicious little snake, and in the current situation he might lash out unexpectedly. You have known him for years. He is at his most dangerous when he feels threatened or humiliated by you, his great rival.'

I laughed, and replied: 'Surely even Philip cannot blame me for this fiasco. It is entirely of his own making.'

Berengaria responded, circling her hands gently on her belly: 'When he is blinded by humiliation and overcome by jealousy of you, he does not necessarily think rationally. We should just be careful. Remember, he has not forgiven you for rejecting Alice, and that was not your fault either.'

I swallowed hard. It was back after almost two years. That wave of nauseous dread that overcame me as the blood ran from my dead father's nose. I felt it again.

I reached out to Berengaria and we made slow tender love in the cushioned luxury of our private pavilion. It was hot outside, but deliciously cool inside. I was gentle, careful not to hurt our baby growing inside her. As we lay there afterwards, I reflected on the imperfection of love attained. I could not feel more strongly, more passionately about Berengaria, and our child to come. But despite the languor of the afternoon spent in the arms of the woman I love beyond anything, with the world seemingly at my feet, the feeling of dread would not entirely fade. My father's dead face, and that stream of blood, would not leave me.

I feel as if I had a firm grip on God's love and that somehow I have let go and it is slipping from my fingers. However hard I try I cannot clench my hand to grasp on to the love. It is strange; only a few days ago I felt positively warmed by the glow of His love. What have I done to deserve its loss?

Perhaps He might be angry at my failure to take Acre at the first attempt. I will just have to take Acre next time, and then move on to Jerusalem. Surely He cannot begrudge me His love if I deliver the Holy Land into His care?

12 July 1191

Acre

I stand here in the staterooms of the castle, dictating to a dusty Armande. Finally we are in a proper building instead of a damned tent. I am leaning with one cheek against the stone of the thick wall, willing its coolness to spread from my face down to the rest of my body.

Through that open door lies Berengaria, asleep, with our precious son growing inside her. If I pause, I can hear the soft rise and fall of her breathing, which is heavier now that she is pregnant in the summer heat. The late evening peace in our rooms contrasts sharply with the frenetic intensity of the last couple of days.

The leaders of the defenders of the city must have had spies in our camp, for they knew exactly how and when to strike at the fissure in our camp.

Two days ago, just after breakfast, a great cheer went up from our front lines. There was a rush to see what all the fuss was about. The city gates had opened slowly and two huge white flags, on long wooden poles were being tentatively brought out. The men thought at first that the city was surrendering. However, the flags were followed swiftly by a small group of ten heavily armed men, surrounding two horsemen clad in shining silver chain mail. They were instantly recognisable as Mestoc and Caracois, the two powerful warriors at the heart of the valiant defence of Acre.

They galloped towards our lines and drew abruptly to a halt in a cloud of dust, some twenty yards short of our men, who stood with crossbows cocked. By this time I was making my way down towards the lines. I gave instructions to be taken forward to the Saracens. We would grant them a truce for the length of the parley, but they would have to return directly to the city afterwards. If any of them attempted to make a run for Saladin's camp, then all of their lives would be forfeit. If they did not go back to the city, I would have them all killed.

I turned back towards camp, making for Philip's pavilion. We needed to talk before meeting Mestoc and Caracois, in order to agree a common line. But again, he refused to see me, sending out a message that he would join me in twenty minutes to see the Saracen leaders. I was enraged. Hubert tried to calm me down, counselling that we should simply see what the Saracen leaders had to offer. Eventually I regained my composure and in due course took my place alongside Philip as we prepared to receive the Saracen delegation.

Shortly after we sat down, the curtain at the front of the pavilion was drawn back and the two warriors entered. They were impressive if contrasting figures. Mestoc is tall, almost as tall as me, and broad-shouldered. His skin looks dark anyway, but his face and his forearms were tanned a burnished brown. The various scars on his forearms stood out pink against the dark skin, and he also had a deep weal of a pink scar crossing his right cheekbone. It looked almost sculpted, sitting proudly above his closely cropped beard. Caracois was shorter and more bull-chested, but he was no less of an impressive figure. Not for him the haughty, aristocratic, slightly disdainful attitude displayed by Mestoc. No, Caracois positively glowered at us in the belligerent manner reminiscent of my first military instructor, Balardier, Mercardier's father. I suspect that this pair, in their different ways, must have hated being here to parley with us. They would have preferred a quick and gloriously defiant last stand on the city walls. But the bonds of fealty are strong. They must have been following Saladin's orders in coming to treat with us.

Mestoc spoke first, reciting from memory what was clearly a pre-agreed script.

The interpreter felt compelled to translate all the tedious flattery and title-giving until it was as much as I could do to restrain myself from urging him to get to the heart of the matter. Finally we got to the nub of it: the Saracens would leave Acre provided that they would be able to do so with all of their arms and all of their goods.

Beside me Philip let out an audible sigh of satisfaction. I scowled at him out of the corner of my eye. Before he could say anything, I spoke: 'Kindly inform the gentlemen that we require that they withdraw that we might discuss their offer.'

Once Mestoc and Caracois had left the pavilion, Philip could hold himself in no longer: 'This is excellent news. Acre has fallen. We move on to Jerusalem and we could be home by Christmas.'

There was a murmur of assent from the assembled knights and nobles on his side of the room. It was matched by a disapproving shaking of heads from the much larger contingent on my side of the room. I could not rein myself in any longer in the face of the frustration of our failure to take Acre at the first attempt, exacerbated by the apparent French indifference to our losses, and now this reckless naïvety. I exploded: 'What do you mean Acre has fallen, you bloody...' I managed to stop myself from insulting him directly, but only just. 'There are no circumstances under which their offer could ever be considered remotely acceptable. If you had ever managed to actually capture a town or a castle then you would of course know this, rather than have it pointed out to you by your master in warfare.'

There was a collective intake of breath on all sides; I knew I had gone too far. It was as if I could see the words floating out of my mouth but I could not lift my arms to drag them back. Once spoken they could never be unsaid.

I ploughed on, waving my right arm to indicate my men massed behind me: 'These men whom you see before you have thrown themselves time and again upon the city walls, risking their lives in battle, suffering terrible illness and hardship in the camp and learning to live off the scraps left behind by dogs. Some of them have been doing this for nigh on eighteen months. And now you would abandon them by forsaking their right to what they have earned. You must know that these men have suffered all of these hardships in order to get their rewards when Acre is sacked.

'If you let the Saracens walk out with everything of worth and with all of their weapons and horses, then what will my men's sacrifices have been for? How will they pay for new swords and new armour? How will they pay for new horses? How will they pay for food and drink? How will they pay for their passage home? You cannot simply abandon them because you are feeling a little homesick and want to be back for Christmas. And, what's more, if you let the Saracens walk out with all of their horses, armour and wealth, then they will simply stand and fight another day when they have recovered and are twice as strong. There is absolutely no way that those Saracens are walking out of Acre with everything they own.'

I knew as I finished, drowned out by the murmurs of approval from my own side, that like the great Caesar before me, the Rubicon had been crossed. Despite the best advice from Hubert and Berengaria, and others, to tread carefully in my dealings with Philip, I had not been able to heed it. He knew it too. His face was white with fury and his hands were shaking. I know that from his earliest days he has not been able to abide confrontation. This whole scene was anathema to him. He lives in a dark world of scheming and plotting, preferring the dagger to the gleaming battle sword. Drag him into the sunlight and he is much diminished.

There was nothing left to say. Philip turned on his heels and stalked out, followed in swift order by his retinue.

I summoned Mestoc and Caracois and informed them politely but firmly that their offer was declined and that they were free to return to the defence of their city. They received the news with equanimity, nodding courteously before turning to depart. I followed them out and watched as they headed towards their city in a cloud of dust thrown up by the hooves of their disappearing horses. I thought to myself that Mestoc was a worthy and honourable enemy. Indeed, under different circumstances, I suspect that we might be friends.

I turned and walked slowly back to camp. The men stood waiting for me; I was not quite sure what their reaction would be. I was certain of their absolute loyalty, of course, but in the tented bars and taverns, when tongues were loosened and opinions more freely expressed, how would they feel then? The answer came as I approached, head bowed and addressed them.

'Men, we are here to take back the Holy Land in the name of the Lord our God, and to avenge those who were massacred here in the rightful defence of the Holy Land four years ago. We are here to do God's work and to build a Christian nation here where Christ walked. We are not here to accept empty castles and poisoned wells from Saracens when they are on the edge of defeat. We need the castles, we need the horses, we need the armour, we need the weapons, we need the money to buy food and drink, we need the ships to bring the supplies, and we need the women.'

The last part raised a cheer.

'We will take Acre, either by force or by unconditional surrender, and when we do, we will be the masters of everything in it. If we choose to let the Saracens live, then that is our choice because it is God's choice. But we will not have terms dictated to us by heathens. We are in this land to build a country to last a thousand years. We must be strong in order to do that. Now go and prepare for another assault on the city. Soon it will be ours.'

There was another loud cheer and the men turned and began to make off to their respective parts of the camp.

Hubert approached and we walked together back to my pavilion, silent, but I could feel the weight of his disapproval. Eventually I turned to him and said: 'There is no way that we could have accepted their terms. Without their goods and supplies, once we were inside we would have been worse off than they are now.'

Hubert nodded in agreement, but I carried on: 'I suppose I could have been a little more diplomatic with King Philip...'

Hubert almost choked on this understatement; then he smiled and said: 'You, sire, are our King and our leader. Your men will follow you to the ends of the earth; in fact, they almost have,' as he spread his arms to indicate the wastelands around us. 'King Philip is here purely to fulfil the letter of his crusading vow and no more. He is not here to rebuild the Kingdom of Jerusalem on a more stable footing, he has come simply to avoid losing face with his own men. Today he lost that face almost completely, when he revealed his hand by saying that he could be home for Christmas. Even if you had not spoken the way you did, he would have lost the respect of his men.

'So do not blame yourself for causing this rift. It was always there. King Philip and you are here for different purposes. The pressures of this kind of existence were always going to widen the fissure.' He smiled and added: 'And I think it is fair to say that that fissure is now a gaping chasm.'

The smile disappeared and his face became grave. 'But, sire, you must be wary of him. He is jealous of you, your stature, your wealth, your army, your wife, and above all he is jealous of the love in which your men hold you. His jealousy is not in itself so bad, but he is also a man with little scruple, he is capable of many evil acts...'

I looked enquiringly at him. Was there some gossip about Philip about which I was unaware? But Hubert was silent then, and I could not really pursue the matter. I accepted his words, but was there really that much that Philip could do to harm me?

As we reached the pavilion, Berengaria stood at the entrance. I swallowed nervously, for she was unlikely to have been impressed by my outburst. But I was surprised by her reaction. She took my arm and reached up to kiss my cheek, whispering: 'I'm proud of you.'

Although she had always counselled caution in dealing with Philip, now that the break had well and truly come, it seemed she reckoned that there was little to be gained by remonstrating with me.

After an hour or so, the bombardment of Acre resumed. But there was now one marked difference. I was receiving reports of an increasing number of Saracens escaping and approaching our lines, begging to surrender and pleading for baptism into the Christian faith. The priests were having to work hard to baptise them all. I had to smile to myself. Was it really that these men had suddenly seen the true light? Was it divine grace that motivated them, or was it utter terror of what was likely to befall them? No matter. As one passing bishop laughed, when I expressed my scepticism: 'Sire, the ways of salvation are many.'

I expect that the turmoil inside the city was significant. We know that those within the walls have been communicating with Saladin's forces up on the hill by means of pigeons carrying messages. A couple of times in the past few weeks our archers have managed to shoot down one of these birds, but the messages were written in code so that we could not define their meaning. The number of birds passing overhead that afternoon increased dramatically. Clearly there was intense discussion going on between the two camps. We know that Saladin has come under extreme pressure from within his own camp to grant the petitions of the besieged in the city and to allow them to surrender. Many of his leading men have family members trapped inside Acre, adding to the pressure.

I ordered the barrage to be intensified. We were at a crucial point now, we needed to apply as much force as possible. I figured that a whole day and a whole night of bombardment would weaken them sufficiently to allow us to mount another assault.

But towards midday the gates creaked open again, and again two white flags of truce cautiously appeared. I ordered the bombardment to cease, to allow Mestoc and Caracois to approach once more. This time, I received them in my own pavilion. There was no sign of Philip, who has been skulking in his own pavilion, with the drapes very firmly drawn.

As the Saracen leaders entered, they were clearly surprised to find only me there to greet them, but they took it in their stride. This time they offered terms that were much more acceptable. They would quit the city, leaving it intact and with no traps and no poisoned wells, and leaving behind the ships in its harbour. They would return to us, within one month, two hundred and fifty Christian hostages whom Saladin is holding elsewhere in the Holy Land. They would walk out with only the shirts on their backs. No horses, no carts, no possessions, no food, no money, no jewellery. They would be granted only their lives.

I hesitated before accepting. Now was the time when our negotiating position was at its strongest. I demanded further concessions. They would have to release two thousand five hundred Christian hostages, return to us the Holy Cross, on which our Lord and Saviour Jesus Christ gave his life for us, and which had been lost four years ago at the Battle of Hattin. Furthermore, they would have to pay us two hundred thousand of their dinars or gold coins. We would hold two and a half thousand hostages for one month until the return of the Holy Cross and the delivery of the two hundred thousand dinars.

Mestoc and Caracois looked a little taken aback by the further demands, but after a brief discussion, they accepted.

I left Hubert to iron out the details and retired to my rooms for an hour with Berengaria. I was exultant. Saladin had been held at bay, Acre was about to fall, great wealth was about to cascade into our coffers. Most importantly Berengaria is with child. It looks as if I will be able to deliver the Holy Land to God in thanks for Him granting me a son.

The rest of the afternoon passed in planning the arrangements. Hubert was very concerned about the discipline amongst our own men. Will they hold back and silently watch as Saracens file past unarmed and undefended? My father's caution to me about allowing the bloodlust of the crowd to be sated came to mind, but I ploughed on anyway, issuing proclamations through the heralds that the Saracens were not to be harmed by word or deed, on pain of death. I also ordered vast quantities of wine to be delivered to our men. If they were all drunk or hung-over, I reasoned, they would most likely fight amongst themselves, rather than threaten the fragile accord with the Saracens.

By sundown everyone in our camp was pretty much drunk. Mestoc and Caracois had returned to the city to prepare the population for its departure, and as the news spread through the city, and as the noise of our armies carousing grew and grew, so the Saracen garrison came up on to the battlements to see what was going on.

It was a remarkable sight. With the accord signed, our camp, sandwiched between the great walls of Acre and the serried ranks of Saladin's army on the hills to the east, was released from the tension of an eighteen-month siege into an orgy of drunken self-congratulation. The Saracens, watching from the battlements and from the hills, must have wondered how on earth they have contrived to lose Acre to us.

In the morning, I ordered the men to be lined up on either side of a path about eighty feet wide, through which the Saracens would walk. At a quarter to ten, on my instructions, the men fell to their knees to thank God for their safe deliverance, to thank Him for the successful capture of Acre, to beg for His mercy on the souls of those who have perished on the Crusades thus far, and to pray for His continued guidance and love.

As our prayers finished, and the men staggered to their feet, the gates of the city opened for the third time in as many days, and the now familiar white flags of truce emerged.

What followed was shocking. Row after row after row of emaciated men, women and children came first. These were clearly not the warriors we had been up against. These were the ordinary inhabitants of the city. The shopkeepers, the merchants, the fullers, the butchers, the clerks. I could not understand at first why their condition was so poor. Then I realised. With dwindling resources, the fighting men must have been granted first access to the food and water, and these men, women, and children were granted only the bare minimum to survive, if even that. I shuddered to think of the difficulties this decision must have posed for Mestoc and Caracois. I admired their single-mindedness in making the decision, but equally I was appalled at the state of these walking skeletons.

So were the men. The ribald cheerfulness of the early morning was silenced by the vision of these pitiful wretches before us.

Eventually the line of these figures thinned out as they made their way painfully slowly up the hill towards Saladin's camp.

Next came the Saracen fighting men. They were stripped of their armour and weapons, but they were still impressive specimens. They all looked straight ahead, dignified even in their defeat.

Lastly came the men who would be hostages. Mestoc, together with twelve hundred of his men, was to be held by Mercardier. Caracois, with his twelve hundred men, was to be under the care of Philip. They could be fairly lightly guarded; they were sworn not to attempt to escape. However, feeding and housing this number of hostages is likely to prove a challenge. For the time being, they will stay in our camp outside the city walls.

And then we moved on into the city ourselves.

The two palaces in the city had already been allocated. The Royal Palace was to be mine. The Palace of the Templars was to be Philip's. The city itself was to be split equally between the men.

Berengaria and I made for the Royal Palace immediately. I wanted to get her out of the summer heat and into the cool of the palace as soon as possible. She affects annoyance at my fussing over her pregnancy, but secretly, I think, she enjoys the attention.

As I stand here, I can hear outside the frenetic activity as the spoils of the city are divided up amongst the men. Once the loot is distributed, they will soon descend into another night of drunken celebration. They deserve it. We have come halfway across the world to take on a fearsome enemy on his own territory. And, for the time being at least, we have won. Thanks be to God.

13 July 1191

Acre

Last night seems to have passed off relatively well. There were a few minor fights over property, and I believe three people died in the fighting, but this is not too bad given the circumstances.

There was one noteworthy altercation, however. As part of the negotiated agreement, King Philip and I are each to fly one banner each from the walls of the castle. We are also to share equally all of the proceeds of the ransom of the prisoners and we will share the two hundred thousand dinars to come. I consider this remarkably generous of me, given Philip's relatively insignificant role in the surrender of the city. Nevertheless, for the sake of demonstrating at least some unity, I had agreed to the equal share.

It appears that last night the supporters of Duke Leopold of Austria planted his banner on the city walls alongside mine and Philip's. I was already in bed by this time, as, I believe, was Philip. My men took great umbrage at this, tearing down Duke Leopold's banner and hurling it from the ramparts down into the ditches dug at the bottom of the city walls. Apparently there was a small skirmish, but no one was killed.

I understand why my men acted as they did. They saw the planting of Duke Leopold's banner as part of an effort to lay claim to a share of the treasure split between Philip and me. Strictly speaking, they were correct. However, tearing down his banner and consigning it to the wilderness outside was a reckless move and I told them so today.

Duke Leopold is the senior surviving nobleman from the remnants of Frederick Barbarossa's great army, which set out so long before our own, but followed the land route through Constantinople and suffered such terrible losses in arriving here.

Duke Leopold will argue for his share of the spoils as the representative of the Empire. However, the facts are that he has barely five hundred knights left, and is not therefore likely to participate equally in the spoils. Even so, there is no need to humiliate him. He is a proud and noble prince, and he and his men have endured genuine hardship up to this point.

By all accounts, he is furious. I have sent messengers to him to try to atone for the actions of my men. But I fear that the damage has been done. Later in the day, I even sent messengers offering him a quarter of my share, but again my emissary came back empty-handed.

I blame myself for allowing myself to get soft. I knew that the first night in the city would be fraught with danger from the point of view of control and discipline. But, instead of supervising it personally, as I have been accustomed to doing for all of my adult life, instead I vanished into the luxury of the Royal Palace to attend to Berengaria and our unborn son.

It is not her fault; she would never have asked me to stay with her. But the fact that she is so precious to me, the fact that she is expecting a child, the fact that I cannot bear to be away from her for too long for fear that something dreadful might befall her, all these things conspired to make me neglect my duty to my men and my duty to my God.

15 July 1191

Acre

Duke Leopold has left Acre to return to Austria, taking almost all of his five hundred knights with him. I tried everything that I reasonably could to dissuade him from going, but he was adamant.

27 July 1191

Acre

I have been to more religious services in the past ten days or so, than in the last three years put together. Every church in the city has had to be rededicated, and Berengaria and Joanna have been insistent that we attend each and every service.

They are of the view that the way in which the Saracens defiled the churches and set them up as their own Muslim places of worship is a disgrace and an affront to God. I smile to myself whenever one or other of them launches into one of their tirades.

If only they knew how badly churches and churchmen, and especially churchwomen, normally suffer in times of war. And that is at the hands of Christians. But I keep quiet, for fear of provoking enquiries into my past misdeeds, some of which may not bear close scrutiny.

28 July 1191

Acre

The negotiations have gone on for weeks in a constant litany of offer and counter-offer, argument and counter-argument, thrust and counter-thrust. In the end, it comes down to raw power, and on that score, for now at least, I am superior.

And so I win the negotiations with King Philip.

Guy de Lusignan will be King of Jerusalem until he dies. Conrad of Montferrat will inherit the kingdom when Guy dies.

Given Conrad's reputation, it might be sensible for Guy to double his personal guard and employ a taster for his food.

But I win the negotiations at a cost. Philip is to return to France. He claims that he has fulfilled his Crusader's vow to the best of his ability. He made the vow when he was in full health, but now, incapacitated by illness, he cannot go on. He claims to have prayed daily on the matter and that God has released him from his vow on account of his sickness.

We know the real truth. Philip has been humiliated here and he cannot bear to stay. He has a greater chance of recovering his honour at home by moving quickly to secure his share of the inheritance of Philip, Count of Flanders. I know that he will move against me at home as soon as he is able. I have already dispatched a party of ten men to make their way home and warn my mother of the preparations that will be necessary.

Philip is already beginning to try to twist the facts of his departure. The rumours spread around his camp are numerous.

I am in league with Saladin, conspiring against Philip.

Berengaria has offered herself to Philip, so as a man of honour he must absent himself if I cannot control or satisfy my wife.

I prefer the company and beds of men, which explains why Berengaria offered herself to him, for with her, and indeed with any woman, I am impotent.

The list goes on.

I can only laugh at such gossip. They are the usual made-up stories of bullies and malcontents the world over, from time immemorial.

31 July 1191

Acre

Philip left today, leaving behind Duke Hugh of Burgundy to represent his interests. He claims to have left Hugh with sufficient money to pay for five hundred knights and for one thousand foot soldiers for three years.

But Duke Hugh came to see me a couple of hours after the King had left, to ask for a loan of five thousand marks to enable him to pay his men!

What Philip has in fact left the Duke is his share of the ransom, which has yet to be collected from Saladin, and there is no guarantee that we will ever collect that money. I felt sorry for Duke Hugh, abandoned by his own lord and forced to turn to another in order to feed his men.

I am not sorry that Philip has gone. Until recently, I thought that he, or more specifically, his men, would be an asset to the Crusade. But now I am sure that we will get on better without him. There is no doubt now about who is in charge, although it will undoubtedly drain my resources still further.

I am, however, concerned about what Philip will be planning back in Europe. Before leaving, he swore an oath reinforcing his promise not to threaten my lands or interests whilst I am pursuing my Crusader's vow. But as he stood there, with his hand on the Bible, I could almost see him thinking that it was a worthless promise, much as was mine, repeated several times, to marry his sister Alice.

12 August 1191

Acre

My first task, as the single leader of this now unified Crusade, has been to try to implement the terms of the accord that I struck with Mestoc and Caracois.

This has not been easy. When Conrad of Montferrat was confirmed not as King of Jerusalem, but as heir to the Kingdom of Jerusalem, he withdrew to Tyre to make sure that his city was secure. He took Philip's prisoners with him, and getting them back here has been troublesome. In the end, I had to dispatch Duke Hugh of Burgundy to fetch them.

Furthermore, in my negotiations with Saladin, conducted by a series of emissaries scuttling back and forth, it transpires that he had not authorised Mestoc and Caracois to agree to the two hundred thousand dinar payment. It appears that he may be as short of funds as Duke Hugh. I suppose this is only to be expected, since he has been in the field for almost four years continuously, and he must have drained his emirs and satraps of money.

So, I have agreed that the two hundred thousand dinars may be paid in instalments. The first instalment of one hundred thousand dinars is due in eight days' time, on the 20th of August.

We cannot delay any longer than that if we are to reach Jerusalem before Christmas. We cannot march directly to Jerusalem, as I am told that the land is too hilly. We will need to stay close to the sea and use the ships to carry supplies. Otherwise we will have a baggage train that is impossibly long to defend. Once we are closer to Jerusalem, we can strike inland.

17 August 1191

Acre

Just when it seemed as if the world was at my feet, it has all crumbled to dust in one single day.

I knew it would.

I have been feeling it in my heart these last six weeks, that feeling of dread. And the worst of it is that I have to pretend as if nothing has happened, to ignore the fact that my whole world has come to an end.

18 August 1191

Acre

My entry yesterday was brief. I could not bring myself to relate the story. I will try to now, even though my head cannot comprehend it. Most of the facts come from my sister, the Princess Joanna.

Joanna and Berengaria were resting in my staterooms in the Royal Palace here in Acre. Berengaria has recently taken to having an afternoon sleep, shortly after lunch each day. She has been finding the stultifying heat too much to bear with the baby inside her.

Berengaria was asleep in bed, wearing only a thin white gown, while Joanna sat on a cushioned bench near the main window, so that she might read by its light. They were alone; the servants had been dismissed. Two men stood guard outside, as usual.

Joanna looked up from her reading, when she heard two dull thumps in quick succession coming from just outside the door. She was not unduly perturbed, but rose anyway to go and have a look. Halfway across the room she stopped as the handle on the thick wooden door slowly began to turn. She stood there dumbstruck as a tall figure in a black hooded cloak moved swiftly across the room to clamp his hand across her mouth and clasp her hands firmly behind her back. He produced a silken scarf from inside his cloak, which he used to tie around Joanna's mouth as a gag to prevent her from screaming. He then pulled out a rope, again from somewhere inside his cloak and forced my sister across the room and down into a chair. Joanna said he was firm and strong but not unnecessarily violent as he then secured her hands and feet by tying them to a chair with the rope. He then crossed the room back to the door where he dragged the two dead bodies of the guards inside.

With Joanna secured to the chair by the rope, and gagged so that she could not call for help, he left her vision unobscured, no doubt so that she could later recount to me the full horror of what was about to occur.

Joanna described his movements as cat-like, quick and decisive yet curiously noiseless. Certainly Berengaria still lay sleeping on the bed, undisturbed by all that was going on around her, unaware of her impending fate.

She was lying face down on the bed and was barely disturbed when the man moved lightly on to the bed to sit on top of her. Joanna said that Berengaria stirred only lightly, presumably thinking that it was me coming to join her in bed.

The man reached down quickly to fix a gag round Berengaria's mouth and secure it with a tight knot at the nape of her neck. Then he produced another length of rope to tie her hands behind her back. She was awake now, aware that all was not well. As the gag was tightened, she began to struggle and by the time the man was tying her hands she was bucking like a wild horse in a vain attempt to kick him off.

With her hands finally secure, he then pulled a long knife from a scabbard on his belt. Joanna describes the knife as being perhaps twelve inches long, with a very thin blade. He leaned down to hold it in front of Berengaria's face, so that she could see it properly before putting it to her throat. The inference was clear: stop struggling or have your throat cut. She stopped struggling.

With relative peace established, the man shifted position to allow him to keep the knife at Berengaria's throat, whilst pulling her nightdress up over her exposed buttocks and prising her legs apart. She moaned in fear at what she thought he was about to do. The man withdrew the knife from Berengaria's throat and brought it to hover at her exposed vagina. He positioned the point so that it was just at the entrance. Joanna tells me that she thought he was just toying with them both and that she was astonished when he shoved the knife hard up into Berengaria's vagina and on into her womb. Three times he did this, with increasing ferocity each time. There was no way our son could survive that.

Then he moved nimbly from the bed and lay quickly on the floor in the Muslim prayer position. He muttered three prayers with his face down on the floor, then raised his torso so that he squatted on his haunches. He took the knife and drew it quickly and firmly across his own throat. He slumped to the floor, which was soon awash with his blood, mingling with that from Berengaria's womb.

It was thirty minutes before they were discovered.

Berengaria has lost a lot of blood but is still alive. Just.

Joanna could not speak for a day.

Our son is dead and I am lost.

19 August 1191

Acre

I have not really been aware of what has gone on in the last two days, or in what sequence.

A few impressions:

Berengaria was read the last rites three times in the night before last. None of the doctors attending her thought she would survive. But she did.

I have seen her, but she barely recognised me. Her eyes were blank, numb with pain. She could not speak; she just turned away from me and lay on her side sobbing. Eventually I left the room. It was not until later that I realised that every muscle in my body had been stiff with tension.

Joanna has started to recover, emerging from the daze of shock. I cannot help myself from wishing that the man had targeted her rather than Berengaria. Why could she not have thrown herself on him, or screamed before the gag was applied? Then my son would have survived.

The man was dead long before Berengaria and Joanna were found. The doctors estimate that he would have died within seconds from the deep gouge across his throat.

The question is: who is he? Why did he do this?

When the cloak was stripped off, he was found to be of Saracen origin, dark skinned, with the Semitic nose typical of Syria and Lebanon. Initially it was thought that he must be some kind of madman, acting alone out of a misguided religious fervour.

Another possibility was that he had been disaffected in his dealings with us. Perhaps he had been a ship's captain who had gone unpaid? Or a scout whom we had in some way offended? But investigations along these lines did not get anywhere.

Then, Hubert had the notion to re-examine the body for further clues. Perhaps blisters or calluses on his hands might reveal the type of trade he was involved in? All that was found was a small Arabic symbol tattooed on the inside of his right forearm. Because the man's skin was dark and because of the amount of dried blood that covered his body, it had been missed first time round.

Hubert told me about the symbol, but I dismissed it as irrelevant; I presumed that it was simply the mark of a sailor or similar. However, Hubert pursued it and eventually found one of our Arab scouts, who knew what the symbol represented. He was clearly terrified, but with a judicious combination of threats of violence and promises of gold, Hubert eventually managed to confirm that the tattoo was the mark of the Hashishiyyin, an Islamic military order. There are two strands to the order: one is based in northern Persia, the other, much nearer to us in Kahf in Syria, in the mountains south of Antioch.

This Syrian sect, known to us as the Assassins, is led by 'the Old Man of the Mountains', or Sinan ibn Salman ibn Mohammed, and they raise funds by selling the services of their trained corps of killers. Often these men are required to sacrifice themselves as part of the killing, and they seem to do so willingly in the expectation of heavenly reward. Apparently they are often under the influence of some kind of drug when they perform the killings, a drug called hashish. The knife they use is usually long and thin, and it has normally been specially blessed for the purpose by the Old Man.

If this man, this Assassin, was commanded to damage me by attacking Berengaria, then who would have ordered the killing? The obvious answer has to be Saladin.

I was shocked; we have established relatively cordial relations given that we are at war with each other. He even sent me some ice that he had had specially brought down from the mountains when he had heard that I was ill. I had had it tested of course, but it had turned out to be pure enough.

But there was no other plausible explanation. Attacking each other's leaders is simply not something that is done in the West. Even in battle, it is very rare for anyone of significance to be killed; there is an unwritten code of looking out for each other, even amongst quite bitter enemies, partly because of the potential ransom price to be gained from a live hostage. A dead one is worth nothing.

But it is different here in the East. The Saracens have a culture of targeting the leaders of their enemies. They liken it to cutting the head off the snake.

So it must be Saladin, or at least someone in his camp. What is strange is that they instructed the Assassin to target my wife rather than me. Perhaps they believe that a leader incapacitated by emotional pain is better for them than simply having one leader replaced by another. Saladin's objective seems to be to delay and prevaricate in the knowledge that the longer the conflict drags on, the more it is to his advantage.

If so, his plan will not work. I am more determined than ever to be ruthless in my pursuit of vengeance. Furthermore, I do not want to give Saladin the satisfaction of knowing that his scheme against Berengaria has caused her to lose our child. I have thus ordered that no one outside a tight-knit circle should know of what has happened.

If truth be told, I believe that I am still numb with shock. I cannot really feel anything at all. Berengaria is alive, but she may well never recover, and our son is dead. I feel as if

I am detached from everything, living in a nightmare. Surely reality and pain will overwhelm me soon?

And where is God in all this? I had been granted Berengaria and a son by His Grace. If they are gone, what is God's purpose for me? Why has He let this happen, when we are here doing His work?

20 August 1191

Acre

A terrible night, followed by an appalling day.

I have not really slept since the incident, which was now three days ago. I know that the doctors and Hubert are concerned about me, but my head seems locked up in an endless cycle of images of Berengaria being knifed, of my son, safe in her womb, screaming in agony as the knife pierces the womb and then his tiny body.

Hubert has proffered me strong drink, to try to ease my state of high agitation, but I have refused it. I know from past experience that strong drink can make me almost dangerously wretched. Given that that is now my condition when sober, I hate to think where it might lead me.

Eventually last night I relented, however.

I felt on the edge. I took Hubert's advice, and inhaled some of the drug, hashish, that they smoke in these parts. The purpose was to try to unlock my head from its cycle of horrific images and to enable me to relax, and hopefully, to sleep. It worked to the extent that I did drift off, but my sleep consisted of nightmares, images that were even more destructive and even more insistent than the imagery I am experiencing during the day.

By the time I surfaced in the morning, still influenced by the drug, and still exhausted by sleep deprivation, the Council of Nobles was waiting for me. They needed a decision on what to do in the negotiations with Saladin. The word is that he is going to be unable to make the payment of one hundred thousand dinars scheduled for today. Although that is not strictly true. He may well be able to pay it, but he is going to try and evade further, in order to eat up our valuable time before the marching season ends. He knows that for us to march out of Acre with two and a half thousand prisoners is well-nigh impossible. Equally, we cannot leave them behind. We simply do not have enough men to guard them and to garrison the city.

There is only one solution. Even if my heart and my head were not full of hatred for him, there would still only be one solution.

I ordered that the hostages be led out of the city in chains as soon as the last of the Noon Bells had tolled. They were to be led out to the plain to the other side of where our camp had been, so that they would be in full sight of Saladin's camp.

There, in line, they would kneel. And there they would be executed, by sword and by lance.

The barons looked at me, aghast at my ruthlessness. Even the most bloodthirsty of them seemed surprised by my implacable resolve.

'You have my orders,' I repeated.

I turned and left. I went out on to the highest part of the battlements and there in the hot sunshine fell to my knees to pray to God.

To pray for what? To turn back time? To allow me to die soon? To find some way out of the terrible massacre that was about to take place? My prayers tumbled out, one after another, with no logic, often contradictory, beseeching God and then blaming Him.

Eventually, as the bell tolled for noon, I was helped to my feet by the captain of the guard. I pushed him roughly away, and made for the highest part of the castle. Once there, I leaned over the walls.

Did I have the courage to jump and end the pain? I did not. Was it fear of the agony of death or was it fear of the dishonour my death would bring?

In the end, it was neither. It was the fear of everlasting damnation that cowed me. I now had an idea of what damnation would be like, and I had no wish to commit myself to an eternity of it.

Then the line of hostages reached the plain. The Saracens up on the hill saw what was about to happen and they tried to mount an attack, but it was easily beaten back. The wailing and the screaming were now intense, even at this distance of over a mile away.

And then the killing began. Two and a half thousand men, butchered in a few hours by perhaps two hundred of our men. Some were killed with a sword to the neck, but since the men were using regular swords rather than special execution swords, this often took several blows. The rest were killed with a lance to the heart. Quicker and easier. That is the death I would have chosen.

I maintained my vigil on the battlements until every hostage had been killed, and the screaming had stopped. I had thought that that would be an end to the misery. But I was wrong. Even worse was the silence now being punctuated by the occasional laughter and joking of my men as they made their way through the corpses, slitting open their stomachs to see if any hostages had swallowed precious stones to hide them from us. Somehow the laughter was more offensive than anything else.

Darkness was beginning to fall when I finally stirred. I marched downstairs and shouted instructions for the Council of Nobles to be convened immediately. As they filed in, I stood glowering from the raised dais that now serves as my throne. Once they were all in, I gave them brief instructions: 'Prepare the men. We march south to Jaffa in two days' time.'

They were surprised, although they should not have been. It will not be easy to assemble everything together;

the men will not be keen to leave. Acre is an oasis after the difficulties of life in the camp.

But leave we must.

I will take Jerusalem, and then I will throw it in God's face.

Sadly, at this point, there is a gap in the diaries. In other cases where there are gaps, it is because the pages in the diaries have become damaged and illegible. But in this case, the writing simply stops.

It is not altogether surprising, since we have seen the inner turmoil with which Richard was wrestling. His faith in God, his purpose on the Crusade, his will to live; all seemed to be at stake in this last entry.

The gap is of some eleven months, which was a period of intense and frenetic activity during the Crusade. Perhaps this was Richard's way of coping.

Richard set out from Acre with his army, leaving behind only a small garrison, with Berengaria and Joanna, to guard the city. They left on 22 August, and in the following days accomplished one of the most outstanding marches in military history. It was eighty miles of unforgiving terrain that faced the army when they set off. They had the sea on one side to protect them, and from which they could resupply each night, but immense discipline was required in order to keep the army together as one tight unit. That Richard was able to instil that discipline was extraordinary in itself. That he was able to do so with an army made up of a ragtag collection of diverse ethnic groups, all speaking different languages, and with no previous history of engaging in a common cause, was even more extraordinary. Especially since he seems to have achieved it without the benefit of any training, and following a period of military activity of a very different kind: the static siege of Acre over the previous eighteen months.

The conditions were very much against the Crusaders too. The heat was extreme, rising at its peak towards 40°C. Uncomfortable even in modern conditions, then it was almost unbearable, given that armour and chain mail had to be worn almost all the time. The soldiers and knights also had to wear additional clothing underneath in order to stop themselves getting burned by the hot metal.

Furthermore, the wells along the route had all been poisoned, so water was in short supply, and the Crusaders believed that drinking undiluted wine in the heat would send them mad.

In the camps at night, the Crusaders were set upon by tarantulas, which gave a painful but not lethal sting. The prevailing view was that noise was effective at keeping the venomous spiders away, so a system was established to maintain a constant noise of pots and pans banging throughout the night, interrupting sleep for already exhausted men.

However, despite these difficulties, the march was a remarkable accomplishment. Perhaps the acknowledgement of how many difficulties there were to overcome made the army unite in a show of discipline that was the marvel of the age.

The men marched or rode in full armour, tightly packed together, enduring constant sniping attacks from Saracen archers and occasional charges from Saracen cavalrymen mounted on small nimble horses. There could be no question of breaking ranks and fighting; the men simply had to endure and carry on.

The Saracens soon developed a further tactic to test the army's resolve. They started using snatch squads to capture small groups or individuals, who would then be taken to Saladin for questioning before being taken to higher ground so that they might be tortured and executed in the full view of their colleagues still marching down by the sea. Maybe this was Saladin's revenge for the executions outside Acre.

Whatever the motivation, its effect was galvanising rather than dispiriting. It made clear to the marching men that surrendering was no alternative. They had to get to Jaffa or they would die, and their best chance of getting there was to stay together.

The apparent impossibility of the task may have suited Richard's purpose. As we can see from the close of the diaries after the attack on Berengaria, he was in a volatile state, so the enforced discipline of this march was probably his mental salvation. But leaving behind Berengaria in a semi-catatonic state cannot have been easy.

Whatever the turmoil in Richard's mind and heart, these next few weeks were his finest hour militarily. Up and down the lines he ranged. Mounted on his huge white charger, clad in full war armour, he urged his men on, to keep their shape, to keep their discipline, all the while breathing defiance at the Saracen archers. One winged him with an arrow, which caught in the shoulder crevice of his armour. He reached up to break it off and left the rump of the arrow stuck in his chain mail for the rest of the day.

His reputation was at its height. He had only to feint a charge at the Saracen horsemen to cause them to scatter and run for their lives. This was a joke that never turned stale, and the men urged him to repeat it again and again.

This went on for sixteen days, with the Crusaders holding their nerve and their discipline, despite the appalling hardships. By this time supplies were running short and it was in the knowledge of this that Saladin elected to give battle at Arsuf. He could not risk Richard getting to Jaffa without attempting to stop him in his tracks. Letting his enemy march for sixteen days straight in the scorching sun was, from Saladin's point of view, a wise tactical move.

The battle itself was a triumph for Richard. Strangely, given his reputation as a warrior, it was the only pitched battle of his career. In Western Europe battles tended to be avoided, as they were too costly in terms of human life.

Here Richard was commanding something in the region of fifteen to twenty thousand men, of which about two to three thousand were knights. The Saracens numbered about thirty thousand men in total, including ten thousand cavalry. The battle commenced with a major Saracen onslaught in an attempt to break the Crusader lines. The lines held, just, but the pressure was so intense that the Master of the Hospitallers in the rear twice requested permission to charge to relieve the pressure. But Richard knew that they had to wait for the right moment. Eventually, triggered by two Hospitallers who could wait no longer, he released the charge. The timing was perfect and the effect was devastating. The heavy cavalry of the Crusaders mowed down vast swathes of the lighter Saracen cavalry, and, crucially, Richard was able to recall the charge before it went too far and became cut off from the main body of the army.

Attack and counter-attack ensued, but gradually the Saracens were beaten off and withdrew, and the Crusaders could resume their march to Jaffa, now only three days away. The Crusaders lost about seven hundred men in battle compared to seven thousand Saracens.

Richard arrived at Jaffa to find it largely demolished by Saladin's departing men, but it was of no great account. They made camp in the orchards outside the city and relished the prospect of the march on Jerusalem. Richard himself was keen to march on to the port of Ascalon to secure this too. But he eventually bowed to the wishes of the majority of his barons and they set about refortifying Jaffa, with the express intent of moving on to Jerusalem. Richard himself went back to Acre to collect Berengaria and Joanna, and to bring further reinforcements to the army at Jaffa.

It is tempting to speculate about Berengaria's mental and physical state, but for this period there is frustratingly little information about her. Maybe it was Richard's intention to keep her out of the public eye.

In any event, Richard spent October and November 1191 in preparation for the march on Jerusalem, whilst engaged in some extraordinary diplomatic manoeuvres with Saladin. At one stage, he even offered Joanna as a potential bride to Saladin's brother, Saphadin. It was almost certainly not a serious offer; for both sides, these diplomatic exchanges were more a way to obtain intelligence about the enemy, than any real move towards a negotiated truce.

This period also sees Richard involved in three episodes that suggest that, even by his standards, he was feeling unusually reckless, perhaps as a result of his grief for Berengaria and his crisis of faith. But what seems reckless to us now, seemed heroic to the men he lead.

In the first incident, on 29 September, Richard had gone hawking with a few attendants, when he fell victim to one of Saladin's snatch squads.

A group of Saracen horsemen attacked Richard's party and then feigned flight. Richard, of course, set off after them, straight into the ambush of a much larger group of Saracen horsemen. As expected, in keeping with his reputation, and with what we now know about his state of mind, Richard fought like a man possessed. Nevertheless, four of his party had already been killed and the situation looked desperate. Then one of the remaining knights, William de Préaux, had a bright idea. In Arabic he shouted that he was the King and how dare they attack him in such a manner. Of course, the Saracen horsemen swarmed around him and captured him, leaving the real King Richard to make good his escape.

Four weeks later, Richard came across some Saracen scouts and set off after them, in sharp contravention of the code of engagement, which he himself had proclaimed only a few days earlier. Six days after that he again recklessly took on an obviously superior force, citing an obligation to come to the aid of anyone under his command.

Were these three incidents typical of life on crusade? The third-party evidence suggests that Richard had gradually become more cautious or mature in his approach, and his diaries confirm this, but these incidents were a throwback to his youth. Was it just a coincidence, or was his recklessness fuelled by his misery?

With Jerusalem now tantalisingly close, progress was frustratingly slow. It took almost three months to rebuild the fortifications at Jaffa and to repair the castles along the road from Jaffa to Jerusalem that were essential to protecting Richard's supply lines. Striking inland meant that they could no longer be resupplied by sea.

But although progress was slow, it was steady, and the Crusaders were able to keep to the timetable that Richard had drawn up. Just before Christmas 1191, the army made camp at Bayt Nuba, twelve miles from Jerusalem.

The conditions were appalling. Torrential rain continually washed away makeshift paths and roads and caused significant outbreaks of illness. The poor state of the roads meant that it was impossible to get supplies through, and hunger again began to become a severe problem. To commence a potentially long and exhausting siege of Jerusalem at this stage would have been foolhardy in the extreme, especially with Saladin's army still lurking nearby and liable to strike at any time.

Reluctantly, Richard gave the order to retreat to Jaffa to regroup. The order was not popular: to come so close and be denied was heartbreaking for those whose ambition was to pray at the Holy Sepulchre and then return home. Therein lay the problem. Capturing Jerusalem was one thing; keeping it once the Crusaders made for home would be an impossible task without secure supply lines.

Morale had been sky-high when the Crusaders were within sight of Jerusalem, but it plummeted on the march back to Jaffa, conducted in further heavy rain and thunderstorms. Richard dedicated himself to rebuilding the fortifications at Ascalon, which he saw as the key to the success of the future Kingdom of Jerusalem. Whilst Ascalon was in Christian hands, it would provide a reliable supply base for Jerusalem, and it could provide a launch pad for potential attacks south into Egypt, which would be essential to keep Saladin pinned down, and away from Jerusalem.

In April 1192, the Prior of Hereford arrived in Ascalon to bring Richard the news he must have been dreading. Richard's brother John was usurping power in England, and King Philip of France was threatening his lands in Normandy. Given that it took a minimum of six weeks for news to reach the Holy Land, the situation could already be worse than when the Prior had set out.

Richard needed to act. He gave himself one more year in the Holy Land, but he also determined to resolve once and for all the issue of the Kingship of Jerusalem. The previous compromise with Guy de Lusignan as king and Conrad of Montferrat as his heir was simply not working. As the man who had lost the Battle of Hattin, Guy could not command the respect the position required and as a consequence Conrad was openly negotiating separately with Saladin. There were still two poles to which factions in the Crusader army could gravitate, so Richard's solution to achieving unity was simple: reduce the two poles to one.

Guy had tried but had been found wanting, thus Conrad would be king. Under his bellicose leadership, the kingdom would have a chance of survival after Richard left. Richard had the decision confirmed at a meeting of the Council of Nobles on 16 April. The idea, ruthless and simple, was a good one. Guy de Lusignan would be compensated by being allowed to buy Cyprus from Richard for forty thousand bezants, discounted from the original asking price of one hundred thousand bezants.

Richard dispatched his nephew, Henry, Count of Champagne, to Tyre to give Conrad of Montferrat the good news. He was quickly crowned and for a short while the Crusaders' prospects looked high.

But, only a few days later, he was assassinated on the streets of Tyre by two young men sent by the Old Man of the Mountains. Elaborate conspiracy theories abounded. Had Richard had a hand in his death? It seems unlikely, having just proclaimed him king. Had Saladin had some involvement? Perhaps. What is known is that Conrad had ransacked a baggage train destined for the Old Man of the Mountains only some two months before, and then twice refused to return the goods. So perhaps it was a case of retribution, pure and simple.

The conundrum was what to do next. In the end Count Henry, a distinguished Crusader himself and nephew of both King Richard and King Philip, volunteered to marry Conrad's widow, Isabella, through whom Conrad had derived his claim to the throne. The wedding took place seven days after the murder – there was no room for political vacuum in the Kingdom of Jerusalem.

To complicate matters further, Isabella was pregnant. When the Saracen negotiating team subsequently enquired as to the paternity of the child, they were told merely that it was the Queen's child. Their reaction was to be expected; one of them wrote to Saladin: 'You see the licentiousness of these foul unbelievers.'

The situation was not unwelcome to Richard. He needed a strong king in order to conclude his Crusade, and to whom he could entrust the kingdom once he left. If not Conrad of Montferrat, then Henry of Champagne would do just as well.

Encouraged by the sudden outbreak of unity, Richard pressed on, capturing Darum after five days of fierce fighting, and marching once again to Bayt Nuba. This time the weather was fine and conditions were good. The Crusaders paused at Bayt Nuba for a month, giving them time to secure their supply lines and send for reinforcements.

Saladin himself was deeply worried and gave the order to poison all of the wells and springs. It was a last desperate throw of the dice, gambling that the Crusaders could not survive without water in midsummer. Every day they needed four pints per man and twenty pints per horse. Normally, armies could sink wells to find water deep in the ground. But unfortunately for the Crusaders, Jerusalem is surrounded by acres of hard rock making drilling impossible.

A further blot on the horizon was the continuing flow of bad news from home, with rumours of a conspiracy between Prince John and King Philip. Underneath the surface, the fundamental problem remained the same: to advance on Jerusalem was to risk everything. Richard called a meeting of the Army Council and a contemporary chronicle records the exact words of his speech:

> *You will not find me leading the people in such a way as to leave myself open to reprehension or shame. Truly it would be the mark of an unwary man if I were to lend myself to any such folly. But, if you see fit to attack Jerusalem, I will not desert you; I will be your comrade though not your lord; I will follow but I will not lead.*

> *Saladin knows everything that is done in our army; he knows our capacity and our strength. We are far off from the coast, and should Saladin come down into the plain of Ramula with his host and cut off our provisions by guarding the ways, would not this, I ask you, be our utter ruin?*

> *Then, however, it would be too late for repentance.*

> *Besides, the circuit of Jerusalem, so far as we hear, is very large and, if our little host were to attempt to close it in on every side, our numbers would not suffice for the siege*

and for the protection of those who bring up supplies. Besides, if I were to sanction any such imprudence while I was leader, and if any misfortune befell us, I alone should be charged with rashness, and be reckoned responsible for the danger of all.

Further, I know for certain that there are some here (and in France too) who are most eager for me to act rashly, and lay myself open to some dishonouring charge.

For these reasons I do not think fit to show any hurry in the conduct of such difficult affairs.

Besides we and our people are strangers, entirely ignorant of the district, its roads and its passes. Therefore I think it better to proceed on the advice of the natives who, we may be sure, are eager to get back to their old possessions, and who know the country.

It seems fit to follow the advice of the Templars and the Hospitallers as to whether we shall advance to the siege of Jerusalem, or to siege Cairo, or Beirut or Damascus. If we adopt their advice our army will no longer be, as it is now, torn apart by such great dissensions.

Richard himself was keen to strike at Saladin in Cairo, figuring that to do so would mean that Jerusalem would then fall like an apple from a tree.

The decision was so important that a formal decision-making process was established. Even Richard recognised that pure military tactics, of which he was the undisputed master, had to be reconciled with the Crusaders' natural wish to fulfil their vows as soon as possible and then return home.

A jury of twenty men was set up consisting of five Templars, five Hospitallers, five Syrians and five French nobles. There were none of Richard's men on the jury, because they would automatically follow their King.

After lengthy consultation the jury delivered their verdict. They concluded that they should head to Cairo and lay siege to it. The French immediately objected, but their problem was that they were reliant on Richard for money and supplies, having long ago run out themselves.

Then, amongst all the dissension, there was finally some good news. Richard's scouts brought him information as to the whereabouts of an enormous caravan of supplies heading to Saladin's army in the hills above Jerusalem. Richard's response was as swift and as devastatingly effective as ever, capturing the entire caravan including four thousand camels and a large number of baggage horses, together with everything that they carried: gold, silver, money, clothing, herbs and spices, and weapons and armour. What a bonus for the Crusaders! It also meant that, for the first time for a long time, the French could finance themselves from their one-third share of the booty.

In the face of the French refusal to accept the verdict of the first jury, another council was formed and this time the process was even more elaborate. Three hundred men were elected, whose job was then to elect a further twelve men. These men then had to elect from their number a final three men, who had then jointly to make a final and irrevocable decision.

Again the decision was to march on Cairo. Again the French did not accept it, and as the army turned back from Jerusalem, the force fragmented. Richard himself was soon back in Acre, having left Jaffa with only a light garrison.

It is in late July 1192 that his diaries resume.

29 July 1192

Acre

It is almost a year since my last entry in this diary. I have just had Armande check the date. So much has happened since the attack on Berengaria, and yet in many ways it still seems like yesterday.

Berengaria still has not spoken. She clearly does not recognise me as her husband, although she sometimes allows me to hold her hand if I take her for a stroll.

She spends hours staring at the sea watching the waves roll in and out. The rest of the time is spent in church, on her knees, elbows resting on the pew in front, her head bowed as if waiting for execution. Maybe that is what she is praying for?

I had hoped that God might rescue her from her misery, that she might find some solace in prayer. But almost a year has passed and there is no sign of an improvement in her condition.

Superficially she remains beautiful. Her face is unchanged, as lovely as ever. But somehow, with no animation, with no spark, with no life in her eyes, the beauty within her has died.

Her womb is dead. There is no chance of children, the doctors tell me. There is no question of sex even. She goes through life without feeling, without any connection, least of all with me.

I do not complain. I have had no urge for sex since the outrage, either with Berengaria or with anyone else.

The more I think about it the more I think that whoever planned this was extremely clever. Berengaria was a softer target than me. And in hurting her, he has damaged me more than any mere physical attack on me could have done.

I feel obliged to spend some time with her each day, but it is indescribably painful to see the person you love so much reduced to nothing. If she derived any benefit from my visits, then I would be happy to continue to put myself through the heartache, but she does not know whether I am there or not.

Joanna and I have been discussing what we should do with Berengaria. It is now clear to everyone around us that she is not well. Still no one knows about the attack; they must assume that her behaviour is shock from a miscarriage of the baby. Certainly no one brings it up in my presence. It might be best for her to go into the care of a nunnery, where she can be properly looked after and she can spend her time in church.

Later:

For the last week I have been making preparations to journey to Beirut in the company of the Templars and the Hospitallers. If we can take Beirut, then we would significantly damage Saladin's ability to encircle us. If we controlled the coast completely, it would mean that Saladin would find it virtually impossible to supply his troops inland.

But these preparations have been interrupted. At seven o'clock this evening, amidst great commotion, a group of four men arrived at the city gates in a terrible state. Their horses were almost dead underneath them, and their clothes were torn to shreds. They had gashes across their faces and forearms. They had ridden straight from Jaffa to Acre, a distance of about seventy miles, and they had managed it in two days. The main routes, such as they are, are threatened by marauding Saracen bands. So they had often had to take routes through the gorse, which accounted for the torn clothing and cuts.

The news they brought was shocking. Saladin, emboldened by our temporary retreat from Jerusalem and terrified that we might take Beirut, the last of his cities along the coast, has attacked Jaffa, trying to ensure that he has at least one port from which he may bring up supplies and reinforcements.

I had left only a small garrison there, together with the majority of those who were sick or injured on our return from Jerusalem. If the messengers have taken two days to get here, the Saracens may already be inside the city. But equally it might take them five or ten days to get into the city. I am certain that the garrison will hold out as long as they can, waiting for relief. They cannot really expect to achieve favourable terms of surrender after the events of Acre.

It is clear we have to leave immediately to try to relieve the city. Henry of Champagne (I still cannot get used to calling him King Henry) will lead a force of Hospitallers and Templars on the land route. I will go by sea, and we will attempt to keep in touch en route via the use of flags and smoke signals. I have already sent seven galleys north to Beirut, and there is no time to call them back. We will have to make do with what galleys we have.

It is interesting how a sudden disaster like this brings out the best in everybody. There has been no hesitation at all in volunteering for either the land force or for my party to go by sea. The only exception is the French, under Duke Hugh of Burgundy. They had brought all of their sick and wounded here to Acre, rather than leaving them in Jaffa, and they cannot be roused to help us to try to rescue our men. I believe Duke Hugh himself is unwell, as no one has seen him for days.

We leave in an hour. God be with us.

1 August 1192

Jaffa

I stand here dictating to Armande, exhausted but exhilarated. Covered in gore and blood, but cleansed in spirit.

We set out three nights ago, in eerie blackness, as there was no moon to be seen, and at first we made good speed with a following wind. But as dawn broke, the wind changed and we were held up off Cayphas. I instructed all the men to kneel and pray for a favourable wind that we might rescue our comrades. There was no immediate effect, but eventually the wind bore round and we were on our way again.

We knew now that we were well ahead of the land force. We could communicate in basic terms with them, first of all with flags, and then as we became more distant, by means of smoke signals. They are held up for some reason. I suspect there are Saracen ambushes all along the route. We had expected as much, which is why we split our forces into the land and sea routes.

We arrived outside Jaffa late last night. It was still extremely dark, cloud cover obscuring whatever light the moon would have given. At first we were despondent; parts of the city were ablaze and the noise, which carried out to us over the water, was a familiar one, the sound of the city being sacked. The occasional pleading screams, followed by the peculiar punctuated cry that accompanies death. The occasional outbreak of laughter as Saladin's troops discovered some booty, or a grain store, or a woman.

We weighed anchor and waited for dawn to assess the scale of our loss. The boy on lookout at the top of the mast of my ship was the first to break the despondent silence, shouting that our banners still flew above the citadel in the north of the city. The men were revived by his shouting, but I was keen to keep a sense of perspective and told them: 'That is exactly what I would do if I were the Saracen in charge: keep flying our banner in the hope of luring us into the city.'

I resolved to wait and see if we could get any further information. I have been caught a number of times in the past year falling for Saracen ambushes. Then the boy at the top of the mast shouted again: 'Someone has jumped from the tower, from the citadel into the harbour below. He is swimming this way.'

We all watched eagerly as the man swam out to us. While he was close to shore he had to swim underwater to reduce the chances of one of the Saracen arrows claiming him. It was a tense thirty seconds or so as we waited for him to surface for breath, before quickly plunging below the water again. Once he was clear of the range of the archers, he began to swim on the surface, but the Saracens were quick to realise the danger and tried to put five or six archers in a boat to give chase. But, just as they were pushing the small boat out through the waves, it caught the swell the wrong way and capsized, spilling the archers into the sea. Through our raucous laughter and cheering, I could see the archers flailing about in the water. They could not swim, and they were terrified, until they realised how shallow the water was and that they could actually stand.

Finally the swimmer made it to the side of the *Esneca Regis* and he was quickly hauled aboard. It turns out that he is a priest who has been with the Crusade for almost two years. Through his panting breath, we managed to discover that the Saracens had finally breached Jaffa's defences yesterday and had butchered everyone left in the main city. Those left there were predominantly too sick or injured to move, for, as soon as it had become clear that the city was about to be breached, Alberic of Reims, whom I had left in charge of the garrison, gave the order to retreat to the citadel, the main tower in the north of the city. The priest told us that it was impossibly crowded, and all of those inside were petrified for their lives.

They had begged for a truce with Saladin, to last until nine o'clock this morning, in the expectation of relief arriving. Alberic of Reims and a number of others had given themselves up as hostages. I expect Saladin had seen no harm in the truce, as it meant he would take all the valuable hostages out of the city without the risk of them dying (and therefore losing their value) when his men stormed the citadel.

It seemed we were just in time. But we had to act quickly. The Saracens were busying themselves on the foreshore below the citadel, trying to fortify it to give themselves some shelter from which they could rain down arrows as we landed. We had to get on the shore before they could build up their defences. Already I could see them dragging timbers across the beach, no easy task in the heavy sand.

We had a brief council at which I issued my instructions. We had no time to gather enough small boats to bring us to shore in the conventional method. We were going to have to drive our ships right up on to the sand and then jump. Fortunately we had with us a man who earned his living as a pilot in the waters around Jaffa. He was able to confirm that there were no rocks in the water near to the beach. Our ships generally ride quite low in the water, so the jump should not be too bad, even in armour, and we had already seen how shallow the water was.

Of course, it was a huge risk. We were not expecting the ships to suffer any great damage from being beached on the sound, but they would be stuck there until the next tide. So, if our beach assault was not successful, there could be no retreat to the ships for a quick escape back out to sea. It was death or glory.

I ordered the ships to turn round briefly and head out to sea. The purpose was twofold. I wanted the Saracens on the beach to believe that we had given up and withdrawn and therefore they would not call up reinforcements. I also wanted the ships to build up sufficient speed to get as close to the beach as possible before running aground.

We could hear the cries of anguish from the citadel as they watched us turn and head out to sea. They were soon drowned out by the jeers of the Saracens on the beach. Looking back to the shore, I could see them dropping their timbers and making their way back up into the city, keen not to miss out on the plunder.

Shortly, we turned about again, and made for the beach at full speed. It must have been quite a sight from the city. We could not hear anything now, we were moving too fast. As we approached the beach, the men moved to the sides of the ship, crouching and bracing themselves for the impact to come.

The *Esneca Regis*, painted red, with my red banner flying atop the mast, was the first to hit the beach. The jolt was not as bad as I had feared. We were just thrown forward off balance by the suddenness of the halt. And then we were overboard, jumping into the sea frothing beneath us.

The ruse of heading out to sea and then charging back in, was, though I say it myself, brilliant. The beach was relatively undefended. Only a few desultory arrows came down on us, and our own crossbowmen on the ships went quickly into action picking off the few Saracen archers up on the walls. The first task was to erect some sort of defensive barricade, which we could use as a staging post in getting from the water to the walls of the city. Luckily the Saracens had done half the job for us, so it was the work of perhaps five or ten minutes to put up an effective barrier.

Now we could call in the archers and crossbowmen, who came ashore carefully holding their equipment out of the water. With them in position, we had covering fire to get to the stone steps leading up into the city. Now, all the rest could come ashore, while I deputed a band to follow me as we made for the steps.

The swimming priest was busy signalling to those trapped in the citadel that, upon my sign, they should break out of the citadel and join us. I wanted to get as many men as I could on to the steps leading up into the city. If I could get two or three hundred men there, before bursting into an unsuspecting city, then the element of surprise could be powerful indeed.

Standing there at the top of the steps, with all these men behind me, I felt alive in a way that I have not felt for a year. I knew that this day was going to be a success, that what we were about to achieve would pass into legend. I felt powerfully that nothing could go wrong. I remember looking down at my sword, Excalibur, in my hand, and knowing with absolute certainty that, for today at least, I was invincible.

With a deafening roar, we erupted into the city, with me at the head, breathing defiance and rage. The Saracens had little chance. They were fully engaged in plundering the city. They had no expectation of attack and were cut down as they stood, some without even time to draw their swords.

We were soon joined by the occupants of the citadel, who came crashing down the steps of the tower and into the streets. As soon as the Saracens fully understood their position, they turned and ran for the gates. Within two hours we had cleared the city of Saracens. The job was done and our euphoria was complete. There was only a tinge of disappointment for the men in that there was no booty to reward them for their efforts: that is the only problem when one takes back one's own city.

The Saracens had withdrawn, but we had no horses with which to pursue them. They are camped within sight, having abandoned their temporary camp just outside the city walls. I determined that we should take over what was, until a few hours ago, their camp as I was worried that if we stayed inside the city, they could easily bring up more sappers to try to bring down the rest of the city walls. If we stay outside the walls they will have to keep their distance.

5 August 1192

Jaffa

After the elation of retaking the city, we have settled down to the hard graft of restoring its defences. It has not been easy, with one eye permanently fixed to the horizon in anticipation of a renewed Saracen attack. It has also not been easy without adequate supplies; there is no building lime to be had anywhere in the region.

There are no horses anywhere, either. There were only three in the city when we retook it, and after an extensive search we have managed to locate another twelve, so we now have a grand total of fifteen horses in the entire force. They are pretty ragged specimens as well, so I have had to take them off the duty of pulling carts of stones, which is now being done by the men. We need to save what horses we have for the defence of the city, whether it is for sending messages from one end of the lines to the other, or for the commanders to ride so that the soldiers may see them.

Never was that requirement clearer than this morning. I had been receiving intelligence of unrest in Saladin's camp.

The loss of Acre and then his defeat at Arsuf had put him under some pressure from his own emirs, who had seen his aura of invincibility tarnished. To some extent, our double withdrawal at the gates of Jerusalem shored up his position, but then the loss of his great caravan and now being chased out of Jaffa by a vastly inferior force has increased this pressure, in particular from the Mamluks and the Kurds.

So they conceived a plan to sneak up in the night and specifically target me. They figure, rightly or wrongly, that removing me will greatly aid their cause. It is flattering, but strange. As far as I knew, Saladin had already singled me out by authorising the Old Man of the Mountains to conceive and execute the outrage against Berengaria. This plot against me now has made me question whether Saladin was in fact involved in the Assassin's attack.

This new attack was fended off, but only by the skin of our teeth. A Genoese happened to be going out into the bush to relieve himself in the night, when he caught sight of a number of helmets glinting in the moonlight a little way off. Racing back to camp, he raised the alarm just in time.

I staggered from my bed, pulling on my chain mail, my helmet and grabbing Excalibur as I went. Outside it was chaos, men stumbling blindly from their tents, eyes full of sleep, and disoriented by the noise and confusion all around. I assessed the situation quickly. We had perhaps two minutes to bring some order to our defence, or we would be overrun. We had only a few horses; there could be no question of a charge or a counter-attack to blunt the thrust of the oncoming Saracens. Today was going to be all about solid defence.

I screamed orders for the men to form up in battle line and to drop down on one knee to give them more support to withstand the charge. They were to dig their long lances into the ground to their side and to hold the lance at an angle to catch the onrushing horses' throats.

The crossbowmen were to be intermingled amongst these lances, and they were to work in pairs, one crossbowman stepping forward to replace the one who had just fired, giving him time to reload. The tighter and more compact our lines, the greater the chance of survival.

Even so, I did not relish our prospects, although I tried not to show it. Mounted on the bedraggled creature that passed for my horse, and riding out in front of the men to try to encourage them, I shouted: 'There is no chance of flight. Since the Saracens have cut off every route, to attempt flight would be to invite certain death. Hold out as stubbornly as you can, for it is the sworn duty of every man here to triumph bravely or to die gloriously. If martyrdom beckons, we will embrace it with a thankful heart. But before we die, let us take vengeance on God's enemies!'

Then, almost immediately they were upon us, with the great clash of arms and the usual chaos as battle was joined. The first wave of horses ran aground on the tips of our lances, and our men leapt on their riders to dispose of them as quickly as possible before the next was upon us.

Wave upon wave came crashing in, and the corpses of horses and men piled up ever higher. In the meantime I was busy with the other mounted men in cutting down those Saracens who had got through. They had clearly been briefed to target me, and to bring me down at all costs. But by the time they reached me, they were often exhausted or injured or both, and it was relatively easy work to dispatch them. I had had Excalibur specially sharpened, and it was slicing into Saracen necks and heads with force and bite.

As the direct charge waned in the face of our defence and the obstacle that the mounds of dead and dying now posed, so the Saracens switched their attack, swarming around us and towards the city to try to encircle us. I led our horsemen, such as they were, back up into the city, clattering and slipping on the cobblestones as we charged through the streets, as I issued instructions about what to expect and how to defend the city walls. The defenders performed valiantly, knowing that they were fighting for their very survival. There were no weak spots and eventually the Saracen attack faded here too. Soon the plaintive notes of their horns summoning them home could be heard drifting across the plain. Against all the odds, we had survived.

This evening a gift arrived from Saladin. A beautiful white charger, reminiscent of my beloved Arthur. There was a note accompanying the gift, written in perfect Norman French, which the messenger handed to me before disappearing.

Malek[6]* Richard,

My men tell me that you are not like other men. They have never seen a warrior so stout, so valiant and so skilled.

It is a shame that a soldier such as you is reduced to riding about on a piebald pony. Please accept this horse as my gift to you.

I should also tell you that I have certain information from our friends in the mountains concerning your recent difficulties. I am sorry for the loss of your son.

It would be an honour to receive you in person so that I may offer this information to you. We might then be able to come to an agreement about how we can share this land, which is so holy to us both.

You will understand that for us to meet might invite the suspicion of those in our camps who are not as weary of this war as you and I. We will therefore need to maintain secrecy.

If you would meet with me, give me a signal by riding this gift around your camp tomorrow. Then we can make discreet arrangements.

---

6   *Arabic for 'king'.

I retired to my tent with Hubert and Henry of Champagne, who arrived this evening by ship from Caesarea. His land force had been held up by Saracen forces and been obliged to turn back, so he had decided to come on by sea.

We tried to consider all of the implications of the offer. Hubert's first thought was that the gift of the horse might be a trick. He had heard some story where a horse had been sent as a gift to an enemy and had been specially trained to bolt back to its original owner as soon as it was mounted. I could not believe that Saladin would stoop to something like that, but I humoured him and let him find one of the squires to test the horse. Sure enough, there were no mishaps.

The real surprise in the note is that Saladin is happy to reveal that he knows about the attack on Berengaria. Given that only six people in our forces know of it – me, Berengaria, Joanna, Hubert, Henry of Champagne and Berengaria's lady-in-waiting – how is that possible? The two doctors who attended her have both since died.

The only explanation is that either Saladin was the person who gave the instruction to the Old Man of the Mountains, or he has been told about it by the Old Man. If he was the person who gave the instruction, why reveal that now? We concluded that he must have recently received information that he wants to pass on, presumably because it aids his cause in one way or another.

I have decided to meet with him. I know of the risks, but for some reason I trust his motives. He, too, has reason to fear the risks. After all he will be in as much danger as me. I suspect, however, that the real danger comes not from each other, but from others within our own sides finding out about the meeting.

I have put Hubert in charge of the arrangements. It is not an easy task. Not only does the meeting have to ensure the safety of both parties, but it has also to remain completely confidential.

In the meantime, I shall ride my new white horse around the camp tomorrow as a signal to Saladin, watching in the hills.

12 August 1192

Jaffa

When the plans had been agreed with Saladin's envoy, and when Hubert Walter was finally satisfied with them, I made a great play of falling ill at the banquet to celebrate the release of Jaffa. In order to provide some explanation for my absence for a few days Hubert had ordered one of my servants to lie in my bed in place of me, feigning a severe fever. No one would want to come near for fear of catching the dreaded fever. The servant was told that he was having to act as a decoy because Hubert had uncovered a plot to murder me in my sleep. He looked less than thrilled to be taking my place, but he knew he had no choice.

Hubert and I slipped out the back of the pavilion, and mounted our horses in virtual darkness. It took me back briefly to that time all those years ago, when I sneaked off at night to join the party sent to arrest Thomas Becket.

We moved out of camp as silently as we could, disguised in the cloaks of the Templars. Once clear of the camp, we moved the horses on more quickly, rushing towards our rendezvous. For me, this was the point of greatest danger, before we reached the Saracen escort deputed to take us on. If we came across a marauding Saracen band, we might be cut down indiscriminately. But we made it safely to the top of the hill where we had agreed to meet. They were already there, waiting, a band of eight Saracen warriors, led by Saladin's brother Saphadin. Hubert and I dismounted as they approached us. These were tense moments indeed. If there were to be a betrayal of trust, then surely it would occur now. This was their great chance to seize me.

They dismounted too. As Saphadin approached I held out my arms and gave him the Kiss of Peace. It seemed to break the tension and as soon as we had exchanged our Templar cloaks for the Saracen cloaks that they had brought with them for the purpose, we remounted, beginning the long journey overland towards the place where Saladin and I were to meet.

We rode through the night, making good speed, stopping once at the fort at Tal Gezer to change horses. Saphadin was careful to make sure that the hood of my cloak was up and that his men sheltered me, so that I might not be recognised. There are not too many blond Saracens in these parts.

By the time dawn was breaking we were just coming up on the hills outside Jerusalem. There she lay before us, shimmering golden in the early morning light. I made a signal to Saphadin that I wished to stop for a moment to take it all in. It was my first view of the city. I dismounted and stood for a while taking in the beauty and splendour of the place where Christ died and ascended into Heaven. I dropped to my knees to say a brief prayer.

When I had finished I turned to find my escort on their knees too, but in the Muslim style facing the rising sun, saying their morning prayers. I smiled to myself. How strange that after all this bloodshed it should come to this, Muslims and Christians praying together within touching distance of the site so holy to them both.

We mounted up again, and rode down into a city just rousing itself for the day. Butchers and bakers were busy laying out their wares. Wagons laden with fruit passed by, and everywhere the pungent smell of the East. What a contrast with my first entry into Paris twenty years ago, when all I could take in was the foul smell of sewage. Here, the air smelled of delicious herbs and spices.

And so we rode up to Calvary and the Church of the Holy Sepulchre, my objective for the past four years. The place where Jesus Christ was crucified for us, and the place where his temporal body now rests. We went in through the south door.

The church had obviously been cleared for the meeting. It was our understanding that Saladin was to arrive incognito as well, but we were an hour early. There was no one else in sight, and as Hubert Walter and I entered, our escort melted away. I made straight for the Rock of Calvary, and, in front of the altar, prostrated myself, lying with my face on the cold stone of the floor.

It felt strange to be in the place I had dreamed for so long of reaching, and yet under such different circumstances to those I had envisaged.

I wish I could say that I felt a surge of divine love, that our sufferings had all been worth it, that somehow I felt instantly close to the Lord. But I did not feel anything, try as I might. There was no blinding light, no revelation.

Soon Hubert prostrated himself too, and as we lay there in the most holy of all places, we silently contemplated our journey.

And then the south door creaked on its hinges, and in came two men. One was Saphadin, and the other was Saladin himself. We advanced towards each other, both with arms outstretched to give and to receive the Kiss of Peace. We then stood back to examine each other.

He is of average height with dark, saturnine features, with the Semitic nose typical of the region. His hair is dark still, despite his age, which I reckon to be about fifty years. He wears a beard, closely cropped, that encircles his mouth, covering his upper lip and his chin only. His cheeks are clean-shaven. He looks more like a distinguished scholar than a great warrior, but it may well be that his age is the cause of this. Clearly he is clever and wise, but he is also ruthless; how else would he have united so many different nations and tribes?

We smiled at each other, the inspection over. He began speaking in Arabic to me, pausing to allow Saphadin, whose command of our language is excellent, to translate: 'I welcome you to this holy site. I trust that you will agree that we keep it in good repair.

'I want to thank you for coming here to meet with me. I understand that it is a risk for you, both in terms of your physical well-being, which I can guarantee, but also in terms of your position with your own supporters, which I cannot guarantee. At least these are risks that we both share.

'I wanted to meet with you to discuss face-to-face the arrangements for a possible truce. Our respective ambassadors have been back and forth a good deal, and we have had some entertaining exchanges, but I think that for both of us a truce is now essential.'

I had smiled a little at his mention of our 'entertaining exchanges', remembering Joanna's horror at my offer of her to Saladin as a bride for Saphadin.

He went on: 'We are both exhausted by this effort, and it is futile to continue. You have pressing problems that need your attention at home, your army is now riven by faction, your resources are depleted and, even if you succeed in taking Jerusalem, you have no realistic prospect of holding it for any length of time.'

I bristled slightly at his analysis of the situation, but he moved quickly on: 'However I have much the same problems myself. I have matters in other parts of my lands requiring my urgent attention. I am sometimes at odds with some of my emirs. Keeping armies of this size in the field is, as you know, expensive in terms of money and supplies.'

He held his arms out as he spoke, suggesting that we were in fact just two simple men who through no fault of their own were beset by problems not of their making. But the thrust of what he said was true. In the current situation, unless someone were to make a calamitous mistake, or unless one or other of us were suddenly to be bolstered by a new and fresh force of significant size, then the result is likely to be a bloody and long stalemate. Although my army was beginning to leak men back to Europe, so too was Saladin's, as his men left for home.

He continued: 'It is not possible for me to agree a permanent peace with you. We can never give up our claim to this land, which is so holy to us. I understand that you will feel the same, so I suggest that a truce of three years is the best outcome.'

We had already been through all of this in our various diplomatic exchanges. This much was already agreed.

The sticking point was Ascalon. Saladin had been demanding it as the price of any truce, as he was desperate to have a port on the coast. Without it, he was hamstrung. It was for exactly that reason that I was unwilling to concede it lightly.

He carried on: 'As you know, I need a port on the coast, but I understand fully your reluctance to concede it. So, again, we stand at an impasse.' I shifted a little irritably from side to side. He must have sensed my impatience. 'I have a proposal to make to you… but it will require your goodwill.'

I was puzzled; what did he mean by this? It was my turn to speak: 'Sire, I thank you for your kind words and for your hospitality and escort today. I share some of your views about the respective situations in which we find ourselves, and I am as eager as you are to find a solution. But, we cannot give up Ascalon, in which we have invested so much time and money, without a substantial concession on your part.'

I held my arms out as I spoke, indicating that the onus was on him to propose a concession.

Saladin looked down at the floor, as if momentarily considering whether to go ahead with what he was about to say. Then he looked up and spoke, quite rapidly now: 'I have a piece of information that I believe is very valuable to you. The problem is, until I tell you, you will not know its value.

'So I will have to rely on your good grace. I believe that this information is worth to you the surrender of Ascalon. What I am going to do is this. I will give you the information, and I will rely on your renowned honour to decide whether you will agree with me and will therefore surrender Ascalon.'

I was surprised by this development, but after a moment's thought, I consented with a nod.

Saladin bowed his head gravely and moved towards me, taking my right arm and leading me to the front pew, where we sat, side by side. Saphadin took a seat in the pew behind us, so that he could continue translating.

Saladin turned to face me and said: 'You already know of the sect called Hashishiyyin, led by Sinan ibn Salman ibn Mohammed. I believe you call him the Old Man of the Mountains. You may know that I have had something of a history with this man. Twice he sent men to kill me, but by Allah's mercy, I was spared.

'Taking my survival as an indication of Allah's support, I raided deep into Sinan's territory with a view to eliminating him altogether as a threat. However, as you know, I was not successful. His mountain forts are virtually impregnable. It was during this period that, for some reason unknown to me, Sinan moved from trying to kill me to trying to warn me off.

'On one occasion, he sent a messenger to try to come to a negotiated settlement with me. The messenger was searched in the normal way, and no weapon was discovered. Since the messenger insisted on delivering the message in person and in private, I dismissed all but two of my most trusted bodyguards. I told the messenger that these two men were the men I trusted the most on Earth, and they could be wholly relied upon. To my astonishment, the messenger then turned to them and said: "If my master were to order you to kill Saladin, would you do so?" To my even greater astonishment, my two guards drew their swords and replied: "Command us as you wish."

'No harm came of it. My two guards sheathed their swords and left with the messenger. That, of course, had been his message, that in the end he could reach beyond any of my defences.

'I settled with him and I have never regretted it. No more waking up to find poisoned daggers on my pillow (which happened not once but twice) and no more sleeping in specially constructed beds elevated above beds of gravel, so that I might hear people coming. In exchange for my peace of mind, I pay him a small tribute each year, and he feeds me a little information from time to time.

'You will know already that his men were responsible for the death of Conrad of Montferrat, who was foolish enough to try to cheat him out of a caravan of goods destined for Sinan. Well, it turns out that Conrad had also been left money by King Philip of France that he was to pay to Sinan on King Philip's orders. But Conrad never paid over the money.'

Saladin continued:

'Sinan was robbed twice by Conrad. Once of the goods, and once of the money from Philip. For the goods he took his vengeance by killing Conrad. And for the money from Philip, he takes his vengeance by informing you that Philip was the man who commissioned the assault on your wife. I am profoundly sorry for it.'

He looked as if he genuinely meant it, his face creased with sympathy and his manner soft as if breaking the news of the death of a father to a loving young son.

I could not take in what he had told me, and half laughed, not knowing what else to do. I think I managed to stammer out: 'You're joking, of course.'

But Saladin shook his head. He was serious.

King Philip, my brother in arms, my former friend, my fellow king, had conceived and executed a plan of such evil that it is scarcely comprehensible.

Saladin saw that I needed a few moments to gather myself. He told me that he would walk around the church with Saphadin, and we would convene again in a few minutes. I nodded, I think. I could not order my thoughts.

After a few moments, Hubert Walter came to sit next to me. Clearly he knew; Saphadin must have briefed him quickly before he and Saladin walked off.

There was nothing to be said. We were both equally astonished. I could sense that Hubert was trying to figure out why he had not even regarded it as a possibility.

My thoughts were more with Berengaria. My beautiful bride, about to flower into motherhood, had been set upon and destroyed, and sentenced to a lifetime of wretchedness and fear. And my utterly defenceless son, the future heir to my kingdom and my lands, had been murdered in his mother's belly.

There was, however, a little sorrow left for me. Before the attack, I was a king on the Lord's business, with a loving wife and an unborn son, on the threshold of greatness, at the peak of my powers. Now I have lost it all. My wife, my son, God's love.

I could feel the shock turning slowly to anger. I clenched my fists, and roared with anguish. It was no brief cry for attention. This was the full-blooded guttural roar of a man who has had everything and lost it. It is the reaction I should have had a year ago, but it never came.

Three times I roared, three times the roar came back to me as an echo through the church, and then silence. I remained mute for perhaps five minutes, and then got to my feet, touched Hubert lightly on the back and said: 'Come on, let's find Saladin.'

We found the brothers examining the Stone of Anointing where Joseph of Arimathea had prepared Jesus' body for burial. They looked up and smiled. I went for a walk around the church with Saladin, with Saphadin walking to the right, so that he might continue translating. This time it was my turn to speak.

'I thank you, Saladin, for your honour in bringing this matter to my attention. You will be aware that it is difficult for me to hear of such a betrayal by my brother in arms. I will have to consider carefully what to do next.

'My instinct is to continue to pursue the truce that we have been discussing. It will allow me to return home for a period to deal with this matter. I trust that we can continue through our embassies to try to agree such a truce?'

'And Ascalon?' he responded quickly.

I had almost forgotten his speech about Ascalon. I was reluctant to give it up, but it is certainly true that Saladin had volunteered an extremely valuable piece of information. I thought for a second. Given that we were not going to be here to enforce the truce, we would have to rely to a certain extent on the goodwill of the Saracens. I made up my mind.

'I will grant you Ascalon, but only in the condition in which we took it. I will have to take down the fortifications we have erected. Otherwise my men will see this as too great a concession.'

He nodded, seeing the logic of my argument, but I went on: 'And I will ask for one more thing: that my soldiers and knights may come here to this sacred place, and pray here at the tomb of Jesus, that they may complete their vows. They will come unarmed, but they should be granted free passage.'

As Saphadin translated my words Saladin looked happy to grant this. He turned and stopped to take my hands in his, saying: 'We have an agreement. Allah be with you, and remain with you always.'

With that, he signalled to Saphadin to remain with us to escort us back, and then he turned and left quickly via the south door.

I spent the long ride back reliving in my head the events leading up to the assault on Berengaria. My small humiliations of Philip had added up in the end. Berengaria and Hubert had both warned me, and I had ignored their counsel.

But I had been in an impossible position. I could not have married the Princess Alice, even if I had not met Berengaria. She had been defiled by my father, who had placed a dying curse on me. But, I suppose, Philip may not have known of this. He may simply have seen his sister being set aside for Berengaria. Then, at Acre, against a backdrop of my much greater resources, he had been humiliated time and time again by his inexperience on the battlefield and in siege warfare.

Yet, however much provocation, whether intentional or not, Philip had had, the attack was still an astonishingly vicious plan to carry out.

As we plodded back through the sandy forests that characterise the land between Jerusalem and Jaffa, I contemplated what life would be like now if Philip had not crumpled. Berengaria would be full of life and fun. Our son would now be about five months old. I would have some purpose and resolve, and, I presume, I would still have my faith in God.

But I could drive myself mad thinking like this. The facts are these. My son is dead. I am married to a woman who is not the woman I loved and made my wife against all the odds. My lands at home are under siege from my brother and my enemy Philip.

What can I do to remedy these facts?

I cannot do anything for Berengaria, other than ensure that she is well treated. Perhaps she will return to me in time, but perhaps not. I cannot bring back my son, and I cannot add to Berengaria's woes by abandoning her to try to find another wife to bear my children.

What I can do is take my vengeance on Philip. That will now be my objective: from the time that I wake up until the time that I go to sleep. I will not rest until I have avenged Berengaria and my son.

18 August 1192
Jaffa

On our return to camp, again at night and again in the cloaks of the Templars, I took to my bed to validate the story of my illness, kicking out the servant who had been my substitute.

I was brought news that Duke Hugh of Burgundy is seriously ill at Acre. This cheered me up, and I ordered wine to celebrate.

20 August 1192
Jaffa

The news arrived from Acre today that Duke Hugh of Burgundy has died. I gave him what I thought was an appropriate period of mourning: fifteen minutes.

Then I emerged from my pavilion to announce that with this news my fever was gone and my temper vastly improved.

2 September 1192

Jaffa

Today we agreed the truce with Saladin, and the mood in the camp is buoyant. I have also managed to ransom William de Préaux, who so bravely shouted out that he was king when we were led into a Saracen ambush. He has had praise and reward heaped upon him.

The men are thrilled at the concession from Saladin to allow them to complete their pilgrimage by worshipping at the Church of the Holy Sepulchre. Some were a little puzzled that I would not be going. I replied haughtily that I would not visit it while it remains in Saracen hands. I feel guilty about the lie, but I have to keep secret the fact that I have already been inside.

There is almost a festival atmosphere as the men prepare for the journey, and I am genuinely delighted to see their anticipatory joy.

8 October 1192

Acre

We leave the Holy Land tomorrow to begin our return to Europe. I feel no sense of regret about leaving, only of anticipation of what is to come. Berengaria and Joanna left for Sicily last week.

One note of caution. Philip, Bishop of Beauvais, who was at Jaffa when I heard the news of the death of Duke Hugh of Burgundy, has apparently headed back to France announcing to anyone who will listen that I was responsible for poisoning the Duke, for ordering the killing of Conrad of Montferrat, and that I have instructed the Old Man of the Mountains to send Assassins after King Philip. O rich irony!

It is not actually a bad idea, but I will prefer to take my vengeance in person.

Apparently, Philip has given orders that I am to be arrested on sight if I am seen in his lands on my return journey. He has persuaded the Holy Roman Emperor to do the same. No matter. We will sail via Cyprus, Corfu and Sicily directly to Barcelona, and then proceed by land up through Navarre into Aquitaine.

I will be home before they know it.

18 November 1192

At Sea

We are sailing late in the year. The Roman writers tell us that no one should sail on the Mediterranean Sea after the 14th of September, but with improved technology most ports now stay open until the 10th of November. It is now already a week later than that.

I have chosen to travel back on an ordinary buss.[7*] Sailing in the *Esneca Regis*, painted bright red as she is, will only make me stand out. If, as rumoured, there is a large price on my head from Philip and the Holy Roman Emperor, then travelling in my normal style is too foolhardy, even for me.

The ship itself is much larger than the *Esneca Regis*, with two tall masts, and it is about one hundred feet long and forty feet wide. I have my own set of rooms, which has windows looking out on the sea. One of my first acts was to ban anyone from throwing the contents of their slop buckets over my side of the ship. The ship itself is supposedly capable of carrying one thousand men, but it seems crowded with the

---

7   *A cargo or fishing vessel used in the Mediterranean.

two hundred or so whom we have on board. About seventy-five of those are ship's crew, so my party is small indeed.

I am fascinated by the process of sailing, particularly into the wind, as almost all of our journey will be. Sailing with the wind is straightforward, but now, into the wind, we are having to tack backwards and forwards, hugging the coastline as best we can. It is difficult work, and dangerous. We take on local pilots who guide us through any particularly treacherous waters, and we always have a lookout stationed in the crow's nest, who can see, on a good day, about ten miles around us. That is normally about two hours' journey time.

The chapels along the coast have lanterns lit at night to show their position to sailors, but it is not an entirely reliable method; wreckers are known to extinguish the lights in the hope of luring unsuspecting ships on to the rocks. The crew, and in particular the pilots, also seem to be able to discern the proximity of the land from the way that the seabirds and, to a less dependable extent, the clouds, behave.

There is also a newfangled invention for use in low visibility to help tell which way is north. It is what is called a magnetic needle. If you put it in a bowl of water, the needle supposedly always points north.[8]* I think it must have been invented by a non-sailor, because at sea, the water slopping about in the bowl with the movement of the ship makes it difficult to tell which way the needle is pointing.

The journey is not comfortable, even though we have much more space than that afforded in normal ships. We have brought our own food with us, but it consists of little more than hard cheese, salted bread and cured meat. There is no hot food unless we stop at night and row ashore. In the sailing season it is possible to cook food on board, but the rising swell as winter approaches means that the ship is tossing too much

---

8   *If a needle is rubbed on a lodestone or other magnet, it becomes magnetized. Once inserted in a cork or a piece of wood, and placed in a bowl of water it serves as a compass. Such devices were universally used as compasses until the box-like compass was invented around 1300. Interestingly, Alexander Neckam, Richard's childhood companion, reported the use of a magnetic compass in *De utensilibus* (*On Instruments*; c.1190), the earliest mention of the compass in European writing.

to risk having braziers on deck. If one were to topple over, the ship would catch fire in an instant.

It took us three days to reach Cyprus, and we put in at Limassol, where we were magnificently entertained by Guy de Lusignan. It appeared that he is having some difficulty in impressing himself on the island, but that came as no great surprise. He is a kind and well-meaning man, but with all the personality and drive of a wet fish flapping about on the dockside. I cannot imagine what it must have been like to serve under him at the Horns of Hattin, facing the might of Saladin's army. No wonder they were almost all slaughtered.

It was also an opportunity for me to revisit the Chapel of St George, where Berengaria and I were married. Sitting there on my own in the chapel, I resolved to renew my vow to avenge her. Perhaps, when vengeance comes, she will be restored to good health and sound mind.

Then, we voyaged on from Cyprus to Rhodes and along the southern coast of Crete, to sail up the western coast of Greece. We put in at Corfu briefly, and mulled over for a while the prospect of staying there for the winter. Most trade passes through there on its way from the East to the West and back again, and, as a consequence, the island is a vital source of information about events in both the East and the West. It was there that the rumours about my impending arrest were corroborated, notwithstanding the fact that I am a Crusader returning home, and therefore in theory have the Pope's blessing to pass through any lands unmolested.

This news means that landing in Italy and travelling back the way we came is no longer possible. I had thought that the Italian route might be an alternative to heading for Barcelona, which now seems very far off given our slow progress against the wind. However, I have sent Hubert home by land across Italy. He will not be recognised, and it will be useful to have him at home before I get there.

What we will have to do now is to head for Marseilles, which is a free city, and take our chances on making a run across southern France to Aquitaine.

20 November 1192

Messina, Sicily

More bad news, this time gleaned from a ship that left Marseilles ten days ago.

Apparently, Raymond, Count of Toulouse, has bands of men in every port along the French coast looking for me, or for news of me. There is a huge reward being offered for information leading to my arrest. I am not quite sure how King Philip has managed to turn Europe against me so completely, but it is certainly making life difficult. I cannot land in Italy. I cannot land in France. I cannot land in Barcelona now that Philip has aligned himself with the Kingdom of Aragon and Catalonia. I cannot go back to England through the Straits of Gibraltar; the currents there all flow from the Atlantic into the Mediterranean and at this time of year the currents are faster than the fastest ship afloat, so we would forever be sailing backwards. Even the oceans are conspiring against me.

So, Europe seems effectively closed to me. I could winter here in Sicily and wait for the spring, but so much could happen between now and then, and I would be an easy target for King Philip and the Emperor as spring approaches.

On land, on a horse, what would I do in this situation? Well, I have done it many times on land. I would double back and find the weakest point in the enemy lines, and try to slip through his lines there. It should be no different at sea. They are looking for me up and down the coast of northern Spain, southern France and Italy. If I double back to Corfu and make my way silently up the coast east of Venice, I could then make my way across land to Saxony, where Henry the Lion, my brother-in-law and old friend, will surely give me shelter from his oldest enemy, the Holy Roman Emperor. There will be relatively little traffic in Corfu at this time of year, as shipping has more or less ceased for winter, so we may be able to get through unnoticed.

At least I know that Berengaria and Joanna are safe. They have landed at Naples and are on their way to Rome under the Pope's personal protection.

6 December 1192

Ragusa[9]*

We are finally ashore. When we spotted two galleys off the coast of Dalmatia, it seemed like a heaven-sent opportunity. I was able to hire them, at two hundred silver marks each, and we were able to disembark quickly from the larger buss into the smaller, more manoeuvrable vessels. It also means that we are not so recognisable; I fear the buss has left a trail across Mediterranean ports in recent weeks. I have left one hundred men on the buss providing cover. What is more, these galleys are much quicker than the buss; with one hundred oarsmen in each vessel, we can cover almost ninety miles per day. At that speed, I figured I may well be able to travel faster than the news of my movements.

But everything comes at a price. For speed we have sacrificed comfort. For anonymity we have sacrificed safety. When we were on board the buss it felt uncomfortable and unsafe. Once we were on the galleys, the buss suddenly seemed like a floating palace.

But we endured the discomforts stoically, making good progress until the fateful bora intervened. This fearsome wind is well known in these parts of the Adriatic, and we had to seek sanctuary ashore. We decided to make for Ragusa, but fell short, landing on the island of Lokrum, about half a mile out to sea from Ragusa.

I fell to my knees as we finally stepped off the small boat that brought a small group of us ashore through the choppy waters, while the galleys anchored in the bay to shelter from the worst of the storm. Lashed by driving rain, we climbed slowly to the top of the hill to see if we could establish where

---

9   *Modern-day Dubrovnik.

we were. After so many weeks at sea, I noticed that my legs had become weaker; so little exercise, and no riding. Eventually, we staggered to the top of the hill, exhausted by the effort of climbing in the icy rain.

It was at the summit that our spirits really sank. It appeared as if the island was uninhabited. There were no signs of any buildings, no paths, no clearings in the dense wood. Dejected, we turned to trudge disconsolately back down, when we heard the deep bass toll of a church bell. To my ear, it sounded like the bell of a monastery summoning its monks to prayer.

Joyfully, we half-ran half-slid down the hill in the direction of the sound. It must have been an astonishing sight for the monks to see ten men, five of them, including me, dressed in the cloaks of the Knights Templar, careering down the hill, whooping and hollering like children.

We were received with the quiet dignity and generosity that are often the mark of a Benedictine monastery. We were just in time for a hot meal, which we ravenously consumed, and we were offered beds or, as the storm was now abating, a boat to row us across to Ragusa.

Although I had fondly imagined myself as secure in my disguise as a Templar, it rapidly became clear as we approached Ragusa in the rowing boat that the city knew exactly who I was. They had come out in their hundreds to the port, shouting and waving to me. The oarsmen from our galleys had clearly come ashore before us and spread the news. Fortunately the plan of doubling back seems to have worked. Here, there was no arrest party to greet us, merely a collection of local notables and dignitaries keen to welcome me to their city.

Somehow they seem to have got wind of a story that, when the storm was at its height, I had promised a large sum to build a church on the spot where I finally made land. Presumably, one of the more imaginative oarsmen had made this up, for I had made no such promise. However, it seemed churlish now to refuse, so I pledged a generous amount towards the rebuilding of the ancient cathedral here in the city.

There was one small problem; I was now running seriously low on funds. Fortunately, not only is Ragusa one of the few places where I am not actively being hunted, but it also has a number of bankers, who are prepared to lend me money against the strength of my name. So I have been able to make good on my undertaking to help with the cathedral, which has led to great good cheer here in Ragusa.

As I dictate this, I reflect that entering the city in the manner in which I did, and then endowing the cathedral, does not really fit with my plan of flitting secretly across Europe.

I need to move on quickly, before the news spreads.

21 December 1192

Vienna

As the bora abated, we judged it safe to reboard our galleys and make north, heading for the coast of Hungary. I was hopeful that I might be able to travel through Hungary undetected, but even if I were identified, I suspect that I might receive a favourable reception there. Although King Bela of Hungary is married to Margaret, the sister of King Philip and the widow of my brother Henry, Bela is known to wish to remain independent of France. Certainly he is much richer and more powerful than Philip and is therefore unlikely to accede to his brother-in-law's every demand. He is also permanently at war with his neighbour, Duke Leopold of Austria, whose territory I am most keen to avoid.

But after only two days, the bora strengthened, and we were driven out from shore into the main sea, out of sight of land. At one stage, things seemed desperate, but I remained calm, confident that we would survive.

Then, after a day and a half of rough seas, we spotted land. The sense of relief was palpable. Land was our haven. But, as we approached, we could see that, far from being a safe haven, the land around here was in fact a dangerous threat. We could not simply hug the coastline and continue on our way. The tide and wind rolled us inexorably in, despite the best efforts of our oarsmen. The shoreline was not rocky or jagged but more like a marshy swamp. If we were going to be shipwrecked, as now seemed inevitable, at least it would be a relatively soft landing.

And so it proved. There were no serious injuries to any of my men, although some of the oarsmen were killed when their oars snagged on the beach and snapped, killing them in their seats.

But the feeling of relief at a safe landing soon gave way to confusion. Where on earth were we? Was this Hungary?[10]* Or was this Italy? We needed to find out where we were, and fast. The disorienting effect of the storm at sea meant we had no idea. The landscape did not give us any clues. The swampy beaches lead straight up into thick forest. There did not appear to be any roads, or indeed any people.

We had no choice but to set off in the direction of the hills in the distance, reasoning that where the ground rose, so the marshy swampland would disappear. We trudged through the dark forest for hours, occasionally believing momentarily that we had come across a path or a road, but soon finding that they led nowhere.

There were ten of us; we had left the ship's crew and oarsmen with the galleys. As the tide came in and the wind changed, they would be able to refloat the vessels and carry on their voyage.

There was some discussion as to whether to continue in our guise as Templars. Five of us were wearing Templar cloaks, and the other five could masquerade as our servants. But was this wise? Templars excite strong passions, either for or against. Perhaps it would be sensible to pass ourselves off as something less controversial. So eventually, we abandoned the Templar cloaks and I was to play the role of Hugo, a rich merchant returning from a pilgrimage to the Holy Land. The others would be my retainers.

---

10   *The medieval Hungarian Empire stretched all the way to the coast, incorporating what is now Slovenia and Croatia.

Finally, we stumbled out of the forest on to an overgrown road just in time, for it was beginning to grow dark, and the terrain looked like wolf country. With our weapons concealed (we were supposed to be merchants, after all, not noblemen), it would not have been enjoyable to continue traipsing through the forest in the gathering darkness.

When we reached the road, we had a decision to make, right or left, east or west. We tossed a coin, a Syrian silver penny. It came out left, east. How different things might have been if the coin had told us to go right.

So on we walked.

After about two hours, growing footsore now, and hungry, we saw the faint lights of a town in the distance. We were cautious in our approach. We still had no idea where we were, or whether a hostile reception awaited. I sent Baldwin of Béthune ahead, whilst we sheltered just off the road, amongst the trees.

He came back after half an hour, reporting that the town was quiet, settling down for the night. There was an inn that looked as if it might provide a temporary refuge, and there was no obvious sign of a guard waiting for us.

So on we went. The innkeeper was rather surprised to see a party of ten men rolling in so late. I expect that normal travellers stick to daylight hours. Nevertheless, he managed to produce a hot meal, some sort of stew. God alone knows what was in it, but we were too hungry to care.

As the food arrived, there was a little confusion amongst our group. Normally, as King, I eat at a separate table from those who are not of royal blood or high office, even if that means that I eat alone. I had spent many hours in recent months on the deck of the ship, eating alone whilst the men shared a table not far away. But this was the first test of our disguise. Would the men and I remember our roles? I did, and I swung my leg over the bench to sit at the table with them, sharing the communal bread with which we mopped up the stew. We dared not produce our knives and spoons to eat, as their value might give us away.

As we ate, William de L'Etang tried to engage the innkeeper. It was laborious work, involving the extensive use of hand signals, and some shouting of the few words we managed to identify that we shared. Eventually, we ascertained that we were in the town of Gorizia. None of us had ever heard of it. Venice lies to the west, Austria and the Holy Roman Empire lie directly north, and Hungary is to the east. We must have overshot the coast of Hungary. What bad luck!

We managed also to identify to him our need for horses. Fortunately here, as elsewhere, horses are so commonly traded that they are almost a form of currency in themselves.

I am fairly sure that one could turn up almost anywhere in the world, gesticulate that one needed a horse, and within minutes horse dealers would appear eager to do business. Gorizia was no different from any other place. The innkeeper whistled for his boy and shouted at him briefly, whereupon the boy disappeared.

Fifteen minutes later he was back with a horse dealer, who with his long face and pronounced jaw reminded me of the old adage that a man eventually grows to resemble his trade. Half an hour later, and we had ten horses all saddled up. They were not, it is fair to say, exemplars of their breed, but they would do.

The next thing we needed was a guide. We debated amongst ourselves for a while and then I decided to send a message to the local noble, ensconced in his castle up the road. His name is Count Engelbert of Gorz. I decided to send him, as a token of my goodwill, a ruby ring that I had purchased at Ragusa, once I had organised my loan. I had bought a few pieces of jewellery there, figuring that they might prove useful in situations such as this.

Again, Baldwin of Béthune was the man selected for the task. We were rather relying on the fact that the Count would be able to speak some Latin, as communicating with him via sign language would have been a much harder than signalling our need for food and horses to the innkeeper.

As we waited for Baldwin to return, the atmosphere rose to one of conviviality. The warmth, coupled with the strong local wine, made us forget for a while the danger of the position with which we were confronted. In fact, so convivial had the evening become, that when the door opened and Baldwin stood there, we had almost forgotten about him. Our hour or two of merriment had been only temporary respite, it appeared.

Count Engelbert, who saw him almost immediately, had treated Baldwin cordially. He had a good grasp of Latin, so they had been able to communicate well from the outset.

Baldwin began by explaining that our party was returning from the Holy Land and our ship had been wrecked within his territories. The party was principally one of pilgrims returning home, but included a rich merchant, Hugo, who offered this ruby ring as a sign of goodwill.

All was going well so far, thought Baldwin, as Count Engelbert leaned forward to take the ring. But, then he paused, turning it over and over in his hand, clearly mulling over in his mind what to do. Then, finally, he spoke: 'I thank you, sire, for your explanation, but I cannot altogether believe it. I am of the opinion that the man whom you describe as Hugo is in fact King Richard. I have heard recent reports that he landed at Ragusa and then swiftly set sail again. It would be a remarkable coincidence if there are two men of such wealth roaming about our lands at this time. I am under instructions from the Emperor to arrest all pilgrims returning from the East until we can ascertain their true identities.'

But then the Count continued: 'However, the King Richard has been remarkably generous to offer me this ring as a gift of honour. As it is a gift of honour, I feel that I cannot betray him. Therefore, I return the ring to you, and bid that you leave my lands at once, so that I have no cause to change my mind.'

As Baldwin recounted this news our mood of happy conviviality dissipated in an instant. We would have to move on straight away, back out into the cold darkness and unknown land. But, better that than arrest.

The innkeeper was paid, generously, and he guided us as best he could. Hungary was no longer a viable option; the range of mountains between here and there was too treacherous. We decided to head northwards to Bohemia where I had heard that the Duke is in dispute with the Holy Roman Emperor. If so, he would be likely to offer us sanctuary. From there it would be an easy trip up to Saxony and my old friend, Henry the Lion. But first, we had some three hundred and fifty miles to get to Bohemia and before that, we had to get past Vienna.

We would make first for Udine. Even in the sign language we were using, I could see the innkeeper conveying his warning for us to be careful. Udine is controlled by Count Engelbert's brother-in-law, Count Meinhard. Would Meinhard be as generous to us as Engelbert had been? Would we be able to rest at Udine and regain our strength?

As we set off into the night, I could not help feeling a sense of foreboding. Our prospects were not good. We were being hunted like boar in the woods by the assembled forces of the King of France and the Holy Roman Emperor. We had no real understanding of the terrain. We had no real sense of where we were going, no guides to help us and no understanding of the local language. We could communicate in Latin, but only with nobles and churchmen, who had all been briefed to look out for us. We were freezing cold, starting to fall ill, and we had no reserves of supplies for the journey, which meant that we had to go into towns to seek food and rest, when I would have preferred to camp and keep clear of the towns where possible. High-speed flits across the countryside to make the most of the element of surprise had become my stock in trade over the years, but this was a different matter entirely.

However, we had to make the best of it, and to trust that luck would carry us through.

As the night gave way to dawn, the gloom lifted somewhat. With dawn came a beautiful, crisp winter morning, and shortly thereafter we spied what must have been Udine, up ahead. We had decided to stick to our original story: we were a merchant and his retainers returning home from the Holy Land.

Our cover was good enough to see us through the city gates. It was a good time to arrive; the guard was clearly half asleep having been on night watch, and the town was beginning to busy itself with the preparations for market. William de L'Etang found an inn that could accommodate us. It was down a side street just off the market square and was less conspicuous than some of the grander establishments in the square itself. We took two rooms to share between the ten of us, and once the horses had been quartered, we collapsed, leaving one man to stand guard on an hourly rotation while we slept.

It was at about two o'clock in the afternoon when we were roused by Baldwin of Béthune, whose watch it was. He whispered urgently: there was a great hue and cry in the town. A group of soldiers led by a minor nobleman was going from house to house making enquiries.

It might just have been the normal business of the town; the authorities searching for a common or garden thief or murderer. But, equally it might not. Perhaps they were looking for us.

We sat silently; the ten of us who had all, in one way or another, distinguished ourselves as soldiers on the Crusade, now cowering in a rented room, waiting for discovery. It was a dramatic fall from grace.

We could hear the soldiers coming down our street. The man in charge was stopping and knocking forcefully on each door and speaking to the occupants in a tongue that was quite foreign to us. He seemed satisfied with each answer, as he kept on moving down the street towards us.

Finally he reached the door to our inn. A firm rap, three times. Just as it seemed as if the innkeeper was never going to get to the door, it creaked on its hinges.

Again the man in charge spoke, presumably asking the innkeeper if he had seen this or that man. The innkeeper replied in what seemed to pass for the negative in these parts, a sort of guttural grunt. The officer seemed satisfied and we could hear him turning away, as the innkeeper started to close the creaking door. We began a collective sigh of relief, but halted as the innkeeper's wife called out to the officer over her husband's shoulder.

The officer turned back, and spoke again to the innkeeper's wife, his voice rising over that of the innkeeper, who was clearly telling his wife to be quiet. The officer had his way, and soon he barked orders to his men, presumably to stay in the street, and we heard the sounds of his boots clumping heavily up the stairs towards us.

Baldwin took up a position behind the door, his knife in his right hand, ready to attack if necessary. I stood to receive the man as the door slowly opened.

'I bid you good day,' said the man standing there. He did not look like a native of this area; he looked more like someone from our part of the world. Norman, perhaps, or English. 'May I enquire as to your business?'

In the tension of the moment, and befuddled by lack of sleep, it was only then that I realised that he was speaking in our tongue, Norman French.

I stammered out the reply that we had agreed as part of our plan. I was Hugo, a merchant, on my way home from the Holy Land. I could sense his disbelief from the outset, but he allowed me to finish.

Then he astonished me, and my companions. He knelt on one knee before me, and said: 'Sire, I recognised you immediately as King Richard. You must be aware that all of the forces in the area are out looking for you. My name is Roger d'Argentan, in Normandy. I am married to the niece of Count Meinhard, in whose lands you stand, and as such I serve him from time to time as an officer. He has commanded me to see if I can locate you. His men, whom I command, are waiting in the street outside. But my loyalty, and that of my family who still live in Normandy, is to you, sire, as our Lord.'

I could not believe our luck. Perhaps we were going to escape after all.

I held out my hand for him to kiss. As he did, I signalled with my eyes for Baldwin to shut the door, so that we could form a strategy. We did not have much time. If we were there too long, Roger's men would grow suspicious and might come after him.

Soon we were agreed. Roger would return downstairs and continue his search. When it was over, he would report to Count Meinhard that he had found a group of pilgrims, but that King Richard was not amongst them. The longer he took, the more time he would buy for our escape, which we would make through the back door, gathering our horses before exiting the city at speed.

I thanked Roger effusively before he left, promising that, on my return, I would honour his family in Normandy.

Once he was out of the door, and we heard him rejoining his men in the street, we began to shuffle as silently as we could downstairs and out the back to the horses. These were tense moments, every sound and creak of a stair board, and every clank of a sword making us pause and hold our breath. But eventually we were astride our horses and riding out through the market, which was just closing up, with carts and horses streaming out of the city gates. Again, our timing was fortuitous.

As we reached the milestone from the gates of the city, I chanced to look back, and glimpsed a pack of horsemen thundering out of the gates in fierce pursuit of something. The chances were that that something was us.

I called the men to order. Swift decisions were required. They were certainly going to catch up with us, mounted on fine cavalry chargers, whilst we had only our workaday horses. But we still had one advantage and we had to use it. No one but Roger had confirmed a sighting of me here. So, if we split the group, with myself, Baldwin and William de L'Etang hiding in the woods, and the other seven men continuing to pose as pilgrims, then we could perhaps give ourselves some more time.

I issued the instructions. Baldwin, William and I, taking advantage of a turn in the road invisible to our pursuers, made off into the forest. About three or four hundred yards in, I signalled a halt and turned to see if I could make out what was happening. It was proceeding as I had thought. Our men were being escorted civilly back into town. There, they would maintain the pretence of being simple pilgrims returning home. I doubt that even the most malevolent of local lords would risk God's wrath by stooping to torture pilgrims who are following their Crusader vows, so I hoped they would be released in a few days.

Once the group was safely back near the city gates, Baldwin, William and I headed back to the road.

Now there were just the three of us. We were heading north into the Alps in mid-December. Our journey would be grim.

And grim it undoubtedly was. As we made our way north, at walking pace on our horses, the air turned distinctly colder, and to make it worse the stiff breeze whistled through our clothing and armour. We were back in our cloaks of the Knights Templar now. The fictional figure of Hugo, the rich merchant, had been discarded.

There were few travellers out on the road. Partly because no sensible person would attempt to travel at this time of year. Partly because the roads were awful. The roads were Roman in origin, in that they carved straight lines through the countryside, rather than following the contours of the land as 'natural' roads tend to do. But they had clearly not been maintained for hundreds of years.

In my lands, each local lord is responsible for the maintenance of roads, and they take this responsibility seriously for the most part. They recognise that good roads lead to more traffic, which leads to more people at the markets where the lords derive significant income from rent. But here, it seems as if the local lords, for year after year after year, have simply abandoned the roads to the wilds.

As a consequence, progress was slow, painfully slow, as we took care to avoid our horses stumbling in the numerous potholes. The few travellers we did come across were of little use to us. Generally, it was a farmer moving from one part of his land to another, dragging firewood or hay. We saw one monk, on a mule, but on closer inspection his robes were dirty and threadbare, and he moved off quickly when we hailed him. No doubt, he had been expelled from some monastery or other, and some time ago to judge from the state of his clothing. Either that, or he had stolen the robes from somewhere.

So it was a desolate journey. We passed the fortified town of Venzone eventually, reading the name of the town from the stone a mile out. Then we had no choice but to take what the innkeeper had described as the Val Canale, the pass through the Alps.

As we turned into it, the magnitude of our task became clear. The Val Canale is little more than a giant riverbed, perhaps half a mile wide, slung almost carelessly between sheer mountains reaching up to the skies on either side. The Val Canale is about forty miles long, we were told by a local priest in halting Latin. When he gathered that our intention was to traverse the pass, his eyes widened, he crossed himself and hurried away as if our madness might somehow infect him.

But, onwards we marched, our spirits rising and falling in a seemingly random pattern. One minute we would be cast down by the oppressive gloom of the mountains bearing down on us from above, and all we could think about was the cold, the exhaustion, the futility. There was the constant dread that a snowstorm would start. We could see snow falling in the upper reaches of the mountains, but it never quite came down into the valley. We were lucky, for if the snows had come the pass would have been cut off, and we would have frozen to death, our bodies hidden until the spring thaw. The next moment we would be chanting bawdy songs and bowling along as if we had not a care in the world. I recall Balardier warning me of this once, the hysteria that is borne of great exhaustion or great fear.

That night, we took refuge in a monastery at Moggio, where we were fed and warmed and given a bed. It was here that we acquired Einhard, a boy of about twelve or thirteen years. He had volunteered to guide us for the rest of the way through the pass. I had been inclined to say no when the monks offered him to us. How much guiding would we need in a pass with only one exit? But then, I thought, we could use his ability to speak the language, send him into towns for food and so on. So I agreed. Einhard was thrilled to be leaving the monastery. It seemed as if the monks were thrilled he was leaving too. He was a little too lively for the contemplative life, it seemed.

Einhard took his job as guide seriously, pointing out every sheet of ice, or sharp crag of rock as we passed. He soon learned to use his tongue a little less extensively, after Baldwin had a bad fall between the rocks and the ice and blamed Einhard for distracting him with his constant chatter.

Then, just when it seemed as if the pass would never end, or at least not before the snow came down the mountain and entombed us all for the winter, suddenly the mountains at our side petered out and we emerged from the pass, skirting the town of Villach and others, to find ourselves at Friesach.

The monks at Moggio had been scathing about Friesach. Silver had been discovered here some ten years ago, and as a consequence it has become a somewhat lawless town, full of the kind of privateers and ne'er-do-goods the Church professes to abhor, although churchmen seem to enjoy its bordellos and brothels as much as the next man. The monks at Moggio had warned us to steer clear, as if its licentiousness might be unsuitable for royal eyes. But, to me, it sounded like the right sort of place in which to lose oneself. The townspeople would be used to all manner of folk passing through.

It was in this optimistic frame of mind that we approached town. The monks had been right, the place was full of brothels and taverns, but despite its anarchic feel, there was still a strong official presence.

Taking our seats in a tavern, mopping up rancid-looking stew with stale bread, we were told that Count Friedrich of Pettau was out, on the orders of Duke Leopold of Austria, searching for men masquerading as returning Crusaders. Our spirits sank. I had thought that here, of all places, we would be inconspicuous.

The tension amongst us ratcheted up a notch, as the now familiar stamp of an armed guard smacked on the cobblestones outside the tavern. I looked at the faces of my comrades. Baldwin of Béthune, features drawn tight, looked exhausted and hollow-eyed, a shadow of the great warrior joyfully beating off Saracen assaults at my side at Jaffa just six months ago. William de L'Etang, probably the finest horseman in our army, sat at my side, shivering under his cloak with fever. I did not fool myself. I knew that I was not exactly looking in my prime either, and I could feel the fever coming on too. William and I needed to find some sanctuary to give us time to recover.

Baldwin read my mind. In fact, generous soul that he is, he even volunteered it as his suggestion, so that I would not feel bad asking. 'Sire, I have a proposal. It is clear that William and you are both suffering from the fever. You need to find somewhere to rest and recover. In order to do that, we need to buy some time, and I am the one who can do that. You and William should go on now, sire, with the boy and find a small village or farm to rest for a few days. Einhard can slip in and out unnoticed and bring food and supplies. In the meantime, I will lead these officers of the Empire a merry dance. All I need is some money to draw attention to myself and to throw them off the scent for a while.'

It was a typically brave and selfless offer. Even in my desperate condition, I felt blessed to have the loyalty of men such as this. I would never normally have accepted, but I am desperate to achieve the vengeance I have sworn for Berengaria. That must come first. So I nodded, stood with William and Einhard, clasped Baldwin on the shoulder as I passed and whispered: 'Farewell, dear friend.'

Up on our horses again, and out once more into the freezing cold of an Austrian winter. Einhard suggested that we move to his home village, and take refuge in the inn of his uncle in Erdberg, a small village near Vienna. I nodded my assent, thinking to ask only an hour or so later how far it was to this village. About three days and nights came the reply. I was sickened. We would never make that in our feverish condition.

But what was the alternative? Weak with sickness, William and I just plodded on, watching the horses step carefully along the worn-out road. Einhard was magnificent, a young boy looking after two battle-hardened warriors reduced to an abject state. We slept in barns, begged food from farms that we passed, and shivered and sweated as Einhard lead us calmly to his home town.

Three days and nights passed in a febrile blur, until finally we arrived at an inn in what must have been Erdberg. I collapsed on to the bed and remember little of the next day or so.

I woke eventually, still swooning with fever, to find William de L'Etang sitting up on the other bed, lacing up his boots. He looked much better. I mumbled a question about where he was going.

'Sire,' he replied. 'I am going ahead to Saxony to find Henry the Lion to see if he will send an escort to come and get you. We are just near Vienna, so it is not far to go now to the Danube. Once I am across the river, it should all be straightforward.'

I smiled feebly at his enthusiasm, and had little stomach for arguing with him. 'Thank you, William. When you meet Henry the Lion, he may ask you to prove that you are indeed who you say you are. When he was exiled from Germany for three years, he came to stay at my father's court. That was, let me see, nine or ten years ago. He was married to my sister Matilda, and took great exception to the troubadour Bertran de Born, who made up a number of songs flattering Matilda. Henry had to smile and laugh at the time so as not to look ridiculous, but he confided to me that he would quite happily skin Bertran alive. If you remind him of this, he will know that you have come from me.'

William was soon off, leaving strict instructions about my care with Einhard. I fell back on the bed and was soon asleep again, the endless days and nights on the road without sleep taking their toll.

Einhard came and went, bringing food and some new clothing, keeping the fire in my room stoked and emptying out the chamber pot from time to time. I was grateful to him; I could not think how I had almost refused to take him from that monastery at Moggio.

On the third day, it was noticeably colder. Einhard's teeth were chattering as he brought in more firewood. He was off to market, he said, although it was so cold he was not sure if it would be taking place. Without thinking, I said: 'Take my gloves, they are lined with ermine, so they will keep you warm. But make sure you don't lose them, boy.'

He smiled, picked them up off the table, and almost skipped out of the door. I was preoccupied. I was feeling much better now. What would be my next move? Would I wait for a possible rescue by Henry the Lion? Would he and William make it to the rendezvous in five days' time?

I did not realise then that by letting Einhard take my gloves, I had betrayed myself. In such small mistakes are great empires lost. A casual act of kindness ends in disaster.

The royal crest sewn into the fine gloves would look odd on a thirteen-year-old German boy in a small country market. So odd that they would attract attention. The wrong sort of attention.

I was not to know this at the time, however. A couple of hours later, I wandered downstairs to find no one around. I entered the kitchen and saw the innkeeper, Einhard's uncle, sitting on a stool by the fire, on which roasted a large, plump chicken. He invited me to have a glass of wine with him by the fire, and I accepted, sitting on a stool on the opposite side. I had not been so warm, or felt so strong in weeks, I mused.

But then this peaceful scene was shattered by the familiar tramp of the boots of an armed guard ringing out over the cobbles. It was a sound with which I had become wearily familiar over the past couple of weeks.

This time, there was nowhere to run. I stayed sitting by the fire, drinking my wine, watching the chicken roast, as the guard entered the inn. The officer came into the kitchen eventually and found me there, apparently at peace.

'There you are!' I snapped to his surprise. 'If you will send for the Duke Leopold of Austria, I will gladly surrender to him.'

The officer was taken aback, but disappeared soon enough, leaving a guard all around the inn, both to make sure I did not escape again, and to ensure the gathering crowd outside was controlled.

Duke Leopold appeared in due course, and the matter was resolved very civilly and with appropriate dignity. He formally announced that he was taking me into custody for my own protection as the relatives of Conrad of Montferrat have sworn a blood oath against me. I presume that that is how King Philip and the Holy Roman Emperor have agreed to manage the story of my arrest.

I smiled and consented, surrendering my sword to him. He knew and I knew that no guard is required once a king has given his word not to try to escape, but the guard remained, mostly to keep the crowd in check.

He had brought a fine horse for me and we trotted to Vienna in fairly good time. I was given some fine rooms in his palace and allowed to dine alone. I did not want to suffer the indignity of being forced to dine in public in enemy hands.

He granted me one other favour. Armande had been left on the buss when we transferred to the two galleys from Dalmatia, so I had no one to whom I could relate my story. He granted a clerk, Walther, who has been taking down notes of my words. I will give the papers to Armande for him to transcribe into my diary in the normal way.

Leopold informs me that tomorrow I am to be moved to Dürnstein, his castle on the Danube. I think he is worried that Henry the Lion may come looking for me, and Vienna is a softer target than the impregnable fortress at Dürnstein.

Unsurprisingly, Richard's diaries cease here for a time.

Armande was making his way across Europe to await Richard at Rouen. The courtesy extended by Duke Leopold of Austria of providing Richard with a clerk seems to have been withdrawn as Richard settled into what he must have known would be a long imprisonment.

On 28 December, seven days after Richard's last diary entry, Duke Leopold informed the Holy Roman Emperor, King Henry VI of Germany, that he had Richard in his possession. He was summoned to Regensburg, and he was to bring Richard with him. Duke Leopold obeyed, but then seems to have feared that Henry would abduct Richard, so he sent him back to Austria. After six weeks of negotiation, Duke Leopold and Henry agreed terms. Henry would ransom Richard for one hundred thousand marks, of which Duke Leopold would receive seventy-five thousand marks. Richard would also be required to provide the Emperor with fifty galleys and two hundred knights for his next assault on Sicily.

Meanwhile, Joanna and Berengaria were in Rome. Contemporary chronicles record that they jointly persuaded Pope Celestine III to excommunicate Duke Leopold. From what we now know from the diaries, it must have been Joanna who achieved this on her own.

Whilst Henry and Duke Leopold argued about the divisions of the spoils, King Philip of France and Richard's younger brother John were busily plotting. John's reaction to the news of his brother's imprisonment was typical. He immediately went to Paris to pay homage to King Philip to secure his support in taking over Richard's lands.

Richard's vassals in England would not be so easily swayed, however. At a Great Council meeting in Oxford in March 1193, they could not agree on what to do in this unprecedented situation. Eventually they sent two Cistercian abbots to Germany to try to find out how the land lay. The abbots finally

*found Richard on his way to the imperial court at Speyer.
Duke Leopold was escorting him there to hand him over to the
Emperor once and for all.*

*At Speyer, Richard was subjected to what amounted to a
trial. He was accused of betraying the Crusade by making a
truce with Saladin, of ordering the assassination of Conrad
of Montferrat and of betraying the Emperor by supporting
Tancred of Sicily. But here Henry had rather overplayed his
hand. Although he was the Holy Roman Emperor, it was an
elected position and his power was not absolute. Germany
at this time was a sea of shifting alliances amongst powerful
princes, such as Henry the Lion of Saxony, and it was not a
foregone conclusion that the Princes would toe the imperial
line.*

*Richard himself spoke at his trial to defend himself against the
charges, and his words clearly resonated with those gathered
to hear him. He began with a gibe at King Philip, whom he
assumed to be behind the charges:*

> *I know nothing that ought to have brought on
> me this anger, except for my having been more
> successful than he [King Philip].*

*He spent a couple of hours recounting for the assembled
nobles and visitors (including Hubert Walter, who had found
his way there) the true story of the Crusade, from the siege
of Acre through to the final truce with Saladin (omitting an
account of their meeting). He dismissed the accusation of
his involvement in the murder of Conrad of Montferrat with
contempt:*

> *I have never before shown such a fear of my
> enemies, that men should believe that I would
> do anything other than take him on myself, if I
> were so inclined.*

He concluded with a robust defence of the decision taken twice outside Jerusalem:

> *I am accused of not having taken Jerusalem. I would have taken it, if I had had the support of my enemies, to make sure that when Jerusalem fell, it remained ours forever.*

The speech was well received. Even the court poet to King Philip, William the Breton, was impressed:

> *When Richard replied he spoke so eloquently and regally, in so lionhearted a manner: that it was as though he had forgotten where he was and the undignified circumstances in which he had been captured, and imagined himself to be seated on the throne of his ancestors at Lincoln or at Caen.*

Richard concluded by walking towards the Emperor's throne and kneeling before him. His years of chivalric training at his mother's court produced a bravura performance that went down well before the Princes, the flower of German chivalry.

Henry, sensing the mood of the court, came down from his throne and gave Richard the Kiss of Peace, to thundering applause from the assembly.

But the glorious rehabilitation was short-lived. Once the Easter court had broken up and departed, Henry began to reconsider. The agreement with Richard was a ransom of one hundred thousand marks. He would be released when seventy thousand marks was paid over and hostages were given for the remaining thirty thousand marks. Hubert Walter and William Longchamps scurried back to England to begin the process, with Richard's mother, of raising the ransom.

But could the Emperor get more? He believed he could, and openly began courting King Philip for a rival offer. Would Philip (and John) offer enough for Henry to release Richard into Philip's custody?

For Richard this would be the worst possible outcome.

He increased his offer to one hundred thousand marks now and fifty thousand marks within seven months. It was a colossal sum, equivalent to a quarter of the wealth of England, and, not surprisingly, it won the day with Henry. An agreement was signed on 29 June 1193. By Christmas that year, Henry had received enough of the money to set 17 January 1194 as the date of Richard's release.

Then, just before the release date, King Philip and John put in a last desperate offer. They offered one hundred and fifty thousand marks for Richard now. Alternatively they would pay Henry one hundred thousand marks now and five thousand marks per month for as long as the Emperor kept Richard prisoner.

The Emperor was tempted and called a conference of the Princes of the Empire.

Nevertheless they held Henry to his agreement with Richard. Not only had they been won over by Richard's performance at court a year earlier, they also felt some guilt at the exploitation of a returning crusader. After all, Duke Leopold was still excommunicated for his sins in taking Richard prisoner.

Finally, on 4 February 1194, Richard was freed at Mainz. His captivity had lasted one year, six weeks and three days.

On 13 March he arrived back in England, landing at Sandwich.

It is at Canterbury that his diaries resume, briefly.

15 March 1194

Canterbury

How delightful to have Armande back with me again at last. As I disembarked at Sandwich, there he stood, modestly, to one side of the quay amongst the fishermen's baskets and nets. I made for him as soon as I saw him, and enveloped him in a great hug. It was then that I noticed how frail he has become. I stood back to examine him, drinking in the changes that a year and a half have wrought.

I stand here dictating to him a record of his own decline. His hair has almost gone, his skin is sallow, and any fat that covered his frame has dropped away. He has told me that he feels as if he is being eaten away inside, and has described the great pain he suffers in his gut, such that he can no longer eat properly. He suspects that he has not long to live. I admonished him firmly at first, but soon the truth sank in. I have asked him to stay with me three more months, whereupon he may retire to his family's lands with a comfortable pension.

Hubert Walter, of course, William Longchamps and other old friends were waiting for me on the dock at Sandwich.

I feel strangely reinvigorated by my incarceration. Now that it is over, I feel that I have to make up for lost time. King Philip and John have conspired against me, but generally my lands have held together well, providing a good springboard from which to fight back against Philip. He has taken many castles and some land from me whilst I have been away, but the situation could have been so much worse.

I came to Canterbury today to pray at the shrine of Thomas Becket. When I was younger, I would have scoffed at the idea, but with my release, I feel as if God is looking kindly on me again and, as a consequence, I am prepared to honour Him. Even if it means lying prostrate at the tomb of a wicked and unprincipled man.

My sense of God's renewed favour was confirmed when I received a letter here from Joanna. She reports that Berengaria is showing small but steady signs of improvement. She has begun to speak a little, and there are indications that she is starting to recognise Joanna. It appears that her memory is slowly coming back to her. Joanna suggests that I should meet with Berengaria again, to see if my presence triggers any further recovery. She warns against holding out too much hope that Berengaria will ever be fully restored, but I cannot give up all hope.

Joanna also tells me of how Berengaria and she were treated well by the Pope, and how he arranged an escort of cardinals to bring them to Genoa. From there, the son of my old rival Count Raymond of Toulouse escorted them to Poitiers. Joanna sings the praises of this man, Raymond of St Gilles, and asks if there is a way in which a union between them could provide me with some security from attack in my southern lands!

How ironic, that in a world where marriage is a political act, both she and I, coming from the most political of families, would choose to marry for love. I resolved to give my consent, but also to warn her that marrying for love is not necessarily a guarantee of happiness. She only has to see what happened to Berengaria.

But in truth, my agreement for her to marry Raymond of St Gilles was also a reward for a much greater favour she has bestowed on me. I heard, whilst in captivity, of the disaster of the marriage of King Philip. It was last summer, eight months or so after my capture, and the news of the calamity had reverberated around Europe. Philip had finally selected a new bride, Ingeborg, who was the daughter of King Canute VI of Denmark. Not only was she supposed to be very beautiful, but she also came with an ancient claim to the Kingdom of England through her ancestor King Canute of England. This claim might have proved useful to Philip if he could have kept me locked up. Joanna and my mother had heard news of this impending marriage, and immediately recognised the threat to me. So they came up with their own scheme.

Saladin died last March, about nine months after our meeting and two months after my capture at Erdberg. On his deathbed, as a final gesture of goodwill to me, he had instructed two of his guards to convey to me one final gift. When these guards arrived in Venice, they found that I had been captured. What should they do? They heard that Joanna was in Rome so they travelled south and passed the gift into her care to give to me when I was released.

Joanna, as is her wont, could not resist opening the gift. Inside the box lay an Assassin's dagger, with its distinctive markings. Saladin had kept the knife with which he had been warned off by the Old Man of the Mountains, and now he was passing it on to me.

Joanna and my mother concocted a plan based on this gift. Ingeborg had spent two years at my mother's court, being educated in French manners and customs, expressly so that her father could marry her off for political advantage in French lands. As a result, my mother was perfectly placed to write to Ingeborg to congratulate her on her forthcoming nuptials and to offer some final pieces of advice about matrimony.

Ingeborg would have been aware already of the need to show to the assembled crowd on her wedding night the evidence that her virginity had been lost, with a display of bloodied sheets. But sometimes there is no blood, my mother advised, so she must be prepared to nick her finger with a knife to provide the required proof. And with the letter my mother enclosed the Assassin's knife, which she claimed had been specially blessed for fertility by the Pope. Make sure that you leave the knife under the pillow on your wedding night, she wrote. The crowds will not wait, she warned.

And so it all fell gloriously into place. I had heard even in captivity the extraordinary story of Philip's marriage to Ingeborg, and how he repudiated her halfway through their wedding night, without giving any explanation. The stories coursing through Europe had been that she must have had some terrible deformity that was only uncovered when she was naked.

The truth was much more prosaic. The poor girl had simply followed her mentor's advice. When Philip saw the knife, his worst fears were apparently realised. He was convinced, even before this, that the Old Man of the Mountains was now in my pay. Seeing the Assassin's knife, placed in his marital bed by his new bride, evidently sparked an extreme paranoiac breakdown.

Ingeborg was repudiated and the marriage was annulled three months later.

I felt sorry for Ingeborg, but I could not help but laugh. Part of my vengeance was being wrought. All praise to my sister and my mother for such an ingenious plot!

Tomorrow, my mother and I set out for London. The first signs of spring are in the air. The whispers are that the unusually warm sunshine is a sign of God's approbation of my return.

17 March 1194
London

Today we attended a service of thanksgiving for my safe homecoming from the Crusade and from captivity. It was held at St Paul's Cathedral, and was a wondrous celebration. The crowds were huge as we processed afterwards down the Strand to Westminster.

19 March 1194
Bury St Edmunds

I am tiring slightly of all the ceremonial, itching as I am to get back into action. My mother and Hubert Walter tell me it is necessary. We are still raising the second part of the ransom money. But I am keen to get on to subduing those parts of the country that are still holding out for John. Nottingham is the most important.

Firstly I have to be seen to be paying my dues. Today I paid a visit to the shrine of St Edmund the Martyr at the abbey here in Bury St Edmunds.

24 March 1194
Nottingham

The castle here is a disappointment. I had heard great things about it, but it has fallen to us in a matter of days. I am pleased that we now have it under our control, but it will need to be substantially rebuilt if it is to be effective in controlling this area. To be fair, the defendants of the castle did not really have their hearts in the job, certainly not after the Earl of Chester hanged a couple of those he had captured, from gallows set up just outside the castle.

I spent a couple of days hunting boar in Sherwood Forest. I am trying to ride more, to regain some of the strength I lost in my captivity. Although I was well treated, I was not allowed to ride. Not out of fear that I might try to escape, but for fear that I might injure myself. I was much less valuable to my captors dead.

So the hunting of boar seems a good way to try to build up my strength. But Sherwood is a curious forest, so dark and gloomy in places, with a mysterious atmosphere. Locals aver that it is the haunt of a band of outlaws, but in two days we did not see them. I did, however, have a strange sensation of being watched the entire time we were in the forest.

11 May 1194
Portsmouth

We have been here for three weeks now, preparing the fleet that will take us to France. I have been occupied with the preparations, but my heart has been lifted inexorably by a letter received yesterday from Joanna.

Armande has copied it out. It reads:

My dear lord and brother, Richard.

I bring you news of your beloved wife, Berengaria. I feel confident in saying that I believe that she is now recovering well from her ordeal.

She is able to talk normally now, and her memory is almost what it was before. She is unable to speak of any of the events in the Holy Land, but she is seeking comfort in her faith. She spends two or three hours a day in prayer.

Physically she is well. Of course, the wounds to her remain grievous. She is certainly unable to bear children, and she may no longer be able to have intimate relations. But her skin is clear and soft, and her eyes have regained some of the spark that they had before, although they can drift off into great sadness at a moment's notice. The sound of children playing delights her, but the sound of a baby crying catches her like a stab to the heart.

So, be assured that she is making progress: still fragile, but certainly stronger than before. I do believe that she may soon be well enough to receive a visit from you.

Your loving sister and obedient servant, Joanna.

Progress, indeed. We are moving forward again.

I had thought I would have to wait until we meet in Heaven to get my beloved wife back. Maybe Berengaria and I will eventually be reunited in love here on Earth after all.

And that is where Richard's diaries finish. The records show that Armande died on the journey from Portsmouth to Barfleur. He was buried in the traditional way at sea, having been sewn into his hammock with two cannonballs for weight.

There are no further diaries of the type we have been reading. Presumably Richard missed the companionable presence of Armande, and could not find anyone to replace him. Or perhaps he chose not to replace him, out of respect for the man who had served him so well.

There is, however, one further piece to the jigsaw of Richard's life. Tucked into the back of the last of the diaries is a letter from Richard to Berengaria. It was written from his bed in the castle of Châlus-Chabrol in Limousin, when he knew he was dying.

At the close of the diaries, Richard still had five years to live, and they were spent in campaigning vigorously against King Philip all over France, recovering the lands that Philip had seized from him when Richard was in captivity. The years were a story of slow but steady gains, culminating in Richard's building of the great castle Château Gaillard, in Normandy. In its construction Richard brought to bear all of his experience of siege warfare. This was to be his legacy, his lasting monument. It was finished shortly before he died in 1199.

Richard himself best tells the story of his death; his letter to Berengaria from his deathbed is evocative of his diaries in its frankness, and it is with this letter that this volume will close.

31 March 1199

Châlus-Chabrol

My dearest Berengaria,

I write this from our camp just outside the castle of Châlus-Chabrol.

We arrived here five days ago and I thought it would be a fairly routine operation against the Viscount of Limoges. It is the type of action I have carried out a thousand times before.

In fact, things were going so well that we had a lively evening dinner, in my pavilion. Mercardier, whom I know is not to your taste, was in good form for once, regaling us with stories from the time when we were on crusade and he was charged with keeping order in my French lands. Not many of the stories would be suitable for your ear, my love, but he kept us all well entertained.

As dinner wound down, I thought I would take one last look at how the siege was progressing before night fell. It might also be a chance to practise the crossbow, of which, as you know, I am most fond.

There was remarkably little happening. The defendants appeared to be on the verge of giving up, and we were reluctant to continue bombarding the castle, as any damage would have to be repaired when the castle becomes ours in a few days.

The only activity came from a man hopping about on the battlements, screaming insults at me. At least, that is what I assumed he was doing. We could not hear him as the wind was in the wrong direction. I was amused by his antics at first, and pushed down the heavy metal shield held by my bearer, so that I might see him properly. I was wearing my helmet, but I had on only a light chain mail.

I held my hands up to applaud him mockingly. It seemed only to enrage him further, which in turn amused me.

Then Mercardier offered me my crossbow, saying: 'With him dancing around like that, I'll wager you a silver mark that you cannot hit him, sire.'

Fuelled by a glass or two of wine, and in good cheer, this seemed like an amusing after-dinner bet. I took Mercardier's outstretched hand: 'You're on.'

I ordered my shield-bearer to stand back to give me more room, then took the crossbow, aimed quickly and loosed off a sighter. Not bad. It struck the wall three feet to the right of the man. For a moment, he looked startled. Then it seemed to drive him to even greater heights of agitation. He ducked down beneath the wall and reappeared, holding up as a shield a large frying pan!

Mercardier and I were beside ourselves with laughter, doubled up, finding it hard to catch our breath.

Then, just as it seemed as if I would not be able to stop laughing, it got worse. He bent down again and picked up a crossbow, which must have been lying at his feet. He clearly was no expert, fumbling with the heavy weapon, but eventually he brought it up to his shoulder. By this time, Mercardier and I were standing there openly clapping his efforts. I felt at no risk; the man obviously had no idea how to operate and aim a crossbow. In fact, I felt nothing but the joy that uninhibited laughter brings.

And then, he loosed off a bolt from the crossbow, and with my arms raised high above my head in applause, I was just a little too late in retreating behind my shield-bearer. As I moved to duck in behind the shield, I was still confident that there was no way an amateur could be accurate over a distance of three hundred and thirty feet. But, in the moments before my head ducked behind the shield, I realised that I was wrong. The bolt was coming in my direction. I tried to accelerate, but my boots scrabbled and slipped in the loose gravel.

And then, suddenly, there it was, a crossbow bolt sticking out of the back of my left shoulder. I was still laughing. This was not unknown. I have often had arrows or bolts stuck in my armour. One just plucks them out. After all, that is what chain mail is for. Mostly the mail takes the brunt of the force, and leaves just a scratch or a cut.

I reached up with my right arm to pull the bolt from my shoulder. It came away in my hand, and it was only after a second or so that I saw that there was no bolt head on the end of it. As I realised that the head must still be stuck in my chain mail, the pain suddenly hit. I dropped to the floor, now in agony. The bolt head was not in my chain mail. It was in my shoulder.

Mercardier quickly understood what had happened and was swiftly at my side to help me up. At this stage, although in pain, I was not really concerned. Four years ago, I had a bad injury just above the knee, when my chain mail rode up. I felt sure that this bolt would not prove more serious than that.

It was not until I was back in the pavilion, with the chain mail lifted over my head, that I could tell from the ominous silence of the men with me that the injury was more serious than I had thought. Mercardier ordered one of the men to find a barber surgeon.

I will not tire you, my dear, with the details of how the barber surgeon tried to extract the bolt. But it is fair to say that his skill was not great. He was summoned from the local town, and I suspect that he had not had great experience with the removal of bolts and arrows. My men held me down, as he thrashed about in my shoulder. I held a leather bit between my teeth, and I will not lie to you, my love, the agony was intense.

Eventually he was finished and sewed up the skin. Even through the haze of pain and brandy (I was on my second flask by now), I could tell that Mercardier was concerned by the quality of his work. No doubt the muscles in my shoulder had been torn or cut, but at least it was my left shoulder. My sword arm is my right arm. As long as it did not go gangrenous, I would still be active.

It was a long, long night. The pain in my shoulder was excruciating, and with every stab I wondered if that was torn muscle screaming, or the first sign of gangrene setting in. I have seen so many cases of soldiers with relatively mild injuries suddenly have their leg or arm turn black or blue. If the limb is not amputated in time, death follows fairly quickly.

Remember the case of my captor, Duke Leopold of Austria? He fell from his horse and had his foot crushed only days before we were due to deliver a part of the ransom to him. The foot rapidly turned gangrenous. Poor Leopold, he could find no one in his entourage with sufficient heart to perform the necessary operation. Even his son Frederick refused. They did not believe the gangrene was so dangerous. Duke Leopold's experience on the Crusade had taught him otherwise.

Eventually he did the amputation himself, with the aid of a servant. He had to hold an axe to his foot, while the servant drove a mallet into the axe. Three blows it took, before the foot was severed. But it was still too late; he died three days later.

Well, my dear, after five days I believed myself to be free and clear. But as I woke on the sixth morning, I knew that something was wrong. The pain of the healing shoulder was still there, but the whole area felt puffy and unnaturally hot. Mercardier came to look at the back of my shoulder. He confirmed that it had turned black. If it were in my arm, I would have a chance. We could amputate my arm. But we cannot amputate my back.

I expect I have three or four days to live, and I write to you now whilst I am still clear in mind. I have sent for my mother, who is nearby. You will have too far to come, my darling, and in any event I would not want you to remember me like this.

I take my leave of you now, Berengaria, with this letter, so that you will always have a record, and so that history will always have a record, of the depth of my love for you.

From the moment I first saw you, illuminated by a shaft of light sent by God, I knew that you would be the crowning glory of my life. The tournaments, the wealth, the fighting, the Crusade, all of my achievements pale into insignificance when set against the backdrop of my love for you.

At first, in the heady early days, my love was of the obsessive kind. I could not bear to be away from the light and the laughter that you brought. The shining sparkle of your bright blue eyes, your fine cheekbones and alabaster skin, your golden hair cut short to the consternation of the older ladies at court. This truly was the love of which the poets sing.

There was no prospect of not spending my life with you, despite the political risk with King Philip and the opposition of every one of our advisers. All of those obstacles were overcome, leading to our wedding in Limassol, hurriedly arranged but all the more to be treasured for its informality.

Then, I recall the wonders of physical love with you, binding us together and culminating in the shining moment on the hilltop above Tyre, when I knew for certain that we would be blessed with a son. This was the apotheosis of my life, on top of the world, brimming with confidence and love and God's favour.

In your wisdom you once told me not to goad Philip, my great enemy and rival, too far or I would push him into lashing out. How I wish I had listened to you! How I wish that Philip were not the devil himself!

Those terrible events at Acre destroyed you. They destroyed me too. You were lost in your world of misery and silence. And I could do nothing to help.

From then on, although there were triumphs, they were borne of a reckless energy for confrontation, with God as much as anyone else. I threw myself into harm's way, praying for deliverance. But it never came, and nor did the ultimate glory of taking Jerusalem.

Eventually I abandoned Jerusalem, to spite God for abandoning you.

Vengeance was then my objective, my consuming passion.

But, I vowed that vengeance would not come with a cowardly instruction to a faraway Assassin. It would come with a slow and painful humiliation for Philip, as I picked away at his lands and his power, emasculating him piece by piece. In many ways, that is a more satisfying revenge, to see him lose, little by little, everything that he loves.

In part, over the past three years as you have come back to life, and illuminated my world, so my desire for vengeance has waned.

The first time I saw you, after Joanna had told me of your improvement and I had come flying to your side, I perhaps expected too much. Coming out to meet you in the rose garden of the Abbey at Poitiers, I was nervous and unsure of how to behave. You were nervous too, and prone to drift off in moments where you were uncomfortable.

You, who had been in the company of women for three years, had not been alone with a man since Acre. Clearly I scared you; clearly I brought back all sorts of difficult memories. I think I made the situation worse trying to take your hands, even trying to embrace you. I had hoped for too much too soon, and when you fled into the sanctuary of the church, I thought I had destroyed any chance we had.

I sat there in the rose garden, the great Crusader King, with tears rolling down my cheeks in an agony of despair and crushed dreams.

When we tried again, a year later, this time I was more circumspect, more gentle, and we made small steps with our polite conversation. I had only intended to visit for two days. I ended up staying for four weeks.

As we sat together in church on the second Sunday after my arrival, you put your hand on top of mine, resting on my thigh. I dared to glance at you. You were looking at me, smiling, welcoming me back into your heart. My spirits soared.

We were together again; although not in the full physical sense. But we slept in the same bed together, and I held you naked against me. It reminded me of those days just before our marriage, when we had lain together but remained celibate for our wedding night. In some ways that was more intimate than sex. The simple naked entwinement of our bodies still held for me more happiness than sex ever could now, and I bless you for your courage.

When I departed again, you remained in seclusion, and I would come back to you every other month during the summer, and then for most of the winter. You were for me the cooling balm to the heat of life outside.

I send with this letter the diaries that I have been keeping all these years. I hope that they will bring you some comfort and some small remembrance of me. When you too die, have the diaries buried with you. They are a record for you and for me of our love and our life.

Do not be sad, my love.

Soon I will be with God. Together we will watch over you, and when the time comes, we will be waiting faithfully for you.

Your loving husband,

Richard

Richard died on 6 April 1199.

Postscript

Berengaria

Berengaria settled in Le Mans, devoting herself to the Church. She funded the rebuilding of the Cathedral of St Julien and a new Franciscan friary, and was heavily involved in the foundation of a new Cistercian monastery at L'Epau, where she was buried on her death, some thirty years after Richard, in 1230.

The effigy on her tomb is of a virgin bride, with her feet resting on a watchful lion. Richard had adopted the three golden lions on a red background as his emblem after his release from captivity. In the effigy she is also holding a book to her breast. Normally this would have been held in a simulated reading position. But this book is shut and held close to her heart. Perhaps this was a clue to the diaries buried with her body.

Berengaria remains the only Queen of England never to have set foot in that country.

Joanna

Joanna had married the man she had fallen in love with, Count Raymond VI of Toulouse, and had given birth to one son, the future Raymond VII.

But at around the time of Richard's death, there was some crisis in the marriage. It is sometimes attributed to Raymond having fallen for the daughter of Isaac Comnenus, recently arrived in their court. Joanna fled to her mother, Eleanor, and was then told of Richard's death.

The news precipitated a breakdown. She went to the Abbey of Fontevraud, where Richard was buried, and demanded to be made a nun, despite being both married and pregnant. She and the baby died in childbirth, although the baby lived long enough to be christened Richard.

Eleanor

On Richard's death, Eleanor, now seventy-seven, assisted John, her youngest son, to establish himself in Richard's lands. There is some evidence that Mercardier assisted her in this. Whilst she was alive, John managed to hang on to his inheritance, but after she died in 1204, his empire began to crumble.

Eleanor was buried at Fontevraud Abbey with Richard.

John

By 1205, six years after Richard's death, John had lost Normandy and Anjou to King Philip, and his reputation had suffered further with rumours of his involvement in the murder of Arthur of Brittany, his and Richard's nephew, and a potential rival.

By 1209, England was laid under interdict, as Pope Innocent III excommunicated John. This enabled John to take control of the Church's revenues and build up a war chest for a renewed campaign against King Philip. But at the Battle of Bouvines in 1214, John was humiliated by his former ally, and came skulking back to England with his tail between his legs.

John was by now so weak that he was forced by the barons into the signature of Magna Carta in 1215.

His death in 1216 was greeted with relief, summed up by the words of Matthew Paris, the Benedictine monk and chronicler: 'Foul as it is, Hell itself is made fouler by the presence of John.'

King Philip of France

Philip outlived Richard by twenty-three years, dying in 1223. He has been widely credited as being one of the most successful of all French monarchs.

Henry VI, Holy Roman Emperor

Henry VI had died unexpectedly of a high fever in September 1197. On his deathbed, he had sought forgiveness for his part in Richard's imprisonment, offering to repay all of the ransom. Indeed, the Pope forbade the burial of his body until the ransom was repaid. It was only with the accession of Innocent III to the papacy in 1198 that Henry's decomposing body was finally laid to rest.

Saladin

Saladin died some nine months after his meeting with Richard, while Richard was imprisoned in Dürnstein. He had seventeen sons to dispute the succession of his brother, Saphadin. However, despite this, Saphadin managed against the odds to hold the Empire together, but without reaching the heights attained under Saladin.

Count Henry of Champagne, King of Jerusalem

In 1197, five years after Richard's departure, Henry faced an attack on Jaffa from Saladin's brother, Saphadin. From a window in his castle he was reviewing his troops in the courtyard below, when an envoy from Pisa entered the room. Henry forgot where he was for a moment as he turned to greet the envoy and stepped backwards, falling to his death through the window.

Isaac Comnenus, Ruler of Cyprus

After his capture by Richard and his imprisonment in silver chains, Isaac was handed to the Knights of St John for safekeeping. He was eventually released as part of the negotiations leading to Richard's release in 1194. Isaac immediately travelled to Constantinople, where he was poisoned as he intrigued against the Byzantine throne.

Mercardier

Although Richard had ordered that the man who had fired the fateful crossbow bolt, Bertrand de Gurdon, should be pardoned, Mercardier had him flayed alive and then hanged. He then set about assisting Eleanor in securing Richard's lands for John, but a year after Richard's death, Mercardier was murdered by a rival mercenary captain in Bordeaux.

Baldwin of Béthune

After Richard's capture and imprisonment, Baldwin continued to serve Richard first as a hostage for the ransom money, and then as his emissary at the German court, playing a pivotal role in securing the election of Richard's nephew, Otto IV, as Holy Roman Emperor in 1198. As a reward for his service, Baldwin was given in marriage a rich widow, the Countess of Aumale, and died peacefully in 1212.

Hubert Walter

Hubert profited greatly from his role as Richard's most trusted adviser and friend.

During his imprisonment, Richard had arranged for him to be appointed as Archbishop of Canterbury in May 1193. At Christmas in the same year, Richard appointed him as Justiciar, in which position he effectively ruled England as Richard's vice regent.

After Richard's death, Hubert saw no realistic alternative to John. As Archbishop of Canterbury he crowned John King of England, and as reward was shortly thereafter appointed Chancellor. He served for five years before his death in 1205, from an infection arising out of an untreated carbuncle on his lower back.

Richard

In his will, Richard asked for his heart to be buried at Rouen, his brain and entrails to be buried at Charroux, and the rest of his body in the family vault at Fontevraud Abbey.

His bones remained there until 1789, when they were dug up by French Revolutionaries and scattered in the fields outside.

His heart remains entombed in Rouen Cathedral.

About the Editor

Chris Manson was educated on a Senior Foundation Scholarship at St Paul's School, London and at St John's College in the University of Oxford where he read history, with the Crusades as a special subject.

He then developed a successful business career at PricewaterhouseCoopers, Andrew Lloyd Webber's Really Useful Group and at Chelsea Football Club.

In 1999 he co-founded sit-up television, which he sold to Virgin Media six years later. He was elected an Ernst and Young Entrepreneur of the Year in 2005, and five years later founded Blott, one of Britain's fastest growing retailers.

He and his family divide their time between homes in Zermatt in Switzerland, Quinta do Lago in Portugal and Oxford, England.

Printed in Great Britain
by Amazon.co.uk, Ltd.,
Marston Gate.